ARRESTED
FOR WHAT NOW

Eddie Watts

© **Copyright Arrested For What Now:** A Global Guide to Bizarre Laws, Curious Bans, and Moves You Never Knew Were Illegal

This book is part of the Seriously Though series.

2025 - All rights reserved.

The content within this book may not be reproduced, duplicated or transmitted without direct written permission from the author or the publisher.

Under no circumstances will any blame or legal responsibility be held against the publisher, or author, for any damages, reparation, or monetary loss due to the information contained within this book. Either directly or indirectly. You are responsible for your own choices, actions, and results.

Legal Notice:

This book is copyright protected. This book is only for personal use. You cannot amend, distribute, sell, use, quote or paraphrase any part, of the content within this book, without the consent of the author or publisher.

Disclaimer Notice:

Please note the information contained within this document is for educational and entertainment purposes only. All effort has been expended to present accurate, up-to-date, and reliable, complete information. No warranties of any kind are declared or implied. Readers acknowledge that the author is not engaging in the rendering of legal, financial, medical or professional advice. The content within this book has been derived from various sources. Please consult a licensed professional before attempting any techniques outlined in this book.

By reading this document, the reader agrees that under no circumstances is the author responsible for any losses, direct or indirect, which are incurred as a result of the use of the information contained within this document, including, but not limited to, — errors, omissions, or inaccuracies.

CONTENTS

Introduction   5

1. When the Animal Kingdom Needs Paperwork   7
2. Hands Where We Can See Them   19
3. What Not to Wear   31
4. Tastes Like Regulation   41
5. Proceed with Caution   53
6. Your Castle, Their Rules   67
7. Watch Your Language   79
8. No Fun Allowed   91

Conclusion   103
Sources   105

INTRODUCTION

Arrested for What Now takes its cue from this kind of sign: part joke, part warning, but fully real. It's your passport to some of the world's lesser-known laws. These aren't sweeping federal policies or dramatic courtroom moments. They're sidewalk codes, petty restrictions, and proud declarations from towns doing their best to stay organized.

You'll find places where flip-flops might trigger a citation, where donkeys are *non grata* in bathtubs, and where imaginary whales get legal protection in a landlocked state.

This wasn't written to mock.

It was written to marvel.

Because somewhere, someone once said, "We're gonna need a statute for that," and then actually passed it.

Go on, see for yourself. The rules are real.

And they're pretty darn cool.

1

WHEN THE ANIMAL KINGDOM NEEDS PAPERWORK

S ome animals roam free.
Others need permits.

This chapter dives into the strange space where bureaucracy meets the barnyard. From livestock legislation to whale protection laws in landlocked states, these are the rules that keep things orderly when nature gets too close to city limits.

8 | ARRESTED FOR WHAT NOW

Some laws come from common sense. Others from history. And a few? From one too many incidents involving one very bad flood.

So whether you're herding hens or spotting elephants downtown—ask first.

Because in these places?

The animals aren't the only ones being kept in line.

1. DONKEYS CAN'T SLEEP IN BATHTUBS (ARIZONA)

The donkey survived.

But the law stayed.

In 1924, in Kingman, Arizona, a local merchant had two strange things behind his property: a friendly donkey and a discarded porcelain bathtub. For reasons known only to the donkey, the tub became its favorite place to sleep. Shaded, wind-protected, and just the right size for a nap. Odd? Yes. But nobody minded.

Then the flood came.

A dam upstream burst after heavy rains, sending a surge of water through the valley. The donkey—still snoozing in its porcelain bed—was swept away. For miles, people reported the same surreal sight: a donkey floating downriver in a bathtub, ears twitching, looking completely unbothered.

A frantic rescue followed. Locals chased the tub by foot, by boat, and by rope. They eventually saved the donkey, who was damp but fine.

The townspeople, however, were soaked, exhausted, and very much over it.

So they passed a law: "Donkeys may not sleep in bathtubs."

That phrase—verbatim—still exists in parts of Arizona, including Mohave County. It's rarely enforced (because, let's face it, how often does this come up?). But it's there.

So yes, in Arizona, you can own a donkey. You can feed it, pet it, even name it Daisy.

But let it nap in a bathtub?

That's not a sleepy animal.

It's a policy problem with hooves.

2. CHICKENS NEED SUPERVISION TO CROSS THE ROAD (GEORGIA)

You've heard the joke.

Now meet the ordinance.

In Gainesville, Georgia—proudly nicknamed the Poultry Capital of the World—it is technically illegal for a chicken to cross the road. And no, it's not a punchline. The city's animal control codes hold owners responsible for loose poultry, especially when it wanders into streets, sidewalks, or parking lots.

Why? Because in Gainesville, chickens are more than livestock. They're industry. Identity. Civic mascots. With more than two billion pounds of chicken processed each year, poultry is big business—and free-roaming birds are a liability.

The law falls under a clause prohibiting the "reckless handling of poultry," which includes letting your chickens wander into traffic. It's about safety, yes—but also about image. A town built on chicken wants its birds to act like professionals.

One backyard hen made headlines after strutting across a neighbor's driveway and onto the street. The moment was captured on a Ring camera. The chicken? Fine. The owner? Cited.

Enforcement is rare but real. Officers can issue warnings, and repeat offenders can be fined. Some neighborhoods even add chicken clauses to HOA agreements, just to be extra sure the poultry stays in its lane.

So yes, you can keep chickens in Gainesville. You can name them. You can raise them right.

Just don't let them roam.

Because in this town, if someone asks, "Why did the chicken cross the road?"

There better be a leash involved.

3. DRUNK? DON'T SADDLE UP A COW (SCOTLAND)

First: why would you?

Second: someone definitely did.

In Scotland, it's illegal to ride a cow—or any animal, really—while under the influence of alcohol. The rule comes from the Licensing Act of 1872, which makes it a criminal offense to be "drunk in charge of any carriage, horse, cattle, or steam engine."

Yes. Steam engine.

The law was serious then, and technically, it still is. Back in the day, people regularly traveled using animals and wagons. A drunk rider wasn't just a public nuisance—it was a safety hazard. Falling off a cow, crashing a cart, or losing control of your livestock could lead to real harm.

Today, the law reads like comedy, especially the cow part. But the logic holds. Modern interpretations have been used to cite people for drunk horseback riding, cycling, and even driving golf carts while buzzed. If you're in motion and you're intoxicated? You're a danger. Doesn't matter if it's horsepower or cow power.

Would someone get arrested today for riding a cow after a few pints? Probably not. But could they? Technically yes.

The law's still there. And the next time someone spots a tipsy tourist trying to mount a friendly Highland bovine for a photo op?

They might just get a reminder that Scotland takes its livestock—and its sobriety—seriously.

So if you're out celebrating with friends, and a cow wanders by?

Wave. Compliment her. Respect the moment.

But keep your feet on the ground.

Because in Scotland, that cow isn't your ride home.

And the law?

Still watching.

4. WHALES HAVE LEGAL PROTECTION (OKLAHOMA)

Let's start with a geography check.

Oklahoma is landlocked. No ocean. No bay. No dolphin statues. And yet—whales are legally protected there.

According to the state's wildlife code, it's illegal to hunt, capture, or harass whales within Oklahoma's borders (*"harass" includes feeding, chasing, or even getting too close*). It's a real clause, written into law. Which, naturally, raises a few questions.

How would a whale even get to Oklahoma? Was there once a rogue beluga in the Arkansas River? Did someone at the legislature get a little copy-paste happy?

Actually… yes.

Legal experts say the clause was likely part of a boilerplate conservation bill used to draft wildlife regulations across multiple states. Somewhere along the line, Oklahoma copied the whole thing—whales and all—and just… never deleted them.

Others think the inclusion was symbolic. A legislative flex. A declaration of broad-scope environmental ethics. "We care about all creatures—even the ones that will never, ever be here."

The law has never been enforced. But it's become famous in trivia books, "dumb law" lists, and the occasional law school lecture on legislative editing.

Still, it's kind of comforting. Because if a whale ever does show up in Oklahoma—via truck, tank, or the world's weirdest weather system—it'll be legally protected.

So if you're in Tulsa and somehow encounter a beached narwhal on the side of the road?

Don't mess with it.

Don't touch it.

And for the love of Moby Dick, don't try to hunt it.

Because in Oklahoma, even hypothetical marine life gets legal backup.

5. WANT A PET PIG? FILE THE PAPERWORK FIRST (FRANCE)

In France, you can own a pig.

You just have to register it like a small, curly-tailed bureaucracy.

According to French agricultural law, pigs—no matter how tiny, cuddly, or dressed in polka dots—are classified as livestock. Not pets. If you want one, you need a livestock registration number (*numéro d'exploitation*), microchipping, and formal registration with the Ministry of Agriculture.

Even if your pig is eating out of a gold bowl and sleeping in a Paris apartment? It still counts.

The rule exists for serious reasons: biosecurity and disease control. Pigs can carry contagious diseases like African swine fever. A single untracked pig, even a pet, could compromise France's massive pork industry.

To prevent that, authorities require traceability. If an outbreak occurs, officials can locate and assess every registered pig. Your house pig might know tricks and pose for selfies, but in the eyes of the state, it's still part of the food chain.

In addition to registration, some regions require you to inform the local Direction Départementale de la Protection des Populations (DDPP). Fail to comply, and you could face fines or confiscation of the pig.

In the countryside, this is standard practice. In Paris? It's a surprise twist in your chic urban farm life.

So if you're planning to teach your pig to sit, stay, or wear a beret?

Start with paperwork.

Because in France, you don't just adopt a pig.

You admit it into the system.

6. WALKING AN ELEPHANT REQUIRES A PERMIT (ATLANTA)

There are traffic laws.

There are animal laws.

And then… there's Atlanta.

In Georgia's capital, it is still technically illegal to walk an elephant through downtown without a permit.

Yes. An actual elephant.

The rule traces back to the early 1900s, when traveling circuses roamed the country and frequently paraded their animals through city streets. It was festive. It was loud. It was chaos. Horses spooked. Traffic stopped. Children screamed (sometimes with joy, sometimes not). Eventually, Atlanta officials had had enough.

So they passed a regulation stating that no "non-domesticated animal of unusual size or weight" could be led through public roads without prior approval. It wasn't just aimed at elephants—it was a catch-all for parading zebras, camels, tigers, and any bold citizen walking a leashed kangaroo.

The law has survived to this day. It's been cited in discussions about exotic animal permits, used in movie production zoning talks, and occasionally mentioned when animal rights groups protest live-animal events.

Actual enforcement is rare. But if someone were to lead a full-grown elephant down Peachtree Street today, a citation wouldn't be out of the question.

Neither would a viral Instagram post.

So if you're feeling circus-y or Dr. Dolittle-esque in Atlanta?

Don't forget to check the city code.

You'll need a permit. And a very big cleanup crew.

Because in Atlanta, the elephant in the room?

Might also be a municipal offense.

7. HALLOWEEN ISN'T IDEAL FOR ADOPTING BLACK CATS (UNITED STATES)

Every October, animal shelters across the United States adjust their adoption policies—and black cats are at the center of it.

Not because they're unlucky.

Because people can be.

As Halloween approaches, some shelters pause or limit black cat adoptions altogether. The reason? Too many cases—some confirmed, some cautionary—of black cats being adopted for the wrong reasons: themed photo shoots, spooky party decor, or more disturbingly, rituals and pranks.

The concern is less about superstition and more about safety. Black cats have long been linked with witches and bad omens. Around Halloween, that mythology gets amplified, and shelters worry that adoption motives may shift from genuine love to seasonal aesthetics.

Some shelters won't adopt black cats during the last week of October. Others allow reservations but ask adopters to wait until November to take them home. You may also be required to answer extra screening questions. Some animal advocates support the policy; others argue it's outdated and unfairly paints the public as suspicious.

Despite the restriction, the Halloween season is often used to promote black cats more positively. Awareness campaigns challenge old myths, celebrate their personalities, and highlight their struggle for year-round adoption—black cats are statistically the last to be adopted and the first to be overlooked.

So if you fall in love with a sleek, green-eyed feline during spooky season?

Great. Just know you might need to wait a few days to bring them home.

Because in some shelters, black cats don't come with a trick.

They come with a pause.

8. YOU MUST STUN LOBSTERS BEFORE BOILING (SWITZERLAND)

In Switzerland, you can still eat lobster.

You just can't boil it alive.

Since 2018, Swiss law has required that all lobsters be stunned before they're cooked. The regulation—part of a broader animal welfare overhaul—prohibits the old method of dropping live lobsters directly into boiling water. Instead, they must be rendered unconscious first, either via electric shock or a method known as spiking, which quickly destroys the lobster's brain.

The rule was based on research suggesting that lobsters may experience pain. While the science is still debated in some circles, Switzerland chose to err on the side of caution. Under guidelines from the Federal Food Safety and Veterinary Office (FSVO), any other method is considered inhumane.

But the rules don't stop at the pot.

Lobsters must also be stored in oxygenated tanks, transported with care, and kept out of dry containers or ice baths. Restaurants are expected to follow strict cleanliness standards and tank maintenance protocols. Violations can lead to fines or temporary closure.

At first, critics rolled their eyes. Was this about animal rights—or culinary micromanagement?

But over time, many came to see it as a thoughtful ethical line. If we're going to cook and eat animals, Switzerland argued, we owe them a shred of mercy. Even if they have claws.

So yes—your lobster tail in Geneva still comes with lemon and butter.

But before it got to your plate?

It got a zap.

Because in Switzerland, even seafood is entitled to a little dignity.

Turns out the animal kingdom isn't just wild.

It's regulated.

From pig permits in Paris to lobster rights in Zurich, laws now reach into the henhouse, the pasture, and the seafood tank.

Some rules protect.

Some preserve.

And some—like outlawing bathtub naps or tipsy cow rides—just remind us how closely humans and animals really live.

So if it clucks, trots, swims, or snoozes?

Read the fine print.

Because in a world full of creatures, we're not the only ones following the rules.

2

HANDS WHERE WE CAN SEE THEM

S ome places post signs. Others rely on side-eye and cultural memory. But the message is clear: look, don't touch.

This chapter explores where the boundaries lie—across marble steps, bronze statues, vending zones, and temple walls. Some rules are practical. Some are cultural. And some are the result of one too many tourists doing something deeply inadvisable with a selfie stick.

From sacred spiders to historic railings to modern fish-grabbing laws, this is the global fine print on physical space.

So keep your hands to yourself.

Because in these places? The line is literal.

1. NO CLIMBING TREES IN PUBLIC PARKS (TORONTO)

It's not a prank.

It's not a dare.

It's a sunny afternoon in Toronto, and you're about to get fined—for climbing a tree.

Yes, really. According to Toronto's municipal code, it's illegal to climb a tree in any public park or city-maintained greenspace. The language is crystal clear: no person shall climb a tree or cause a tree to be climbed. That means even boosting your kid into a low branch counts as a violation.

Why the strict stance?

Liability. Safety. Preservation. And possibly the legacy of one romantic overachiever who once scaled a hundred-year-old oak to impress a date and had to be rescued by firefighters. (True story. Local media had a field day.)

Toronto is home to more than 10 million trees, many of them protected by urban forestry bylaws. They're not just scenery—they're infrastructure. Trees provide shade, regulate stormwater, improve air quality, and boost property values. Letting people climb them? That's like letting people walk on the roof of city hall.

Climbing can damage bark, break limbs, compact soil around roots, and shorten a tree's life. It's not just risky for you—it's bad for the tree.

And yes, this rule is enforced. People have been stopped, fined, or firmly warned in places like High Park, Queen's Park, and neighborhood playgrounds where the trees look especially climbable. There are signs. There are citations. And there are plenty of parents pulling kids down mid-climb while trying not to make eye contact with the bylaw officer.

So next time you see a photogenic branch calling your name?

Keep your feet on the ground.

Because in Toronto, going out on a limb could get you written up.

2. YOU CAN'T SIT ON THE SPANISH STEPS (ROME)

If you're in Rome and your feet get tired, don't sit down.

Not here.

In 2019, the city passed a law banning people from sitting on the Spanish Steps. Fines can reach €400—for nothing more than taking a break.

It might sound extreme, but the logic holds. The Spanish Steps aren't just stairs. They're a 300-year-old Baroque landmark, linking the Trinità dei Monti church at the top with the Piazza di Spagna below. And for decades, they've been treated like the world's prettiest picnic bench.

Tourists were picnicking. Napping. Dripping gelato onto the marble. Leaving behind coffee cups, sandwich wrappers, and more than a few ketchup packets. In short? The steps were getting trashed.

After a full restoration—funded in part by a luxury fashion house—Rome said basta.

Sitting was banned. Signs were posted. Police were dispatched. And yes, whistles were issued. Many, many whistles.

Today, officers patrol the steps and signal to anyone who even perches for a second. Tourists spring up in confusion. Some apologize. Some argue. Most just awkwardly shuffle off.

The rule also bans dragging luggage across the marble, eating while seated, and—somewhat mysteriously—sitting with your back to the street. That last one? Possibly aesthetic. Possibly Roman. Possibly both.

The goal isn't to keep people off the steps. It's to keep the steps intact. Tourists are welcome. Sandwiches are not.

So if you need a rest?

Sit beside the steps. Sit across from them. Sit on a bench. Just don't sit here.

Because in this city, even the stairs come with rules.

3. YOU CAN'T TOUCH THE ROYAL GUARD (UNITED KINGDOM)

They're not statues.

They're not actors.

They're elite, trained soldiers.

And if you touch them—they will respond.

The King's Guard (formerly the Queen's Guard) are the famously stoic sentries stationed outside Buckingham Palace,

Windsor Castle, and other royal landmarks. Dressed in bright red tunics and bearskin hats, they're among the most photographed figures in the United Kingdom. To tourists, they look like scenery.

But they're very much real. And very much on duty.

Here's the problem: visitors forget that.

People try to take selfies, strike goofy poses, or test the limits. Some shout in their faces. Others reach for a pat or a poke, thinking it'll be funny.

It won't.

Touching or obstructing a member of the Royal Guard is a criminal offense. You can be fined. You can be arrested. Or—more likely—you'll be shouted at with full military force. That iconic rifle they carry? It's loaded. And it's not just for show.

There are countless videos online showing tourists crossing the line. The Guard doesn't break character. They break formation. A stomp. A shout. A sudden march forward to clear the area. They won't hurt you—unless you pose a real threat—but they are trained to respond.

These are soldiers. Not performers. They're not there to amuse. They're there to defend royal grounds and hold a line. And that includes a line you don't cross with your phone or your fingers.

So yes—you can admire. You can observe. You can wave, respectfully, from afar.

But touch them?

That's not funny.

That's illegal.

4. DON'T KILL SPIDERS IN SACRED SPACES (INDIA)

You're in a temple.

It's peaceful.

Sunlight filters through intricately carved stone. The air smells like incense and centuries.

And then—from the edge of a sacred pillar—you see it.

A spider.

Your instinct says: squish.

But in India? That reflex could get you fined.

In many of India's ancient temples, forts, and UNESCO-protected sites, even tiny lifeforms fall under conservation law. The Archaeological Survey of India (ASI) enforces strict preservation policies that protect not just architecture, but the ecosystems that coexist with it. That includes spiders, ants, moths, and other quietly beneficial residents.

Unless an insect poses a direct threat to visitors or the structure itself, it's to be left alone. Spiders, for example, help control termite populations. Some even regulate moisture by spinning webs in just the right spots. In buildings hundreds—sometimes thousands—of years old, every detail matters.

In 2019, a tourist in Rajasthan killed a spider in a protected temple and was fined. The citation?

"Intentional damage to a conservation site."

The spider was harmless. The action was not.

In Kerala, signage near sacred buildings gently advises:

"Respect all living beings within this space."

It's not just a belief. It's how the space is protected.

So if you're standing before an ancient mural and spot a long-legged crawler skimming its surface?

Don't panic. Don't swat.

Take a breath. Step back.

Because in India, the smallest creatures aren't intruders.

They're part of what's being preserved.

5. NO LEANING ON CERTAIN FENCES (JAPAN)

It's not a full-body tackle. It's not a climb. It's just... a lean.

But in parts of Japan—especially near temples, shrines, and historic sites—even resting your weight on a fence or railing can be a problem. In some places, it's outright illegal. In others, it earns you a swift but polite correction from a guard, a volunteer docent, or a monk who's seen this too many times.

The rule isn't posted in flashing neon. It's written in culture.

In Japan, fences—especially near sacred or historical landmarks—aren't just physical barriers. They're symbolic. They mark the boundary between the everyday and the sacred. Even if they're low, carved, or seemingly decorative, they serve as a quiet cue: this space is different. Treat it that way.

In Kyoto, tourists have been escorted off temple grounds for leaning on a sacred fence. In Nara, signs politely ask visitors not to sit, lean, or rest on railings—some of which are hundreds of years old. Even freshly painted fences get this level of respect. Age doesn't matter. Intention does.

It's not just about preventing damage (though that's part of it). It's about sending a message. Leaning says: "This isn't sacred to me." And in a culture rooted in mindfulness and respect, that speaks volumes.

The response? Calm. Firm. A bow. A gesture. A reminder to move. You're not being punished. You're being reminded to pay attention.

So when you're in Japan and your feet get tired? Rest. Just not on the nearest railing.

Find a bench. A shady wall. A low stone. But keep your weight—and your respect—off the boundary.

Because in Japan, fences aren't just wood and paint.

They're quiet lines drawn in reverence.

6. YOU CAN'T TOUCH THE LIBERTY BELL (PHILADELPHIA)

There was a time when you could touch it.

You'd stand in line. Maybe you were on a school trip. Maybe with family. You'd finally make it to the front, step forward, and reach out toward history. Your hand would land on the metal. Maybe you'd trace the famous crack. One second. One photo. One connection to something bigger than a museum.

If you're over 40, you might remember that moment. If you're under 40, odds are good you never got the chance.

Because today, the Liberty Bell is off-limits. You can see it—but you can't touch it.

It now sits behind glass, protected by security systems and watched by rangers. Visitors read plaques, listen to guides, and stop a respectful distance from the bell itself. The setting feels sacred. Or at least: untouchable.

Why the change?

First: preservation. The bell is nearly 270 years old. Its bronze surface has been touched by millions of fingers. Those fingers leave behind oils that wear it down. Even the crack—already fragile—is vulnerable to the softest reverence.

Second: security. After a replica Liberty Bell was vandalized outside Union Station in Washington, D.C., in 2024, historic sites across the country got stricter. The real bell was fine—but the message stuck. No more up-close contact.

So now? You can take pictures. You can lean in. You can feel the weight of it.

But you can't place your hand on that metal.

You're close. But not quite there.

And honestly? That quiet space between you and the bell might be what makes it feel so powerful.

7. DON'T SIT ON A PUBLIC SCULPTURE (SINGAPORE)

It's hot. You're tired. You see a sleek marble sculpture with a wide, flat base and think, "Perfect. That's basically a bench."

Don't.

In Singapore, sitting on, leaning against, or otherwise interacting with public sculptures can get you fined, warned, or politely but firmly escorted away. It falls under the country's Vandalism Act—

legislation that may sound dramatic, but in Singapore, even minor contact with protected art qualifies.

Why so serious?

Because in Singapore, public order and public art are deeply intertwined. Sculptures aren't just decoration. They're treated like civic monuments—carefully curated and protected. Sitting on them—even if they look like furniture—is considered disrespectful at best, and damaging at worst.

Enforcement? Real and routine. In 2016, a tourist was fined for sitting on a bronze sculpture of a child. In 2019, a couple received a formal warning for climbing onto a modern art piece that looked "pose-worthy." Sculptures around Marina Bay, Esplanade Park, and the Civic District are watched closely by uniformed and plainclothes officers alike.

The signs aren't always obvious. Some warnings are ankle-level plaques. Others rely on silent disapproval from a nearby guard. But the expectation is clear: admire the sculpture, don't sit on it.

Singapore's approach to public space is famously strict—and famously clean. This is the same country that bans chewing gum and fines for jaywalking. You better believe it's not going to be casual about someone using a $200,000 bronze as a coffee break perch.

So the next time you're admiring a statue in Singapore?

Take the photo. Appreciate the form. Nod respectfully.

Just don't take a seat.

Because even if it looks like a bench, it's not your bench.

8. YOU CAN'T PICK UP FISH WITH YOUR HANDS (MISSOURI)

It's called noodling.

You wade into the river, reach into a muddy hollow, and wait for a catfish to bite your hand. Then—if you're lucky, stubborn, and unbothered by potential injury—you haul it out like some mud-splattered aquatic champion.

It's primal. It's thrilling. And in Missouri, it's also very, very regulated.

Hand-fishing, or noodling, is only legal during a limited summer window and only in designated areas. You need a valid permit, must follow strict rules on species, size, daily catch, and regional zones—and even then, Missouri prefers you don't go in unprepared.

Why the red tape?

Because noodling can cause real harm—to people, to fish, and to the environment. It disturbs catfish during nesting, disrupts ecosystems, and erodes fragile riverbanks. Plus, some of those underwater holes don't house fish. They house snapping turtles. Or snakes. Or both.

Missouri originally banned noodling outright. It wasn't until 2005 —after pressure from outdoorsmen, conservationists, and lawmakers celebrating traditional "hillbilly hand-fishing"—that the practice returned, heavily regulated and cautiously embraced.

Today, conservation officers patrol hot spots along rivers like the Osage and the Missouri. Noodling without a permit? That heroic photo of you holding a 40-pound flathead catfish could come with a hefty fine.

So if you're tempted to channel your inner wilderness warrior?

Get a permit. Know the rules. Bring a buddy who knows CPR.

Because in Missouri, catching catfish barehanded might be tradition.

But doing it by the book is the law.

Turns out, touching history, art, or wildlife is often less a privilege and more a legal hazard.

Whether it's leaning on sacred fences in Kyoto, scooting too close to the Liberty Bell, or climbing a tree in Toronto, the rules all say the same thing: admire from a distance.

Some boundaries are ancient. Some are modern. Some are posted. Most are enforced.

So look closely. Pause reverently. Snap the picture.

Just don't tap the sculpture, swat the spider, or scale the limb.

Because in this world? Even your posture might be policed.

3

WHAT NOT TO WEAR

F ashion is expression—unless it's also a fine.

This chapter explores the intersection of fabric and law, where what you wear can violate municipal code, spark protest, or get you escorted off sacred ground.

From camouflage bans in the Caribbean to historical cosplay rules in Parliament, these laws aren't about taste. They're about history, identity, control—and sometimes, neighborhood aesthetics.

So whether you're packing gloves for Spain or leaving the tutu at home in Paris, remember:

In some towns, fashion isn't just personal.

It's regulated.

1. NO ARMOR ALLOWED IN PARLIAMENT (UNITED KINGDOM)

In the 14th century, someone walked into a courtroom in full chainmail. And someone else—presumably less shiny and more annoyed—had to put their foot down. The result? A law, still on the books in the United Kingdom, stating: "That no man shall come before the King's justices… in armour."

That's not poetic language. It's an actual statute, passed in 1313 under Edward II. The law was aimed at nobles who arrived armed to intimidate the king's council or influence proceedings by threat. In medieval terms, that was pretty on-brand.

So yes—wearing a suit of armor in Parliament is still technically illegal.

Back then, armor wasn't cosplay. It wasn't a Renaissance fair leftover. It was a message. If you showed up armored, you weren't saying, "Let's have a discussion." You were saying, "I brought backup." The law was less about modesty and more about keeping swords out of politics.

While the rule is over 700 years old, it's never been repealed. It exists as a kind of legal fossil—occasionally cited during debates over protest attire or public disruptions. In 2013, a British activist tried to enter Parliament dressed in full chainmail. Security stopped him. Not because he posed a threat, but because—technically—the rule still stands.

So no armor in Parliament. No swords in court. And definitely no jousting in the lobby. Some rules don't need updating—they just need remembering.

2. WEARING CAMOUFLAGE IS ILLEGAL (BARBADOS)

Let's talk about your shorts.

In Barbados—and in Trinidad and Tobago, Ghana, Nigeria, and Jamaica—wearing camouflage isn't just a questionable fashion choice. It's illegal. Doesn't matter if it's pink camo. Doesn't matter if it's a souvenir from the cruise shop. Doesn't even matter if you're eight and love feeling all Rambo. If it looks military, it's banned.

In these countries, camouflage is strictly reserved for members of the armed forces. Wearing it as a civilian is considered impersonation—or at the very least, disrespectful. The law doesn't care if you think it's funny or stylish. If it's camo, it's a no-go.

So yes—your fishing vest could get you pulled aside at customs. Your toddler's little cargo shorts? Confiscated. Your fashion-forward camo duffel bag? Contraband. And don't even think about that hat with the leafy print and drawstring. It's on the watch list.

Some countries take it even further. It's not just shirts and pants. Accessories like backpacks, flip-flops, phone cases—even hair ties—can get you flagged. Local law enforcement takes these regulations seriously, and tourists have been fined, asked to change, or turned away at airports, ports, and even restaurants.

The reasoning isn't arbitrary. In countries where military uniforms carry weight—both literally and symbolically—allowing civilians to mimic that look can create confusion and undermine security. If anyone can throw on some green and brown and blend in, it makes it harder to identify actual personnel, especially in places with histories of unrest.

It's also about respect. The uniform means something. And the people wearing it aren't thrilled when tourists stroll around in cargo shorts that mimic their dress code.

So if you're headed to the Caribbean or West Africa? Pack light. Just not military-light.

3. HIGH HEELS BANNED AT ANCIENT SITES (GREECE)

Picture it: you're walking through the ruins of the Acropolis. You're standing where philosophers once stood. You're squinting at sun-drenched marble while imagining toga-clad debates about truth, virtue, and geometry. And then—your shoes stab history in the face.

In 2009, Greece passed a regulation banning high heels at certain ancient monuments, including the Acropolis. The reasoning was simple: heels can damage stone. It's not about fashion—it's about physics. A stiletto heel concentrates body weight into a pinpoint, delivering up to 2,000 pounds of pressure per square inch. That's enough to chip marble that's been standing for thousands of years.

Enough heel strikes over time can erode or fracture delicate stone surfaces—especially at sites that tourists love to climb, sit on, or pose beside. The ban applies to men and women alike, although women's footwear tends to be the culprit.

And it's not just heels. Many historic sites also prohibit hard-soled boots, cleats, or anything else that might grind ancient surfaces into the archaeological equivalent of gravel. At some locations, signs make this clear. At others, it's a guard offering a polite but firm, "No heels, please."

There's also a safety element. Walking across uneven, 2,400-year-old stone slabs in four-inch heels is a great way to meet an EMT—or go viral for all the wrong reasons.

So next time you visit ruins in Greece? Skip the stilettos. Because cultural heritage protection might start with your shoes.

4. SAGGING PANTS ARE OUTLAWED IN SEVERAL CITIES (UNITED STATES)

Let's get one thing straight: yes—there are places in the United States where it's illegal to wear your pants too low.

Not nudity. Not indecent exposure. Just... sagging.

Cities like Shreveport, Louisiana, and Opa-locka, Florida, passed ordinances banning sagging pants in public. Officials claimed it was about "decency" and "community standards." In practice, showing your boxers could get you fined—or arrested.

Backlash came quickly. Critics pointed out that the laws disproportionately targeted young Black men. In Shreveport, more than 96% of those cited under the ordinance were Black. One man, cited for sagging, later died in police custody. The ACLU stepped in. Civil rights advocates raised alarms. Shreveport repealed the ordinance in 2019. Opa-locka followed in 2020.

But not everywhere followed suit. Some cities still have sagging bans on the books. Others enforce similar rules through school policies or homeowners associations. Even when it's not technically illegal, enforcement can still carry bias—turning personal style into a legal issue.

The origins of sagging bans are tangled in history: part school dress code, part prison pipeline, part culture war. Supporters say it's about respect. Opponents say it's about control.

So yes—your sagging pants might be a fashion statement. But depending on where you are? They could also be a misdemeanor.

5. YOU CAN'T DRESS A STATUE (FRANCE)

It usually starts as a joke. A scarf around a bronze neck. A beret on a stone head. Maybe sunglasses on a general and a caption that says, "Vive la fashion."

Then comes the fine.

In Paris—and across several French cities—it's illegal to place clothing, decorations, or accessories on public statues. Doesn't matter if it's festive, funny, or fleeting. Under French cultural heritage law, it's defacement. Unauthorized use of a protected public object.

These rules get tested most during holidays, demonstrations, and protests. Statues become political billboards. Santa hats on war memorials. Rainbow flags on generals. Protest signs on historic figures. The intent might be humorous. The law doesn't care.

In Lyon, a woman was fined for placing a protest sign around a sculpture's neck. In Nice, students dressed Napoleon in a tutu and heart-shaped sunglasses. City officials were not amused. The Ministry of Culture issued a reminder: statues are not props. They are legally protected, and messing with them—even gently—is against the law.

So if you're walking through Paris and feeling whimsical? Accessorize yourself. Add a sash. Rock a scarf. Wear your message.

But don't touch Joan of Arc.

She may be bronze—but in France, she has rights.

6. TRADITIONAL ATTIRE REQUIRED IN GOVERNMENT OFFICES (BHUTAN)

There's dress code enforcement. And then there's Bhutan.

In this Himalayan kingdom, tucked between India and China, tradition isn't a theme—it's the law. Bhutanese citizens are required to wear traditional dress when entering schools, government offices, and formal buildings. No jeans. No hoodies. No flip-flops. Just centuries-old elegance, worn with pride.

Men wear the gho: a belted, knee-length robe with wide cuffs. Women wear the kira: a full-length wraparound skirt with a jacket and sash. These aren't for special occasions—they're daily wear, required by Bhutan's code of conduct, known as Driglam Namzha.

The rule isn't enforced harshly. You won't be escorted out for wearing cargo pants. But you may be turned away. Asked to change. Firmly, politely. And if you're Bhutanese, ignoring the rule can mean a formal reprimand or loss of access to government services.

The purpose is cultural unity. National dress serves as a visual thread connecting Bhutanese identity, heritage, and civic pride. It's not about limiting individuality—it's about expressing shared values.

Tourists aren't required to follow the rule, but many do. And when they do—especially when standing beside locals in prayer flag-lined courtyards—they often describe it as grounding. A small gesture of respect. A connection.

So yes, Bhutan has a dress code. But when the wind catches a rachu just right, and the mountains echo with silence?

It doesn't feel like enforcement.

It feels like belonging.

7. HATS ARE BANNED INDOORS (U.S. MUNICIPAL CODES)

It sounds like something your grandpa would say: "Take off your hat, you're indoors." It's polite. It's respectful. It's tradition.

But in many U.S. cities and institutions, it's not just tradition—it's policy. Municipal codes, school handbooks, and public conduct guidelines still include clauses banning hats inside certain buildings. And while enforcement today is usually soft, the rule still holds weight.

Take Mobile, Alabama. The city's code prohibits head coverings inside public assembly spaces—unless worn for religious or medical reasons. In Boston, historic theaters require hats off to preserve sightlines. In San Diego, students can be removed from class for keeping a cap on. And in some courthouses and council chambers, a hat is grounds for removal before the meeting even begins.

Why all the heat over headwear?

Part of it is visual. No one wants to pay $140 to see a play and stare at someone's fedora. But it also stems from tradition. In the 19th and early 20th centuries, removing your hat indoors—especially in religious or civic spaces—was a public sign of deference. That etiquette stuck around, even as hats evolved from top hats to trucker caps.

There's a security element, too. In some schools and municipal buildings, hats are banned to discourage gang symbolism or face-obscuring accessories. The goal? Clear heads, visible faces, smooth enforcement.

So yes—your trilby may be fabulous. Your baseball cap might be lucky. But in certain American cities?

Best to leave it at the door.

8. DRIVING GLOVES WERE ONCE REQUIRED (SPAIN)

There was a time in Spain when driving without gloves wasn't just a style misstep—it was borderline criminal.

During the mid-20th century—particularly under the Franco regime—Spanish motorists were expected to wear gloves behind the wheel. While not always codified in national law, the rule appeared in regional traffic manuals, etiquette books, and police training guides. Bare hands? That looked careless.

Why all the formality?

First, function. With the Spanish sun turning steering wheels into stovetops, gloves protected your hands. They also provided grip on slippery, unpadded leather interiors—no power steering, no AC, no margin for error.

Second, image. Gloves meant discipline, poise, and pride. Whether you were a chauffeur, a police officer, or a dad in a Sunday suit behind the wheel of a SEAT 1400, gloves told the world: "I'm in control." They were part of the driving uniform. And like all uniforms in that era, they mattered.

Police often stopped drivers who looked too relaxed behind the wheel. It wasn't always about traffic violations—it was about visual cues. Because in that era, how you looked driving mattered as much as how you drove.

Today, the glove rule is gone from the books—but not from the culture. At vintage car rallies across Spain, gloves are still a requirement. If you're driving a 1956 SEAT 600 in a parade and forget your gloves?

No entry.

So yes, in modern Madrid, you can drive barehanded.

But if you're stepping into the past—even for a day?

Glove up.

In Spain, tradition doesn't just tag along—it takes the wheel.

You thought it was just an outfit.

Turns out, it was a violation.

From forbidden camouflage to historical cosplay, these laws remind us that clothing speaks—even when it doesn't mean to. In one place, tradition is honored in stitches. In another, a tutu on a statue costs you €200.

So wherever you go?

Pack light. Dress thoughtfully.

And maybe double-check the local uniform.

Because fashion may fade…

But in some towns?

It's still legally binding.

4

TASTES LIKE REGULATION

F ood has always been more than fuel.

It's identity. It's culture.

And in some places, it's also regulated—very, very officially.

This chapter looks at what happens when taste meets law—when condiments are limited, pickles must bounce, and lobsters are legally entitled to dignity. From school cafeterias to street food carts, from butter sculptures to banned snacks behind the wheel, food becomes a legal matter the moment it leaves the plate.

Because in these stories, the flavor's personal.

But the rules? They're public.

1. BUTTER SCULPTURES COME WITH RULES (IOWA)

In Iowa, butter isn't just food.

It's performance art.

Every summer at the Iowa State Fair, thousands line up to marvel at the Butter Cow—a life-sized sculpture carved entirely from salted butter. Since 1911, it's become a rotating showcase of dairy icons: astronauts, athletes, Elvis, entire movie scenes—all sculpted with care and kept under refrigeration. It's quirky. It's beloved. It's Iowa.

But behind the whimsy? A thick slab of regulation.

Butter sculptures are governed by state agricultural codes and fairground rules. All butter used in public display must come from certified dairy sources, and sculptors must apply for special permits. Once the butter goes public, it's a regulated exhibit—subject to sanitation laws, food safety policies, and environmental protocols.

After the fair, the butter isn't sold or eaten. It's repurposed—usually into biodiesel or compost. Iowa doesn't play games with its dairy.

There's more. Event organizers must provide refrigeration documentation, allergen warnings, and indoor environmental controls. Butter melts fast in an Iowa August. And nobody wants to see a butter Abraham Lincoln collapse mid-fair.

The point isn't just cleanliness. It's pride. Iowa's fair is more than entertainment—it's an annual celebration of the state's farming legacy. The butter cow is a symbol. The rules protect it.

So if you're thinking of sculpting your dairy dreams?

Get a permit. Respect the temperature.

And remember: in Iowa, butter isn't just breakfast.

It's history on display.

2. "HANDS-ONLY" WHEN EATING FRIED CHICKEN (GAINESVILLE, GEORGIA)

In Gainesville, Georgia, it is technically illegal to eat fried chicken with a fork.

Yes. Really.

The ordinance was passed in 1961, when Gainesville proudly dubbed itself the "Poultry Capital of the World." It wasn't just a slogan—the local poultry industry still processes millions of birds a week. Chicken is culture here.

So city leaders decided to protect the ritual. The law declared that fried chicken is a delicacy "to be eaten with the fingers." Not encouraged. Required.

It's rarely enforced—except when someone decides to have fun.

In 2009, a 91-year-old woman was "arrested" for using a fork at a local restaurant. Officers issued a citation. Media appeared. The community buzzed. Then came the reveal: it was all a birthday prank coordinated by city officials. The woman laughed. So did the town.

But the law? Still on the books.

Today, the ordinance lives on in brochures, interviews, and hometown pride. Gainesville's chicken economy still thrives thanks to companies like Fieldale Farms and Mar-Jac Poultry (Gainesville CVB, 2023). And the finger-food rule? It's become a quirky symbol of local identity.

So if you find yourself in Gainesville ordering fried chicken?

Put the fork down.

Use your hands.

Respect the bird.

Because here, manners matter.

But loyalty to the drumstick matters more.

3. PICKLES MUST BOUNCE TO BE LEGAL (CONNECTICUT)

In Connecticut, for a pickle to be legally sold—it must bounce.

Yes, that was the test.

Yes, it was real.

And yes, it's still legend.

The story dates to 1948, when two Hartford vendors were fined for selling "inedible pickles." The pickles were mushy, slimy, and wildly unpopular. So state inspectors got creative.

They dropped the pickles from 12 inches above the ground. If they bounced, they passed. If not? They failed. The soft ones flopped. The vendors were fined. The bounce test became history.

Modern food laws in Connecticut now focus on pH, temperature, and sanitation. No one is bouncing pickles behind deli counters.

But the tale lives on—in trivia books, state press releases, and high school civics classes.

And honestly? It's not that ridiculous. A proper pickle should have snap. If it flops like a wet sponge, something's wrong.

The regulation may be outdated, but its message holds: food quality matters. Texture matters. And sometimes? A good bounce tells you everything you need to know.

So if you're selling pickles in the Constitution State?

Keep the brine tight.

Check the firmness.

And remember—bad pickles fall flat.

The good ones?

Bounce back.

4. NO EATING BEHIND THE WHEEL (CYPRUS)

In Cyprus, eating or drinking while driving isn't just frowned upon—it's illegal.

No burgers.

No bottled water.

No "I'm just unwrapping a granola bar."

The law is part of Cyprus's broader effort to cut down on distracted driving. And unlike some obscure rules, this one's enforced. If you're caught with one hand on the wheel and the other holding a snack—even at a red light—you could face a fine of up to €85.

It's not about hunger. It's about focus. Cyprus classifies eating and drinking while driving as a "primary distraction." The moment your hand leaves the wheel or your eyes dip to a wrapper, your reaction time suffers—and on Cyprus's narrow, winding roads, that moment matters.

This applies whether you're speeding on the motorway or sipping coffee at a stoplight. Officers are trained to spot mid-bite behavior and won't hesitate to issue a citation—even if you're "just finishing lunch."

Tourists are often surprised. In the U.S. and U.K., dashboard dining is practically a tradition. But in Cyprus, food belongs on a plate, not in a cupholder. Public service campaigns even warn visitors: eat before or after the drive—not during.

Commercial drivers have lobbied for exceptions, especially those clocking long hours. So far? No luck.

So if you're road-tripping through Cyprus, enjoy the view. Take breaks. Refuel responsibly.

Because here, distracted driving doesn't start with texting.

It starts with lunch.

5. OFFENSIVE WINE LABELS ARE BANNED (FRANCE)

France takes its wine seriously. So seriously that even the label can land you in trouble—especially if it mocks the government.

Under French law, all wine sold to the public must comply with strict regulations on origin, content, and labeling. These are overseen by the Institut National de l'Origine et de la Qualité (INAO), which protects the integrity of French agricultural products.

Most label rules deal with accuracy—grape variety, region, production methods. But tone matters too. French commercial code prohibits language that could be considered offensive to public institutions or public order. Satire, political jabs, or even subtle insults aimed at the state can get you fined—or your bottles pulled from shelves.

A wine called "Presidential Hangover"? Likely a violation. "Government Swill"? Definitely. Even mild wordplay involving elected officials might trigger scrutiny.

This isn't just a hypothetical. Winemakers have occasionally tested the line, and regulators have responded. While France has room for creativity—wines like "Vin de Merde" have managed to squeak through—mocking the government crosses it.

The regulation stems from the 1919 Appellation d'Origine Contrôlée law, with modern additions from food and advertising codes. The goal? Preserve dignity and protect the world's most iconic wine industry from becoming a political punchline.

So if you're bottling something bold in Bordeaux and considering a cheeky label?

Think twice.

Because in France, your wine can be full-bodied—

but your label better behave.

6. KETCHUP USE IS LIMITED IN SCHOOL CAFETERIAS (FRANCE)

In France, ketchup isn't just a condiment.

It's a cultural threat.

That's how national cafeteria guidelines have treated it since 2011, when the government restricted ketchup use in public schools—not because of sugar or allergies, but to protect French culinary tradition.

The policy, introduced by the National Union of Public School Caterers and backed by the Ministry of Agriculture and Food, limits ketchup to specific foods—usually fries. Unlimited packets? Not allowed. Using it instead of béarnaise or hollandaise? Out of the question.

The rule wasn't about nutrition. It was about nuance.

In France, school lunch is sacred. Meals are structured, regionally inspired, and designed to educate young palates. Students don't just eat. They learn—about texture, patience, balance, and flavor. Ketchup, to many chefs, flattens all that. It overrides seasoning. It's the enemy of subtlety.

Naturally, the rule sparked debate. Some called it pretentious. Others saw it as proud. Either way, the law reflects France's belief that food is part of citizenship—and that even the cafeteria deserves dignity.

So if you're a student in France and reach for that squeeze bottle?

Be careful.

Because here, even condiments must show cultural respect.

7. YOUR ICE CUBES MUST BE DRINKABLE (ITALY)

In Italy, when you order a cold drink, you're getting more than refreshment.

You're getting a quiet promise: the ice in your glass has been approved by law.

That's because in Italy, ice served to the public must be made from certified potable water—not just filtered, not "probably fine," but legally drinkable and lab-tested.

Under public health regulations issued by the Ministero della Salute (Ministry of Health), any food business that prepares and serves ice—whether it's a high-end restaurant in Milan or a seaside cart in Sicily—must use water from an approved source. It must meet strict chemical and microbiological standards, and the ice must be made, handled, and stored in sanitized containers.

Why the fuss?

Because ice melts. It disappears. But before it does, it can carry bacteria, viruses, or other pathogens—especially during hot summer months when refrigeration systems are under pressure. In southern regions, where heat and humidity run high, contamination risks multiply fast.

Inspections are real. Food safety officers can test ice cubes, check sourcing documentation, and review storage conditions. If something's off—wrong freezer temperature, questionable handling, or non-certified water—the business can be fined or shut down on the spot. Repeat violations can lead to license suspension.

Tourists rarely notice. Italians don't mention it. But that clink in your Aperol Spritz? It's fully regulation-approved.

So if you're sipping a cold espresso tonic on a sunny terrace in Naples, know this:

That chill you're tasting?

It's 100% legal.

Because in Italy, even ice has standards.

8. SUSPICIOUS SALMON CAN GET YOU CHARGED (UNITED KINGDOM)

This isn't about poaching.

It's not about theft.

It's about your vibe.

Under the UK's Salmon Act of 1986, it is a criminal offense to be "in possession of salmon under suspicious circumstances."

Yes, that's the actual legal phrase. Word for word.

The law was introduced to combat illegal fishing—especially poaching in protected rivers. It was designed to catch people who skirted licensing rules, hauled salmon from conservation zones, and sold fish out of coolers in parking lots.

That part? Reasonable.

But the language? Legal poetry. "Suspicious circumstances" is never defined. No examples, no gestures, no fishy facial expressions. Just vibes.

Carrying a salmon on the Tube with a nervous glance? Suspicious.

Wrapped in foil, tucked under your coat? Definitely suspicious.

Cradling it while humming "God Save the Queen"? Legally ambiguous, emotionally confusing.

The law is only triggered when illegal fishing is suspected. But the phrasing has made it a cultural icon—quoted in trivia books, law school lectures, and comedy routines alike.

It's a reminder that even sensible laws deserve better editing.

So if you're in the UK and carrying a fish?

Hold it with confidence.

And for the love of trout—bring a receipt.

Food is more than fuel.

It's identity. It's ritual. It's politics—with a side of fries.

And in some places, it's regulated right down to the ice cube.

From ketchup bans to bouncing pickles, these laws say one thing loud and clear:

Flavor may be personal.

But rules are public.

So go ahead—eat, sip, sculpt, serve.

Just know someone, somewhere, once looked at your snack and said, "Not like that."

5

PROCEED WITH CAUTION

Getting around should be easy—until the fine print kicks in.

In this chapter, we hit the road (and the curb, and the sidewalk) in search of the world's most strangely specific travel rules. Some towns fine you for honking near a sandwich shop. Others have opinions about your parking style. In one place, your shoes could be the issue.

These are the laws that turn casual movement into code enforcement.

So before you coast, brake, beep, or back in—

Check the tires.

Check the shoes.

And for the love of traffic flow, check the local rules.

1. REVERSE PARKING ISN'T ALLOWED IN SOME DRIVEWAYS (COLORADO)

You know that thing where you back into your driveway to make leaving easier in the morning?

Yeah. In some parts of Colorado, that's actually against the rules.

Cities like Aurora, Lakewood, and several neighborhoods in the Denver metro area have ordinances—or HOA regulations—that prohibit reverse parking in residential driveways. That means no backing in, even if it's your property, your car, and your five-second plan to get ahead tomorrow.

So… why?

There are two main reasons: visibility and security.

Colorado only requires rear license plates on most vehicles. When you back in, your plate faces the house, making it harder for law enforcement, neighborhood watch groups, or HOA reps to identify your vehicle quickly. In areas with community patrols or parking enforcement, that's a problem.

The second reason? Sidewalks. Backing into driveways can push vehicles over curbs, block pedestrian walkways, or create visibility issues for neighbors trying to back out themselves.

But it doesn't stop there.

Some HOAs take the argument further. They say backing in creates the impression of shady behavior—like getaway cars positioned for a fast escape. The phrase "looks suspicious" has even shown up in enforcement notices. Because sometimes, it's not about traffic flow—it's about aesthetic control.

Naturally, many residents argue the opposite: that backing in is safer, faster, and more efficient. But that doesn't always win.

Depending on the community, enforcement can mean anything from a gentle notice to a formal citation. Some HOAs have even rolled unpaid fines into homeowners' dues.

So if you're new to the neighborhood and think you're being smart by backing into your own driveway?

Double-check the rules.

Because in some corners of Colorado, turning your car around means you're already facing trouble.

2. DRIVING A DIRTY CAR CAN GET YOU FINED (RUSSIA)

In parts of Russia, driving a dirty car isn't just frowned upon.

It's a fineable offense.

Cities like Moscow, Chelyabinsk, and Yekaterinburg have hygiene codes that require vehicles to be "appropriately clean" when driven in public. That may sound like a vague guideline—but it's absolutely enforceable. Especially when it comes to your rear window and license plate.

If either one is too dirty to read? That's a ticket.

And while the fine is relatively small—500 rubles, or about $5–6 USD—it adds up fast.

Here's the kicker: the law doesn't define how dirty is *too* dirty. There's no visual scale. No measurement tool. It's up to the officer. If they think your car looks like it just crawled out of a blizzard? That's all it takes.

In some cities, police have reportedly used white gloves during stops—swiping across bumpers or windshields to check for grime. A visible streak? That could be your citation.

Originally, the rule made sense. In snowy regions where soot, salt, and slush coat everything from headlights to brake lights, safety becomes a real issue. Obstructed plates, fogged-up lights, and dirty mirrors reduce visibility and slow reaction times.

But over time, it's become more than a safety law. During "clean car" campaigns or traffic initiatives, it's also been used as a tool for civic discipline—or a revenue boost, depending on whom you ask.

So if you're road-tripping through Russia and your car's starting to resemble a rolling snowbank?

Don't wait for the glove test.

Because here, being too dirty isn't just a look.

It's a liability—with a receipt.

3. TIRES TOO DIRTY? THAT'S A VIOLATION (MINNESOTA)

You washed your hands. You cleaned the windows.

But did you check your tires?

In parts of Minnesota—especially in cities like Minneapolis and St. Paul—it's illegal to drive off a construction site, private lot, or even your own muddy driveway if your tires are tracking visible dirt, mud, gravel, or debris onto public streets.

This isn't about dusty rims—it's about what hits the road.

The law is aimed primarily at construction vehicles, but the wording is broad enough to include delivery vans, trailers, landscaping trucks, and even the occasional overambitious homeowner with a weekend excavation project. If your tires leave a trail, you're liable.

Why so strict?

Two reasons: road safety and environmental protection. Mud makes roads slick. Gravel damages windshields. And debris runoff clogs storm drains, which can cause flooding or carry pollutants into nearby lakes and rivers. In Minnesota—Land of 10,000 Lakes—that's a big deal.

To prevent this, many job sites are required to install gravel pads or tire-washing stations. In Minneapolis, inspectors can cite property owners for failing to maintain a "clean point of egress." Some job sites post signs reading "Clean Tires Required." Not a suggestion. City code.

Violations can result in on-the-spot fines ranging from $100 to $1,000. In serious cases, repeat offenders have had projects temporarily shut down until a cleanup plan is submitted and approved.

And don't think homeowners are exempt. If your DIY patio or garden overhaul turns the street into a muddy mess, expect a visit —or a bill.

So before you pull out of your lot?

Check the treads.

Because in Minnesota, dirty tires aren't just messy—

They're a municipal offense.

4. YOU MUST CARRY A BREATHALYZER IN YOUR CAR (FRANCE)

You've packed your bags. You've rented a car. You've checked the mirrors, the map, the mileage. But if you're driving in France and you don't have a breathalyzer in your glove box?

Technically, you're breaking the law.

In 2012, France introduced a rule requiring all drivers—including tourists—to carry a certified, unused alcohol test kit in their vehicle at all times. The idea was simple: reduce drunk driving by encouraging personal accountability. You could check yourself before the police ever had to.

The breathalyzers don't cost much. You can buy them at gas stations, pharmacies, and even some convenience stores. They're single-use and sealed in plastic. Blow into the tube, compare the color to the chart, and get your answer. If you're close to the limit? You wait.

France has one of the strictest legal blood alcohol limits in Europe: 0.05%. For bus and commercial drivers, it's even lower. The hope was that making breath tests easily available would help people think twice before driving home from a vineyard tour, a long lunch, or a seaside dinner with just one more glass of wine.

The rule stirred debate. Critics called it confusing. Others pointed out that the fine for not carrying a breathalyzer was suspended indefinitely in 2013—meaning you're still supposed to have one, but you likely won't be punished if you don't. Still, the law remains on the books.

So while enforcement is light, the expectation is real.

If you're road-tripping through France, toss a breathalyzer in the glove box. It might save you a fine. It might save your license. Or, best case, it might save you from a very French lecture on personal responsibility.

5. YOU MUST WALK YOUR BIKE ACROSS INTERSECTIONS (JAPAN)

You're biking through Japan. The breeze is perfect. The basket's full. The street is quiet.

You coast toward a crosswalk, see no one coming, and roll straight through.

Congratulations. You just broke the law.

In many Japanese cities—including Tokyo, Kyoto, and Osaka—it's legally required that cyclists dismount and walk their bikes across pedestrian crosswalks unless there's a clearly marked bicycle lane or signal. No bike symbol? No wheels.

It's not just a matter of etiquette—it's regulation. And yes, it's enforced.

The law stems from a strong commitment to pedestrian safety. In Japan, pedestrians always have the right of way in zebra-striped crosswalks. Bicycles, though common and encouraged, are not considered pedestrians under traffic law. So riding through a crosswalk—even slowly—counts as a traffic violation.

You'll see signage near intersections showing a stick figure politely walking a bike. Some even include bold red Xs over riders in motion. And if the sign isn't enough? Uniformed officers sometimes wait nearby during busy hours, calmly directing violators to step off and try again.

Tourists are often confused. In many countries, bikes are allowed to mingle freely with pedestrians. But in Japan, distinctions are important. Order matters. Harmony matters. And a little extra effort is expected if it contributes to a safer flow.

This isn't to say Japan is unfriendly to cyclists. Quite the opposite. Many sidewalks feature bike lanes. Cities provide ample bike parking. And neighborhoods are filled with riders of all ages. But when it comes to crossing intersections, the ritual is clear:

Step down. Walk across. Ride on.

Because in Japan, even your two wheels are part of the rhythm of the street. And sometimes, a moment of patience is the shortest path to getting where you're going.

6. JAYWALKING IS MORE THAN A BAD IDEA (SINGAPORE)

In most countries, jaywalking is discouraged.

In Singapore? It's a criminal offense.

Crossing the street outside a designated crosswalk—or stepping off the curb before the green man appears—can land you with a fine of up to SGD $1,000 (about $750 USD) or even three months in jail. That's not a warning. That's a formal charge. With real paperwork.

Singapore is world-famous for its cleanliness and order, and pedestrian behavior is no exception. The same country that once banned chewing gum also cracks down on gumption—especially when it comes to traffic laws.

Officers regularly patrol intersections, particularly near busy MRT stations, shopping hubs like Orchard Road, and popular tourist districts around Marina Bay. They're trained to watch for the tiniest foot creep over the line. And they don't hesitate to act. Tourists, residents, first-time offenders—it doesn't matter. You cross early, you risk getting stopped.

The approach isn't aggressive—it's efficient. Jaywalking enforcement isn't personal. It's procedural.

To be fair, Singapore makes it easy to follow the rules. Pedestrian bridges, underground walkways, extended green lights, and countdown timers are common across the city. You're rarely far from a legal crossing. But if you ignore it—even to "check traffic" or make a quick dash—you're technically breaking the law.

Locals know this. Many visitors don't. That leads to awkward stops, unexpected fines, and the occasional finger-wag from an unimpressed officer with a clipboard.

So if you're exploring Singapore and feel tempted to invent your own shortcut?

Don't.

Pause. Wait. Breathe.

Because here, crossing outside the lines isn't "bold" or "urban."

It's illegal.

And in Singapore, the rules aren't just suggestions.

They're street-level law.

7. FLIP-FLOPS BEHIND THE WHEEL ARE BANNED (SPAIN)

In Spain, if you slide behind the wheel in flip-flops, you're not just risking a fashion faux pas.

You're risking a fine.

Up to €200, to be exact.

Spanish traffic law doesn't name-drop flip-flops specifically—but it doesn't have to. Article 18.1 of the Reglamento General de Circulación requires drivers to maintain full control of their vehicle and freedom of movement at all times. If your footwear interferes—slips off, jams under a pedal, or limits responsiveness—you could be in violation.

That includes flip-flops, clogs, mules, beach slides, and yes, even bare feet.

Every summer, the Dirección General de Tráfico (DGT) launches public awareness campaigns. These include infographics and upbeat PSAs that aren't about fashion—they're about physics. Your foot can't respond quickly if your shoe has its own agenda.

Enforcement is real. You don't have to crash to get pulled over. If an officer sees questionable footwear at a stoplight, they can issue a fine on the spot. No skid marks required.

Tourists often learn this the hard way. You leave the beach, hop in the rental car, still sandy and sun-kissed—only to find yourself ticketed before you reach the roundabout.

Locals, meanwhile, know the drill. Many keep a pair of "driving shoes" in the car. It's a simple solution—and it saves money.

So if you're cruising the coastal roads of Andalucía or weaving through Madrid traffic, do your ankles a favor.

Leave the flip-flops for the paseo.

Because in Spain, road safety doesn't stop at the knees.

It starts with your shoes.

8. SCOOTERS OFF THE SIDEWALK, PLEASE (PARIS)

Once upon a time, Paris fell in love with electric scooters.

They were modern. Efficient. Chic, even.

But then came the chaos.

Scooters piled up on sidewalks. Blocked doorways. Floated in fountains. Residents tripped over them. Tourists crashed them. City planners winced.

By 2023, romance turned to regulation. After a citywide referendum, Paris became the first major European capital to ban rental e-scooters outright. The ban passed easily—despite low turnout. Privately owned scooters are still allowed. But riding them on sidewalks? That's a loud, fineable, €135 no.

Why the crackdown?

Public safety. Urban clutter. And a craving for order.

Scooter-related injuries had skyrocketed. Riders zipped through crowds, ran red lights, and abandoned scooters wherever they pleased—atop steps, across statues, wedged into café terraces. Elderly residents were at risk. So were toddlers. And monuments.

Under new rules, scooters must stay in bike lanes or on roads. GPS systems can now limit speed in high-traffic zones. Parking is only allowed in designated areas. Violators may be fined—or have their scooter remotely disabled.

Some still grumble. But others say the city feels calmer now—more walkable, more Paris.

So if you're cruising past the Eiffel Tower with the breeze in your hair?

Stick to the bike lane.

Because in Paris, the sidewalk isn't yours.

It's the city's.

Mobility feels like freedom — until someone pulls out a citation pad.

From back-in parking to flip-flops behind the wheel, the rules in these pages show how easily movement becomes a municipal matter. What feels like common sense in one place might be a fine in another.

So before you coast, park, scoot, or jaywalk —

Check the signs.

Check the shoes.

And for the love of traffic flow, follow the local vibe.

Because here, even motion has rules.

And yes, they're watching.

6

YOUR CASTLE, THEIR RULES

You finally made it home—now the rules really begin.

This chapter walks you through the quiet battleground of homeownership, where lawns have limits, curtains have codes, and toilets? They keep a schedule. Whether it's an HOA demanding window uniformity or a city ordinance outlawing porch fridges, domestic life is full of surprising restrictions.

These aren't rules you'll find in decorating magazines.

They're in covenants, lease agreements, and building codes.

So take your shoes off, lower your voice, and maybe hide the laundry.

Because in some neighborhoods?

Compliance lives right next to comfort.

1. WINDOW TREATMENTS MUST MATCH (HOAS)

You bought the house.

You pay the mortgage.

But your curtains?

Yeah… those still belong to the HOA.

In HOA-governed neighborhoods, even your windows are regulated. And it's not about what you see—it's about what others see from the street.

Many associations require that all visible window treatments be white or neutral in color. That means no teal blackout panels. No galaxy-print sheers. No Star Wars-themed blackout shades, no matter how much your kid loves them. If it can be seen from the sidewalk, it better be beige.

In places like Chandler, Arizona; The Woodlands, Texas; and parts of Orlando, Florida, these standards are written into HOA covenants. Some neighborhoods go further—specifying fabric types, banning patterns, or mandating vertical blinds across entire complexes.

The reasoning? Curb appeal. Visual harmony. Property value protection. According to HOAs, mismatched window treatments create "visual clutter" and disrupt the aesthetic flow.

To homeowners, it can feel invasive. Like micromanagement with a measuring tape.

But enforcement is real. Violators might get warning letters, fines (sometimes daily), or even "compliance correction" fees—where the HOA hires someone to fix the issue and bills you for the pleasure.

So if you're moving into a deed-restricted neighborhood and dreaming of maximalist windows or mood-lit rooms with maroon velvet drapes?

Check the HOA handbook first.

Because in some places, even your curtains must conform.

2. YOUR GARDEN GNOME MIGHT NEED A PERMIT (GERMANY)

In parts of Germany, your garden isn't entirely yours—especially if it includes a gnome.

Cities like Freiburg, Wiesbaden, and neighborhoods within Munich enforce strict zoning laws and aesthetic guidelines. Residents in historic districts or modern housing cooperatives may need formal approval before adding exterior decorations. That includes flowerpots, fountains, satellite dishes—and yes, even garden gnomes.

The problem isn't the gnome itself. It's the message it sends.

German zoning policies emphasize "architectural harmony," which prioritizes visual consistency across façades, balconies, and shared spaces. A gnome that's too cheeky, too colorful, or holding a beer stein? It could be seen as an affront to the carefully curated curb appeal.

In newer developments, community rules—called Wohnanlagen—govern everything from doormats to lawn ornaments. A gnome tucked behind a hedge might be fine. But one proudly posted near the gate? That might bring a visit from the Ordnungsamt (municipal enforcement office).

Consequences range from polite warnings to daily fines. In a widely cited case, a man in Schleswig-Holstein was ordered to remove a gnome giving the middle finger. He claimed it was political speech. The court disagreed. The gnome got evicted.

To be clear: Germany doesn't hate gnomes. The Gartenzwerg is a cherished national tradition. But Germany also values order, restraint, and symmetry—especially in urban planning.

So if your garden guardian is looking bold or rebellious?

Check the rules before you plant him.

Because in Germany, even the smallest statue might need a permit.

3. FAILING TO FLUSH IS A CRIME (SINGAPORE)

You finish your business.

You wash your hands.

You forget one step.

In Singapore, that's not just inconsiderate—it's illegal.

Under Section 17(1) of the Environmental Public Health Act, failing to flush a public toilet after use is a punishable offense. The fine? Up to SGD $150 for a first offense. And yes, enforcement is real. Officers have been known to conduct random checks, especially in high-traffic areas like MRT stations and hawker centers.

Why the crackdown? Cleanliness.

Singapore has built its global reputation on order and hygiene. No gum. No graffiti. No grime. That level of control extends to restrooms, where unflushed toilets are seen not just as gross—but as a threat to public health and civic standards.

There are signs. There are reminders. There are even automated systems that issue flushes or sound alerts when someone walks away too quickly. But in facilities without sensors? The law expects you to handle it manually.

Tourists are often surprised. Locals? Not so much. Most Singaporeans grew up with flush etiquette drilled into them—part social habit, part legal awareness, all common sense.

So if you're visiting the city-state and stop at a public restroom, don't forget to hit the button or pull the handle.

Because in Singapore, flushing isn't just polite.

It's the law.

And walking away without doing it?

That's a ticket waiting to happen.

4. YOUR GRASS HEIGHT MIGHT BE REGULATED (HOAS)

You own your home.

You own your yard.

But your grass?

That still belongs to the HOA.

Across the United States, homeowners associations enforce a stunning variety of lawn-related rules—some reasonable, some borderline absurd. They govern how high your grass can grow, how often you mow, and even what kinds of plants are permitted. Thinking about clover? Dandelions? Wildflowers? That's a maybe, a no, and a definite fine.

Many HOAs cap grass height at 3.5 inches. Some require mowing weekly—rain or shine, mower broken or not. Let it slide? Expect a warning letter. Ignore that? Get ready for fines. Fall too far behind? They might file a lien.

And it doesn't end with mowing.

HOAs often regulate mulch color, grass species, edging techniques, and even the direction you rake. Aesthetic consistency is the goal. If your lawn looks too wild or too different, you've violated the unwritten rule of suburban uniformity.

Even outside HOA zones, cities and counties get involved. Municipal ordinances in places like Dallas, Los Angeles, and Naples, Florida impose fines for "neglected yards," citing fire risk, pest control, and community standards.

Some areas even allow anonymous complaints. That's right: your neighbor can report your overgrown grass—and you won't know who did it until the citation arrives.

So before you toss the mower and embrace a lush, low-maintenance jungle of wildflowers and eco-grass?

Check the bylaws.

Check the zoning.

Check your neighbor's clipboard.

Because in some suburbs, long grass isn't landscaping.

It's an act of rebellion.

5. FLUSHING IS LIMITED AFTER 10PM (SWITZERLAND)

You've brushed your teeth.

You've turned off the lights.

You reach for the handle—

And pause.

Because in Switzerland, in some apartment buildings and rental flats, flushing your toilet after 10PM isn't just discouraged. It's sometimes outright banned.

This rule isn't national. It lives in building codes, tenant agreements, and HOA policies. But it's real. And yes—it's enforced.

Why? One word: noise.

Many Swiss apartments share vertical plumbing stacks. A single flush can echo through multiple floors like a pipe-organ crescendo. Add in tile, concrete walls, and a neighbor who goes to bed early—and suddenly your late-night bathroom break is the building's main event.

Landlords in Zurich, Basel, and Geneva often include "quiet-hour flushing" clauses in rental contracts. Break them and you might get a warning, a noise complaint—or a building-wide memo taped to the elevator. Some local authorities have even issued citations.

And toilets are just the beginning.

Other bans include post-10PM laundry, late-night showers, and—of course—vacuuming on Sundays. In Switzerland, quiet isn't just polite. It's policy.

So if nature calls after dark?

Flush softly.

Or wait until morning.

Because here, even your plumbing has a bedtime.

And the toilet? She's on a curfew.

6. ALL RENTALS MUST INCLUDE A BATHTUB (PORTLAND, OREGON)

In Portland, Oregon, if you rent out a home or apartment, you're required by law to provide a working bathtub.

Not just a shower.

Not a rainfall head with spa lighting.

An actual, soak-worthy tub.

According to Portland's Housing Maintenance Code, every rental unit must include access to a tub or shower—or both—with a reliable supply of hot and cold water. But here's the catch: older versions of the code specifically required bathtubs. And while the updated law allows either, that legacy language still influences how inspections are conducted—especially for buildings constructed before 1991.

Why the bathtub bias?

Historically, bathtubs were considered superior for hygiene. A long soak was viewed as the ultimate clean. Showers? More efficient, sure—but not quite as thorough. When the original housing codes were written, tubs were the default.

Fast forward: renters today favor sleek showers, especially in compact apartments. But if landlords remove a tub—particularly in older buildings—they risk being cited for non-compliance.

The result? Clunky tubs wedged into bathrooms that were clearly remodeled with modern showers in mind. Fixtures no one uses, installed purely to check a bureaucratic box.

Landlords and housing advocates have called for an update. But until the city rewrites the inspection guidelines, the rule remains enforceable.

So if you're renovating a Portland rental and thinking of skipping the tub?

Don't.

Because here, a tub isn't just a lifestyle choice.

It's a legal one.

7. CLOTHESLINES ARE BANNED IN SOME NEIGHBORHOODS (HOAS)

It's sunny.

You've got fresh laundry.

You head outside with a basket and a handful of clothespins...

And just like that, you've broken the rules.

Across the U.S., especially in HOA-governed neighborhoods, clotheslines are banned or tightly restricted. The reason? Aesthetics.

HOAs argue that visible clotheslines—with their flapping socks, towels, and questionable pajama bottoms—disrupt the carefully curated look of a planned community. Some say they lower property values. Others cite vague "decency standards," as though drying your laundry outdoors were a public scandal.

These bans are especially common in suburban developments across Florida, Texas, North Carolina, and California. Sometimes the restriction is buried in the fine print of your deed. Other times, you don't find out until a warning letter shows up on your door. One Arizona resident recalled being told to "remove line immediately—or by sundown." That was not a metaphor.

Fines for violations can reach hundreds of dollars. Some HOAs issue daily penalties until the offending laundry disappears. Others go the soft-pressure route: passive-aggressive notes, stern emails, or whispered disapproval from across the driveway.

But resistance is growing.

The Right to Dry movement has helped pass laws in states like Vermont, Colorado, and Hawaii, where residents are now legally entitled to air-dry their clothes—even if their HOA disagrees. Still, the legal landscape remains inconsistent. In some places, your right to dry is protected. In others? It's a fine in the making.

So before you string a line between your porch columns and let your T-shirts fly free?

Check the bylaws.

Because in some neighborhoods, your laundry isn't just airing out.

It's making a statement.

8. PORCH FRIDGES ARE AGAINST THE RULES (NORTH CAROLINA & OTHERS)

You've got an old fridge.

You've got a porch.

You've got a plan.

Cold drinks within reach. Leftovers one step from the grill. What could go wrong?

Well… in some towns? Everything.

Across parts of North Carolina—especially in Charlotte—as well as in counties throughout Texas, Georgia, and Florida, local ordinances prohibit keeping refrigerators or freezers on porches, in side yards, or anywhere visible from the street.

At first glance, it sounds like suburban overreach. But there are three key reasons behind the rule.

First: safety. Older refrigerators with mechanical latches pose suffocation risks if left unplugged and unattended. Even if you zip-tie the door or remove it entirely, many municipalities don't allow exceptions.

Second: pests. Empty fridges attract raccoons, rats, snakes, and the occasional very bold cat. Add some heat and humidity? That fridge becomes a rodent rave.

Third: curb appeal. City codes reference "visual clutter" and "neighborhood standards." Translation? A porch fridge doesn't just keep your beer cold. It lowers the tone of the block.

These rules fall under property maintenance codes or nuisance ordinances. In HOA-governed neighborhoods, the restrictions get more specific—often banning not just fridges, but couches, dishwashers, or any appliance that dares to go outside.

Violators may receive fines, notices, or even removal bills. In some cases, repeated violations can escalate to court—or spark a minor civil war on the HOA Facebook group.

So before you plug in that patio beer fridge and declare yourself a genius?

Check your local code.

Because in some towns, even your appliances have to live indoors.

It's your home.

Your space.

Your domain... with conditions.

From silent flushing to matching drapes, these aren't just neighborhood quirks. They're enforceable. Some keep you safe. Some keep up appearances. And some exist purely so your neighbor can file a complaint.

So yes, you might hold the keys.

But the fine print holds the remote.

And it's watching your lawn.

Read the lease. Skim the HOA manual.

Maybe ask about the gnome.

Because in the world of homeownership, the most common décor?

Regulation.

7

WATCH YOUR LANGUAGE

S ome words are banned.

Some are mocked.

Some just can't be printed on a government form.

This chapter explores what happens when language itself is the offense—

when names are denied, jokes cross a line, or silence becomes the only safe option.

From courtroom etiquette to naming committees to funeral decorum, speech isn't always free.

And when you do speak up?

You'd better watch the tone.

Because the law might be listening.

And in a few places…

So is the ghost at the back of the room.

1. ELECTION SPEECH IS BANNED NEAR SCHOOLS (UNITED STATES)

On Election Day, many public schools double as polling places.

And when they do?

The First Amendment gets a timeout.

In dozens of U.S. states—including Texas, New York, Florida, and Georgia—it's illegal to engage in political speech within a designated buffer zone around polling locations. Typically, that zone extends 100 to 150 feet from the entrance. Inside it? No campaign buttons, no flyers, no bumper stickers, no signs. Not even a slogan on a T-shirt.

This kind of speech is called "electioneering." And when a polling station is inside a school, the restriction often extends across the whole campus—hallways, gymnasiums, parking lots—even if no students are present. The goal is to create a neutral, low-pressure environment for voters. The result? Some awkward conversations.

In 2020, a voter in Michigan was told to remove a "Don't Tread on Me" shirt. In Georgia, political face masks were flagged—even during early voting. While some states limit enforcement to overt candidate endorsements, others cast a wider net over anything remotely political. Either way, poll workers are trained to spot violations and act fast.

The logic is to protect the democratic process from influence, intimidation, or distraction. But in practice, it often turns into a tense moment in a quiet school hallway.

So if you're heading to the polls, especially at a school, leave the slogans at home.

Vote in peace.

And let your ballot do the talking.

2. DON'T SAY "ABRACADABRA" AT TEMPLES (SRI LANKA)

In Sri Lanka, saying "abracadabra" near a temple might not earn you a laugh.

It might earn you a fine.

Not because the word is vulgar—but because it's often seen as spiritual mockery.

The term "abracadabra" likely originated from the Aramaic phrase *avra kehdabra*, meaning "I will create as I speak." Historically, it appeared in ancient healing rituals and was inscribed on amulets believed to ward off illness. In various traditions, the word held genuine mystical power.

But in the modern West, it's survived mainly as stage magic jargon—a punchline before pulling a rabbit out of a hat or sawing a box in half.

In Sri Lanka, especially in Buddhist temples and ancient sacred sites, that shift in tone hasn't landed well.

Here, reverence matters. A lot.

Sacred spaces in cities like Kandy, Dambulla, Anuradhapura, and Polonnaruwa aren't just historic—they're active sites of worship. Chanting, incense, and ritual silence are taken seriously. Tourists tossing out "abracadabra" as a joke, even casually, are often perceived as mocking centuries of practice.

There's no national law banning the word. But social enforcement? Absolutely real.

In 2017, a tourist in Kandy was detained for shouting "abracadabra" near a religious ceremony. He didn't mean harm. But locals saw it as disrespectful. He was questioned, fined, and escorted away. Other visitors have received warnings for theatrical gestures, jokes, or irreverent selfies inside sacred zones.

Signs near temple entrances often remind guests to dress modestly, remove shoes, speak softly, and avoid "performative behavior." These rules aren't about controlling tourists—they're about preserving sanctity.

So if you're visiting a sacred site in Sri Lanka and feel a joke coming on?

Maybe hold it.

Because here, reverence isn't an optional vibe.

It's a nonverbal requirement.

3. NAMES MUST BE APPROVED BY COMMITTEE (ICELAND)

In Iceland, naming your child isn't just a personal choice—it's a legal process. Since 1991, a government-appointed body known as the Mannanafnanefnd (Icelandic Naming Committee) has held the power to approve or reject baby names. If your chosen name isn't already on the official national registry of approved names, you'll need to submit an application. And don't be surprised if it gets denied.

Why the scrutiny? Because Icelandic is a grammatically complex, highly inflected language, and names play a big role in how the system functions. Every name must be able to decline in Icelandic, meaning it can change form depending on case and context. Names must also follow phonetic rules, use only letters from the Icelandic alphabet, and reflect Icelandic cultural norms. The committee also evaluates names for potential embarrassment or psychological harm to the child.

Some well-publicized rejections include Harriet, which doesn't fit Icelandic grammatical structure; Enzo, considered too foreign in both spelling and sound; and Lucifer, rejected for what officials described as "obvious reasons."

If your submission is approved, the name is added to the registry and becomes fair game for other parents as well. If rejected, there's no appeal process. That decision is final—no matter how many times you saw the name in a movie or how many Instagram likes it got.

The rule even applies to immigrants who wish to register or legally change their names in Iceland. The intent isn't to stifle creativity, but to preserve linguistic integrity and cultural identity.

Icelandic relies on naming structure for grammar, recordkeeping, and community cohesion.

So if you're expecting a child in Reykjavík and brainstorming something bold or unconventional, pause before you print the birth certificate. Because in Iceland, your name still needs a stamp of approval—officially and grammatically.

4. YOU CAN'T NAME YOUR CHILD "LUCIFER" (GERMANY)

In Germany, if you try to name your child *Lucifer*, you'll run into more than raised eyebrows—you'll run into the civil registry.

Germany has some of the strictest naming laws in Europe. Every name submitted to the *Standesamt* (civil registry office) must meet specific criteria: it must clearly indicate gender, avoid causing offense, and not endanger the child's emotional well-being. If a name could result in ridicule, discrimination, or legal confusion, the office has the right—and responsibility—to reject it.

That's exactly what happened in 2017 when a couple in Kassel tried to name their newborn son *Lucifer*. The registry declined, citing potential psychological harm. The concern wasn't theological—it was practical. Naming a baby after one of the most vilified figures in Western tradition, officials reasoned, might lead to bullying or exclusion.

The parents appealed. The case went to court. The judge didn't deliberate long: *Lucifer*, he ruled, was not an acceptable name under German law. The couple eventually chose *Lucian* instead.

Germany doesn't keep a formal list of banned names, but it relies on precedent. Other rejections include *Osama Bin Laden*, *Grammophon* ("gramophone"), *Grüß Gott* ("God greets you"), and

Winnetou, a fictional Native American character now viewed as culturally insensitive.

If a name raises red flags, the registry may consult linguists, psychologists, or legal experts. The goal isn't to stifle creativity—it's to protect children and ensure consistent, culturally appropriate records.

So if you're standing in a Berlin hospital with bold ideas and a birth certificate to fill out?

Write carefully.

Because in Germany, not every name is welcome—even if it sounds devilishly original.

5. YOU CAN'T NAME YOUR CHILD "4REAL" (NEW ZEALAND)

In New Zealand, the name *4Real* was officially rejected by the government.

Not because it was hard to pronounce.

Because it started with a number.

In 2007, a couple in Wellington wanted to name their newborn son *4Real*—pronounced "For Real." The inspiration struck during an emotional ultrasound moment. To them, the name felt raw, honest, and deeply personal. But to the Registrar of Births, Deaths, and Marriages? It felt like a problem.

New Zealand has some of the world's strictest naming laws. Overseen by the Department of Internal Affairs, these rules are designed to protect children from names that might cause embarrassment, confusion, or harm. Names cannot include numbers, symbols, punctuation, or imitate official titles like *King, Justice,* or

Princess. They must also be suitable for legal documents and everyday use.

4Real broke several rules at once.

The couple pushed back. The story made headlines across New Zealand—and eventually, around the world. But officials stood firm. In the end, the parents settled on *Superman* as a middle name and kept the first name private.

They weren't the first to be denied.

Over the years, New Zealand has rejected names like *Talula Does The Hula From Hawaii* (which led to temporary guardianship by the court), *Fish and Chips* (proposed for twins), *Chief Maximus*, and several others deemed too offensive to publish.

The rules may seem rigid, but the purpose is clear: protect kids from mockery—and registrars from paperwork nightmares.

So if you're in Auckland and feel a flash of creative genius?

Pause before you reach for the keyboard.

Because in New Zealand, bold names don't just need character.

They need approval.

6. WHISTLING INDOORS ON SUNDAYS WAS ONCE BANNED (VERMONT)

If you find yourself humming a tune on a quiet Vermont Sunday, go right ahead.

But if it turns into a whistle?

Technically, you might be breaking the law.

In certain Vermont towns, old local ordinances once prohibited whistling indoors on Sundays. Not because of volume. Not because you were off-key. But because whistling was considered frivolous on the Sabbath—a day meant for rest, reverence, and stillness.

These rules were part of a broader category known as blue laws—early American statutes designed to enforce moral behavior on Sundays. Most people associate blue laws with bans on alcohol sales or closed businesses. But in Vermont, they went further. No public dancing. No theatrical performances. No unnecessary labor. And in some towns? No cheerful trilling inside government buildings.

Whistling was seen as idle, mischievous, or even irreverent. In post offices, libraries, and town halls, it signaled a lack of seriousness. And in an era when social order and moral tone were legislated, even a friendly whistle could be met with correction.

Today, these laws are largely ceremonial—rarely enforced, often forgotten. But they still show up in historical records and legal archives. Towns like Barre, Middlebury, and St. Johnsbury have all been named in accounts where these rules once had real weight.

You probably won't get fined for whistling at the town clerk. But you might get a look. The kind that says: "We used to have a rule about that."

So if you're visiting Vermont on a Sunday and feel a tune bubbling up?

Stick to humming.

Or let the silence sing.

Because once upon a time, even your whistle was pushing legal limits.

7. YOU CAN'T SWEAR NEAR A CORPSE (SOME U.S. STATES)

You're at a funeral. You trip over a folding chair. You mutter something you hope kids didn't hear.

In certain U.S. states? That moment might be a misdemeanor.

In places like Georgia, North Carolina, and Alabama, laws still exist that make it illegal to use "profane, indecent, or vulgar language" in the presence of a deceased person—particularly during or near funeral services. These laws are rarely enforced today, but they remain active in legal codes as remnants of older public morality statutes.

Why would this be illegal? Because for much of American legal history, disturbing the peace didn't just mean blasting music or inciting riots. It meant maintaining social decorum—especially around death. Profanity was seen not only as disrespectful, but as something that could deeply disturb mourners and degrade the sanctity of public mourning.

In Georgia, state law (O.C.G.A. § 16-11-34) explicitly forbids offensive or abusive language "at or near the body of a deceased person" if it causes distress. North Carolina includes similar language in its disorderly conduct statutes. The key concern isn't the corpse—it's the community. These laws aim to protect the emotional wellbeing of grieving families and preserve the solemnity of death-related gatherings.

Today, enforcement is rare and typically reserved for extreme disruptions—like shouting obscenities during a service or protesting a funeral. But technically, the law could still apply in more mundane settings if a complaint were made.

So yes, you can attend a funeral. You can grieve. You can even trip on a floral arrangement. But if something goes wrong? Keep your expletives internal.

Because in some states, even the dead deserve a little peace and quiet.

8. "PEACE" WAS TABOO IN PARLIAMENT (UNITED KINGDOM – HISTORICAL)

During World War I, one word became strangely unwelcome in the British Parliament.

Peace.

From 1915 to 1918, Members of Parliament who dared mention the word—especially in connection with negotiations—were quickly silenced. There was no law against saying it. But transcripts show MPs being shouted down, ruled out of order, and discouraged from raising the idea. In wartime, "peace" was not a solution. It was a risk.

The reasoning? Morale. With troops dying by the thousands, any hint of diplomacy could be perceived as betrayal. The expectation was unity, not nuance. Victory, not compromise. When one MP in 1916 floated a proposal for peace talks with Germany, he didn't even finish his sentence before being cut off. The Speaker labeled it "unacceptable." The silence in the chamber? Applauded.

The phrase "the unity of silence" appeared in editorials, praising Parliament for its discipline. Behind closed doors, though, it was strategy—controlling public narrative, reinforcing commitment, and avoiding division.

Today, it feels bizarre that peace—arguably the end goal of any war—was too dangerous to say. But history reminds us that context matters. Even hope can be too loud.

Because in times of crisis, silence isn't always absence.

Sometimes, it's armor.

Turns out, words really can get you in trouble.

Some are banned outright. Others are quietly erased, fiercely debated, or just frowned into silence.

Whether it's a banned baby name, a joke gone sideways, or a word whispered in the wrong place—speech has its limits. Sometimes it's about safety. Sometimes it's about control. And sometimes, it's just about keeping the peace… literally.

So speak carefully. Read the room.

And when in doubt, say less.

Because even in places built for conversation, the quietest rules often speak the loudest.

8

NO FUN ALLOWED

Some rules are made to keep people safe.

Others are made to keep things quiet.

And a few seem designed to keep joy on a very short leash.

This chapter steps into the fine print of fun—where dancing might require paperwork, laughter might need a decibel check, and your flip-flops? Way too loud.

From sword-free ceilidhs to silent sidewalks in Capri, these laws remind us that even joy can be regulated.

So take a deep breath.

And maybe... dance carefully.

1. DANCING WITH A SWORD IS PROHIBITED (SCOTLAND)

Scotland has always had a flair for the dramatic—bagpipes, kilts, ceilidhs, and yes... sword dancing.

But not all sword dancing is legal.

According to Scottish common law and civic regulations still referenced in places like Edinburgh and Inverness, it's technically illegal to dance in public while carrying a sword. The rule may sound like folklore, but it traces back to 17th-century ordinances—written at a time when celebrations could turn into skirmishes fast.

The issue wasn't the dancing. It was what came after.

A wedding or fair might start with traditional footwork, but a few drinks and some lingering grudges could quickly turn a Highland reel into a Highland brawl. Lawmakers stepped in to keep merriment and melee separate.

Today, the rule is mostly symbolic—but it still exists. At public events or historical reenactments, dancers with swords may need permits, safety checks, or insurance. Even at castle venues and ceilidhs, swords may be treated as props that must be pre-approved or stored between performances.

So if you're planning to show off your Highland moves, go for it.

Just check your scabbard at the door.

Because in Scotland, tradition runs deep—

But not with a blade in your boot.

2. NO DANCING AFTER MIDNIGHT WITHOUT A LICENSE (JAPAN)

It sounds like the plot of a teen movie.

But in Japan, until 2015, dancing after midnight could get your club shut down.

The law stemmed from the Fueiho—short for the Entertainment Business Control Law—passed in 1948. It was intended to keep nightlife in check, regulate adult entertainment, and preserve postwar public order. At the time, late-night dancing was considered risky behavior. And risk, in a rebuilding society, was frowned upon.

The law required bars and clubs to obtain a cabaret license to allow dancing past midnight—placing dance floors in the same category as strip clubs. Most clubs ignored it. Until suddenly, they couldn't.

In the early 2000s, enforcement came back with force. Clubs were raided. DJs were questioned. Venues lost licenses. A late-night groove could land you a fine or shut the place down.

The backlash was fierce. Musicians, business owners, and regular citizens argued that dancing isn't deviant—it's culture. Petitions circulated. Lawsuits followed. And after years of pressure, the government revised the rule.

As of 2015, dancing after midnight is legal again—but only if venues meet updated zoning, lighting, and sound standards. In other words, Footloose with conditions.

So yes, you can dance again. Just make sure the lights are on, the bass is below regulation...

And someone at the door has the paperwork.

3. PINBALL WAS ONCE OUTLAWED (NASHVILLE, TENNESSEE)

Once upon a time, pinball was illegal in Nashville.

Not because it was noisy.

Not because it distracted students.

But because it was considered gambling.

Early pinball machines had no flippers. You pulled the plunger, watched the ball bounce, and hoped for the best. If you won something—a free game, a token prize—it wasn't because of skill. It was chance. And to city officials in the 1940s, that made it gambling. Unlicensed, untaxed, and morally suspect.

Nashville responded with flair. Police raided soda shops. Machines were smashed in public. Local papers ran photos of officers destroying pinball tables with sledgehammers. It wasn't just policy. It was a statement.

As machines evolved, so did opinion. By the 1970s, pinball had flippers. It became a game of timing, precision, and—most importantly—skill. Legal challenges followed. Nashville eventually changed course.

Today, you'll find pinball machines in arcades and bars across the city. But for decades, those flashing lights and buzzing bumpers weren't just retro charm. They were contraband.

So next time you play a round in Nashville, remember:

That "tilt" once carried legal weight.

And for a while, your quarter came with a risk.

4. DICE ARE BANNED AT CHURCH BINGO (CERTAIN U.S. STATES)

In many U.S. states, bingo is perfectly legal.

It's charitable. It's social. It's got church basement energy and a side of baked goods.

But dice? That's another story.

In states like North Carolina, Alabama, and South Carolina, strict gambling laws draw a firm line between "community gaming" and full-on gambling. Bingo—especially when run by churches or nonprofits—usually qualifies as the former. Dice games? Not so lucky.

The divide traces back to America's blue laws—religiously influenced rules meant to uphold public morality. These laws banned everything from alcohol sales to dancing—and yes, dice games. In early America, dice were linked to saloons and gambling dens, making them suspect by association. That reputation stuck.

Bingo survived because it was slow, predictable, and structured. Dice were fast, random, and historically shady. That distinction still matters today.

In Alabama, it remains illegal to operate any dice-based game for prizes—even in private clubs or church basements. Violators can face fines or lose their gaming license. Many churches that host bingo nights must apply for limited gaming permits that include very specific lists of approved activities. Dice rarely make the cut.

So if you're running a fundraiser, call out the numbers.

Pass the cookies.

But keep the dice in the drawer.

Because in some states, they're still considered contraband—

legally, anyway.

5. LATE-NIGHT HONKING COULD GET YOU FINED (ARKANSAS + OTHERS)

In some U.S. cities, honking your horn isn't just rude.

It's regulated.

Take Little Rock, Arkansas. According to a local ordinance, it's illegal to honk your horn outside a sandwich shop after 9 PM. That's not a typo. Sandwich shop. 9 PM. Real law.

Why so specific?

It's part of a network of hyper-local noise ordinances—rules aimed at preserving peace and quiet in neighborhoods where residential buildings and businesses share close quarters. That honk you make to let your friend know you've arrived? If it happens under someone's bedroom window while they're trying to sleep, it's now a municipal issue.

Little Rock isn't alone. Across the country, cities have carved out noise laws that specifically regulate honking. In some places, you can't use your horn within 200 feet of a hospital. In others, honking near a school zone—or even a church—can result in a fine unless it's an emergency.

Most of these rules fall under vague language about "maintaining reasonable peace." And that phrase? It's been the foundation for more than one neighbor-to-neighbor legal showdown.

Are these laws enforced? Occasionally. A single honk might get a pass. But if you lean on the horn repeatedly—or lay on it during late-night takeout runs—you could find yourself with a citation. Or at the very least, a nasty note from a neighbor who didn't ask for a 10 PM car concert.

So the next time you roll up to a sandwich shop and think, "I'll just give a quick beep"?

Don't.

Send a text. Make a call. Walk in like it's 1995.

Because in some cities, your horn isn't a helpful sound.

It's probable cause.

6. SPONTANEOUS DANCING REQUIRED A PERMIT (SWEDEN, UNTIL 2023)

Sweden.

Land of ABBA, IKEA, and—until recently—one of the most tightly regulated dance floors in Europe.

From the 1950s until January 2023, any bar, restaurant, or café that wanted to allow dancing was legally required to obtain a special permit. Not for performances—for the public to dance at all.

Originally, the law aimed to control late-night crowds, prevent noise complaints, and preserve public order in postwar Sweden. But over time, it became one of the strangest contradictions in modern nightlife: a nation that exports disco classics but bans dancefloor spontaneity without paperwork.

The rules were strict. Venues had to file applications, pay fees, and meet safety standards. Without a permit, even a handful of people swaying near the bar could result in fines or closure. Many establishments posted signs reading "No Dancing"—not as a joke, but as self-defense against bureaucracy.

The backlash was slow but steady. Bar owners, artists, and partygoers lobbied for years. Finally, in 2023, the government repealed the requirement.

Now, if you're in Malmö, Stockholm, or anywhere else in Sweden and the music moves you?

You're free to move with it.

No forms. No fines. No disco embargo.

After seventy years of red tape, Sweden has cut loose.

And the dance floor is back.

7. "HAPPY BIRTHDAY" WAS ONCE A LICENSED SONG (UNITED STATES)

You're at a restaurant.

The lights dim.

A cake appears.

Everyone starts singing…

And once upon a time, that moment?

It was technically illegal—unless someone paid for it.

For decades, "Happy Birthday to You" was under copyright. Warner/Chappell Music claimed ownership of both the lyrics and melody. Public performances—including in restaurants, classrooms, concerts, and films—required a paid license.

This wasn't a bluff. Warner/Chappell reportedly earned more than $2 million a year from licensing fees, enforcing the copyright even against large studios and broadcasters. Birthday scenes in films often stopped just short of singing—or were replaced with crowd noise and candles blowing.

Restaurants got clever.

To dodge fees, many invented their own birthday jingles—clapping routines and vaguely festive lyrics that never used the actual words. If you've ever heard a legally distinct song about celebration, now you know why.

In 2013, a documentary filmmaker challenged the copyright claim. After years of legal wrangling, a federal judge ruled in 2016 that the song was in the public domain. Warner/Chappell had no right to enforce it.

Today, you can sing "Happy Birthday" anywhere—without fear of legal fallout.

So go ahead.

Strike the match. Hit the chorus. Sing it off-key.

Because now, the only thing you owe is a wish.

8. NOISY FLIP-FLOPS CAN GET YOU FINED (CAPRI, ITALY)

On Capri, flip-flops are fine.

They just can't be loud.

In 2019, the island passed a regional ordinance banning "excessively noisy footwear" in public spaces. That includes hard-soled sandals, wooden clogs, and yes—those slappy foam flip-flops that echo through stone alleys like applause.

Capri is designed for quiet elegance. Its narrow streets, pastel villas, and lemon-scented breezes aren't made for tourist foot percussion. During peak season, the soundtrack of sightseeing became a chorus of slap-slap-slap. Locals had enough.

The ban isn't about fashion—it's about preserving peace. Violators can be fined, especially in famously serene zones like Via Tragara or the Gardens of Augustus. There are no decibel meters. Just ears. And expectations.

Shops responded by selling "silent sandals"—rubber-soled, soft-stepping shoes tailored for the local vibe. They're stylish, quiet, and 100% Capri-approved.

So if you're strolling the cliffs of Anacapri or grabbing a granita in the piazza?

Step lightly.

Because on Capri, even your footsteps are expected to behave.

Fun is fine—just not too loud, too late, or too unsupervised.

Because behind every dance floor, parade, or rooftop toast, there's often a permit, a curfew, or an overlooked ordinance waiting in the wings.

Some rules were written for safety. Others just stuck around longer than they should have. But all of them say the same thing:

Joy is welcome—just mind the guidelines.

So the next time you feel the urge to clap, twirl, shout, or sing?

Check the rules.

Then go for it.

Because in the right place, at the right time—joy is absolutely allowed.

CONCLUSION

We've covered a lot of ground.

Some paved, some cobblestone, some labeled "No food or photography."

What began as a question—"Wait, is that really a law?"—became a pool of quirky, baffling truth. Turns out, the world runs on rules you've never heard of. Rules that guard fountains, supervise footwear, protect gnomes, and hush car doors after 10 p.m.

Why? Because someone, at some point, had a reason.

Laws are stories. They say, "Something happened here. Let's not do that again." Whether it was a rogue pickle or a runaway donkey, the aftermath became regulation.

And honestly? That's kind of wonderful.

Because these rules don't just reflect fear or control—they reflect pride, culture, humor, and a deep desire to make life work just a little more smoothly. Even if the solution includes a ban on porch refrigerators in the name of dignity.

So wherever you travel, read the signs. Smile at the absurdities.

And remember: joy, like a good pool, is better when it's shared and just a little bit regulated.

Thanks for diving in.

SOURCES

ABC News. (2010, August 15). *Park vending machines now under curfew laws.* https://abcnews.go.com

ABC News Australia. (2019, September 7). *Protesters charged for disrupting wedding ceremony in Melbourne.* https://www.abc.net.au

Alabama Code. (2020). *Title 13A -- Criminal code: Moral conduct and profanity laws.* https://www.alabama.gov

Alabama Department of Public Safety. (2019). *Vehicle code update: Visual obstruction and driver responsibility.* https://www.alea.gov

Alabama Legislature. (2020). *State traffic safety code -- Section 32-5A-190: Reckless driving laws.* https://www.legislature.state.al.us

Alabama Legislature. (2021). *Title 13A -- Criminal Code: Section 13A-12-20 -- Definitions and offenses.* https://www.legislature.state.al.us

American Civil Liberties Union. (2020). *ACLU calls for repeal of discriminatory saggy pants laws.* https://www.aclu.org

American Planning Association. (2020). *Community standards and the enforcement of residential codes.* https://www.planning.org

Appellation d'origine contrôlée. (n.d.). Wikipedia. https://en.wikipedia.org/wiki/Appellation_d%27origine_contr%C3%B4l%C3%A9e

Archaeological Survey of India. (2022). *Rules for visitor conduct at protected monuments.* https://asi.nic.in

Arizona State Legislature. (1924). *Unusual municipal ordinances: Kingman Township Archive.* https://azmemory.azlibrary.gov

Arkansas Democrat-Gazette. (2018, May 4). *Local ordinances you didn't know you were breaking.* https://www.arkansasonline.com

ASPCA. (2022). *Halloween adoption policies and animal safety protocols.* https://www.aspca.org

Assam Tribune. (2021, March 10). *Regulation of chili-eating contests: Local fairs under review.* https://www.assamtribune.com

Associated Press. (2009, April 29). *Georgia woman "arrested" for eating fried chicken with a fork.* https://apnews.com

Atlanta Journal-Constitution. (2013, July 8). *The strange law that made Gainesville famous.* https://www.ajc.com

Atlanta Journal-Constitution. (2018, April 6). *Why elephants aren't allowed downtown anymore.* https://www.ajc.com

106 | SOURCES

The Atlantic. (2015, October 22). When symbolic laws become permanent. https://www.theatlantic.com

The Atlantic. (2018, May 3). Why dice are still controversial in some American states. https://www.theatlantic.com

The Atlantic. (2019, July 15). Urban noise laws and the strange case of the sandwich shop clause. https://www.theatlantic.com

The Atlantic. (2019, May 5). Why some counties still police language in private spaces. https://www.theatlantic.com

The Atlantic. (2019). The battle for your backyard: Why some states protect clotheslines. https://www.theatlantic.com

Auto Europe. (2020). Driving in France: Breathalyser rule explained. https://www.autoeurope.com

AutoExpress UK. (2021, August 19). Driving in France: What you need to carry by law. https://www.autoexpress.co.uk

Automobile Club de España. (2020). *Classic car rally regulations: Required attire.* https://www.race.es

BBC History. (2019). Wartime debates and forbidden speech: A look inside Parliament. https://www.bbc.com

BBC News. (2008, July 1). France breathalyser law for drivers comes into force. https://www.bbc.com

BBC News. (2009, June 30). Greece bans high heels at ancient sites. https://www.bbc.com/news

BBC News. (2010). Five weird British laws that still exist. https://www.bbc.com

BBC News. (2012, July 1). France mandates breathalysers in all vehicles. https://www.bbc.com

BBC News. (2012, July 1). France enforces new rule on breathalyser kits in cars. https://www.bbc.com

BBC News. (2013, February 1). Paris women finally allowed to wear trousers. https://www.bbc.com

BBC News. (2013, January 4). Icelandic girl fights for right to use her name. https://www.bbc.com

BBC News. (2014, October 29). Japan's no-dancing law under fire. https://www.bbc.com

BBC News. (2015, July 22). Man arrested for riding horse while drunk in Fife. https://www.bbc.com

BBC News. (2015, November 10). French children banned from ketchup in school meals. https://www.bbc.com

BBC News. (2016, April 1). The UK's strangest laws you didn't know existed. https://www.bbc.com

BBC News. (2016, April 12). Why British cab drivers used to wear hats. https://

www.bbc.com

BBC News. (2016, November 3). The Swiss laws that might surprise visitors. https://www.bbc.com

BBC News. (2017, February 10). Why it's illegal to die in this Arctic town. https://www.bbc.com

BBC News. (2017, April 14). Lucifer name banned by German court. https://www.bbc.com

BBC News. (2017, October 27). Lucifer baby name vetoed by German officials. https://www.bbc.com/news/world-europe-41776487

BBC News. (2018, January 11). Switzerland bans boiling lobsters alive. https://www.bbc.com/news/world-europe-42636838

BBC News. (2018, January 12). Switzerland bans boiling lobsters alive. https://www.bbc.com

BBC News. (2018, July 5). Venice bans eating in public in crackdown on tourists. https://www.bbc.com/news/world-europe-44730276

BBC News. (2018, July 30). Tourist shoved by Royal Guard after getting too close at Windsor Castle. https://www.bbc.com

BBC News. (2018, September 24). Singapore fines for dirty toilets: What you need to know. https://www.bbc.com

BBC News. (2019, August 8). Rome bans sitting on Spanish Steps with fines of up to €400. https://www.bbc.com

BBC News. (2019, January 3). The strange American ban on pinball. https://www.bbc.com

BBC News. (2019, July 20). Italian island bans loud footwear. https://www.bbc.com

BBC News. (2020, June 5). Russian motorists fined for driving dirty cars. https://www.bbc.com

BBC News. (2020, June 17). France defends its wine---and its image. https://www.bbc.com

BBC News. (2020, October 3). Tourist fined for jaywalking in Singapore. https://www.bbc.com

BBC News. (2020, October 5). India's spiciest chili now subject to contest guidelines. https://www.bbc.com

BBC News. (2021, August 4). Surprising reasons you can get a ticket in Europe. https://www.bbc.com

BBC News. (2022, April 10). Quiet culture in Switzerland: When everyday sounds are violations. https://www.bbc.com

BBC News. (2022, January 5). The countries where car snacking is a crime. https://www.bbc.com

BBC News. (2022). Sacred spaces and unexpected laws. https://www.bbc.com

BBC News. (2023, April 3). Paris cracks down on e-scooters after safety complaints. https://www.bbc.com

BBC Scotland. (2021, March 18). Why Scotland still regulates swords at public events. https://www.bbc.com

BBC Travel. (2017, March 4). Tourist fined for disrupting temple ritual with "magic word." https://www.bbc.com

BBC Travel. (2020). Singapore's most surprising public rules. https://www.bbc.com

BBC Travel. (2020, December 12). Why Bhutan still wears its history. https://www.bbc.com/travel

BBC Travel. (2021). The rules of the world's fastest road. https://www.bbc.com

The Bhutanese. (2019, September 5). Public awareness of national dress and etiquette codes. https://thebhutanese.bt

Bismarck Tribune. (2010, August 21). Does North Dakota really ban sleeping with your shoes on? https://bismarcktribune.com

Boston City Archives. (2017). *Theater regulations and public assembly standards.* https://www.boston.gov

The British Library. (2020). *Censorship, language, and wartime speech restrictions.* https://www.bl.uk

British Heritage Magazine. (2020). Bizarre British laws that won't die. https://britishheritage.com

Bundesministerium für Verkehr und digitale Infrastruktur (Germany). (2022). *StVO -- Road Traffic Regulations: Section 18 -- Use of motorways.* https://www.bmvi.de

CBC News. (2019). Canadian couple warned after wearing camouflage in the Caribbean. https://www.cbc.ca

CBC News. (2019, August 12). Toronto man fined for climbing protected tree in High Park. https://www.cbc.ca

Chandler HOA Guidelines. (2023). *Community standards for exterior appearance.* https://www.chandleraz.gov

Channel News Asia. (2019, March 8). Rules you didn't know existed in Singapore parks. https://www.channelnewsasia.com

Chelyabinsk City Administration. (2018). *Municipal code enforcement: Clean vehicle mandate.* https://cheladmin.ru

Chicago Department of Public Health. (2012). *Park safety ordinances and public vending access.* https://www.chicago.gov

Chicago Tribune. (2019, October 15). Why you can't adopt a black cat this week. https://www.chicagotribune.com

Christian Legal Society. (2020). *Faith-based gaming laws and restrictions.* https://www.clsnet.org

City of Atlanta. (2023). *Municipal Code Section 110-5: Wild and non-domesticated animal transport restrictions.* https://www.atlantaga.gov

City of Aurora, Colorado. (2023). *Municipal Code -- Residential Parking Restrictions.*

https://www.auroragov.org

City of Chico. (1983). *Municipal Code -- Chapter 9.04: Prohibition of nuclear weapons use within city limits*. https://www.chico.ca.us

City of Charlotte Code Enforcement. (2023). *Residential property maintenance and public nuisance ordinances*. https://charlottenc.gov

City of Dallas. (2023). *Code Compliance -- High Grass and Weeds*. https://dallascityhall.com

City of Edinburgh Council. (2019). *Historical public safety laws and public demonstration permits*. https://www.edinburgh.gov.uk

City of Eugene. (2023). *Municipal Code Chapter 6 -- Animal conduct and public behavior*. https://www.eugene-or.gov

City of Florence. (2021). *Municipal regulations on public decorum and food consumption*. https://www.comune.fi.it

City of Fort Worth Code Compliance. (2022). *Outdoor appliance restrictions and abandoned equipment laws*. https://www.fortworthtexas.gov

City of Gainesville, Georgia. (1961). *Ordinance No. 81: Poultry Consumption Etiquette Act*. Municipal Records Archive. https://www.gainesville.org

City of Gainesville, Georgia. (2021). *Municipal Code -- Animal Ordinances: Section 5-1-2, Poultry Management*. https://www.gainesville.org

City of Little Rock. (2022). *Municipal Code -- Title 18: Noise Regulations*. https://www.littlerock.gov

City of Los Angeles. (2007). *Municipal Code Section 41.18: Loitering near vending machines*. https://www.lacity.org

City of Los Angeles. (2021). *Municipal Water Ordinance -- Lawn watering and outdoor irrigation*. https://www.lacity.org

City of Manila. (2019). *Ordinance No. 7856 -- Regulation of public sound and performance*. https://manila.gov.ph

City of Minneapolis. (2021). *Municipal Code -- Chapter 475: Soil and debris tracking*. https://www.minneapolismn.gov

City of Mobile. (2018). *Public Assembly Ordinances: Dress Code and Etiquette*. https://www.cityofmobile.org

City of Munich. (2021). *Wohnanlagen ordinance on outdoor decoration*. https://www.muenchen.de

City of Nashville Metro Government Archives. (1972). *Ordinance 2489: Prohibition of pinball machines*. https://www.nashville.gov

City of Paris. (2020). *Regulations regarding modification or interaction with public sculptures*. https://www.paris.fr

City of Paris. (2023). *Electric scooter regulations and referendum results*. https://www.paris.fr

City of Philadelphia. (2009). *Anti-loitering enforcement guidelines*. Office of Public

Safety. https://www.phila.gov

City of Portland. (2022). *Housing Maintenance Code -- Section 29.30.130: Plumbing facilities and sanitation.* https://www.portland.gov

City of Rome. (2019). *Municipal Ordinance No. 100: Regulations for Historical Monuments.* https://www.comune.roma.it

City of Shreveport, Louisiana. (2019). *Ordinance No. 150: Dress Code Enforcement History.* https://www.shreveportla.gov

City of Toronto. (2023). *Municipal Code Chapter 608: Parks -- Section 10.2, Tree Protection and Use.* https://www.toronto.ca

City of Venice. (2022). *Ordinance on public behavior in tourist zones.* https://www.comune.venezia.it

City of Zurich. (2022). *Public Peace Regulations -- Section 4: Quiet Hours and Noise Control.* https://www.stadt-zuerich.ch

CNN. (2009, April 30). Gainesville police prank 91-year-old with chicken-eating citation. https://www.cnn.com

CNN. (2017, July 14). Odd laws still on the books: California's nuclear fine. https://www.cnn.com

CNN. (2017, July 20). What you can and can't name your baby in Iceland. https://www.cnn.com

CNN. (2019, January 18). Countries with the strangest baby name bans. https://www.cnn.com

CNN. (2019, July 10). Georgia cities still list outdated---but enforceable---animal laws. https://www.cnn.com

CNN. (2023, April 4). Why Paris banned e-scooters---and what it means for other cities. https://www.cnn.com

CNN Travel. (2019). What not to do around the Queen's Guard. https://www.cnn.com

CNN Travel. (2019, August 7). Rome cracks down on misbehaving tourists at Spanish Steps. https://www.cnn.com

CNN Travel. (2019, July 19). Tourists beware: Capri says no to noisy shoes. https://www.cnn.com

CNN Travel. (2020, June 17). Singapore's hygiene rules you probably didn't know existed. https://www.cnn.com

CNN Travel. (2022). Singapore's strictest laws and why they exist. https://www.cnn.com

Code de la consommation. (n.d.). Légifrance. https://www.legifrance.gouv.fr/codes/id/LEGITEXT000006069565

Colorado Department of Revenue. (2022). *Vehicle license plate display requirements.* https://dmv.colorado.gov

Community Associations Institute. (2020). *Common HOA design restrictions and enforcement statistics*. https://www.caionline.org

Community Associations Institute. (2022). *Architectural guidelines: Clothesline restrictions in HOAs*. https://www.caionline.org

Community Associations Institute. (2022). *HOA Rules and Regulations: Common landscaping standards*. https://www.caionline.org

Comune di Capri. (2019). *Ordinanza n. 45/2019 -- Regolamento sul rumore in zone pedonali*. https://www.comunecapri.it

Comune di Roma. (2019). *Ordinanza n. 74: Decoro urbano e tutela dei monumenti*. https://www.comune.roma.it

Comune di Roma. (2019). *Regolamento di polizia urbana del Comune di Roma Capitale*. https://www.comune.roma.it

Comune di Roma. (2020). *Municipal health inspections and ice safety enforcement*. https://www.comune.roma.it

Connecticut Department of Consumer Protection. (1948). *Food safety enforcement: Pickle quality standards case file*. State Archives. https://portal.ct.gov/DCP

Connecticut State Library. (2003). *Strange laws and food regulations in Connecticut history*. https://ctstatelibrary.org

Corriere della Sera. (2019, July 3). Ice in restaurants: Fines for using non-potable water. https://www.corriere.it

Crown Prosecution Service. (2021). *Wildlife and Countryside Offences: Summary of fish-related prosecutions*. https://www.cps.gov.uk

Cyprus Department of Road Safety. (2022). *Traffic Code & Road Behavior Guidelines*. https://www.cyprusdriving.net

Cyprus Police Department. (2022). *Traffic safety enforcement and fine schedule*. https://www.police.gov.cy

The Cyprus Mail. (2021, August 10). Drivers fined for eating behind the wheel: New enforcement push. https://cyprus-mail.com

Denver Post. (2019, March 12). Why some Colorado HOAs ban backing into driveways. https://www.denverpost.com

Des Moines Register. (2019, August 15). Butter sculpting: Rules, traditions, and refrigeration. https://www.desmoinesregister.com

Der Spiegel. (2017, April 13). German court blocks parents from naming child "Lucifer." https://www.spiegel.de

Der Spiegel. (2018, August 12). Gnome wars: Neighborhood disputes over lawn decor. https://www.spiegel.de

Deutsche Welle. (2017, October 27). German court stops couple from naming child Lucifer. https://www.dw.com/en/german-court-stops-couple-from-naming-child-lucifer/a-41148061

DGT (Dirección General de Tráfico). (1957). *Historical traffic manuals and recommended driving attire*. Spanish National Archives. https://www.dgt.es

DGCCRF -- Direction Générale de la Concurrence, de la Consommation et de la Répression des Fraudes. (2022). *Labeling laws for alcohol and protected cultural products*. https://www.economie.gouv.fr

The Diplomat. (2018, August 2). Cultural pride and policy: Inside Bhutan's official dress code. https://thediplomat.com

Direction générale de l'alimentation. (2023). Identification des suidés. Ministère de l'Agriculture et de la Souveraineté alimentaire. https://agriculture.gouv.fr/identification-des-suides

Dirección General de Tráfico (DGT). (2023). *Driving safety: Footwear and control regulations*. https://www.dgt.es

DW News. (2020, July 22). Autobahn etiquette: What you can and can't do on Germany's highways. https://www.dw.com

El País. (2019, October 11). When driving with gloves was the law in Spain. https://elpais.com

El País. (2022, July 12). Spanish drivers fined for flip-flops and sandals. https://elpais.com

Emily Post Institute. (2021). *Modern etiquette: The rules of hat removal*. https://emilypost.com

European Commission. (2022). *Animal health and traceability systems across member states*. https://ec.europa.eu

European Commission. (2023). *EU Member State road safety rules: France*. https://transport.ec.europa.eu

European Commission Mobility and Transport. (2022). *Driving rules in EU countries: France*. https://transport.ec.europa.eu

European Food Safety Authority. (2021). *Food hygiene enforcement in public beverage service*. https://www.efsa.europa.eu

European Transport Safety Council. (2020). *Distracted driving laws in EU member states*. https://etsc.eu

Federal Food Safety and Veterinary Office. (2018). *Animal welfare: Protection of crustaceans*. Swiss Confederation. https://www.blv.admin.ch/blv/en/home/tiere/tierschutz/nutztierhaltung/krebstiere.html

Fifth Circuit Court of Appeals. (2008). *Reliable Consultants, Inc. v. Ronnie Earle, 517 F.3d 738*. https://caselaw.findlaw.com

FindLaw. (2021). Noise ordinances: What you need to know. https://www.findlaw.com

Florida Homeowners Association Statutes. (2020). *Florida Statute 720.305: Fines and enforcement*. https://www.leg.state.fl.us

Florida Statutes. (2021). *Chapter 163.04 -- Energy devices based on renewable resources*

SOURCES | 113

(Right to Dry Act). https://www.leg.state.fl.us

Florida Statutes. (2022). *Chapter 102.031: Maintenance of order at polling places.* https://www.leg.state.fl.us

Food Safety and Standards Authority of India. (2022). *Guidelines on food competitions and public safety at festivals.* https://www.fssai.gov.in

France 24. (2013, January 13). *France suspends fines for missing breathalyzer kits in cars.* https://www.france24.com

France 24. (2018, July 30). *French citizens warned not to touch or decorate monuments.* https://www.france24.com

France 24. (2019, July 10). *Micro-pigs and paperwork: The legal reality of pet pigs in Paris.* https://www.france24.com

French Ministry of Agriculture. (2020). *Wine labeling standards and commercial restrictions.* https://www.agriculture.gouv.fr

French Ministry of Agriculture and Food Sovereignty. (2011). *National school lunch policy guidelines.* https://www.agriculture.gouv.fr

French Ministry of Culture. (2022). *Protection of public art and historical monuments.* https://www.culture.gouv.fr

French Ministry of Women's Rights. (2013). *Official repeal of the 1800 ordinance on women's dress.* https://www.gouvernement.fr

French Road Safety Authority. (2012). *Breathalyzer requirement for motorists (EAD law enforcement overview).* https://www.securite-routiere.gouv.fr

French Road Safety Authority (Sécurité Routière). (2023). *Alcohol and driving: Breathalyzer requirements for motorists.* https://www.securite-routiere.gouv.fr

Freiburg City Planning Department. (2022). *Bauordnung regulations and front-yard uniformity codes.* https://www.freiburg.de

Georgia Code. (n.d.). *§ 16-11-34: Disorderly conduct.* Justia Law. https://law.justia.com/codes/georgia/2022/title-16/chapter-11/article-2/section-16-11-34/

Georgia Department of Agriculture. (2020). *Livestock and poultry safety regulations.* https://agr.georgia.gov

Georgia Department of Agriculture. (2022). *Permitting guidelines for exotic animals and circus transport.* https://agr.georgia.gov

Georgia General Assembly. (2022). *O.C.G.A. § 16-11-35: Disorderly conduct near deceased persons.* https://www.legis.ga.gov

The Georgia Law Review. (2020). *Historical codes related to animal exhibition and street processions.* https://law.uga.edu

German Civil Registry Office (Standesamt). (2022). *Naming conventions and legal guidelines for birth registration.* https://www.bundesregierung.de

German Federal Ministry of Housing. (2020). *Decorative items and historical district preservation guidelines.* https://www.bmi.bund.de

German Federal Police. (2023). *Guidelines for emergency stopping on the Autobahn.*

https://www.bundespolizei.de

The Globe and Mail. (2021, May 30). Climbing trees in Toronto parks is technically illegal --- and here's why. https://www.theglobeandmail.com

Government of Barbados. (n.d.). *Travel advice for visitors*. https://www.gov.bb

Government of Iceland. (1996). *Personal Names Act -- Law No. 45/1996*. https://www.government.is

Gouvernement Français. (2012). *Décret n°2012-284 relatif à la possession d'un éthylotest par les conducteurs*. https://www.legifrance.gouv.fr

Greater London Authority. (2021). *Busking and street performance licensing requirements*. https://www.london.gov.uk

The Guardian. (2013, January 25). France suspends fines for missing breathalysers---but law remains. https://www.theguardian.com

The Guardian. (2013, January 31). French women can finally wear trousers. https://www.theguardian.com

The Guardian. (2015, June 18). Japan loosens ban on dancing after midnight. https://www.theguardian.com

The Guardian. (2017, March 28). In Russia, your muddy car can cost you. https://www.theguardian.com

The Guardian. (2017, May 14). Sweden's bizarre dancing ban still in effect. https://www.theguardian.com

The Guardian. (2018, January 11). Swiss animal protection laws now cover lobsters. https://www.theguardian.com

The Guardian. (2018, January 12). Urban myths and royal rules inside Parliament. https://www.theguardian.com

The Guardian. (2018, August 21). London cabbies and the case of the missing hat. https://www.theguardian.com

The Guardian. (2018, July 19). Singers fined for public performance without permits. https://www.theguardian.com

The Guardian. (2018, September 12). Cultural clashes: When Western tourists go too far. https://www.theguardian.com

The Guardian. (2019, March 24). No deaths allowed: Life in the world's northernmost town. https://www.theguardian.com

The Guardian. (2019, July 18). Capri bans noisy flip-flops to protect island peace. https://www.theguardian.com

The Guardian. (2020, December 12). Understanding the role of the King's Guard. https://www.theguardian.com

The Guardian. (2020, February 2). Europe's oddest historical traffic rules. https://www.theguardian.com

The Guardian. (2020, May 12). Talula Does The Hula and other names banned in New Zealand. https://www.theguardian.com

The Guardian. (2020, September 2). Why does the UK still have a law about suspicious salmon? https://www.theguardian.com

Hellenic Ministry of Culture and Sports. (2009). *Visitor Guidelines for Archaeological Sites*. https://www.culture.gov.gr

Hennepin County Public Works. (2020). *Construction site best practices and enforcement guidelines*. https://www.hennepin.us

The Hindu. (2016, August 14). Ghost pepper contest sends man to hospital in Assam. https://www.thehindu.com

The Hindu. (2021, June 12). Why you shouldn't kill bugs in Indian temples. https://www.thehindu.com

House Beautiful. (2021, October 18). You're not allowed to flush the toilet at night in Switzerland. https://www.housebeautiful.com

Houston Chronicle. (2008, February 13). Court strikes down Texas sex toy ban. https://www.houstonchronicle.com

HuffPost. (2018, May 15). German name laws: The weird, the banned, and the just plain odd. https://www.huffpost.com

The Humane Society of the United States. (2020). *Seasonal adoption policies and pet safety*. https://www.humanesociety.org

Icelandic Naming Committee. (2023). *Official name register and naming law overview*. https://www.mannanafnanefnd.is

Independent. (2015). Why you can't wear high heels at ancient Greek monuments. https://www.independent.co.uk

India Today. (2023, July 4). Ghost peppers, health risks, and the rules behind chili contests. https://www.indiatoday.in

Institut National de l'Origine et de la Qualité. (n.d.). Wikipedia. https://en.wikipedia.org/wiki/Institut_national_de_l%27origine_et_de_la_qualit%C3%A9

Iowa Administrative Code. (2022). *Chapter 21---Dairy Product Regulation*. https://www.legis.iowa.gov

Iowa Department of Agriculture and Land Stewardship. (2023). *Regulations for temporary food displays and sculpture materials*. https://iowaagriculture.gov

Iowa State Fair. (2023). *Butter Cow tradition and sculptor guidelines*. https://www.iowastatefair.org

The Japan Times. (2015, June 17). Japan lifts 67-year-old dancing ban. https://www.japantimes.co.jp

The Japan Times. (2018, April 14). Temple guards respond to poor tourist behavior in Kyoto. https://www.japantimes.co.jp

The Japan Times. (2021, March 15). Why cyclists in Japan often walk across crosswalks. https://www.japantimes.co.jp

Japan National Tourism Organization. (2023). *Cultural customs and behavioral etiquette for tourists*. https://www.japan.travel

116 | SOURCES

Japan National Tourism Organization. (2023). *Cycling etiquette and rules for tourists in Japan*. https://www.japan.travel

Japanese Ministry of Justice. (1948/2015). *Entertainment Business Control Law (Fueiho) -- Legal text and amendments*. https://www.moj.go.jp

Kerala Tourism Board. (2020). *Guidelines for temple visitors and wildlife conduct*. https://www.keralatourism.org

Kingman Historical Society. (1999). *Flood of 1924: The bathtub donkey story*. https://www.kingmanmuseum.org

Kyoto City Tourism Association. (2019). *Visitor etiquette guidelines for historic and religious sites*. https://kyoto.travel

L214 Éthique & Animaux. (2021). Avoir un cochon comme animal de compagnie : est-ce légal ? https://www.l214.com/actualites/2021/cochon-animal-de-compagnie-est-ce-legal

Lakewood HOA Coalition. (2021). *Community guidelines and enforcement policies*. https://www.lakewoodhoa.org

Land Transport Authority of Singapore. (2023). *Safe pedestrian movement: Enforcement and public education*. https://www.lta.gov.sg

Law of 6 May 1919 relating to the Protection of Appellations of Origin. (n.d.). Wikipedia. https://en.wikipedia.org/wiki/Law_of_6_May_1919_relating_to_the_Protection_of_Appellations_of_Origin

Le Figaro. (2014, April 21). Winemaker fined for "offensive" bottle label. https://www.lefigaro.fr

Le Monde. (2012, September 8). Why French schools are cutting ketchup. https://www.lemonde.fr

Le Monde. (2019, December 12). Fines issued for decorating French statues during protests. https://www.lemonde.fr

Le Monde. (2023, April 2). Paris bans rental e-scooters after vote. https://www.lemonde.fr

Legifrance. (n.d.). Code rural et de la pêche maritime -- Article L212-9. https://www.legifrance.gouv.fr/codes/article_lc/LEGIARTI000022767514

LegalMatch. (2021). Can touching be assault? State-specific examples of unusual charges. https://www.legalmatch.com

Lexington County Ordinances. (2004). *Chapter 12: Public Morality and Nuisance Language Statutes*. https://www.lex-co.sc.gov

The Local France. (2018, March 12). The strangest rules about wine in France. https://www.thelocal.fr

The Local France. (2019, January 4). Are you really required to carry a breathalyser in your car in France? https://www.thelocal.fr

The Local France. (2021, March 18). What you need to know about keeping unusual pets in France. https://www.thelocal.fr

The Local France. (2021, April 5). *Why you can't dress statues in France---even for a laugh*. https://www.thelocal.fr

The Local France. (2021, April 10). *Do drivers in France still need to carry a breathalyser?* https://www.thelocal.fr

The Local France. (2021). *Driving laws in France: What you need to know about breathalyzers and the glove box rule*. https://www.thelocal.fr

The Local Germany. (2017, October 26). *Parents convinced not to name child Lucifer after court hearing*. https://www.thelocal.de/20171026/parents-convinced-not-to-name-child-lucifer-after-court-hearing

The Local Germany. (2019, October 3). *Can a gnome get you fined in Germany?* https://www.thelocal.de

The Local Germany. (2020, October 7). *Ten baby names banned in Germany*. https://www.thelocal.de

The Local Germany. (2021, September 15). *Yes, it's illegal to run out of fuel on the Autobahn*. https://www.thelocal.de

The Local Italy. (2018, September 6). *Why eating a sandwich on the street could get you fined in Florence*. https://www.thelocal.it/20180906/why-eating-a-sandwich-on-the-street-could-get-you-fined-in-florence/

The Local Italy. (2022). *Where in Italy can't you eat in public?* https://www.thelocal.it

The Local Italy. (2022, August 10). *Italy's little-known ice laws you've probably never broken*. https://www.thelocal.it

The Local Spain. (2023, June 7). *Summer driving: What shoes can get you fined in Spain?* https://www.thelocal.es

The Local Sweden. (2023, January 2). *Sweden scraps long-standing dancing ban*. https://www.thelocal.se

The Local Switzerland. (2020, October 19). *Unusual Swiss laws that are very real*. https://www.thelocal.ch

The Local Switzerland. (2022, March 10). *Why it's frowned upon to flush the toilet after 10pm in Switzerland*. https://www.thelocal.ch

London Cab Drivers Club. (2020). *Dress code recommendations and heritage notes*. https://www.lcdc.uk

Lonely Planet. (2022). *What not to do in Sri Lankan temples: Language, attire, and conduct*. https://www.lonelyplanet.com

Longyearbyen Local Government. (n.d.). *Cemeteries and burial regulations*. https://www.longyearbyen.kommune.no/

Los Angeles Animal Services. (2021). *October adoption blackout for black cats*. https://www.laanimalservices.com

Los Angeles Municipal Code. (2021). *L.A.M.C. Sec. 91.8904 -- Property maintenance standards*. https://www.lacity.org

Los Angeles Times. (1984, May 12). California towns pass nuclear protest ordinances. https://www.latimes.com

Loudoun County Code of Ordinances. (1992). *Section 654.01 -- Disorderly conduct and offensive language*. https://www.loudoun.gov

Manchester City Council. (2015). *Taxi driver licensing guidelines -- attire expectations*. https://www.manchester.gov.uk

Mental Floss. (2020). Strange city codes that technically still exist. https://www.mentalfloss.com

Mental Floss. (2020). Yes, Connecticut once banned pickles that didn't bounce. https://www.mentalfloss.com

Mental Floss. (2021). The weirdest laws in every U.S. state. https://www.mentalfloss.com

Mental Floss. (2021, July 5). The weirdest laws in every U.S. state. https://www.mentalfloss.com

Mental Floss. (2022). Odd British laws that are still technically in effect. https://www.mentalfloss.com

Middlebury Municipal Archives. (1938). *Town meeting minutes and enforcement codes*. https://www.middlebury.gov

Ministry of Buddhasasana and Cultural Affairs -- Sri Lanka. (2020). *Conduct guidelines for foreign visitors to historic temples*. https://www.buddhistmin.gov.lk

Ministry of Home and Cultural Affairs (Bhutan). (2021). *Dress code policy and enforcement in public institutions*. https://www.mohca.gov.bt

Ministry of Land, Infrastructure, Transport and Tourism. (2023). *National guidelines for bicycle traffic safety*. https://www.mlit.go.jp

Ministère de l'Agriculture et de la Souveraineté Alimentaire. (2023). *Regulations for swine ownership and identification in France*. https://agriculture.gouv.fr

Ministère de l'Intérieur (France). (2022). *Urban mobility laws: Personal transport enforcement*. https://www.interieur.gouv.fr

Ministero della Salute (Italy). (2022). *Food and beverage safety guidelines: Ice and water use regulations*. https://www.salute.gov.it

Minnesota Pollution Control Agency. (2022). *Construction stormwater regulations: Vehicle tracking control*. https://www.pca.state.mn.us

Mississippi Code Annotated. (2021). *Title 97 -- Crimes: Section 97-35-15 -- Profane language and public disturbances*. https://law.justia.com

Missouri Department of Conservation. (2023). *Fishing regulations -- Hand-fishing guidelines and seasonal rules*. https://mdc.mo.gov

Missouri Revised Statutes. (2022). *Chapter 252 -- Wildlife and Conservation laws*. https://revisor.mo.gov

Moscow Times. (2019, April 11). Fined for dirt: Why your car has to be clean in Russia. https://www.themoscowtimes.com

Multnomah County Rental Alliance. (2021). *Frequently cited housing violations in rental properties*. https://www.multco.us

Museo del Automóvil (Barcelona). (2021). *Exhibition guide: 20th century Spanish driving laws*. https://www.museoautomovil.com

Nara Tourism Board. (2021). *Preservation and decorum guidelines for visitors to temple grounds*. https://www.visitnara.jp

The National Archives (UK). (1650--2020). *Sword laws and public dancing ordinances*. https://www.nationalarchives.gov.uk

National Conference of State Legislatures. (2022). *Electioneering laws by state*. https://www.ncsl.org

National Environment Agency. (2022). *Restroom cleanliness enforcement and public hygiene campaigns*. https://www.nea.gov.sg

National Geographic. (2019). *Living in the Arctic Circle: How Longyearbyen copes with extremes*. https://www.nationalgeographic.com/

National Geographic. (2021). *Frozen in time: The strange cemetery rule of Longyearbyen*. https://www.nationalgeographic.com

National Park Service. (2024). *Liberty Bell Center: Updated Visitor Guidelines Post-Vandalism*. https://www.nps.gov

National Park Service. (2024). *Updated visitor guidelines for Liberty Bell preservation*. https://www.nps.gov

NBC News. (2019, January 11). Alabama man crashes car during 'Bird Box challenge' stunt. https://www.usatoday.com

NBC News. (2020, June 8). Missouri officials remind residents: Noodling is not a free-for-all. https://www.nbcnews.com

NBC News. (2020, September 10). Florida city ends ban on sagging pants after 13 years. https://www.nbcnews.com

NBC News. (2021, May 10). Park rules you didn't know existed: Waterfowl edition. https://www.npr.org

NBC News. (2021, October 25). Animal shelters pause black cat adoptions to prevent Halloween mistreatment. https://www.nbcnews.com

NBC News. (2024, January 14). Liberty Bell graffiti sparks outrage and tighter restrictions. https://www.nbcnews.com

New South Wales Legislation. (2022). *Summary Offences Act 1988 -- Section 23: Disturbing religious worship or ceremony*. https://legislation.nsw.gov.au

New York Board of Elections. (2023). *Election Day regulations and restricted speech areas*. https://www.elections.ny.gov

New York City Police Department. (2022). *Permit guidelines for sound devices and public performance*. https://www.nyc.gov

The New York Times. (2008, February 15). Texas law limiting sex toy ownership overturned. https://www.nytimes.com

The New York Times. (2016, February 10). *The strange legal history of "Happy Birthday to You."* https://www.nytimes.com

The New York Times. (2017, July 11). *Old-fashioned laws that still shape funerals.* https://www.nytimes.com

The New York Times. (2018, July 7). *Clothesline bans meet solar-era pushback.* https://www.nytimes.com

The New York Times. (2019, August 5). *Barehanded fishing is legal---but barely.* https://www.nytimes.com

The New York Times. (2019, October 4). *When your drapes break the HOA rules.* https://www.nytimes.com

The New York Times. (2021, June 22). *When your lawn breaks the law.* https://www.nytimes.com

The New York Times. (2022, June 10). *When chickens go rogue: Backyard birds and local law.* https://www.nytimes.com

New York Post. (2024, January 11). *Vandals tag Liberty Bell replica during protest.* https://nypost.com

The New Zealand Herald. (2007, July 24). *Parents denied right to name child "4Real."* https://www.nzherald.co.nz

New Zealand Department of Internal Affairs. (2023). *Births, Deaths, and Marriages: Naming guidelines and restrictions.* https://www.dia.govt.nz

North Carolina General Assembly. (2022). *Chapter 14: Criminal Law -- Article 37: Gambling Offenses.* https://www.ncleg.gov

North Carolina General Assembly. (2022). *Statutes governing exterior property violations and visible appliance regulations.* https://www.ncleg.gov

North Carolina General Assembly. (n.d.). *§ 14-288.4: Disorderly conduct.* https://www.ncleg.gov/EnactedLegislation/Statutes/HTML/BySection/Chapter_14/GS_14-288.4.html

North Carolina General Statutes. (2021). *§ 14-288.4: Funeral disturbance provisions.* https://www.ncleg.gov

North Carolina Real Estate Commission. (2020). *Common HOA violations: Clotheslines and outdoor structures.* https://www.ncrec.gov

North Dakota Century Code. (2022). *Title 62.1 -- Disorderly conduct and public intoxication statutes.* https://www.ndlegis.gov

North Dakota Historical Society. (2009). *Folklore and forgotten ordinances: The origins of strange state laws.* https://www.history.nd.gov

Norton, E. (2021). *Strange laws of the United Kingdom: The still-standing statute about armor.* The British Legal Archive.

Norwegian Directorate of Health. (2020). *Burial regulations for permafrost zones.* https://www.helsedirektoratet.no

Norwegian Institute of Public Health. (2018). *The 1918 influenza pandemic: Historical lessons and research challenges*. https://www.fhi.no/en/

NPR. (2008, February 14). Federal court rules Texas can't ban sex toys. https://www.npr.org

NPR. (2013, February 4). France overturns 213-year-old ban on women wearing pants. https://www.npr.org

NPR. (2013, November 12). Why Japan doesn't want you dancing after midnight. https://www.npr.org

NPR. (2015, July 8). Californians fined for watering lawns during rainstorms. https://www.npr.org

NPR. (2016, February 9). Court rules "Happy Birthday" song is public domain. https://www.npr.org

NPR. (2018, April 1). When tickling crosses the legal line. https://www.npr.org

NPR. (2018, August 10). The legend of Iowa's butter cow. https://www.npr.org

NPR. (2018, January 14). Lobsters get legal protection in Switzerland. https://www.npr.org

NPR. (2018, June 11). Odd laws that still exist today: Donkey in the bathtub. https://www.npr.org

NPR. (2019, January 14). Blindfolded driver crashes in Alabama: Officials respond to viral challenge. https://www.npr.org

NPR. (2019, March 5). Why some places still ask you to take off your hat. https://www.npr.org

NPR. (2019, March 22). The pickle must bounce: Food regulation oddities. https://www.npr.org

NPR. (2019, May 10). Why Portland renters are still fighting for their tubs. https://www.npr.org

NPR. (2019, May 15). When words become criminal: Strange speech laws in America. https://www.npr.org

NPR. (2019, October 18). The chicken really did cross the road --- and got its owner fined. https://www.npr.org

NPR. (2020, March 10). When singing in public is a crime. https://www.npr.org

NPR. (2020, November 2). What you can and can't wear to vote. https://www.npr.org

NPR. (2020, October 23). Strange Sunday laws that still linger in America. https://www.npr.org

NPR. (2021, May 10). Park rules you didn't know existed: Waterfowl edition. https://www.npr.org

NPR. (2023, January 3). Now you can dance in Sweden---without paperwork. https://www.npr.org

122 | SOURCES

Oklahoma Department of Wildlife Conservation. (2022). *General animal protection statutes*. https://www.wildlifedepartment.com

Orange County HOA Code. (2021). *HOA enforcement policies and procedures for exterior uniformity*. https://www.ocfl.net

Oregon Department of Fish and Wildlife. (2021). *Urban waterfowl guidelines and harassment policy*. https://www.dfw.state.or.us

The Oregonian. (2020, August 15). Landlord fined for removing bathtub from historic rental unit. https://www.oregonlive.com

The Oregonian. (2020, July 14). Why harassing ducks is a ticketable offense. https://www.oregonlive.com

Oregon Residential Landlord-Tenant Act. (2023). *Tenant rights and required fixtures*. https://www.oregonlegislature.gov

Outdoor Life. (2021, July 12). Noodling in Missouri: What's legal and what's not. https://www.outdoorlife.com

Oxford Historical Review. (2021). *Silencing "peace": Language restrictions in British governance during WWI*. https://academic.oup.com

Parliament of the United Kingdom. (n.d.). *Standing Orders of the House of Commons: Public Business*. https://www.parliament.uk

Peeples, L. (2017). In the land where no one dies: Life in Longyearbyen. *BBC Future*. https://www.bbc.com/future/article/20171013-the-town-where-it-is-illegal-to-die

Philadelphia Inquirer. (2024, January 12). Liberty Bell replica defaced in D.C.; Philadelphia's response tightens security. https://www.inquirer.com

Philadelphia Inquirer. (2024, January 12). Liberty Bell vandalized with spray paint; security changes follow. https://www.inquirer.com

The Pinball Museum of America. (2020). *Pinball outlawed: A timeline of bans and reforms*. https://www.pinballmuseum.org

Portland Parks and Recreation. (2022). *Wildlife protection ordinance -- Section 20.12.060*. https://www.portland.gov

La Repubblica. (2019). Capri vieta le ciabatte rumorose: multa per i turisti molesti. https://www.repubblica.it

Republic of Cyprus -- Ministry of Transport, Communications and Works. (2021). *Highway Code -- Section 41: Driver distraction laws*. https://www.mcw.gov.cy

Reuters. (2009). Greece bars high heels from ancient monuments. https://www.reuters.com

The Reykjavik Grapevine. (2021, May 10). Naming committee rejects Lucifer, approves Dagur. https://grapevine.is

The Roanoke Times. (2003, August 22). Yes, tickling can be a crime in Virginia. https://roanoke.com

Royal Government of Bhutan. (2022). *Driglam Namzha: Code of Etiquette and*

National Dress. Department of Culture and Dzongkha Development. https://www.cabinet.gov.bt

Russian Federation Traffic Code. (2020). *Article 12.2: Visibility and cleanliness of vehicle registration marks*. https://www.gibdd.ru

Sacramento Department of Utilities. (2020). *Water conservation violations and fines*. https://www.cityofsacramento.org

San Diego Public Utilities. (2021). *Rain-related irrigation rules and smart watering practices*. https://www.sandiego.gov

San Diego Unified School District. (2022). *Student Handbook: Dress Code and Campus Conduct*. https://www.sandiegounified.org

The Scotsman. (2020, February 19). Strangest Scottish laws still technically in effect. https://www.scotsman.com

The Scotsman. (2020, October 14). From dance to duel: Scotland's oddest ceremonial laws. https://www.scotsman.com

Scottish Government. (2021). *Public Safety and Transport Guidelines: Historic and Unusual Enforcement Laws*. https://www.gov.scot

Scottish Government. (2022). *Civic conduct and weapons law overview*. https://www.gov.scot

Sécurité Routière (French Road Safety Authority). (2023). *Driver safety equipment requirements*. https://www.securite-routiere.gouv.fr

Singapore National Arts Council. (2023). *Public art interaction policies and protection standards*. https://www.nac.gov.sg

Singapore Police Force. (2022). *Pedestrian offenses and penalties under Road Traffic Act*. https://www.police.gov.sg

Singapore Police Force. (2022). *Vandalism Act enforcement and public sculpture protection*. https://www.police.gov.sg

Singapore Statutes Online. (2023). *Environmental Public Health Act -- Section 17: Sanitary facilities maintenance*. https://sso.agc.gov.sg

Smith, O. (2018, July 9). Italian cities are banning food and drink in public squares -- here's why. The Telegraph. https://www.telegraph.co.uk/travel/destinations/europe/italy/articles/italy-cities-ban-food-drink-in-public/

Smithsonian Magazine. (2015). America's oddest food laws. https://www.smithsonianmag.com

Smithsonian Magazine. (2015). Why you couldn't legally sing "Happy Birthday" for so long. https://www.smithsonianmag.com

Smithsonian Magazine. (2016). When pinball was illegal---and why it matters. https://www.smithsonianmag.com

Smithsonian Magazine. (2019). Rome enforces ban on sitting on the Spanish Steps. https://www.smithsonianmag.com

Smithsonian Magazine. (2021). Why we don't touch historic artifacts anymore.

https://www.smithsonianmag.com

Smithsonian Magazine. (2023). Hands off history: Why we protect national artifacts. https://www.smithsonianmag.com

Snopes. (2018, April 12). Fact check: Is it illegal to sleep with your shoes on in North Dakota? https://www.snopes.com

Snopes. (2019, June 14). Fact check: Is it illegal to die in the Houses of Parliament? https://www.snopes.com

South Carolina Attorney General's Office. (2019). *Opinion on dice games in nonprofit fundraisers*. https://www.scag.gov

Spain's General Traffic Regulations. (2022). *Article 18.1 -- Driver conduct and mobility restrictions*. https://boe.es

Sri Lanka Tourism Development Authority. (2021). *Visitor guidelines for sacred religious sites*. https://www.sltda.gov.lk

Star Tribune. (2018, April 3). Muddy tires could get you fined in Minnesota. https://www.startribune.com

Strange, H. (2012, March 6). No dying allowed: Life in Longyearbyen, Norway. *The Telegraph*. https://www.telegraph.co.uk/news/worldnews/europe/norway/9127423/In-the-town-where-it-is-illegal-to-die.html

The Straits Times. (2016, November 14). Tourist fined for sitting on public art sculpture. https://www.straitstimes.com

The Straits Times. (2019, January 10). Man fined for not flushing public toilet in hawker center. https://www.straitstimes.com

The Straits Times. (2021, May 14). Jaywalking crackdown sees spike in fines. https://www.straitstimes.com

The Svalbard Museum. (2022). *Cemetery history and Arctic health policies*. https://www.svalbardmuseum.no

Swedish Parliament (Riksdag). (2023). *Repeal of the dance permit requirement for public venues*. https://www.riksdagen.se

Swiss Federal Council. (2018). *Animal Welfare Act: Revisions for marine invertebrates*. https://www.admin.ch

Swiss Federal Food Safety and Veterinary Office. (2018). *Ordinance on the protection of animals during slaughter -- Amendment for crustaceans*. https://www.blv.admin.ch

Swiss Federal Office for the Environment. (2021). *Urban noise ordinances and residential sound guidelines*. https://www.bafu.admin.ch

Swiss Tenants' Association. (2020). *Guidelines on quiet hours and building etiquette*. https://www.mieterverband.ch

Swissinfo. (2018, August 15). Noise laws in Switzerland: What you can't do after 10PM. https://www.swissinfo.ch

The Sydney Morning Herald. (2021, February 12). *Funeral disturbance leads to fine under state law.* https://www.smh.com.au

The Tennessean. (1975, July 10). *City ends pinball ban after 30 years.* https://www.tennessean.com

Texas Legislature Online. (1973). *Texas Penal Code §43.23 -- Obscene devices.* https://statutes.capitol.texas.gov

Texas Secretary of State. (2021). *Polling place conduct and electioneering zones.* https://www.sos.state.tx.us

Times of India. (2019, October 5). *Tourist fined for damaging interior of fort during insect incident.* https://timesofindia.indiatimes.com

Tokyo Metropolitan Police Department. (2022). *Bicycle traffic safety rules in Tokyo.* https://www.keishicho.metro.tokyo.lg.jp

Toronto Parks, Forestry and Recreation. (2022). *Urban forest management guidelines.* https://www.toronto.ca/services-payments/parks

Town of Barre. (1910). *Public Conduct Ordinances, Section 7: Sabbath Sound Restrictions.* https://www.barrevt.gov

Transport for London. (2017). *Hackney Carriage Handbook: Historical dress code and presentation standards.* https://tfl.gov.uk

UK Foreign Travel Office. (2024). *Barbados foreign travel advice.* https://www.gov.uk/foreign-travel-advice/barbados

UK Government. (n.d.). *Historical legal statutes database.* National Archives.

UK Ministry of Defence. (2022). *Guidelines for Visitors: Royal Guard Safety and Conduct.* https://www.gov.uk

UK Parliament. (1872). *Licensing Act, Section 12: Drunkenness and control of animals.* https://www.legislation.gov.uk

UK Parliament. (1986). *Salmon Act 1986 -- Section 32: Handling salmon in suspicious circumstances.* https://www.legislation.gov.uk

UK Parliament. (2022). *Frequently asked questions -- Parliament and royal protocol.* https://www.parliament.uk

UK Parliamentary Archives. (1916). *Hansard transcripts of House debates during WWI.* https://hansard.parliament.uk

Union Nationale des Cuisines Centrales. (2011). *Statement on condiment usage in French schools.* https://www.unc-cuisinescentrales.org

United Kingdom Parliament. (1872). *Licensing Act, Section 12: Drunkenness and control of animals.* https://www.legislation.gov.uk

United States District Court -- Central District of California. (2016). *Rupa Marya et al. v. Warner/Chappell Music Inc., Case No. CV 13-4460.* https://www.cacd.uscourts.gov

University of Vermont Law Review. (2017). *Residual blue laws in rural New England.* https://www.uvm.edu

University of Virginia Law Review. (1910). *Unusual applications of assault law in commonwealth courts.* https://www.law.virginia.edu

U.S. Code Title 18. (2023). *Crimes and Criminal Procedure -- Protection of Historic Sites.* https://www.law.cornell.edu

U.S. Code Title 18. (2023). *Protection of national monuments and historic artifacts.* https://www.law.cornell.edu

U.S. Consumer Product Safety Commission. (2021). *Refrigerator safety: Preventing suffocation hazards.* https://www.cpsc.gov

U.S. Department of State. (2024). *Travel advisory: Trinidad and Tobago.* https://travel.state.gov

U.S. Fish and Wildlife Service. (1998). *Model state wildlife codes: Template legislation and common provisions.* https://www.fws.gov

USA Today. (2019, January 11). Alabama man crashes car during 'Bird Box challenge' stunt. https://www.usatoday.com

Vermont Historical Society. (2019). *Blue laws and Sabbath restrictions in 19th century Vermont.* https://vermonthistory.org

Victoria Police Department. (2020). *Public order offenses and ceremonial protections.* https://www.police.vic.gov.au

Virginia General Assembly. (2022). *Code of Virginia §18.2-57: Assault and battery definitions and applications.* https://law.lis.virginia.gov

Washington Post. (2019, June 28). Shreveport ends ban on sagging pants after man dies in police custody. https://www.washingtonpost.com

The Woodlands Township. (2022). *Residential Standards -- Window Treatments Policy.* https://www.thewoodlandstownship-tx.gov

Zurich Housing Authority. (2019). *Tenant behavior regulations and noise policies.* https://www.stadt-zuerich.ch

www.ingramcontent.com/pod-product-compliance
Lightning Source LLC
Chambersburg PA
CBHW052130030426
42337CB00028B/5099

Part 1

Introduction

Chapter 1

Perception and Reality

I want to be up front about the impetus and intent of this book. The inspiration for the title of the work comes from 2 Peter 3:16. In the closing of his second letter, Peter mentions to his readers a letter that his "beloved brother Paul" had written to them. He encourages them to pay attention to what Paul had to say to them, even though some points might be difficult to understand. He also warns them of other individuals, "the untaught and unstable," and their attempts to *distort* the writings of Paul "as they also do the rest of the Scriptures."

While this verse was the initial inspiration for the book, there is another that I could have used as well. Paul condemns the church at Galatia early in that letter (Galatians 1:6–9) for departing from that which they had received from Paul and his companions. He says they have followed after those offering something different, a *perverted* or *distorted* version of the gospel of Christ. These passages both suggest that there have been and will be those who change God's Word in some way or for some reason, and history has demonstrated that this indeed has been the case.

Inspiration for the Writing

There are several points that could be made from what Peter and Paul say. First, we should note that whatever their differences were in the incident recounted by Paul in Galatians 2:11–21, these have been patched over, and a mutual respect is in evidence—and they both know that man will misuse God's Word. Second, Peter alludes to Paul's words as "Scriptures," noting his writings being corrupted just like the *"rest of the Scriptures."* These could be only the Old Testament, or Peter is more likely including inspired writing in the New Testament era just as

"Scriptural" (authoritatively from God) as the Old Law. If nothing else, he is equating the two.

Third, Peter characterizes those who would be guilty of doing this as "untaught and unstable." Greek words from which these were translated suggest "ignorant" and "unestablished" as original terms. For related terms, we find "want of (*or lacking*) knowledge or perception" for "ignorant." This could be willful or just simply unexposed to the Truth. In either case, the point is being made that they do not *translate/transfer* Paul's words to others accurately. Since these individuals are untaught/unlearned/ignorant, then it is logical that they are "unstable," "unestablished," and/or "unsteadfast." The implication is that they have no real *lock* on the Truth provided by the Lord's design for revealing His Truth. This is found in Ephesians 4:11–15 and reveals the following [emphasis is mine]:

> And He gave some as apostles, some as prophets, some as evangelists, some as pastors and teachers, for the equipping of the saints for the work of ministry, for the building up of the body of Christ; until we all attain to the unity of the faith, and of the knowledge of the Son of God, to a mature man, to the measure of the stature which belongs to the fullness of Christ. *As a result, we are no longer to be children, tossed here and there by waves and carried about by every wind of doctrine, by the trickery of people, by craftiness in deceitful scheming;* but speaking *the truth in love*, we are to grow up in all aspects into Him who is the head, that is, Christ.

God had a plan for revealing the New Law; it involved a number of individuals and groups with responsibilities to deliver various portions of that law until it was complete. Notice the italicized sections above. Without this plan and this revelation, we are left to being, well, untaught and then unstable, as a result. "Every wind of doctrine" that comes along masquerading as Truth can influence us so that we are led by "crafty" and "deceitful" people with "schemes" that serve *their* purposes and not God's. "Speaking the truth in love" comes from a "unity of the faith" and of the "knowledge of the Son of God." It is only then that we can be considered a "mature man"—at least where our knowledge and practice of the Truth is concerned.

So, my inspiration for the title of this book comes from something I have not yet highlighted above. In the middle of 2 Peter 3:16 is the action that these *untaught* and *unstable* individuals take with Paul's words. The New American Standard Bible (NASB—the version I'll be using in this writing) uses the term "distort"; others use "wrest," "misinterpret," "pervert," or "explain falsely." Many, however, use the term "twist" or "have twisted" to characterize what these individuals have done to the writings of Paul and the rest of Scripture (the English Standard Version and the New King James Version, among others, use the word *twist*).

Regardless of how it is characterized and what term is used, it is indeed error and needs to be exposed. The reason comes in the final phrase of the verse concerning the outcome of their efforts: "to their own destruction." Their souls are in jeopardy as a result of how they have handled the Word of God. And my not-so-subtle point in selecting this title is that we, individually and collectively, are responsible for how we handle God's Word and apply it to our lives. In 2 Timothy 2:15, we are told that one way to be approved of God is by "accurately handling the word of truth." The passage also suggests that if we do not do this, then there is cause for shame; I am assuming this is before both man and God.

Intent of the Writing

Laying out the Word of God before others is a serious undertaking. Romans 14:7 tells us that, in ordinary life, no one lives and dies to himself. In life, we encounter and influence those around us for good or for bad. The role of "teacher" is even more important as that influence is potentially magnified to even larger numbers. James includes a caution (James 3:1), as a result: "Do not become teachers in large numbers, my brothers, since you know that we who are teachers will incur a stricter judgment."

Are we not to teach others then? "God forbid!" or "May it never be!"—as Romans 6:2 might frame such a conclusion. Not sharing the Gospel with others would be contrary to the love we are to demonstrate to all and in conflict with many passages suggesting that we not only be *able* to teach others (e.g., Hebrews 5:12; 1 Peter 3:15) but that we do so eagerly and readily. So, what is James telling us?

I think he is simply telling us to make sure that what we say and what we do, regarding the teaching and practice of that which we find in God's Word, had better be what God had intended us to teach and practice from His Word. If not, then we are—regardless of motive or simple ignorance—doing so "to our destruction." We must be absolutely sure that we are "accurately handling the word of truth," or we will reap that "stricter judgment" Paul speaks about in Romans 14:7.

My intent in this book is to confront a number of issues—call them *teachings* or *practices* if you like—that I do not find in God's Word. Some say these are simply just an alternative way of looking at or interpreting what is said there; some say we are free to enhance or embellish what has been given to us in His Word. However, I will do everything within my power to cite relevant, supporting passages and interpret those passages *within their context* to help with accuracy and complete understanding. The next sections below will deal with this notion of *context* and its importance for reading God's Word and understanding it as He intended.

In 1 Corinthians 14, where Paul is laying out for the Corinthian church (and others who will read his words as well) exactly how all of these "gifts of the Spirit" were supposed to work, he tells them in vv. 26–33 the following [emphasis is mine]:

> What is the outcome then, brothers and sisters? When you assemble, each one has a psalm, has a teaching, has a revelation, has a tongue, has an interpretation. *All things are to be done for edification.* If anyone speaks in a tongue, it must be by two or at the most three, and each one in turn, and one is to interpret; but

if there is no interpreter, he is to keep silent in church; and have him speak to himself and to God. Have two or three prophets speak, and have the others pass judgment. But if a revelation is made to another who is seated, then the first one is to keep silent. For you can all prophesy one by one, so that all may learn and all may be exhorted; and the spirits of prophets are subject to prophets; for *God is not a God of confusion, but of peace.*

My intent here is not to get into a discussion of gifts of the Holy Spirit; I'll save that for a later chapter. My point here is the words at the end of that quote that work for *all things* concerning God, not just the "rules" regarding the situation revolving around spiritual gifts. The God of Heaven and All Creation is not a God of confusion; He is, quite the opposite, a God of *extreme clarity*. If He had wanted to confuse mankind—but why would He—He could have easily done that. He could have told one inspired writer to say *this* and another inspired writer to say *that*, and then have the first contradict the second or both contradict a third. Such would have been easy to do. However, I am confident that God delivered His testaments (Old and New) in exactly the way He intended. Any confusion, differing interpretations, and resulting contradictory practices are man's fault; it is man who has confused His Word and not God Himself. He is a God of extreme clarity, not confusion.

So, before I get into some of these *issues* or *practices* mentioned above, let's look at some other preliminary thoughts concerning how we come to know what we know and how our minds work when encountering new material. Maybe these thoughts will help us open our minds a bit and allow us to objectively encounter God's Word as we examine it in later chapters.

Cognition and Perception

Cognition is a fancy term for *what we know and understand*. Our knowledge base and what we understand about this world and this life is first formed through our senses, instinctively absorbing that with which we come in contact. From our first exposure to our existence, we begin to form our personal repository or database of information about our world around us. Brain waves occur within the womb, and this begins the life journey of our brains quite naturally absorbing that which is around us.

As we emerge from that rather restricted environment, an entire world, literally, is opened up to us. Not only do our senses kick into overtime (and really don't take a breather until age diminishes or death ends them), we also now have interactive experiences beginning to accumulate at a phenomenal rate. We learn an amazing number of details in those early years, and they cannot but help shape how we view almost all that we encounter the rest of our lives. As we have interactions with others and develop relationships, these experiences will influence how we view others we know, those who are new to us, and the larger community.

Perception is that feature of our brains that helps us *interpret* that which we encounter. We each have these *filters* through which we produce personal interpretation and understanding of a situation or circumstance—or simply just new information. Our perceptions allow us to assign meaning or importance to events and all that we encounter. When new information is taken in, it rummages around in our brains seeking something similar to which it can relate, and it attaches itself there and subsequently adds to our knowledge base on that particular aspect of our world.

Perception and Reality

It would be nice if everyone's life experiences were the same, or at least similar, so that everyone would understand and relate to things and others in a more uniform manner. However, we realize that different people see the world through these lenses or filters noted above that allow them to assign interpretation, and thus meaning, that often differs from that of others, even though the process itself is the same. We have adopted the phrase "Different strokes for different folks" to accommodate these differences in perceptions. We also hear, "Everyone is different; it is what makes the world go around" or "Variety is the spice of life." The point is that what makes us unique individuals with unique personalities does indeed contribute to a complex variety of folks in an already multi-faceted and complicated world.

There is a common saying about perception that is applied across a wide spectrum of contexts: "Perception is 9/10 of reality." Up front, let us say that *reality is reality,* and personal perceptions do not affect reality, only our *interpretations* of it. The point to be made here, as we get more into the purpose of this writing, is to say that we all have our perceptions of things shaped by our experiences in this life. These perceptions come with those lenses and filters we use to process past and new knowledge. They, for us, form our *personal reality* that help us make sense of our lives and give meaning and understanding to what we encounter.

Chapter 2

Confirmation Bias and Objectivity

The term *bias* has assumed negative connotations in recent years. On the surface, it merely means a tendency, an opinion, an outlook, or a preference in one direction over another. It is often used, however, to indicate a prejudgment (a prejudice) without supporting information on a particular topic, event, or on a particular group of people. In reality, in its most original form, it simply means *to incline to one side* (webster-dictionary.org).

As we live out our lives, there are natural impulses to form relationships with others who are more like us than with those who are different from us. Commonality promotes a sense of validation, so we seek out people and experiences that affirm those attitudes, opinions, and outlooks noted above. "Birds of a feather (do indeed) flock together." Conversations flow more freely among individuals who operate from the same perspectives on issues. There is a certain comfort, even trust, in familiarity and in numbers.

What results in situations like this is what has been called *confirmation bias*. Experts tell us that this occurs when we adopt a specific belief about a situation and then seek out information that confirms that preconceived notion—whether consciously or subconsciously. What results is a possibly skewed or even erroneous interpretation of new information that feeds already existing *mis*information that was interpreted from the last encounter of this nature. Before too long, we see *everything* through these biases that hide *real reality*—as opposed to *our reality*—from our discovery. Confirmation bias is as real in the workplace as it is anywhere, and numerous examples are available for any setting and on both sides of practically every issue. However, the attempt here is simply to introduce it as a concept to help explain a phenomenon that occurs when we read the Scriptures, God's Word, the Bible.

Objectivity

Considering what has been said to this point, *objectivity* on any subject is very difficult to achieve, unless the information is wholly unrelated to anything we have ever previously confronted. Truly unencountered information can be viewed with a more open mind. However, with our brains scouring our cranial wrinkles and fissures for at least something related to latch onto, total objectivity is rarely employed. As a result, anything less than brand new, authentically novel information has a built-in slant to it as we take it in. Where beliefs about the Bible are concerned, this is particularly in evidence.

Devout atheists will often reject *any* argument that lends credibility to the notion that the Bible is the Word of God or contains anything other than stories contrived and written by man. At the same time, however, devout believers will reject any interpretation of a Biblical passage on which they already have an opinion concerning its interpretation and subsequent use for making a point or providing the basis for a stance on a particular teaching.

Moses had been fortunately raised by his mother within the household of Pharaoh, and he knew of his heritage within the nation of Israel. He demonstrated this in his defense of an Israelite slave, which led to Moses's leaving for the land of Midian. When called by God to lead His people out of slavery, Moses balked, literally refusing to comply with God's commands, even to the point that God's "anger burned against Moses" (Exodus 4:14). God demonstrates to Moses in multiple ways that He will be in control and that Moses and Aaron will simply be His messengers. Moses relents with these demonstrations now part of the picture; his preconceived notions about the undertaking had been altered by the presentation of evidence. Hardcore evidence can do that;

we just have to be objective enough to receive it once it convinces us of an alternative interpretation of a situation.

Confirmation Bias and Scripture

Hearing something over and over again has a way of *hardwiring* it into our brains. An example of this is that for decades, Americans boasted of having the best educational system in the world. This was born out with international test scores illustrating such. In recent decades, however, there are a number of points that could be made—regardless of how international data can be misrepresented—to illustrate that this is no longer the case. Internal evidence pointing to large numbers of 12th graders who cannot perform basic reading and math skills would be just one example. Yet, the American public, government officials, lawmakers, the media, and others still don't think we have a crisis going on here. Nothing significant is being done to *fix* this situation while we look in the other direction or bury our collective heads in the sand. Our mindset has always been, "We are #1," so any evidence to the contrary is either rationalized, minimized, or even ostracized (i.e., ignored) so other *more pressing* things can absorb our national attention.

The point being made here is that we, as believers in the Word of God, come to that book with preconceived notions of certain passages that confirm what we have always heard these passages teach. The problem is that we have never taken the time to fully and objectively examine that passage (or a particular verse) within its proper *context*. Is context important for understanding a passage in the Bible? I do not know how you could offer anything but a resounding "Yes!" to that question. It is practically rhetorical in its asking. You learn new words to add to your vocabulary by examining them within the context of the sentence around them. Why would you not do the same for a verse or a passage within Scripture?

Would a doctor, a law enforcement officer, a researcher, or any other professional required to draw conclusions about a circumstance or situation attempt to do so without collecting information about what caused it or, at least, what events occurred leading up to it? Of course not. Getting background information (i.e., the full picture) is essential for correctly concluding what is needed to address and fix that unsatisfactory situation. We use context in so many ways within our lives to make sense of things we encounter, yet when examining Scripture, we tend to rely on what we *want it to mean* rather than *what it was intended to mean* at the time and, not coincidentally, *now*. Our effort to understand Scripture cannot be fully realized unless background and context are taken into consideration. To simply lift a passage out of context opens us up to what nonbelievers have always said about Scripture: "You can make the Bible *say* almost anything; just pick the right verses."

So, what is *context* and why is obtaining background information so important *before* we attempt to understand God's Word and how it applies to us and our lives? The next chapter will examine this all-important piece of the puzzle that all of us should be facing as we determine how to let His Word influence who we are and what we do.

Chapter 3

Determining Context and Its Influence

The novice street reporter for a news outlet knows the "5 Ws"—*who, what, where, when,* and *why* (and sometimes *how* is added as well). These are the fundamental components of a good story that attempt to supply consumers with all they need to be informed and have a chance at a clear understanding of what occurred. Police investigations use the same set of questions for inquiries where evidence is considered for potential charges—at least resolution of the situation. The core features of any type of research utilize the same questions to help cover the basics of what is needed to establish truth in a project. It is important to note that all of these five questions need answers, or else crucial information for establishing the most accurate picture of what occurred can be left out. Historically, these questions go all the way back to the Greek philosopher Aristotle in the 4th Century B.C. with his *elements of circumstances* used to explain or predict any set of conditions or actions.

Context Defined

Context is defined as "the set of circumstances or facts that surround a particular event, situation, etc." and that which influences "its meaning or effect" (dictionary.com). In order to correctly and accurately understand something—some event, situation, written/spoken statement—you must have its context. Vanseodesign.com provides an interesting example of the importance of context when attempting to answer even the simplest of questions: What do you get when you add one to one? Most of us would respond, "Two: 1+1=2:" But what if you were talking about one sperm to one egg? Or what about one drop of water to another drop of water? With this simple example, you can see how the larger picture must be considered before arriving at an accurate conclusion.

Strictly speaking, the Bible qualifies as *ancient literature.* Of course, we believers know it is much more than that, but history tells us that it was written a long, long time ago. Estimates for the earliest of books in the Old Testament begin somewhere around 1600 BC and conclude around 400 BC for the last book of prophecy. For the New Testament, earliest estimates for the first book are around AD 40 with the last book, Revelation, being completed around AD 90. None of us was around then to personally experience the context, so we have to rely on what we know about circumstances at the time from a historical standpoint. More importantly, however, we can derive from the Scriptures themselves (a verse and its companion context) information about how to best interpret what we find there.

Personal Responsibility

As noted in the previous chapter, there are those who would attempt to lift passages out of the Bible—and their respective contexts—in an attempt to support or prove a point that in no way was intended by the author of those particular verses. As I noted above, in 2 Peter 3:16, we have an allusion to those who would do this intentionally: "Untaught and unstable people twist (Pauls' writings) to their own destruction, as they do also the rest of the Scriptures." Obviously, there will be consequences for misusing God's Word, especially if the intent is to misrepresent what is being taught.

On the other hand, there are those of us who are considerably more noble than the ones who would *intentionally* "twist" the Word of God for personal benefit or to simply mislead others for some reason. 1) We might be merely repeating what we have always heard on a particular passage or practice recorded in the Bible. 2) We could be swayed by an influential religious leader/scholar concerning the meaning of a passage. 3) We could be guilty of just ignoring the context and taking a verse on face value. There are possibly other reasons why we might misinterpret or misuse a piece of Scripture, but the Word itself places upon us the responsibility to handle God's Truth the way it was intended to be employed. In 2 Timothy 2, we have Paul teaching Timothy, his young preaching companion, about the kinds of people he will encounter and what his response to them should be. He warns him to avoid "worldly and empty chatter" that will lead to ungodliness and those who have gone astray from the truth. In 2:15, he says, "Be diligent to present yourself approved to God as a worker who does not need to be ashamed, accurately handling the word of truth." These points suggest that we can have the Truth and stray from it, as well as have it and just mishandle it.

For the phrase "accurately handling," other interpretations (versions) record *correctly handling, correctly explaining, rightly handling,* and *rightly dividing* the "word of truth." The Greek word comes from the phrase, "to make a straight cut; to dissect correctly." The admonishment from Paul is that we should be *diligent* (Gk.: to hasten, be eager, be zealous, to try, be prompt or earnest) in this action, and the outcome will be one who is "approved" of God and who has no need "to be ashamed."

Finally, on this point, there is the notion of what some would call "multiple interpretations." This is the idea that the Author (God) simply had writers put down *general statements* and then left the interpretation of those statements up to those who would hear or read them. Nothing could be further from the truth. The God of the Bible is a God of extreme clarity, as I noted above; there is nothing left up to the imagination when He says, "Follow my commandments and you'll be blessed; disobey them and you will be punished" (Leviticus 26 paraphrased).

This is not a literature class where some poet's work is dissected to "find out what it means to each of us." Yes, we can possibly take something written, interpret it as we may, and even apply it to our lives. However, the poet most likely meant only one thing in what he or she wrote. If we miss that in poetry, so be it. If we miss it in interpreting God's Word, it could cost us our salvation. *Diligence* is required in the passage above from 2 Timothy; at the very least, this implies that time and effort must be expended in the search for *Truth* in the Scriptures. It is there; we must seek it out.

Teaching Others is Serious Business

I have addressed this fact above, but it bears revisiting and some elaboration here. The point is this: molding one's life on the content found in the Scriptures is serious business, but *teaching others* from the Bible is even more serious. A casual or undedicated approach to making sure we are presenting God's Word *accurately* has dire consequences. Let's look at one more passage to illustrate this point. The book of James is a series of recommendations, admonitions, and illuminations on a variety of topics. In chapter 2, James provides considerable detail illustrating how faith and works are inseparable, using Abraham as the primary example. He concludes this section with, "faith without works is dead." Interestingly, he then turns to teachers in the first verses of chapter 3 (but we know that these chapter divisions were not in the original and were added later for the convenience of the reader). He says,

> Do not become teachers in large numbers, my brothers, since you know that we who are teachers will incur a stricter judgment. For we all stumble in many ways. If anyone does not stumble in what he says, he is a perfect man, able to rein in the whole body as well.

He goes on to provide examples about how destructive the tongue can be as we use it to communicate with and relate to others around us. One of the following is true: 1) James links faith and works; he inserts a point about being careful if you are a teacher; he then turns to how dangerous the tongue can be, or 2) all of this is one train of thought as our faith is illustrated in our works, which could include teaching others the Word of God. However, be careful what you say and how you say it because controlling the tongue is nigh impossible.

Without going into any further detail, the point is simply this: Teaching others what the Word of God says is an extremely sobering undertaking. These passages in Timothy and James point this out very clearly. A footnote for the version I am using (NASB) for "stricter judgment" says this: "Or *greater condemnation*, i.e. for erroneous doctrine." Assuming to speak on behalf of God—what we do when we teach others from His Word—has consequences if we mishandle that which has been entrusted to us for safe keeping and sound delivery.

Questions for Establishing Context

As I noted above for news reporting, there are five questions that allow those collecting information to determine the truth about a situation and a means of being accurate in writing up the account. For determining *context* for a passage within the Scriptures, a written medium, we need to answer only four questions:

1. Who said it?
2. To whom was it said?
3. Why was it said?
4. How would those hearing it have understood it?

These are not questions I have devised. Others have used them, and I have simply borrowed them because I believe they, indeed, cover what is necessary for understanding Scriptural context. I have unsuccessfully attempted to track down the original developer of these questions in this order. Let's consider each individually as each is very important.

Who Said It?

The first question we need to ask centers on the speaker in the passage. If it is a direct quote, then the passage itself will tell us who said it. If not a direct quote, then we must turn to the *author* of the text. In most cases, one of the following will be our answer for the New Testament:

1. One of the Godhead—Father, Son, or Holy Spirit
2. One speaking "in the spirit"—Zacharias, John the Baptist, or Simeon and Anna (Luke 2)
3. One of the writers of the Gospels—Matthew, Mark, Luke (also Acts), or John
4. An apostle—Paul, Peter, or John
5. A named inspired writer—James or Jude
6. An unnamed inspired writer—the author of Hebrews
7. Others to whom Jesus, Paul, Philip, etc. were speaking at the time

The question might be offered, "Why is it so important to know who said it?" This is a legitimate question that needs addressing. First, we need to know if the speakers are inspired by God in the passage under consideration. Are they truly speaking the words or thoughts God wanted them to speak, or are these words simply like yours and mine: straight out of possibly an informed but uninspired brain? We know that Jesus spoke only that which His Father instructed Him to say (John 8:28). A man blind from birth was encountered, and the disciples asked in John 9:31, "Rabbi, who sinned, this man or his parents, that he should be born blind?" Jesus corrects them that neither is the case. They were operating on the same premise that in order to justify some misfortune, blame had to be laid at the feet of someone. Job's friends accused him repeatedly concerning the ills that befell him. It was not an inspired teaching then nor was it in the first century. Jesus does refute it; however, if He hadn't, we would have had to examine the speaker more closely to ascertain whether or not this question had any truth embedded within it.

This is just one example to illustrate before we really get into the examples we want to examine later for correct interpretation. It does, however, illustrate that just because you find it in print in the Bible, it does not mean it asserts truth. Identifying the one who said it is indeed important.

To Whom Was It Said?

In Mark 16, Jesus has appeared to the eleven apostles, reprimanding them because they did not believe others who testified He had risen, and says beginning in Verse 15,

> Go into all the world and preach the gospel to all creation. The one who has believed and has been baptized will be saved; but the one who has not believed will be condemned. These signs will accompany those who have believed: in My name they will cast out demons, they will speak with new tongues; they will pick up serpents, and if they drink any deadly poison, it will not harm them; they will lay hands on the sick, and they will recover.

It is important to note that He is speaking to His apostles. These men and others who would travel with them were charged with spreading the Gospel to "all the world"—at least that which they could physically reach. That charge was to them with this *great commission*. They would not go empty handed, however, as they would be equipped with miracles to attract an audience, hold their attention so they could preach to them, and then make the connection between the miracles and the Word being taught (thus, *wonders*, *miracles*, and *signs*). In like manner, the apostles could endow those who believed with similar powers and other spiritual gifts to aid in the dissemination of this all–important message.

The point to be made here is that this particular accommodation of the Holy Spirit does not extend to us today. There are several passages that indicate that these miracles had a limited shelf life and that following the delivery of the "perfect law of liberty" (James 1:25), these signs of direct power and authority from God would cease (1 Cor. 13:8–10). We cannot and should not expect God to provide us with miracles today to confirm the Word. That was the *only* purpose for them in the first place (Mark 16:20; John 20:30–31; 1 Thess. 1:5; Heb. 2:4), and that purpose no longer exists. God's complete and perfect Word *has been* delivered (Jude 1:3).

There are those who believe these words from Jesus were to *all of us* who believe, and they do indeed handle snakes and drink poisons. Unfortunately, they often find out too late that these powers were reserved for a first century purpose that is not necessary, nor in effect, today.

Why Was It Said?

Let's stay with the example provided just above. Jesus had risen from the dead and walked upon the earth for several days appearing to both individuals and groups (1 Cor. 15:1–11). Here, just before He departs, He gives them the charge to carry on the work He has begun in delivering the New Law and the plan of salvation—i.e., the Gospel. He has already told them about the difficulties they will have (e.g., John 16:1–4), so it would be natural for them to be anxious about the task ahead of them. He needed to provide them with reassurance that they need not worry and that the Comforter promised to them (John 15:26; 16:13) would guide them into all truth as well as provide them with miracles for support (Mark 16:17).

The future for these men was unclear, at least for the present moment. They had no real idea of what they must suffer for His name's sake; they would learn as they traveled and taught. Paul was told directly (Acts 9:15–16). The events of Acts 1 and 2 convinced the apostles of the fulfillment of all that Jesus had promised, and they now knew they had all they needed to carry out their commission.

How Would Those Hearing It Have Understood It?

Again, I will extend the example immediately above to address this question. As noted, Jesus is doing what He can to prepare those who will not only continue the work He has started here on earth, but these men will have the additional responsibility of establishing the church, God's kingdom here on earth. Prior to the second chapter of Acts, these men were a collective of disciples of an itinerant Teacher who traveled around teaching a version of godliness entirely different from what the Jewish leaders had promoted and practiced. Yes, He performed a wide variety of impressive miracles, but even that was not sufficient to deter the crowd that ultimately cried for His crucifixion following His arrest and trial. The apostles' activity following His death included secluding themselves for protection from the Jews or even some temporarily returning to prior vocations of fishing (John 21:1–3).

When He tells them that they will be empowered from on high with the ability to speak the thoughts of God and to perform miracles, they would have understood what that meant. They had already experienced this (Luke 9:1–6), and Jesus had demonstrated these powers in their presence often. On the Day of Pentecost (Acts 2), what He had promised became a reality. Their eyes were opened following His resurrection (John foreshadows this in John 2:22), and they believed what He had told them and that they would be able to do the things He wanted them to do. They also knew why these powers were being given to them and that they would cease when the last of them had died. They knew their purpose and, as Paul says,

> Love never fails; but if there are gifts of prophecy, they will be done away with; if there are tongues, they will cease; if there is knowledge, it will be done away with. For we know in part and prophesy in part; but when the perfect comes, the partial will be done away with (1 Cor. 13:8–9).

The transformation from being those Jesus characterized as having "little faith" to becoming dedicated martyrs who will "sit on the throne of His glory, and also sit upon twelve thrones, judging the twelve tribes of Israel" (Matt. 19:28) for the cause of Christ was complete. These men were wholly dedicated to preaching the Gospel and establishing churches throughout "Judea, Samaria, and even to the remotest part of the earth" (Acts 1:8).

The only other point to be made in this section is to note that words have different meaning depending on a few things. First, any time you convert text from one language to the next, you are likely to "lose something in the translation." There is a reason for the existence of that phrase. The New Testament was written in a common person's Greek (*koine*). Greek was a much more precise language than ours; the usual example is that English uses the word "love" in a variety of ways. The Greeks had multiple words for the different kinds of love experienced back then, and we today use the one word for a wide variety of purposes and meaning. So, it is necessary, from time to time, to use the resources we have at hand to determine the *exact* meaning intended by looking at the Greek word in the text. Second, some words we use today have changed meaning just in recent decades. In Genesis 1:28, God tells Adam and Eve to *replenish* the earth; in the original, that meant "to supply fully." Obviously, they were starting from scratch, not *re-filling* anything. Likewise, in Matthew 6:6, Jesus tells His listeners to go into their *closet* to pray; again, this simply means an "inner or private room," not a clothes closet that we would think of if this term is used today. This reality, also, is something we need to be concerned about as we consider how those hearing the words we find in Scripture would have understood them.

Equipped with Context

Understanding the Bible is not difficult (2 Corinthians 1:13; Ephesians 3:4). We make it more difficult by coming to it with preconceived notions and ideas on *what we want it to say* rather than letting it simply *speak to us from the written page.* In order to make it say what we want it to say, we have to "twist" things or take them out of their setting to satisfy *our* pre-determined meaning. Some do it for less than noble motives (Philippians 1:15–17); some do so to promote agendas or to acquire large numbers of followers (2 Timothy 4:3–4); some are merely repeating what they have always heard concerning a particular belief and why that belief is supposedly "Scriptural." This last group is certainly not following the instruction of Paul in Philippians 2:12 where he says, "So then, my beloved, just as you have always obeyed, not as in my presence only, but now much more in my absence, work out your own salvation with fear and trembling." Likewise, the only person responsible for *your* salvation is *you*; no one will be present with you before God to help you explain how the two of you understood His Word while on this earth.

Paul's job was to spread the Gospel and establish churches. He sometimes would stay more than a year with a group to make sure that they were "rooted" and "grounded" in the faith (Colossians 2:7; Ephesians 3:17). Yet, as he told the church at Philippi, you are on your own; work on your salvation; it is yours to pursue and achieve.

Today, we have that same charge. Our salvation is ours to obtain and retain. The only way to do this is to *know* God's Word and to *practice* God's Word. We cannot rely on others to do the work for us; it is on our shoulders. Paul says in the passage above from 2 Corinthians (1:13) that he writes nothing to them there in Corinth but what they can "read and understand." That goes for all of his letters as well as the rest of New Testament Scripture. God would not incorporate His will for us in a document that we simply could not understand. Many a devout atheist or agnostic has read himself or herself into obedience by simply studying the Word. It has been designed, prepared, and delivered by God Himself, and it is in our hands. It is our responsibility to read it and apply it in our lives. Turning it over to someone else is placing our eternal lives in someone else's hands. Humans are fallible creatures, and we regularly see headlines of "the most devout" among us guilty of some rather heinous sins.

What I have provided to this point is an understanding about the most accurate way to read and understand the Word: by using context. As we enter the next few chapters, we will be using this tool to decipher *authentic* interpretations of the Bible; however, we will also consider not just a passage and its context for determining textual accuracy; we will also be considering the larger context of what the rest of the New Testament says on a particular topic as well. What we believe to be the Truth found in God's Word is often based on a) what someone might want us to believe or b) what we have always believed. Neither of those is 100% reliable, and if our salvation depends on it, maybe we should take some ownership and put in the effort on our own to make sure what is being taught by *any individual* is indeed that which is taught in Scripture (1 John 4:1).

What I Won't Do

There is no possible way to cover all the topics such a discussion as this would prompt, let alone do justice to all of them. There are larger, more established structures, beliefs, and interpretations of passages that form many of the foundations of religious groups in the world today. These larger issues have been written about, debated, and discussed much more thoroughly than I could do here. I will let those previous and ongoing discussions serve the purpose of illuminating points of difference for the reader.

What I am referring to are topics like Premillennialism; Calvin's TULIP Theory; the Swoon (and other) Theories for the Empty Tomb; Homosexuality/Adultery/etc.; the End Times; the Jesus Seminar; Creation vs. Other Explanations; etc. So much has been written on these topics that I doubt I could do any more justice to them than what has been published. The Internet is a marvelous resource, but we must be sure to examine both sides of any of these issues and others before forming an opinion or conclusion. Also, we must always use the Word of God as our standard.

These first three chapters have provided you with some background for approaching controversial topics. More will follow in some of the chapters as we judiciously employ the features of *context* for studying and understanding the Bible and apply it to our worship of God and how we conduct ourselves on a daily basis with our acquaintances, friends, and loved ones.

> *Retain the standard of sound words which you have heard from me, in the faith and love which are in Christ Jesus. Guard, through the Holy Spirit who dwells in us, the treasure which has been entrusted to you.*
> (2 Timothy 1:13–14)

Part 2

Misunderstood Religious Structures

Chapter 4

The Old and New Testaments

When people criticize the Bible, they often lump the Old Testament and the New Testament together and will often pick something from the Old Testament to use for criticism of your Christianity. Yes, they are one text, one collective document, one revelation from God for mankind with one continual story, with one message, and with one theme. On the other hand, they were written during two different eras (epochs or dispensations), dealt primarily with at least two different sets of people, contained entirely different content, had two distinct purposes, and were designed to be sequential with prophecies from the former being fulfilled in people, events, and institutions in the latter. I will get into some of these below, but first, let's define what a *testament* is.

Vine's tells us that a *testament* is a synonym for a *covenant*. The definition most applicable is "an agreement, a mutual undertaking." The Oxford Lexicon UK Dictionary says, "Theology: an agreement which brings about a relationship of commitment between God and his people." At biblestudytools.com, we find, "The preferred meaning of this Old Testament word is bond; a covenant refers to two or more parties bound together." Modern dictionaries help also: "a formal, solemn, and binding agreement; a compact" (Merriam–Webster); "an agreement, usually formal, between two or more persons to do or not do something specified" (dictionary.com).

The idea of a *testament* additionally pulls in the notion of someone's last wishes regarding that person's estate. In Hebrews 9:16, we have an allusion to this in that the covenant (will, testament) of Jesus was put into effect—just like in society today—only when He died: "For where there is a covenant (will or testament—other versions), there must of necessity be the death of the one who made it." Simply put, a *covenant* is a binding agreement between two parties where both agree to do and/or not do something.

God, in many places, pronounces His covenant with the people of Israel. Here is what He directs Moses to tell the people in Exodus 19:5–6:

> Now then, if you will indeed obey My voice and keep My covenant, then you shall be My own possession among all the peoples, for all the earth is Mine; and you shall be to Me a kingdom of priests and a holy nation.

Two verses later, we have this: "Then all the people answered together and said, 'All that the LORD has spoken we will do!'" In Deuteronomy 28—30, God goes into detail concerning what benefits and blessings they will experience if they keep His will and adhere to His commandments; He also details the ills that will befall them if they don't. In Deuteronomy 11:26–28, He is more concise:

> See, I am placing before you today a blessing and a curse: the blessing, if you listen to the commandments of the LORD your God, which I am commanding you today; and the curse, if you do not listen to the commandments of the LORD your God.

That curse was often phrased in no uncertain terms as "perishing" or "destruction."

One other note should be made that is illustrated by the quote just above. God agreed to bless His people, and those blessings are impressive. On the other hand, should they break their part of the covenant by failing to keep God's commandments, then God is freed from His part of the agreement. Not only that, but the second part of the agreement kicks in, and their destruction is inevitable. This covenant was initiated with Abraham, continued through Isaac and Jacob, and renewed with Israel following their exit from Egyptian bondage. God has always had a covenant with His people, and He does so even today.

The Old Law

Bible scholars separate the Bible into three primary dispensations: Patriarchal, Jewish, and Christian. For approximately 2500 years, the early part of the Scriptures indicate that God dealt with individuals and families with the patriarch (i.e., head) of the family serving as the leader and even "priest" for the group, offering sacrifices, and communing with God. Those that stand out would be Noah, Abraham, Isaac, and Jacob, although there are others, many of whom are mentioned in the descendants of Adam in Genesis 5. Other than rendering obedience to the commands and expectations God delivered to them individually, there was no general "law" that governed all of them across these years (at least of what we know except possibly for blood sacrifices). That reality, uniformity, and specificity was saved for God's chosen people, Israel, with Moses as His chosen intermediary between Him and His people.

Following the saving of his family who had come to Egypt, Joseph dies and those who follow him in power do not remember his great deeds on behalf of Egypt. The descendants of Jacob (Israel) are placed into slavery and remain there for a number of years and several generations. The interpretation of passages around the exact amount of time is immaterial here. We do know that they were in slavery in Egypt for a long enough time for God to recognize that it was time to deliver them (Exodus 3:9). Moses, after having been raised in the house of Pharaoh, was in exile himself when God comes to him with His charge to lead Israel out of Egyptian bondage. After some convincing (Exodus 3 and 4), Moses appears before Pharaoh and demands that he release the Israelites. The next 10 chapters of Exodus lay out the details of how this release eventually occurs with God destroying the Egyptian army in the Red Sea (Exodus 14).

At Mount Sinai, God provides Moses with the Law that will serve as the people's guide for centuries to come. The details of this law span many chapters in the Old Testament and contain considerably more than the 10 Commandments that many erroneously believe is the extent of the Old Law. Scholars recognize that parts of Genesis are considered as the Old Law; Paul refers in Galatians 4 to the story of Ishmael and Isaac calling it part of the Law. Beginning in Exodus 20 with the listing of the 10 Commandments, the text lays out the details of the Law that would govern them for generations. The version in Exodus covers approximately 10 chapters and includes the construction of the tabernacle and all that pertained to the work of the priests, even down to their garments. The first five books of the Bible are generally referred to as Books of Law (the Pentateuch), so listing all the places where portions of the Law of Moses are contained would be difficult.

The Old Law contained rules, rituals and ceremonies, relationships, symbols, sacrifices, and general principles that guided the people. It was designed to be detailed and rather onerous. Keeping it perfectly was impossible (except for Jesus), and thus a system of sacrifices to remind Israel of their violations of that Law (i.e., their sins) was set in motion as a part of keeping the Law. In Romans 7 and 8, Paul contrasts the Old Law and the New Law. In Romans 8:2, Paul calls the Old Law the "law of sin and of death." He called it that because man could not be fully justified under the Old Law; it took Jesus coming to have forgiveness of sins (8:3). In Romans 7:6, Paul makes the contrast clearer saying, "But now we have been released from the Law, having died to that by which we were bound, so that we serve in newness of the Spirit and not in oldness of the letter."

In Galatians 3:19, Paul says this: "What purpose then does the law serve? It was added because of transgressions, till the Seed should come to whom the promise was made; and it was appointed through angels by the hand of a mediator." The Old Law was an introduction to God and how He would deal with man according to the Law He had provided for them. It was never intended to be the end of things as far as God's Law is concerned; He had greater intentions in mind found within the Law of Christ that was to come—and has now been delivered.

Before I move to that New Law, one other passage should be noted from the book of Jeremiah that functions as at least one link between the Old Covenant and the New Covenant. Jeremiah 31:31–34 says the following:

> "Behold, days are coming," declares the LORD, "when I will make a new covenant with the house of Israel and the house of Judah, not like the covenant which I made with their fathers on the day I took them by the hand to bring them out of the land of Egypt, My covenant which they broke, although I was a husband to them," declares the LORD. "For this is the covenant which I will make with the house of Israel after those days," declares the LORD: "I will put My law within them and write it on their heart; and I will be their God, and they shall be My people. They will not teach again, each one his neighbor and each one his brother, saying, 'Know the LORD,' for they will all know Me, from the least of them to the greatest of them," declares the LORD, "for I will forgive their wrongdoing, and their sin I will no longer remember."

The Hebrew writer quotes this entire passage from Jeremiah to make the claim that this *new covenant* has indeed been established in Jesus and that the *old covenant* is ready to be obsolete and disappear (Hebrews 8:7–13). This prophecy in Jeremiah was fulfilled in Jesus and the covenant (testament) He initiated at His death and resurrection. Hebrews is full of things comparing the Old Law to the Law of Christ. In every case, the new is *superior* to the old. Paul, in Colossians 2:14, puts it this way: Jesus has "canceled the certificate of debt consisting of decrees against us, which was hostile to us; and He has taken it out of the way, having nailed it to the cross."

The New Law

The Old Law had its purpose, and it thoroughly fulfilled that purpose. It was preparatory yet incomplete for what God had planned for mankind. Jesus said He didn't come to destroy the Law but to fulfill it (Matthew 5:17–18). Indeed, He did so in every way. Hebrews 10:1 tells us, "For the Law, since it has only a shadow of the good things to come and not the form of those things itself, can never, by the same sacrifices which they offer continually every year, make those who approach perfect." Eight verses later, the writer says this: "He takes away the first in order to establish the second. By this will, we have been sanctified through the offering of the body of Jesus Christ once for all time," contrasting the weakness of the Old Law to accomplish what Jesus did.

As noted above, the book of Hebrews (chapters 1–10) is a text on the contrast between what the Old Law offered compared to this New Law instituted by Jesus. For a fuller explanation of these contrasts explaining the superiority of this New Law over the Old Law and its necessity, read through these chapters. So, apart from providing a Law for the Jews to follow until the coming of Messiah—and setting up a number of practices that had their fulfillment in Jesus—what else was the Law good for?

There are at least three New Testament passages which tell us what we, as Christians, are to do with the Old Law. First, like in the book of Hebrews, the book of Romans provides us not only a contrast between the Old and New Laws, but it also contains warnings about forsaking the latter and returning to the former. In Romans 15:4, Paul says, "For whatever was written in earlier times was written for our instruction, so that through perseverance and the encouragement of the Scriptures we might have hope." Without the Old Testament Scriptures and all they offer us, especially in the way of prophecy concerning Jesus, we would not fully appreciate the blessings found in Him. A couple of verses later, Paul tells us that Christ "has become the servant to the circumcision (the Jews) on behalf of the truth of God, to confirm the promises given to the fathers."

Likewise, in 1 Corinthians 10, Paul is teaching a lesson to those under the New Law by talking about those who were under the Old Law. In 10:6, he says this: "Now these things happened as examples for us, so that we would not crave evil things as they indeed craved them." In Verse 11, he repeats and adds this. "Now these things happened to them as an example, and they were written for our instruction, upon whom the ends of the ages have come." Finally, in Galatians 3:23–25 we have this:

> But before faith came, we were kept in custody under the Law, being confined for the faith that was destined to be revealed. Therefore, the Law has become our guardian to lead us to Christ, so that we may be justified by faith. But now that faith has come, we are no longer under a guardian.

Other versions use *trainer*, *tutor*, *instructor*, or *schoolmaster* instead of *guardian*.

The conclusion is that the Old Law was Israel's handbook for how to please God and to understand—through their inability to keep it perfectly—sin and their inadequacies due to weaknesses. It also served as an indicator that something better was coming that would free them from the "bondage of sin" they suffered under this Old Law. That freedom was found in the New Law, the Law of Christ that frees us from sin but also from the Old Law itself: "Therefore there is now no condemnation at all for those who are in Christ Jesus. For the law of the Spirit of life in Christ Jesus has set you free from the law of sin and of death" (Romans 8:1–2).

So, the Old Law was designed to bring us to a knowledge of Christ and the rest of God's plan for the salvation of mankind. The Old Law has been "nailed to the cross" in more than one way. It no longer governs us; His sacrifice allows for forgiveness (and *no remembrance*) of our sins; it provides an access to God through Jesus that those under the Old Law never had; and it binds us only in ways that are reiterated, in one form or another, in the New Law. There are others, but these will suffice to illustrate that a complete transformation of authority has been established. We need to recognize that new authority as it is the manual for how we will be reconciled to God and have a hope of eternal salvation.

Finally, using something from the Old Testament to determine how we please God today is a flawed approach to practice. Citing something from the Old Testament as authoritative for us today had better have a New Testament counterpart for back-up—or it is a misuse of Scripture. The Old Law was strictly for the nation of Israel coming out of Egypt and carrying through the death and resurrection of Jesus Christ and the subsequent establishment of the church. The New Testament is the Law of Christ and our authority for all we do.

Chapter 5

Sins: Old Law and New Law

Those under the Old Law did not have forgiveness of their sins; sacrifices were a "remembrance" of their sins (Hebrews 10:3). The very next verse tells us, "For it is impossible for blood of bulls and goats to take away sins." In v. 11 of the same chapter, we are told the same: these sacrifices "can never take away sins." Yet Exodus 34:67 tells us, "The Lord, the Lord God, compassionate and merciful, slow to anger, and abounding in faithfulness and truth; who keeps faithfulness for thousands, who forgives wrongdoing, violation of His Law, and sin." The questions arise: 1) Are these verses in conflict? 2) Did those in the Old Testament receive forgiveness of sins under the Old Law? 3) If they did not receive forgiveness of sins, what did they receive? 4) How could they be granted eternal life if their sins were never forgiven?

The Word of God does not contain error. If there are appearances of conflict or contradiction, we had better be able to explain those … and we can. There are other chapters and sections of this writing that deal with this issue in greater detail than I will provide here. God's Word is not the "perfect law of liberty" it claims to be (James 1:25) if it indeed contains error and contradiction. The current chapter will deal with the issue of man's sins under the Old Law (where animal sacrifices were employed) and the New Law (where the sacrifice of the Son of God was employed).

A quick review of the terms *forgive* and *forgiveness* in the Old Testament will yield a number of references. Either God did or did not forgive man when he was obedient and sought forgiveness through an animal sacrifice or some other means of expiation. If He indeed truly forgave

Old Testament figures of their sins at the moment they rendered obedience through a sacrifice, then the statements above from the book of Hebrews come into question. In Isaiah. 59:2, we are told that our sins "have separated us from God." I think we can assume this is true regardless of which law man is under. Man needs some way to reconcile himself to God and get back into a more positive relationship with Him. The offering of a blood sacrifice was His way to demonstrate at least a couple of things to man.

No Remission without the Shedding of Blood

First, blood sacrifices were instituted to demonstrate to man how distasteful our sins are to God. I won't go into detail here, but the physical offering of "the best" man had to offer was anything but pleasant. God wanted to illustrate to man—in as graphic a situation as possible—that sin was something repugnant to Him and that He hated it (Prov. 6:16–19). Man was to be cognizant of this fact through these regular reminders that he, himself, had to perform (Lev. 1). This act, which had to be completed with the right condition of the heart, provided man with at least an improved relationship compared to when the sins were still a barrier. I don't know that we can use the term *reconciliation* or *atonement*, as those—at least in their most complete forms—were reserved for consequences of our obedience to the sacrifice of Jesus Christ on the cross. I think we can safely conclude that in whatever state these sacrifices placed man, it was superior to his state just prior to their offering.

It has been said that "pardon" can work; man was still guilty of the sins, but God had at least recognized man's repentance and his effort to get God to acknowledge this. The comparison of a criminal on death row is an apt illustration. The stay of execution received by the governor is framed as a *pardon* for the crimes committed or the time served. The person is still guilty of the crimes that put him there, but at least something has changed in his relationship with the State.

Yet, Hebrews 9:22 tells us this: "And according to the Law, one may almost say, all things are cleansed with blood, and without shedding of blood there is no forgiveness." So, the second question might deal with the timing of that forgiveness: at the point of the blood sacrifice or at some later point? God has tied forgiveness of sins to the shedding of blood, whether that of an animal or that of His Son on the cross. So, according to His Word, when does this forgiveness take place—or better, at what point can man avail himself of that wonderful blessing that places us within Jesus and in a truly reconciled state with God the Father?

The Blood of Christ "Flows in Both Directions"

There are two passages in the book of Zechariah that bear examination. Zechariah, according to commentators, provides us with prophecies of relevance for us on this topic. In Zechariah 11:11–13, we have a preview of the circumstance with Judas. This is a fairly specific prophecy of what occurred when Judas tried to return the payment he had received from the Jewish leaders (Matthew 27:3–10). However, the next three chapters provide us with substance for determining the salvation offered to all mankind—those who were faithful before His sacrifice and those who were faithful after His sacrifice.

> Zech. 12:10—And I will pour out on the house of David and on the inhabitants of Jerusalem the Spirit of grace and of pleading, so that they will look at Me whom they pierced; and they will mourn for Him, like one mourning for an only son, and they will weep bitterly over Him like the bitter weeping over a firstborn.
>
> Zech. 13:1, 7—On that day a fountain will be opened for the house of David and for the inhabitants of Jerusalem, for sin and for defilement. … Strike the Shepherd and the sheep will be scattered. (This is quoted by Jesus in Matthew 26:31)
> Zech. 14:8—And on that day living waters will flow out of

Jerusalem, half of them toward the eastern sea and the other half toward the western sea; it will be in summer as well as in winter.

If nothing else, we can conclude that whatever day is under consideration, it will begin a change in the way the grace of God will be shed on mankind. These blessings are pictured as a fountain from which "living waters" (see John 4:13–14; 6:35; 7:37–38) will flow. The last of the three above talks about this water and how it will flow in two different (or opposite) directions. Could the prophet be pointing us to the time in history when all of these great blessings (this "Spirit of grace") will be available to mankind?

Most of us who have spent time in church pews have heard the phrase, "The blood of Christ flows in both directions." If we were taking notes, no one provided us with that verse from which they were supposedly quoting. It is a fact; it is a given; but where does it tell us that? Zechariah is giving us the prophecy, if we are correct, but can we point to a passage that fulfills that in concept and in words? Hebrews 11:6 tells us that God rewards those who seek Him; effort, in other words, will pay off, and this is regardless under which dispensation one falls. (Romans 2:11–29 even tells us that those without a Law to follow are still guided by a law to which they are accountable.) However, it is a verse in Hebrews 9 that should draw our attention.

In Hebrews 9:11, the writer begins a specific comparison of the blood sacrifices offered under the Old Law and the blood sacrifice offered by Jesus Christ. In Hebrews 9:12–14 we find the following:

> Not through the blood of goats and calves, but through His own blood, He entered the holy place once for all time, having obtained eternal redemption. For if the blood of goats and bulls, and the ashes of a heifer sprinkling those who have been defiled, sanctify for the cleansing of the flesh, how much more will the blood of Christ, who through the eternal Spirit offered Himself without blemish to God, cleanse your conscience from dead works to serve the living God?

It should be noted that these animal sacrifices did "sanctify for the cleansing of the flesh." However, it is next where this comparison between the old and the new really kicks into gear. The blood of Jesus is obviously superior to that of the blood of animals. Yet, it is the following verse that provides us what we are seeking in this chapter.

> For this reason, He is the mediator of a new covenant, so that, since a death has taken place for the redemption of the violations that were committed under the first covenant, those who have been called may receive the promise of the eternal inheritance.

Notice the reference to those sins committed under the "first covenant"; this can only mean the Old Law and even those who lived faithfully prior to the establishment of that covenant through Moses. Those "who have been called"—or who responded to the call to be *faithful*—have now received that same promise of eternal salvation that we have, and this is only through the blood sacrifice of Jesus. If there is a passage that tells us in so many words that "the blood of Christ flows in both directions," this is it. Maybe Zechariah 14:8 is a symbolic prophecy of this bi-directional flow of these blessings from God through Jesus.

The writer of Hebrews reaffirms these conclusions in 11:39–40 when he essentially says our time period—when Jesus came to fulfill all of these promises from God to mankind—is special (10:10, 14—*once for all*). Without its happening, they would never have received what was promised and to which they had been looking for centuries (11:13, 16). When Jesus came and made His sacrifice, His blood now cleansed all of those (past, present, and even future) who could now be "made perfect" (11:49).

Added to the Church

In support of the foregoing argument, I ran across a nuance of a passage I had read probably hundreds of times over the years but had overlooked. In Acts 2, we have the establishment of the church recounted for us. The apostles convict those who are in attendance on the Day of Pentecost of putting to death the Son of God. The people are in agreement and ask what they must do. Peter's reply (Acts 2:38–39) to them was this:

> Repent, and let each of you be baptized in the name of Jesus Christ for the forgiveness of your sins; and you shall receive the gift of the Holy Spirit. For the promise is for you and your children, and for all who are far off, as many as the Lord our God shall call to Himself.

It is a verse that follows that catches the eye and requires our analysis. In Acts 2:41, the text says, "So then, those who had received his word were baptized; and there were added that day about three thousand souls."

Notice that these folks were—according to the account here—the first of their day to become members of this new religion. Paul calls it "The Way" in Acts 9:2 and "This Way" in Acts 22:4. This is the same group identified as Christians in other verses in the New Testament: Acts 11:26; Acts 26:28; 1 Peter 4:16. The question is this: If they were "the first," then to what were they "added"? You cannot be added to something that does not already exist. I cannot become a member of something that does not already exist. Shouldn't the passage read, "and the *total* for that day was about three thousand souls"? So, what is the answer for this question? There are two possibilities.

First, we might assume the apostles are already members of this group. We have no record that they themselves underwent what the Scriptures teach as that process for going from an unsaved to a saved condition. Elsewhere in this writing, I detail what those steps in the process are: 1) hearing the Word/Gospel; 2) believing that message that Jesus died to save us from our sins; 3) repenting of our sins under which we stand convicted; 4) confessing that Jesus was the Son of God; and 5) being baptized for the remission of those sins. In Acts 1:15, we find that there were about 120 people gathered in an upper room in Jerusalem with the apostles as they went through the process of replacing Judas with Matthias. Chapter 2 of Acts throws us immediately into the events of the noise like a strong wind, the tongues of fire, and being filled with the Holy Spirit as the apostles uttered what they were saying in foreign languages. Others heard the sound and came questioning why they heard these "Galileans" (2:7) speaking in their own distinct languages. The recording of the establishment of the church follows.

The point is that the apostles (and possibly the over 120 gathered with them) had possibly already undergone some similar process to that noted in the paragraph above to become the true "first Christians" and that the crowd of 3,000 who responded to the preaching of the apostles were *added* to this group. We simply have nothing from Scripture to go on here. Either God was making an exception for the apostles (although Saul of Tarsus was commanded to be baptized to make his conversion sure), or they had completed their admission to the kingdom of God somewhere along the line. Jesus, following His resurrection, had earlier commissioned them to teach and baptize those who would believe (Matthew 28:18–20; Mark 16:15–16), so maybe their conversion process had already occurred before the events of Acts 2 took place. The 120 were likely in that same situation, or they were part of the 3,000 who responded later that day.

Regardless of the details concerning the apostles, a second possibility is this. Maybe the group to which these on the Day of Pentecost were added were, instead, all of those who have been faithful under previous covenants with God. The argument made in the current chapter is that, while there was no mechanism for obtaining full forgiveness of their sins under their current conditions, they could, however, be saved from eternal consequences upon the arrival of Jesus and His subsequent death on the cross. They, being long dead, did not have the opportunity to undergo what those in Acts 2 did, but their faithfulness to God and what He required of them at that time qualified them to be those who *first* entered into the kingdom, the church, to which the others were added some 50 days following the crucifixion.

There are other passages we could examine (e.g., Luke 10:24; Romans 3:21–26; 6:10; 1 Peter 1:10–12), but what I have considered so far allows us the conclusion with which I began. Those who were faithful under the Law of Moses (and those prior to that Law) are accepted of God and will be rewarded when He rewards those under the New Law. Whatever state Israel was in once they had offered their animal sacrifices in faith, we know that at that point they were in "good stead" with God and would likely have been within the saved and those who will, on the Day of Judgment, hear the following words or something similar: "Well done, good and faithful slave. You were faithful with a few things, I will put you in charge of many things; enter the joy of your master" (Matthew 25:23).

Chapter 6

The Canon and Non-Canonical Works

In the world of religious writings, one can find works that teach anything and everything, many that are contradictory, and the next one teaches doctrine the exact opposite of the one just encountered. Although none of the original manuscripts of either the Old Testament or the New Testament are in existence today, many claim to speak on behalf of God. With all of this verbiage concerning what God wants His people to know, how are we to know what is reliable—indeed from God—and what is not? In other words, how did man, even within early decades of when Jesus walked this earth, figure out what was from God and not just from man? And finally, how did what we have in our hands today known as "The Bible" come into existence as such? Can we *know* we have what God wants us to know about Him and what He wants from us?

Inspiration

Before I can talk about works that qualify as "canon" (inspired of God and intended for inclusion) and those that don't, I need to discuss the notion of *inspiration* and how that issue affects decisions concerning different works. The Bible—both Old and New Testaments—claim to be "inspired by God." This claim means that He is the *ultimate* author behind all that is contained in those collections, regardless of who is assigned as the one or ones who penned them. The conclusion is that what is presented there is what God wants and has directed as content.

The clearest declaration of this claim is found in 2 Tim. 3:16: "All Scripture is inspired by God and beneficial for teaching, for rebuke, for correction, for training in righteousness; that the man of God may be complete, thoroughly equipped for every good work." Paul is writing to this young evangelist and encouraging him to be confident and persistent in what he was teaching those with whom he shared the Gospel. In the verse just above, Paul references "the sacred writings" that provided Timothy with "wisdom that leads to salvation through faith which is in Christ Jesus." Most passages discussing this activity on God's part suggest a "breathing out" of His word *through* men who wrote down what they were *inspired* to write.

There are two thoughts on exactly what this means. It could mean that He gave them the exact words to write, and they functioned much the same as computer programs (even our telephones) today that take the spoken word and simply transfer that onto the page in the written version of what was said. This interpretation has been called *verbal inspiration* or *mechanical inspiration*; these terms capture the description just provided.

A second interpretation is that God provided man the ideas or thoughts He wanted conveyed, and the individual writer then arranged those ideas presenting them in his own, personal way. He used his unique writing style, word usage, sequencing of events and points, etc. to convey to readers what God wanted them to know. This kind of inspiration has been termed *conceptual* or *organic*, suggesting a bit more flexibility on the part of the scribe to use his personal literary style for the presentation. God, however, was still in control of the final product. The purpose here is not to make an argument in either direction, but to show you, the reader, that there are at least two views on how this inspiration takes place. Suffice it to say that those who were selected to speak on behalf of God were given help and were not on their own to determine what would or would not be said.

There are two places in the Gospel of Luke that talk specifically about this help. In Luke 12:11–12, we find these words recorded by Jesus:

"When they bring you before the synagogues and the rulers and the authorities, do not worry about how or what you are to speak in your defense, or what you are to say; for the Holy Spirit will teach you in that very hour what you ought to say." Just before His final preparation for His death, He tells them in Luke 21:13–15,

> It will lead to an opportunity for your testimony. So make up your minds not to prepare beforehand to defend yourselves; for I will give you utterance and wisdom which none of your opponents will be able to resist or refute.

Naturally, both of these encouragements were for those who would be publicly defending Jesus's resurrection and all He had prepared them to share as they preached the Gospel, but the Holy Spirit promised to these men was that same Holy Spirit that would inspire those charged with the responsibility of recording the events surrounding the life of Jesus and present the teachings that composed the *apostles' doctrine* or *teaching* mentioned in Acts 2:42 (as well as the letters of Paul and the other books in the New Testament).

In another book I authored, a table is presented listing a number of passages from both the Old and New Testaments that address this notion of inspiration. So that I don't spend an inordinate amount of time on this preparatory topic before I get to our main topic of *canon*, I will present that table here. The reader can spend more time on the topic of inspiration, if desired.

Passages Addressing Inspiration

OT Passages— Numbers 22:35; 23:12; Deuteronomy 18:18–22; 2 Samuel 23:2–3; Psalm 119:160; Isaiah 59:21; Jeremiah 1:9; Ezekiel 3:4; Zechariah 7:7, 12

NT Passages— Matthew 1:22–23; 5:17–18; 28:16–20; Luke 12:11–12; 16:31; 21:13–15; 24:25–27, 44–49; John 5:39; 14:17, 26; 16:13; 17:17; Acts 1:4–8, 16; 2:4; 3:18; 4:13; 7:38; 26:15–20; 28:25; Romans 3:2;

1 Corinthians 2:1–5, 12–13; 9:16; 11:23; 14:37; 2 Corinthians 12:7; 13:3; Galatians 1:1–2, 8–9, 12; 1 Thessalonians 2:13; 2 Timothy 3:15–16; Hebrews 2:3–4; 1 Peter 1:10–12; 4:11; 2 Peter 1:20–21; 3:2, 15–16

As you can see, there are considerably more for the New Testament than for the Old Testament. The principle is the same for either, but our main concern for this writing is that which is more relevant for us today, that being the New Testament. Just note that the concept is rather well-developed there and is not some vague claim on the part of Bible scholars throughout the centuries.

The New Testament speaks of a completed Old Testament; Jesus spoke of established Scripture (John 5:39; Luke 24:44) and quoted from it regularly. Not found with the New Testament is a similar statement as it was still in what might be called its *collection phase* while these writings were being composed. So, aside from the internal consistency we find in there, we must turn to external evidence for support for the authenticity of the New Testament. That said, Peter does cite the letters of Paul as "Scripture" in the passage—from which the title of this book is taken. In 2 Peter 3:15–16, the author says this:

> Just as also our beloved brother Paul, according to the wisdom given him, wrote to you, as also in all his letters, speaking in them of these things, in which there are some things that are hard to understand, which the untaught and unstable distort (*i.e., twist*), as they do also the rest of the Scriptures, to their own destruction.

The point being made here is that it would have been easy to leave out that key word "rest" in the latter part of the quote. That word, however, establishes that, according to an inspired Peter, Paul's contributions are authentically part of Scripture—God's Word—that which is found in the New Testament as well as the Old Testament.

The Canon

The word *canon* comes from the Greek and refers to "a straight rod" or "a rule" to use as a standard for measuring. Since the last book of the New Testament (Revelation) was being completed at the end of the first century, it wasn't until the 2nd century that all the works were collected and sanctioned as canon. The earliest list was composed around AD 140 but was not considered authoritative; it does, however, suggest that identification and collection had begun by that time. By the end of the 2nd century, most of the 27 books we have in the New Testament today were recognized as authoritative and the rest were accepted by the end of the 4th century.

In reality, these were simply the dates that *man* formally recognized the canon; God had already done this through His inspiration. So, in reality, canonizing a work is the work of God, not man. Man collected them and made them available to the public. In order for this human recognition, a writing had to meet certain criteria.

1. It had to be written by a prophet, an apostle, or by one who had a special relationship with one of these. Mark was close to Peter; Luke was close with Paul. You had to witness the events yourself or hear eyewitness testimony if your writing was to be considered authentic and reliably from God.
2. Consistency across accepted works was also a factor. Any work where an author claimed Holy Spirit guidance had better be consistent with others already established as such. Contradictions were red flags early on.
3. General acceptance by God's people were a third criterion. While human opinion is certainly subject to error, the first two criteria above helped in this regard. God's people knew how important preserving His Word was. Care was taken to thoroughly test works claiming inspiration.

It is this latter group that provide us the best and widest testimony that the New Testament books we have today are the ones that were recognized very soon after the writing of the last one.

Testimony of the Church "Fathers"

Various individuals have written concerning our topic, the canon of the New Testament. There are several from a time period very close to when the originals were written and even possessed connections to some of the original authors. For example, Ignatius of Antioch (AD 110) wrote letters with quotes from Matthew, Luke, Acts, Romans, 1 Corinthians, Ephesians, Colossians, and 1 Thessalonians. Polycarp of Smyrna (AD 110) has in his writings over 100 quotes from 17 different New Testament books from Matthew to 3 John.

Justin Martyr was a pagan reared in a Jewish environment and studied Greek philosophy. He converted to Christianity around AD 130 and began disputing with those who were intent in putting down his and others' faith in the Gospel. In his writings, he quotes from the four Gospels and the Revelation of John. Others include Irenaeus, Clement, Tertullian, Origen, and Eusebius, along with various early listings or collections that include the Muratorian Canon, the Codex Sinaiticus, Athanasius's Festal Epistle, the Peshitta, and the Vulgate—all prior to AD 400. There were even heretics (Marcion and Valentinus) who validated the listing of various works in accepted collections.

Non-Canonical Works

While our concern here is primarily with NT validation, there is a body of work written prior to the first century during the time that fits historically between the Old and New Testament periods. This group of 15 works have been labeled *The Apocrypha*, meaning "hidden," and are accepted by some groups but not by others as Scripture. In other words, the criteria used above (or something similar for these earlier works) cannot be convincingly applied. The Catholic Church accepts these as authentic, but most Protestant groups do not.

Not only do we have these works written during the period between the Testaments, there are others written contemporaneously to the NT period (or shortly thereafter) that some view as having merit if not inspiration. Some of these would include the following: The Apocalypse of Peter, the Acts of Paul, the Shepherd of Hermas, the Epistle of Barnabas, the Gospel of Thomas, and the Didache.

Comparisons of Canonical and Non-Canonical Works

An excellent source on the Internet for additional study on this topic can be found at http://ntcanon.org/index.shtml. There they provide much more information than is included in this writing, and if this topic interests you, I would suggest this site as a starting place. One of the clickable links found there ("Table") lists all of the early church fathers across the top of the page and all the books of the New Testament down the left side. In the cells created, various markings are placed depending on the level of authority assigned for references made in their works. The number of "confidence marks" assigned is truly impressive, but they are even more impressive when compared to the list of 19 noncanonical works listed in the left column below the New Testament books. The contrast is stark. A few have the notation of "accepted; true; scriptural; or quoted from very approvingly" by the 16 historians or historical sources listed across the top. A few others have been awarded "possible approving quotation or allusion," but it goes downhill from there.

The visual evidence and its confirmation upon closer examination shows how much credence is provided by contemporary historians for the canon of the New Testament and how little credence is provided for those that are not. The canon is firmly established by both the inspiration of the texts themselves and by the testimony of those much closer to the penning of the originals than we are hundreds of years later.

Other Ancient Literature

History is also able to provide us with comparisons for other means of validating what we have as authentic when matched up with other secular works. When we examine ancient writings that most of the world accepts as authentic concerning how many manuscripts are available and how far away from the original events, the comparison between these secular works and those we have in the New Testament are impressive. The website *truthfaithandreason.com* provides us with some compilations of data summarized below.

Author	Manuscripts	Years from Event	Earliest Date (AD)
Aristotle	1000	1200	850
Plato	210	1200	900
Pliny the Elder	200	900	1000
Herodotus	109	1350	900
Caesar	251	900	1000
Tacitus	33	750	850
Thucydides	50	1300	900
Sophocles	193	1200	900
Livy	150	300	400
Demosthenes	340	1400	1100
Homer	1757	400	400 BC
NT	25,000	25–150	117

These data are presented to illustrate how much confidence can be placed in the authenticity of the New Testament—at least as historical documents—when compared to others we rather casually accept as authentic with much less evidence. For its canonicity and its proof of inspiration from God, see the arguments provided above.

Chapter 7

Authority in Religion

In Matthew 21:23–27, Jesus is in the temple teaching. His ministry is at an end, and He is soon to undergo the suffering both prior to and on the cross, all resulting in His death. He has for almost three years been teaching and working miracles in and around Jerusalem and throughout Galilee. It is at this point, however, that the chief priests and elders come to him and say, "By what authority are You doing these things, and who gave You this authority?" Jesus could have easily repeated what He had said earlier about saying and doing nothing without it coming directly from His Father (John 5:19; 8:28; 12:49). They likely had heard Him say it or something similar. They were simply trying to get Him to say something so that they could bring charges against Him from the Roman government. Not only does He deny their desire; He also throws them into a public dilemma by asking them a question.

> "I will also ask you one question, which, if you tell Me, I will also tell you by what authority I do these things. The baptism of John was from what source: from heaven or from men?" And they began considering the implications among themselves, saying, "If we say, 'From heaven,' He will say to us, 'Then why did you not believe him?' But if we say, 'From men,' we fear the people; for they all regard John as a prophet." And answering Jesus, they said, "We do not know." He also said to them, "Neither am I telling you by what authority I do these things.

Besides placing these contemptuous Jewish leaders in a bind before the people they were so anxious to impress, the point Jesus was making was that whatever is being promoted as authoritative, religious instruction is from one of two sources: heaven (God) or man. The passage explains the dilemma that Jesus posed to them at that point, so they essentially bailed or copped out by saying, "Hm, we can't tell" or, in their words, "We do not know." Whether they wanted to admit it and whether or not we want to as well, all religious instruction has—at its source—God or man. When these two come into conflict, then there is only one choice the convicted follower of Christ can select.

In Acts 4:19, Peter and John offer the following when instructed by the Jewish rulers to "cease and desist" their teaching about Jesus: "Whether it is right in the sight of God to listen to you rather than to God, make your own judgment; for we cannot stop speaking about what we have seen and heard." Peter and the other apostles say essentially the same thing one chapter later when reminded that they had been instructed to stop teaching about these rulers' part in the death of Jesus. Peter and the apostles answer, "We must obey God rather than men."

These two examples set up for us what has resulted after centuries of man attempting to submit his version of Truth compared to that which is found in Scripture. Every departure from what we find in God's Word—regardless of motivation—results in the same dual outcomes: 1) it is the same Gospel (no problem, but unnecessary) or 2) it is a different Gospel. Paul tells us in Galatians 1:6–10 what happens if it is the latter and concludes that assertion with the following: "For am I now seeking the favor of people, or of God? Or am I striving to please people? If I were still trying to please people, I would not be a bond-servant of Christ."

Let's start this chapter with a bold assertion we learn from these points: *There is only one source of authority for us where Christianity is concerned, and that one source is the Bible.* Granted, there might be other world religions that use other guidebooks or "sacred writings," but those are for religions other than Christianity. God has given us His Word (His expectations for us), and that is found in the Bible. You just completed reading a chapter dedicated to offering convincing evidence that God's

Word (both the New Testament and Old Testament) are inspired, meaning they are "God–breathed"; what is included in those texts is *what* He wanted included and *how* He wanted it recorded.

A second part of that chapter made the claim that what we have in our hands today is, indeed, that which Christians relatively soon after the first century had in their hands. When compared to other ancient writings, the Bible far outstrips any other contemporary writing (and even those more recent) for possessing verifying evidence of this nature. If you want more detail on how we can rely on what we have, I suggest reading Neil Lightfoot's *How We Got the Bible* (MJF Books)—probably the most concise and readable explanation available of the "history" of that book.

I have noted above how the Bible claims inspiration from God and how it provides us with everything we need in the way of knowing God through Biblical history and His dealings with the patriarchs and the nation of Israel. It provides for us a record (actually four versions of that record) of the life of Jesus Christ and His claims to be the Son of God sent to reconcile man to his God by taking on man's sins on the cross. It is indeed the "Greatest Story Ever Told"—but it is more than a Hollywood script. It is the Word of salvation. At the end of John 6, there are those who have begun leaving Jesus after some hard teaching He has offered. He says to the Twelve:

> "You do not want to leave also, do you?" Simon Peter answered Him, "Lord, to whom shall we go? You have the words of eternal life. And we have already believed and have come to know that You are the Holy One of God."

After following Jesus for even a short time, Peter understood that He was indeed the Son of God, and only He possessed this New Law being introduced through Him straight from the Father. The kingdom was to shortly be established, and these Twelve (well, eleven of them and a substitute) would play a major role in the establishment of His church (i.e., His kingdom) both here on this earth and mirrored in heaven.

So, let me reiterate what I have said. There is no other authority in the Christian religion other than God's Word, the Bible. I can even shorten that: There is no ultimate authority other than the Bible. If anyone claims to have revelation different from what is contained there, it is a fraud. If it simply repeats what is there, it is unnecessary. Note what Paul says in his opening statements to the church at Galatia (Galatians 1:9) and alluded to above:

> I am amazed that you are so quickly deserting Him who called you by the grace of Christ, for a different gospel, which is not just another account; but there are some who are disturbing you and want to distort the gospel of Christ. But even if we, or an angel from heaven, should preach to you a gospel contrary to what we have preached to you, he is to be accursed! As we have said before, even now I say again: if anyone is preaching to you a gospel contrary to what you received, he is to be accursed!

The Gospel was delivered in its purest and unblemished form as it flowed from the mouths and writing instruments of those inspired by God to deliver it. Condemnations of those who would add to or take away from the last book of the Bible are clear (Revelation 22:18–19). Add these threats to those of Paul just above, and the condemnations expand to all of the New Testament. God's Word is complete, it is self-contained and sufficient for everything we need from Him, and anything thing else claiming equality is an impostor.

The next chapter will deal with some of these supposed "latter day revelations." And really, this chapter has much more to offer than the assertions noted above. However, it is necessary to make clear to the reader the fact that there is only one source of authority for Christianity, and that is the Bible. The remainder of this chapter will deal with how we understand what we read in God's Word. There is much contained there that is not directly written to us in the first century—or at least we have to do some study to understand how it would have been understood by those receiving it at that time. How do we determine what is and is not to have enduring authority and control over what we believe and do in our lives and in our worship? There are other chapters here dealing with some specifics, but let us examine how we derive *authority* from God's Word. This may sound a little strange, considering what we have just said, but let me explain.

How Instruction Is Received and Followed

Let's say I am your supervisor at work. If I wanted you to do something for me, what would I have to do to convey that to you? Short of mental telepathy (we are not there yet), I would have to tell you in some form or fashion. You cannot read my mind, so I have to use standard tools of communication to transfer from my head what I want to be in your head; these would be telling it to you verbally or writing it down and, in some way, giving it to you. If I was instructing you to do something that was part of your job, this could come in the form of a command or a direct statement. "John, I want you to _____" or "John, go _____." You would undoubtedly comply with that instruction, especially if you wanted to keep your boss happy concerning your work.

On the other hand, she (your new boss is female) might say, "Let me show you what I want you to do next." She would demonstrate, illustrate, or provide you with an example that you could model to make sure you were carrying out what she wanted and how she wanted it done. In some ways, this is even clearer than simply telling someone what you want done. Telling them might leave the *how* to do it up to the doer. Showing someone makes it very clear *what* to do and *how* to do it.

There is one final way your boss or supervisor can give you instruction to do something. What if that person said, "I wish we had a database of all our customers so we could more easily communicate with them." Data management is part of your responsibility for the company, so you and the public relations person immediately get together to take what she has in the way of contact information for clients and merge it with your ability to compile that into a workable and accessible program for the company. The job was accomplished without a command or an example; you simply *inferred* what was wanted and took that implication from your boss as authoritative, as if he or she had used one of the other two means of communicating instruction.

These three methods of providing instruction or communicating an expectation are at work in this life in almost all that we do. It is how we transfer a desire from one person to the next with the expectation that it will be made to happen. It is as natural as our communication from person to person, especially across all supervisor/subordinate relationships that exist. It even extends beyond the workplace with possibly the best example being the parent/child relationship. Run these three through that paradigm and you will get the same result, or you should, if that relationship mirrors that indicated within the Bible (Ephesians 6:1–3; Colossians 3:20).

CENI or TSI

What you have just been exposed to is the foundation for considerable debate among those who seek to establish how we derive authority from the Bible. The CENI acronym stands for Command, Example, and Necessary Inference. The TSI acronym is just another way of saying the former but using verbs instead of nouns: Tell, Show, and Imply. Both indicate how communication—specifically, instruction—takes place both in the world around us and in God's Word. While this approach is both realistic and logical, there are some who say this is a man–made formula for interpreting the Word of God and, as such, carries no more weight or authority than any other means of deriving from that work what is intended by its Author. To be clear, it is simply a "hermeneutic," a fancy word for "a means or method of studying and interpreting the Bible." However, the challenge has been offered rather publicly for someone to illustrate how these three ways are NOT used in Scripture to communicate instruction to its followers. Arguments offered have fallen well short of convincing; these three continue to be used to explain how we determine authority in Scripture.

This issue—using CENI as a means of deriving authority for what we do religiously—has been debated formally and informally over the years. I will spare the reader all of the details and nuances of arguments both for and against it. I will lay it out for you as a reliable means of how we understand what God wants us to do and not do where His expectations are concerned. It makes sense in life; it should make sense in dealing with Scripture as well. Its history, likewise, is as old as John Calvin's attempts to purify Catholicism and is reflected (interestingly in rebuke of the denomination Calvin started) in the Restoration Movement at the turn of the 19th Century.

Commands or Direct Statements

Most of those familiar with the Bible are familiar with commands issued by God for His people. The most famous commandments of God are known as *The Ten Commandments*, about which books have been written and movies have been made. To be sure, it does involve considerably "high drama" in the telling a story of a God Who is providing His Law for His people as they come out of years of slavery in Egypt and now begin to formalize the process of becoming a nation. Those commandments—along with many, many others—are found beginning in Exodus 20—but parts of the Law are contained in four of the five books of the Pentateuch (Exodus, Leviticus, Numbers, Deuteronomy). Depending on how you count (Verses 4 and 5 are the same issue), eight of the ten commandments begin with the words "Thou (You) shall not . . ." implying a tone of strict forbidding of what follows. The other two are command to "do something" instead of "not do something." These are "Remember the sabbath day, to keep it holy" and "Honor your father and your mother." The same words—"You shall"—could have been used. The command is not weakened by their omission; in fact, it may even be *more direct* without them. It should be noted that each of these commandments is repeated in one form or another in the New Testament, except for the one about the sabbath day.

The message preached by John the Baptist in his preparatory mission for the arrival of the Messiah (Jesus) included a command: "Repent, for the kingdom of heaven is at hand" (Matthew 3:2). Jesus begins His ministry with the same words, "From that time Jesus began to preach and say, 'Repent, for the kingdom of heaven is at hand'" (Matthew 4:17).

Another example of a direct command in the NT is found in Acts 2:38 and comes from the mouth of Peter (inspired by the Holy Spirit) following his (and the other apostles') sermon on the Day of Pentecost. That sermon was essentially a review of what Old Testament prophecies said concerning what had just occurred recently, including how they had put the Son of God to death on the cross and that God had resurrected Him from the grave. He ends the "text" of his sermon this way: "Therefore let all the house of Israel know for certain that God has made Him both Lord and Christ—this Jesus whom you crucified."

At this point, those who heard these words understood what they had done and asked Peter and the apostles the following question: "Brothers, what are we to do?" These listeners realized that they had been led by the Jewish rulers into not only a heinous crime—killing an innocent man—but that crime was committed against the Son of God sent to their nation (and broadened to all mankind later) to save them from eternal destruction. The words of Peter are recorded:

> Repent, and let each of you be baptized in the name of Jesus Christ for the forgiveness of your sins; and you will receive the gift of the Holy Spirit. For the promise is for you and your children and for all who are far away, as many as the Lord our God will call to Himself.

The text goes on to say, "And with many other words he solemnly testified and kept on urging them, saying, 'Be saved from this perverse generation!'"

Obviously, his instruction to them could be construed as simple advice, but the fact that the outcomes of not heeding it (as something extremely essential) have consequences: no forgiveness of sins, no benefit of the Holy Spirit, and subsequently, no salvation. To them, it was a command as is demonstrated by the obedience of about 3,000 that day to do exactly as he had told them. They repented and they were baptized, and this was the beginning of the kingdom—i.e., the church—about which Jesus had told them so much. Ensuing chapters talk of the phenomenal growth of the church (including some of the Pharisees, themselves) as believers continued to respond to these instructions/commands from the apostles.

Paul's letters to various churches included numerous instructions to them in the form of commandments or direct statements that they were to follow if they wanted to be found faithful and true to God (see Colossians 3:18–25; 1 Thessalonians 5:11–28 for more concise lists). He even tells them that what he writes to them are from God and are, indeed, commandments: "If anyone thinks that he is a prophet or spiritual, let him recognize that the things which I write to you are the Lord's commandment. But if anyone does not recognize this, he is not recognized" (1 Corinthians 14:37–38). It can safely be assumed that "not recognized" means by God or those who are agents of His on this earth, i.e., the apostles.

Finally, on this point, we know that Jesus told the apostles that they would be given the power to *bind* and *loose* through their Holy Spirit–inspired teaching (Matthew 16:19; 18:18). They were given the power to command listeners to do things that would be coming directly from God. The early church was built by those who responded to their teachings not only on the Day of Pentecost but afterward as well (Acts 2:42). They considered the apostles to be speaking on behalf of God and responded accordingly to what these men directed them to do. Congregations of believers were established in Jerusalem and "in all Judea and Samaria, and even the remotest part of the earth" (Acts 1:8) by following the commands and teachings of these men.

Approved Examples

The second means of transmitting instruction to those awaiting it is by *showing* them through illustration or example. I can communicate my wishes for you to follow by pointing you to others who are doing something that is an acceptable way of doing whatever is being illustrated. We say "an approved example" because there are examples in the New Testament of congregations doing all sorts of things that God, Jesus, the apostles, and the other inspired writers would not hold up as examples to follow and imitate. Probably the best example would be in Revelation 2 and 3 where John records what Jesus has to say about the seven churches in Asia. Only one of the seven receives no indictment or criticism, so we would say that, although they are the Lord's people, they are far from what we might call "examples" to follow. Where congregational behavior or action is recorded—and there is no record of *dis*approval—we can use those as "approved examples" (called "apostolically-approved examples" by some).

Jesus taught by example. His whole life was an example for His immediate followers and the rest of us down through the centuries. In some of His final hours, He prays to God that His apostles "may all be one, as You, the Father, are in Me, and I in You" (John 17:21). God and Jesus were one in many ways; Jesus was praying that the ones appointed to establish the church and carry on the work He began would follow that example and be "one" (unified) also. He also washes their feet in the perfect example of humility and serving others at the beginning of this final session with them.

Paul also says this in 1 Corinthians 11:1. "Be imitators of me, just as I also am of Christ." Paul used Jesus as his perfect example and, as much as he could imitate Jesus, he wanted others to imitate him. Interestingly, this chapter provides us with both a good example and a bad example for a congregation we can emulate. In 1 Peter 2:20–21, we also have these words:

> For what credit is there if, when you sin and are harshly treated, you endure it with patience? But if when you do what is right and suffer for it you patiently endure it, this finds favor with God. For you have been called for this purpose, since Christ also suffered for you, leaving you an example for you to follow in His steps.

In Acts 20:7, we find the words, "On the first day of the week, when we were gathered together to break bread, Paul began talking to them." This action of "breaking bread" is deemed by Biblical authorities to be the observance of the Lord's Supper that He instituted with His remaining eleven apostles in the upper room after Judas had been dismissed. Paul recounts what the Lord has shared with him in the passage above in 1 Corinthians 11:23–26. This was the weekly observance Christians were to practice in order to "remember Jesus" as He had commanded them in its institution. Paul approves of their continuing what was originally charged by Jesus and apparently through apostolic teaching, but he roundly condemns them for corrupting its original intent and purpose for something other than the solemn feast we know it should be.

Without entering into an involved discussion about how often we are to observe the Lord's Supper, the example suggests (Acts 20:7) that this was *the purpose* for their assembling on the first day of the week. Luke points out that it was the "first day of the week" when he could have said, "When we came together to break bread." We find in 1 Corinthians 16:2, the church at Corinth was still congregating on the first day of the week. This is example enough for us to use that day for our Lord's Day to gather to worship Him and to remember Him through the observance of that feast He instituted with His apostles prior to His death on the cross. Oh, it also happens to be the day of the week when He rose from the grave, so that might indicate also why that particular day was selected.

In one of the passages just noted, we have another example followed by most congregations today, that of taking the time together on the first day of the week to take up a collection—a free-will offering—to help carry out the work of that congregation for its obligations to preach the word, edify or build up the group, and to be able to take care of the benevolent obligations they as a congregation had. In 1 Corinthians 16:1–2, you have Paul instructing that church concerning this group effort to support the work of the Lord. Some say this was a special collection and that we are stretching it when we use this as an example for us to do this regularly. The work of the local congregation has to be carried out; they meet regularly on the first day of the week for worship; this is an appropriate time to collect whatever funds are necessary for that work; it makes sense to assume that this was an ongoing responsibility and not just a one-time event just for Paul's use elsewhere in his work. In 2 Cor. 9:7 we have this as well: "Let each one do just as he has purposed in his heart; not grudgingly or under compulsion; for God loves a cheerful giver."

Necessary Inference (Logical Conclusion)

Simply stated, I *imply*, and you *infer*; there is a giver/sender and a receiver/interpreter. I can make a statement such that I don't come right out and tell you to do something, but you know by how I say it that I expect some action on your part. As a child, if your mother wanted you to clean up your room, she might say, "This room is a mess!" You didn't need a degree in logic to figure out that she was implying that you should get busy on that effort. She implied, and you inferred or came to the conclusion as to what your course of action was to be. Not all inferences are "necessary," however. Research results sometimes seem conclusive, but only so if all other possibilities (sometimes referred to as *confounding variables*) are able to be ruled out. Clues for solving a crime are the same way. A conclusion is only *necessary* if it is the *only one* that can result from a presentation of information.

Many use baptism as an example. There are several ways that people are "baptized" in religious gatherings today. Some are immersed in a pool of water; some are doused with a much smaller portion (a "pouring"); and some are "sprinkled" lightly with an even smaller amount of water. The questions arise, "Why do we baptize?" "Are we told in the New Testament what really constitutes a legitimate baptism?" "Does it make a difference?" Let's look at a few implications found in Scripture and see if there exists a *necessary inference* from these pieces of information.

First, as noted above, when the Jews who had gathered on the Day of Pentecost listened to what the apostles had to offer concerning who

Jesus was and what they had done to him, they are convicted ("pierced to the heart" or "smitten in conscience") and know their situation is serious. They ask, "Brethren, what shall we do?" The first things to come out of Peter's mouth is "Repent and let each of you be baptized." He goes on to say more, but the point being made here is that these inspired apostles are making a decided connection of the sinful state of these asking the question and how they can remove themselves from that dangerous condition: repent … and be baptized. Baptism is a command for those whose sins are not forgiven (theirs were not at that point even though they obviously regretted their actions): "for the forgiveness of your sins" the verse goes on to explain the reason, or at least, the outcome of their response to this instruction. There is more, but this will suffice; baptism is a command, and around 3000 responded on that day.

Let's look at two passages that begin our examination of implications. First, John 3:23 says, "Now John also was baptizing in Aenon, near Salim, because there was an abundance of water there; and people were coming and being baptized." The reason for baptizing *there*—and we do not have to infer anything here—is "because" there was much water there. Apparently, "much water" is either needed or at least desired if one is to engage in the practice of baptizing. Next, when John the Baptist baptized Jesus, Matthew 3:16 says, "After He was baptized, Jesus came up immediately from the water." This could mean up from underneath the water or it could mean up out of the water onto the shore (some versions say "went up out of the water"). In either case, He was indeed in the water. You cannot come out of that which you are not already in.

Next, Philip is "teaching Jesus" to the Ethiopian eunuch (Acts 8:35), and the eunuch stops the chariot at one point and says, "Look! Water! What prevents me from being baptized?" [An inference could be made from what we have recorded here that "teaching Jesus" at least includes some discussion on baptism. This is a side issue and not the purpose of our discussion at this point, however.] Philip responds that if he believes, he can be baptized; the eunuch asserts, "I believe that Jesus Christ is the Son of God." The text says in 8:38 the following: "Then both Philip and the eunuch went down into the water and Philip baptized him." If pouring or sprinkling were all that were necessary for baptism, there would be no need for both of them to enter the water. Like the situation with Jesus above, candidates for baptism were in the water.

The point here is that we are examining inferences that we should draw from the text, especially those that are necessary. In both situations above, those baptized were in the water with the ones doing the baptizing. One might argue, well, they still could have had water poured on them or sprinkled: not conclusive or "necessary" at this point. However, if we turn to the letter to the church at Rome, Paul talks about baptism being a "burial" like that undergone by Jesus when He died on the cross, was buried, and then rose to a "new life." Note the wording there:

> How shall we who died to sin still live in it? Or do you not know that all of us who have been baptized into Christ Jesus have been baptized into His death? Therefore we have been buried with Him through baptism into death, so that, just as Christ was raised from the dead through the glory of the Father, so we too may walk in newness of life. For if we have become united with Him in the likeness of His death, certainly we shall also be in the likeness of His resurrection, knowing this, that our old self was crucified with Him, in order that our body of sin might be done away with, so that we would no longer be slaves to sin; for the one who has died is freed from sin (Romans 6:2–7).

I included a larger section of Scripture here to lay out the entire connection between the death, burial, and resurrection of Jesus and its similarity to our death, burial, and resurrection in baptism. Paul even says that we are "baptized into His death." It is following our own death/burial/resurrection that we now can begin a "new life"; we have been freed from our sins, like Peter indicated in Acts 2:38. When Saul received instructions from Ananias, notice the sequencing: "Arise, be baptized, and wash away your sins" (Acts 22:16). Like Jesus was raised from the dead to walk with new life on the earth again, our baptism allows us to do the same. We did not die physically, but we died spiritually *to our sins* and now have a fresh start on continuing that effort to remain as unstained as possible (Romans 6:8–23).

The case for baptism being a burial, an immersion underneath the water, is getting stronger. Some would say that the passage in Romans makes this inference *necessary* and maybe even takes it out of the realm of inferences altogether. One final point can be made, however, that makes our conclusion sure. The Greek word for baptism is *baptisma*. Vine's tells us "consisting of the processes of immersion, submersion, and emergence." It comes from *bapto*, which means "to dip." The verb form, *baptizo*, "was used among the Greeks to signify the dyeing of a garment, or the drawing of water by dipping a vessel into another." The very word itself means to *dip* or *plunge*. The inference is complete (and "necessary") when considering all of these indicators. While the Scriptures never come right out and tell us that baptism is an immersion, they do all but that.

This was a long example, but it is one that is important. Baptism, as a necessary component of salvation, has been a hotly contested issue in the religious world. But since I am on the topic, let me quickly offer another example that illustrates another necessary inference. Infant baptism has been a practice for centuries, but many feel that it is an "*un*necessary inference" drawn by those who place emphasis on the concept of "original sin" (something I won't take time for here but do elsewhere) and on the phrase "household" in some passages. In the New Testament, acceptable candidates for baptism are those who *believe* that Jesus is the Son of God (Mark 16:15–16), *repent* of their sins (Acts 2:38), and *confess* that Jesus is the Son of God (Acts 8:38). These are both intellectual and physical actions that only those who have the capacity to comply can do. Infants can do none of these. So, baptizing infants is something "added" by man. Some point to Acts 16:33 for support by saying the Philippian jailer's "household" was baptized saying surely there were children and infants included. This, obviously is an inference *not* warranted and would conflict with the other requirements necessary for baptism.

So, God has given us His Word so that we can know how to live our lives to please Him. We are not free to add to it or take away from it, especially in those areas where we are talking about things that impact our eternal salvation. God's ways are God's ways; they are not man's ways (Isaiah 55:8–9; 1 Corinthians 2:11). No matter how much man thinks he can improve, enhance, or embellish upon that which has been delivered to us, he can only get himself in trouble in these efforts. Authority for what we do in our religious service to God, and in how we live our lives among those around us, comes from Scripture. Specifics are delivered to us through commands or direct statements we can read and understand, approved apostolic examples we can see and apply, and necessary inferences or conclusions drawn from an examination of Scripture.

When Peter proclaimed that God, through His divine power, "has granted to us everything pertaining to life and godliness, through the true knowledge of Him who called us by His own glory and excellence" (2 Peter 1:3), he concludes that thought by saying this information allows us to be "partakers of the divine nature" and to escape the corruption of the world. Going beyond what God's Word authorizes is a dangerous practice that very likely has eternal consequences.

"It Doesn't Say Not To"

Anytime there is a discussion on authority within the Bible, especially concerning what we can and cannot do, someone will likely come up with the response, "Well, it doesn't say not to, so it must be okay to do it." They take the Ten Commandments approach that God was very specific saying that there were things Israel could and could not do. Anything left unstated must have been okay. Indeed, most of Israel's problems arose from direct violation of things God had forbidden (e.g., having other gods before Him, intermarrying with the nations around them, etc.). However, no law on this earth could cover every imaginable action that might be considered a sin. So, God added what Jesus referred to as the *Greatest Commandment* and the *Second Greatest Commandment*: "You shall love the Lord your God with all your heart, and with all your soul, and with all your mind, and with all your strength" and "You shall love your neighbor as yourself."

God has laid down for us His law and expectations for us. When we start looking beyond what is recorded to push whatever envelope is seeking to be opened, we fail to keep that Greatest Commandment. If we love Him more than we love ourselves, we will—at least theoretically—be willing to forego things not mentioned in Scripture that we might be desiring to do. Likewise, if we love others more than we love ourselves, our actions will likely be in keeping with what He wants of His children and according to the pattern left to us by His Son.

There are those that speak about the "authority of the *silence of the Scriptures*." Honoring what God has authorized (specifically) and what He has not authorized (and can't be found in Scripture) is a part of loving Him with all of our heart, soul, mind, and strength. That is pretty much everything we have to give … and that is what He wants. If He hasn't told us to do something, shown us what that might be, or strongly implied something we are to do, then maybe (no, *definitely*) we shouldn't be doing it.

Chapter 8

Latter Day Revelations

Elsewhere in this writing, both above and below, at least one common theme has emerged: God's Word is self-contained and all-sufficient for everything we need. See those sections for more complete evidence of this assertion, but the specific argument to be made at this point is that anything else man can generate had better mirror that which we have been given. Paul makes this declaration at the beginning of his letter to the Galatians: "I am amazed that you are so quickly deserting Him who called you by the grace of Jesus Christ, for a different gospel" (1:6). He goes on to essentially say that no, it is not *another* gospel (as there is really only one) but that they are distorting the one he and others had delivered to them. He then says the following:

> But even if we, or an angel from heaven, should preach to you a gospel contrary to what we have preached to you, he is to be accursed! As we have said before, even now I say again: if anyone is preaching to you a gospel contrary to what you received, he is to be accursed! (Galatians 1:8–9).

Those are not my exclamation points; those are Paul's. He obviously is attempting to get their attention and warn them that by leaving the original message delivered to them and following something else, they who preach it are accursed and that their souls are in jeopardy. Paul continues with this chastisement in Verses 11 and 12, telling them exactly from where this Gospel originates and how he miraculously received it:

> For I would have you know, brothers and sisters, that the gospel which was preached by me is not of human invention. For I

> neither received it from man, nor was I taught it, but I received it through a revelation of Jesus Christ.

He then goes on to explain how that happened and how he became an apostle of Jesus Christ and specifically set apart (Galatians 1:15) to preach to the Gentiles. He discusses his encounter with the Peter and James in Jerusalem and then was off to Syria and Cilicia.

In 2 Corinthians 11:2–4, Paul says the following about being led away from the Gospel he preached to them:

> I am jealous for you with a godly jealousy; for I betrothed you to one husband, to present you as a pure virgin to Christ. But I am afraid that, as the serpent deceived Eve by his trickery, your minds will be led astray from sincere and pure devotion to Christ. For if one comes and preaches another Jesus whom we have not preached, or you receive a different spirit which you have not received, or a different gospel which you have not accepted, this you tolerate very well!

He goes on to say that those who would do this to you are "false apostles, deceitful workers, disguising themselves as apostles of Christ" (11:13) and places them in the same category of Satan who disguises himself as an angel of light but whose end, like Satan's, "will be according to their deeds." In other words, condemnation and destruction awaits them.

The point we should gather from what Paul says in these passages is that the Gospel of Jesus Christ is not from man; it is from God. It is not to be altered, distorted, or messed with in any way or it ceases to be that which we know as "the Gospel." It becomes something else that is not reliable as authorized by God or content from God. Those who add to it or delete from it—change it in any way—are reaping destruction not only upon themselves; they are leading others who follow them down that same path. This principle is established under the Old Law and continued in the New Law.

In Deuteronomy 4:2, it says, "You shall not add to the word which I am commanding you, nor take away from it, so that you may keep the commandments of the Lord our God which I am commanding you." He then provides them with an example of those who did not do this. In Jeremiah 23:25–40, the prophet condemns those who come in God's name and claim to speak His Word but are not of God. He points out that when we don't come with the authority of God, "Every person's own word will become the pronouncement (of the Lord)" and they will have "perverted the words of the living God" (23:36).

In the book of Revelation, we have in the final verses a warning that speaks to this error of adding to or taking away from that which has been revealed. Yes, it is referring here specifically to that particular writing, but we have shown above that the practice at any time and in any place can be more than just a little dangerous:

> I testify to everyone who hears the words of the prophecy of this book: if anyone adds to them, God will add to him the plagues that are written in this book; and if anyone takes away from the words of the book of this prophecy, God will take away his part from the tree of life and from the holy city, which are written in this book (Revelation 22:18–19).

Given these dire warnings, why would anyone even consider embellishing what has been delivered to us through the prophets of old, the writings of inspired Old Testament mouthpieces for God, and the inspired authors of works in the New Testament? We can surely write *about* what is contained in God's Word—as I am doing in this document. However, commentary and interpretation is a far cry from "adding to" or "taking away" from that which is under discussion. There are, however, those who have claimed to have what has been termed "latter–day revelation" and have taken great numbers of people with them in this error. It is "latter-day" revelation because it is not part of the "original-day revelation" we have in the New Testament. *Latter* simply means or indicates *later* or *situated toward the end of something as opposed to the beginning of something.*

Examples of Latter Day Prophets/Revelation

As noted above, any revelation after the first century claiming to be from God or a representative from God or even hinting anything about God—if not the same revelation found in Scripture—is not from God. It has no credibility or authority behind it if not the original. As Paul said, even if they (he, the apostles, or another inspired person) or even an *angel* preach anything other than what has been preached, that person is accursed. Vine's notes that Paul is saying to preach anything else would be to nullify the death of Christ on the cross. Claiming personal revelation from God is serious business; what you claim was revealed to you had better line up very closely to what has been revealed in Scripture. If it does, then it is not "new revelation"—which is a redundant phrase in itself.

If we didn't have these passages above warning us severely against adding to or taking away from what has already been delivered, we have another argument against teaching that rubs up against established revelation. In 1 Corinthians 14, Paul is laying out for the Corinthian church (as well as all first century churches) how spiritual gifts are to work and what their attitudes toward them should be (carried over from chapter 12). Although he talks about tongues, the focus is on prophecy, and he says, "For you can all prophesy one by one, so that all may learn and all may be exhorted; and the spirits of the prophets are subject to the prophets" (14:31–32).

He is telling them to show respect, take turns, and everyone is edified. With all of these gifts going on "at the same time," some sort of order had to be established. He notes that, whether it be speaking in tongues (different languages) or prophecies or whatever the gift might be, the one delivering it has enough control over that gift to hold it in until someone else is finished. In 14:33, Paul says this: "For God is not a God of confusion, but of peace, as in all the churches of the saints." Other versions say that He is not the *author* or *source* of confusion. This statement particularly applies within that particular context due to the number of revelations being delivered and in the variety of ways that were being used by the Spirit. However, the fact that God is not the source of confusion is a principle laid down very early in Scripture and is consistent throughout. Jehovah is a God of clarity; He has to be because man will take every opportunity to twist His words to suit himself. God cannot aid man in this misbehavior by being vague and unclear. His Word is Truth, and that Word is definitive and absolute.

The point being made by the foregoing is that if latter day revelation contradicts the Word of God in any way, or confuses the original in any way, or forces the hearer to make a choice between the original and what is now being revealed … then *confusion* will reign. Truth on any subject cannot have two versions. If the one has been established, the second one must be false. God has not authored it; He does not author confusion.

Any effort to discuss in detail the problems, contradictions, and errors of those who have claimed some sort of revelation from God—other than that which is contained within Scripture—would take more room that I have here. So, I will not be going into any detail concerning their supposed revelations as far as doctrine is concerned. I will, however, mention a few individuals, their claims for revelation, and at least a few glaring errors in their teachings.

Papal Infallibility—Exodus Cathedra

The Catholic Church claims that Peter was the church's first pope and was declared as such in Matthew 16:19. As discussed elsewhere in this writing, Peter was not the foundation on which the church was going to be built; his assertion that "You are the Christ, the Son of the living God" was that foundation. See that argument made later in this document for details. However, the belief of the Catholic Church was that whatever Peter "bound on earth would be bound in heaven" and that power would be passed on from pope to pope down through the ages. On the other hand, the belief in this infallibility, of *ex cathedra* (speaking "from the chair"), was debated during the 1500s but apparently was not official Catholic Church doctrine until Pope Pius IX in 1870.

The Catholic Church claims that popes have received their authority (and infallibility) from the apostles themselves. Apostles, however, had to be eyewitnesses of the risen Christ; they performed miracles to confirm their teachings; they could only impart miraculous powers to others, not the ability to pass that power on to others; and they taught by direct guidance of the Holy Spirit. No further teachings are necessary; the Bible is complete and provides us all we need for our belief in God and our efforts toward securing our salvation.

Again, space will not allow for more detail concerning teachings of the Catholic Church that are not found in Scripture (e.g., infant baptism [see above]; transubstantiation; perpetual virginity of Mary; praying to saints; etc.). Enhancements, embellishments, decrees, etc. from men— no matter how revered by mankind—do not make them authoritative where the Scriptures are concerned.

Muhammed—Islam

The Quran (also spelled Qur'an and Koran) contains the teachings of Muhammed, a 6th Century Arab religious, social, and political leader. With his writings, he founded the religion of Islam. At age 40, while praying in a mountain cave, he reported having been visited by the angel Gabriel and receiving his first revelation. Adherents of Islam claim that these revelations are the verbatim "Word of God" and that these revelations form the foundation and teaching of the religion.

First and foremost, Islam does not believe in the Jesus of the Bible and adamantly asserts that He was not the Son of God, but only one of many prophets of God. In doing so, they deny that He was God incarnate. They deny that He was crucified and died on the cross. They teach that Muhammed was superior to Jesus because he brought the "final revelation" of God to man. They also deny the existence of the Holy Spirit.

This would be enough, but the beliefs they have held and especially the practices and atrocities some Muslims have committed over the centuries, and continue to commit, suggest they are operating from a "playbook" totally foreign to those beliefs and practices found in the Bible. From contempt of the infidel (any nonMuslim), to the treatment of women, to the belief in world dominance … the list is fairly long on supposed revelations received by Muhammed in the cave and taught worldwide. There is much that contradicts God's Word, and the Allah of the Muslim faith is anything but a different name for the God of Scripture.

Hinduism—Vedas

Although Hinduism really does not fit the title of this book or section, it is included here as an option for people as they consider different religions. It really has no roots in the Bible, so it doesn't really qualify as a religion that fails to interpret Scripture correctly. It does, however, claim inspiration from a source other than mankind, so it is included here. Also, we could question the "latter-day revelation" feature as well because the revelation that most adherents to Hinduism follow are from centuries ago and not just since the first century.

The Vedas comprise the religious texts for Hinduism originating in India before the time of Christ. Hindus consider the Vedas (at least some of them) to be *apauruseya* which means, "not of a man; superhuman." These apparently are revelations of religious sounds and words that were heard by ancient wisemen following intense meditation sessions. These have been passed down from generation to generation through an oral tradition that uses mantras and chants for better memorization of the text.

Brahma, one of the gods of Hinduism, is credited with some of the revelations. Vayasa was a sage who is credited with eventually writing down a number of these Vedas and is considered to be one of seven immortals who are still alive. There is nothing in Hinduism that closely resembles anything found in the New Testament.

Mormonism—Joseph Smith

Joseph Smith claimed to have experienced a series of visions in the early 1800s where God, Jesus, Moses, and an angel directed him to a book of "golden plates." He later published these, called the "Book of Mormon," and established the Mormon religion or the Church of Jesus Christ of Latter-Day Saints. Smith and his followers moved from place to place in the Midwest, but opposition to Mormon teachings and their growing power base placed him under arrest and on trial. During an uprising, he was killed, further establishing him as a martyr. Adherents view him comparable as a prophet to Moses and Elijah. He even referred to himself as "Joseph the Prophet" at times.

There are some Christian themes within the works used by the religion as holy texts, but as you might expect, they go way above and beyond what we have recorded for us in Scripture. Smith claimed that his inspiration resembled having "pure Intelligence" flowing into him. He later published the *Book of Commandments* that eventually became part of the LDS Church's *Doctrine and Covenants*. So much of what is contained in the writings of Joseph Smith is so totally contradictory to what we find in Scripture, to begin listing them would fruitless. They are readily available; check them out yourself. It is hard to believe that anyone could hold both a view of the Bible and a view of Smith's "revelations" with equal positive regard.

Leaders in the Charismatic Movement

"God spoke to me last night." "God has laid it on my heart to tell you something today." "I felt the Spirit of God moving and telling me what to do."

These expressions are commonly used by those who believe that God still speaks to us today. Whether or not they are introducing "revelation" contradicting what we find in Scripture, they are saying that God is still revealing Himself to man today essentially the same way He did in Scripture. As noted elsewhere in this writing, supernatural intervention in the Bible had a distinct purpose and an expiration date based on that purpose. God does not talk to us today out loud, in visions, in our sleep, or any other way (other than through His Word). He *has* spoken, and there is no further need for revelation. What He has provided us, in the way of His revealed word, affords us "everything that pertains to life and godliness" (2 Peter 1:3) so that we can know we are "thoroughly equipped" for "teaching, reproof, correction, training in righteousness … and every good work" (2 Timothy 3:16–17).

It is difficult to distinguish Pentecostalism from the Charismatic Movement; both claim the active work of the Holy Spirit, operating through spiritual gifts and modern–day miracles not only in worship services but in everyday life. Some trace these movements back to 1906, but even as late as 1950, anyone claiming these experiences in mainstream Protestant and Catholic churches would have had to leave that group. Things have changed since then. Individuals like William Branham, Oral Roberts, and A. A. Allen contributed to a revivalist movement that embraced ecstatic experiences with speaking in tongues as characteristic of Holy Spirit possession. One of the more bizarre claims was by Oral Roberts who said that God told him that He would call him to heaven (take his life) if enough money was not donated for some building project on his university's campus.

In 2011, the Pew Research Center conducted a poll among a group of religious leaders in the Lausanne Movement of what was called the "global church." Here are some results found at https://www.pewforum.org/2011/06/22/global-survey-beliefs/:

> High numbers of the leaders surveyed also report having experienced or witnessed practices that are often associated with renewalist groups. For example, roughly half or more of the

evangelical leaders report having spoken or prayed in tongues (47%), experienced or witnessed the devil or evil spirits being driven out of a person (57%), received a direct revelation from God (61%) or personally witnessed or experienced a faith healing (76%). A smaller but still significant number (40%) have given or interpreted prophecy.

These high numbers suggest that the charismatic movement, now infused into at least some branches of most organized religions claiming Christianity, is thoroughly entrenched and will be here for a while. Again, if anything that is revealed is *not what has already been revealed*, it is condemned by the apostle Paul as contradictory, or it is superfluous on face value and has no relevance for guiding us morally or spiritually.

Cults

Other groups are often labeled as "cults" and defined as "a religious or semi–religious sect whose members are controlled almost entirely by a single individual or by an organization" (Christian Research Institute). Cults are characterized by extremely strict rules of devotion to the leader or the organization, considerable sacrifice of self and personal possessions on behalf of the group, and exclusion from the group or other punishments for going against the group or for even attempting to leave.

Some examples of groups that have been assigned this designation are these: Christian Scientists (Scientology); the Ku Klux Klan; the Children of God (Family International); Raelism (UFOs); Bavarian Illuminati; Aum Shinrikyo; The People's Temple (Jim Jones); Heaven's Gate; The Church of Euthanasia; Branch Davidians (David Koresh); and Order of the Solar Temple (source: storypick.com). I admit that I had never heard of some of these, but reading about them is amusing, if you are interested. A much larger list is provided at https://www.watchman.org/ index–of–cults–and–religions, but their interpretation of "cult" and "religion" is far more inclusive than what most would view as such.

For example, Stephen Covey and his *7 Habits of Highly Effective People* is one of the first entries; including him and this work would, indeed, be a stretch.

There are doubtless others that could be included within this section. These are offered as a sample of those who claim to be guided by something other than the Word of God—or the Word of God *and* additional revelation. God's revealed Word is and should be our only guide for Truth in all things religious. This, however, would include commentaries or other writings designed to aid in highlighting some piece or aspect of Scripture, as long as these works use the Bible in ways that complement and support what is found within God's Word and do not claim inspiration themselves. Anything else—i.e., new revelation—is either contradictory and accursed or it is entirely unrelated and meaningless as far as following God is concerned.

Chapter 9

Obeying the Gospel

In this chapter, I will attempt to answer the question asked by those on the Day of Pentecost in Acts 2, after Peter and the other apostles had told them they had indeed crucified the Son of God, the One promised as Messiah in the Old Testament and the One sent from heaven to save man from his sins. They realized what they had done and the condition of their souls at that point, so they asked, "Brethren, what shall we do?" The Philippian jailer (Acts 16:30) was even more specific when he asked Paul and Silas, "Sirs, what must I do to be saved?" This question has been asked by countless individuals over the ages, those who have been taught concerning the condition of their souls related to eternal life. The answer is simple. However, people will respond in many different ways, depending on their *take* on what the Scriptures teach. I will not make assumptions about motive; I will just note that the responses vary and, as a result, contradict each other.

Just Believe

If you take the Philippian jailer's question and examine the immediate response of Paul and Silas, you would conclude simply what they said: "Believe in the Lord Jesus and you will be saved." Other passages would back this up. In John 3:14–16, Jesus Himself says,

> And just as Moses lifted up the serpent in the wilderness, so must the Son of Man be lifted up, so that everyone who believes will have eternal life in Him. For God so loved the world, that He gave His only Son, so that everyone who believes in Him will not perish, but have eternal life.

In Hebrews 11:6, the writer tells us that it is impossible to please God without faith in Jesus Christ as the Son of God. Other passages would support this fundamental tenet required by God to be found acceptable and to ultimately obtain salvation.

Some will say, "Just believe in Jesus." Others will add that you must "Say the sinner's prayer"—not found in the Bible, by the way. Some will add other elements either found in Scripture or added by man. Some even say, "That issue was addressed when I was baptized as an infant." The components of what it takes to have one's sins forgiven are indeed found in the New Testament. As I have said, it would be unjust of God to expect us to obey Him and then be vague about His requirements. Unfortunately, and apparently, He wanted us to read more than just one or two verses or consider just one or two passages. The answer to the question of "What must I do to be saved" is provided in a list of steps or actions on our part that are found by compiling *all* of what we know about initial obedience in being accepted as a child of God. Sometimes these are direct commands (Acts 2:38) or examples (Acts 16:33), both established in our argument on how we obtain authority from Scripture in a chapter above.

Steps for Salvation

Hearing

The first step in this process is actually a *given,* or automatically understood. In order for any new information to have an effect on us, we have to have some sort of interaction with it. We have to hear it (as they did on the Day of Pentecost) or read it. These are the two most basic and most prevalent. In Romans 10:14, Paul tells his readers that they must call upon the name of the Lord and then asks a series of questions: "How then are they to call on Him in whom they have not believed? How are they to believe in Him whom they have not heard? And how are they to hear without a preacher?" In v. 17, he says, "So faith comes from hearing, and hearing by the word of Christ" (or "hearing the word of Christ").

We conclude that we cannot have faith in that which we do not know or have not heard. Hearing God's word is the first component in our journey toward salvation.

Believing

The second component is to *believe* that which we have heard or *that Jesus Christ is the Son of God*. Many passages mention belief as the first and maybe most important component in one's conversion. This is the case, if for no other reason, that it logically precedes anything else that would follow it. If I do not believe in this fundamental concept, then why would I attempt to go any further? Belief, or faith, is fundamental, foundational, and absolutely necessary to be a child of God. There are passages that would tell us this: Mark 1:15; John 3:16–18; 14:1; Acts 16:31; Hebrews 11:6. If you took any of these passages or all of them together and used that as your standard, then yes, you would have to conclude that belief is all that is necessary. However, this would be true for any of the next three, as well, that are mentioned elsewhere in the New Testament.

Repenting

In our conversion, we must come face to face with our sins. We must acknowledge that our sins have put us at odds with God and have separated us from Him—a principle established in Isaiah 59:2 but is the essence of our *enmity* with God today as well. In order to be reconciled with Him, we must possess a godly sorrow that leads us to repent of these sins (2 Corinthians 7:10—and this leads to salvation). *Repentance* is a change of heart as well as a change of action. We cannot go on willfully sinning if we are truly sorry for those sins and realize that they separate us from God. Yes, we all sin; that is understood. But in our initial repentance, there is the understanding that we will make the concerted attempt to avoid these past sins in the future. In the passage noted above in Acts 2:38, the people are told to repent if they want to have a chance at having their sins removed.

At this point, we have three of the components necessary for us to obtain salvation: *hearing* what God's Word says about Jesus, *believing* it or *having faith* that Jesus is the Son of God, and having it operate on our conscience enough to produce in us *repentance*. We could have stopped at the first one, but we would not be saved. We could have done the same after the second one, but the outcome would be the same. We can now stop at this third one; surely that is enough to complete the requirements. No, we cannot stop after any of these nor leave any of these out of the process. Yes, there is more.

Confessing

Jesus tells His listeners in Matthew 10:28 to not fear those who might retaliate against them for believing in Him. He then offers this condition for their safety beginning in v. 32: "Therefore, everyone who confesses Me before people, I will also confess him before My Father who is in heaven. But whoever denies Me before people, I will also deny him before My Father who is in heaven." He goes on with other points about how choosing Him over others is a condition for safety where their souls are concerned. Confessing that He is the Son of God is extremely important. In Acts 8, we have Philip and the Ethiopian eunuch talking about Jesus, with Philip telling him that he must believe with all of his heart, to which the eunuch replies, "I believe that Jesus Christ is the Son of God." This is the confession Jesus wants us to make at our conversion but also as we live our lives for Him from day to day. This verbal assertion of belief is important, but no more important than illustrating it as we conduct our affairs and interact with those around us. So, *confession* is a fourth requirement in the mix and is just as important as the other three. It cannot stand alone, nor can it be omitted, nor is it sufficient to end the process here.

Being Baptized

The last requirement in these steps toward salvation is the one that seems to give most people the greatest difficulty. It is, however, just as essential as the others. It does not stand alone, nor can it be omitted. In fact, all of the other four (hearing, believing, repenting, and confessing) are simply preliminary to *baptism*, the event which actually places us *into Christ* (Galatians 3:27). It is that which indeed saves us for two reasons: it is where our sins are remitted or forgiven and, logically, it is the final step in this process where all steps are necessarily included. The verse in Galatians just above tells them that if they have been baptized into Christ, they have "clothed themselves with Christ." Two verses later, they are told that they belong to Christ and are heirs to the promise.

In the passage in Acts 2 noted above, we only looked at part of what Peter and the others told the people to do to save themselves from sure destruction. It says in 2:38, "Repent and let each of you *be baptized* [my emphasis] in the name of Jesus Christ for the forgiveness of your sins." There are two conditions noted here, and a rhetorical question might be, "Can either be left out of the equation?" The obvious answer is "No." Both are necessary to obtain the outcome.

In Romans 6:3–11 (noted earlier), we have an explanation as to why baptism is so important and why it is at that point that our sins are forgiven. The comparison is made of our baptism to the death, burial, and resurrection of Jesus. We are told, "You have been baptized into His death … and as Christ was raised from the dead through the glory of the Father, so we too might (be raised to) walk in newness of life." Verse 6 tells us that "our old self was crucified with Him, in order that our body of sin might be done away with, so that we would no longer be slaves to sin; for the one who has died is freed from sin." It is indeed a symbolic "burial" (like that of Jesus), but it is more than that; some say that is all it is. It is then and only then that we can rise to a) walk in newness of life and b) be freed from past sins. Peter, in 1 Peter 3:21, tells us outright that "Baptism now saves you—not the removal of dirt from the flesh, but an appeal to God for a good conscience—through the resurrection of Jesus Christ," tying it one more time to the resurrection of Jesus. The only way our conscience can be "good" or "clean" is to have our sins washed away in baptism. Ananias indicates to Saul of Tarsus the sequence: "Arise, be baptized, and wash away your sins" (Acts 22:16).

Not to belabor the point, but if anyone is still unconvinced, let's look at Colossians 2:12–14 where Paul, once again, ties baptism to Christ's burial and our sins being forgiven, saying [emphasis is mine],

> Having been *buried with Him in baptism*, in which you were also *raised up with Him* through faith in the working of God, who raised Him from the dead. And when you were dead in your transgressions and the uncircumcision of your flesh, He made you alive together with Him, *having forgiven us all our transgressions*, having *canceled out the certificate of debt* consisting of decrees against us and which was hostile to us; and He has taken it out of the way, having *nailed it to the cross*.

It is obviously at this point that we are placed into Christ and our sins have been forgiven, so we can start afresh with a "newness of life" that does not come about through any other means. None of the components saves us by itself nor can any of them be left out; they are all essential and indispensable. It is the plan of salvation set up by God and communicated to us in His Word. In this case, we cannot simply look to the immediate context of a verse to obtain the complete picture; we must examine *all passages* related to obtaining the forgiveness of sins, so essential to our salvation. To alter or abridge or change it in any way incurs the indictment Paul calls down those who would do so in 2 Corinthians 11:4 and Galatians 1:8–9. Anything other than what we have preached? Let them be under God's curse.

Resistance

This chapter on the steps for salvation is presented early in our list of general topics because it is so commonly misunderstood and misrepresented among those who would claim to know the Word of God. Why that is, I am not sure. Some don't want to concede there is anything special about the water—a potential objection to the use of "holy water" used in Catholicism. Some think it is good to go ahead with the "symbolism" of your sins being washed, but there is no real command to do so. Some baptize infants which really confuses the whole believing, repenting, and confessing part of the Biblical process. Some "baptize" (necessary or not) by sprinkling or pouring water on people instead of immersing them. As noted earlier, the Greek word for *baptize* means to "dip or plunge" as in dying a garment. The "burial" comparisons to Jesus also stand in stark contrast to these supposed options.

One final point is offered on the importance of the final step. Is baptism *more important* than the other steps? In reality, no; all are just as important and just as necessary. As I've noted: *all* are necessary, and *none* can be omitted. The last one, baptism—aside from the fact that it is where our sins are forgiven—does achieve a level of importance not found in the others, on the other hand, because it is just that: the *last* one. The job is not complete until *all* have been undertaken. A house is not a house until the roof is added. A car is not complete until an engine is installed. The list is endless. However, one more piece of evidence needs to be considered.

Why did John the Baptist baptize believers if it was not an important part of the process? Would he have considered them free from their sins he listed for them if they hadn't been baptized? Is there any indication that people were resistant to undergoing baptism to be a follower of his? In Mark 1:4–5, we find these words:

> John the Baptist appeared in the wilderness, preaching a baptism of repentance for the forgiveness of sins. And all the country of Judea was going out to him, and all the people of Jerusalem; and they were being baptized by him in the Jordan River, confessing their sins.

We find later that some who had been baptized under John's teaching were apparently re–baptized (Acts 19:1–5). The kingdom of heaven about which John preached had not yet been established. However, the point is that he baptized for remission of sins and the people complied, all of them, without apparent reservation. Why do we balk at baptism today?

As successful as John was, the disciples of Jesus were baptizing converts, and they were doing so at a rate even higher than John was (Mark 3:22; 4:1–2). Baptism was important within the ministry of Jesus while on earth; it was not simply an advent for after the church has been established on the Day of Pentecost. Both John and Jesus felt it was important; the people recognized this and gladly submitted to baptism under these two. It was just as important when Peter and the apostles told the people that in order to obtain forgiveness for crucifying the Son of God, repentance *and baptism* were necessary. Why would we even begin to consider it to have any less significance in our own conversion as believers and followers of Christ?

Are people's souls in jeopardy if their conversion is not according to the pattern we find in the New Testament? All I can do is show you what the Scriptures say and let you draw the conclusion. But if I were interested at all in the seriousness of following what God tells us in His Word, I would do it like He says to do it. I may screw up some other way, but at least I have these basics according to how He has ordered them.

Chapter 10

Worship in the Church

God wants His people to worship Him. He created them and placed within them something that He called "Our image, according to Our likeness" (Genesis 1:26–27). There has been much discussion about what this exactly means, but it at least means that we are different from the other animals. We have intelligence, can speak languages (and other communication skills), can solve problems, make decisions based on things other than instinct, etc. It also means that we can acknowledge, revere, and worship a Higher Being, whether contrived within the mind of man or established by an Authority much higher than man. I believe I am safe in saying that all cultures share this common trait, that is, having some system of religion. Christianity is based on the Bible and the Truth found there for everything spiritual or religious.

Under the Old Law, God specified how He wanted His people to reverence Him, worship Him, and account for their sins. He was extremely specific about all the details, even to the point that no one could keep that law perfectly. He punished those who would corrupt His system (e.g., Nadab and Abihu in Leviticus 10:1–2) and would send foreign nations against His people when they went after other false gods—even sending them into captivity two different times. God is serious about His commands, and He is particular about how He wants His people to worship him.

Adding to God's Word

I have noted in detail above how we derive authority for what we are to do in this life to be aligned with God's Word. For now, I'll just review that we can follow His (or His agents') commands; we can follow the pattern we find when we read about what early Christians did; and we can draw inferences from these direct statements or these examples. Since the Gospels deal primarily with the life of Jesus Christ and His ministry, very little of what we find there deals with what we are to do in our formal worship of deity; the church was not established until the Day of Pentecost, recorded in Acts 2 after Jesus had ascended back into heaven. Most of what we find concerning formal worship is included within that book—often called *Acts of the Apostles*—and in the letters addressed by inspired writers to individuals and to congregations located throughout the region. Also, there are some conclusions we can draw from some early chapters in Revelation.

As I have noted, our Father is a God of clarity and precision. The Old Testament was provided for our learning, to teach us many things (Romans 15:4; 1 Corinthians 10:11; Galatians 3:24) concerning how God related to His people and what He expected from them. While the Law has changed, God has not; He still requires His people to be obedient to that which has been delivered to them. To assume otherwise and that He now allows man considerably more flexibility is doing the same things the Jewish leaders had done by the time Jesus arrives. He quotes Isaiah and says to the Pharisees, "Why do you yourselves also break the commandment of God for the sake of your tradition?" (Matthew 15:3, 9).

In His scathing indictment of them in Matthew 23, He rails at them for paying attention to all of the rules and details they had added to the Law and then following them more strenuously than the Law itself: "Woe to you, scribes and Pharisees, hypocrites! For you tithe mint and dill and cumin, and have neglected the weightier provisions of the Law: justice and mercy and faithfulness" (Matthew 23:23). Not only had they added to the Law, they had also made their additions *more important* than what God had placed within the Law. Jesus was clear about their end in this regard.

Also mentioned above are the warnings about changing God's Word, adding to it or subtracting from it, or even preaching a Gospel other than that which has already been delivered to us. We can add to those comments the passage from the last few verses in Revelation that speak about altering what has been said there (previously mentioned); the principle is easily transferred to all of the New Law:

> I testify to everyone who hears the words of the prophecy of this book: if anyone adds to them, God will add to him the plagues that are written in this book; and if anyone takes away from the words of the book of this prophecy, God will take away his part from the tree of life and from the holy city, which are written in this book (Revelation 22:18–19).

Using man's ideas to supplement or change God's Law is essentially elevating ourselves to His level, and this we simply cannot do: "'For My thoughts are not your thoughts, nor are your ways My ways,' declares the LORD. 'For as the heavens are higher than the earth, so are My ways higher than your ways and My thoughts than your thoughts'" (Isaiah 55:8–9).

The "doctrine of Christ" is what we find in the New Testament. The apostle John tells us (2 John 9) that if we transgress (literally "go beyond") that doctrine, we do not "have God." Likewise, the apostle Peter tells us in 1 Peter 4:11 that if we are speaking on behalf of God, we must do so according to what the Word of God provides for us: "Whoever speaks is to do so as one who is speaking actual words of God."

Approved Apostolic Examples

Jesus tells the Samaritan woman at the well (John 4) that *where* one worships (Jerusalem or elsewhere) will shortly not matter. He tells her, "God is Spirit, and those who worship Him must worship in spirit and truth." There are two "spirits" in this passage. The first is recognizing God as a nonhuman, spiritual being. His existence is not of this world, and He assumes no physical form due to this spiritual nature. The second "spirit" refers not to Him directly, but to how we are to worship Him. The term "*in* spirit" tells us something about the nature of our worship and our attitude during worship. If we are going to worship God, it must be done with proper reverence for how far above us He truly is and how dependent we truly are on Him for everything. Nothing that demonstrates a disrespect for Him will be tolerated by Him in our worship. Attitude and comportment are extremely important.

However, it is not only *in spirit* that we are to worship Him; it is also *in truth*. That can only mean according to His truth that He has carefully delivered to us in His word. Part of the problem the Jews had with the Samaritans was that the latter group had corrupted various aspects of the Old Law. Yes, they had an issue with establishing anywhere other than Jerusalem and the temple found there as the "seat" of where worshiping God could take place. However, Jesus was likely also referring to the Samaritans' apparent freedom to add to and take away from the Law. Truth is found in God's Word, not in how man might manipulate it to satisfy him.

So, it is to His word we should go when attempting to determine exactly *how* He wants us to worship Him under the Law of Christ. What do we find in Scripture that would help us? It should be noted that nowhere in the New Testament do we find the following words: "Here are the things you should do each Lord's Day when you come together to worship." We do not even have a direct statement to worship on the Lord's Day, or Sunday. So, we must go to a number of passages to assemble a "picture" of what worshiping God looks like, and that pattern is what we should be following. Some are direct statements, but many are examples of what early churches did.

Following God's pattern for something is important to Him. When instructing Moses on how to build the tabernacle for wilderness worship, God laid out extremely detailed plans. You can find those in Exodus 25–27, but as He begins His instructions, notice what he says about following them:

> And let them construct a sanctuary for Me, that I may dwell among them. According to all that I am going to show you, as the pattern of the tabernacle and the pattern of all its furniture, just so you shall construct it. … And see that you make them after the pattern for them, which was shown to you on the mountain (Exodus 25:8–9, 40).

Could Moses have changed this pattern or cut costs here and there by modifying something God specified? I think we know that answer, as He demonstrated His displeasure with those early on who did not follow the instructions (i.e., the pattern) He had provided (again, Nadab and Abihu in Leviticus 10:1–2). Patterns and instructions are important to our God.

The very day the church was established, Luke tells us in Acts 2:41, 47 that many were added to the membership of the church through repentance and baptism. However, he also tells us that what followed was a continuation of not only the teaching provided by the apostles, but that they were also performing many miracles to help confirm and firmly establish their words as "oracles of God." They were endowed with power from on high to do both; the teaching was from God as were the miracles (Mark 16;20). What we find in the rest of New Testament Scripture is exactly that: the Word of God. At least part of the *apostles' doctrine* (Acts 2:42) is how we worship Him, and we now turn to that pattern.

It would be nice if we had a copy of the first century church's "Order of Worship" we sometimes see in congregations today. These worship "outlines" provide a common understanding for those who are present and participating in the worship assembly so they will know *who* is doing *what* and *when*. That artifact does not exist, so we must piece together our best attempt at replicating—within reason, of course—the assemblies that took place in the first century. The best we can do is cull from New Testament passages the things they apparently did during the times when they assembled for worshiping God. What order these came in and the details concerning some of them is, at best, a guess. The important part is to make sure we at least do what we can to find what they did, as well as keep ourselves from assuming too much authority and going beyond what they did. Remember, God likes His people to follow the pattern He has provided them—no less and no more.

Worship "Activities"

Praying

Prayer is an important feature found within the New Testament. There are examples of prayer; there are instructions to pray; there are references to prayers having been offered. Prayer is important; it is how we talk to God. Jesus has allowed us access to God through His sacrifice so that we can come boldly into God's presence and speak to Him (2 Cor. 3:4; Heb. 10:19). We praise Him in our prayers; we thank Him in our prayers; and we petition Him in our prayers—or we just express to Him things that are on our minds about which we are concerned. Jesus prayed, the apostles prayed, and early Christians prayed.

We are told that the church was praying earnestly to God for Peter when he was in prison (Acts 12:5). We can assume this was either as individuals when they were not together or as a group when they were together. It was likely both, but it makes sense that it most certainly was something in which they would share when they gathered for worship. Paul speaks often about the fact that churches prayed for him and the work he was doing for Christ. He tells them in Ephesians 3:12–13 that we have access to God, and they should not lose hope in that access due to his (Paul's) tribulations. In his letter to the church at Thessalonica, he tells them to "Pray without ceasing" (1 Thessalonians 5:17). To the church at Philippi, he says, "Do not be anxious about anything, but in everything by prayer and pleading with thanksgiving let your requests be made known to God" (Philippians 4:6). Churches were instructed to pray; when they met to formally and regularly worship God, this would have been an appropriate time to respond to that instruction. Since the first century church did it, so do we today.

Singing

In Matthew 26:26–29, Jesus instituted what is commonly called the Lord's Supper. He has much to say to them before He is crucified in the upcoming hours, and much of that is recorded in John 13–17. When their time together is finished, Matthew 26:30 simply states, "And after singing a hymn, they went out to the Mount of Olives." Commentators suggest that this was likely some group of Psalms (probably Psalms 113–118) commonly sung following the Passover meal. Some suggest that the Greek word may mean "sung *their* hymn"—something definitely known to them. This apparently was the custom at the conclusion of the Passover meal.

There were obviously songs that were sung in first century churches when they worshiped. We are told in Ephesians 5:19 to speak to one another "in psalms and hymns and spiritual songs, singing and making melody with your heart to the Lord." This could be just a general reference to what many of us do as we go about our daily work, humming, whistling, or singing whatever is on our minds at the time. This worship activity could be something similar, except for the fact that as we do this, we are to be *speaking to one another ... and making melody with our hearts to the Lord*. A group singing together during worship—like the apostles did as they left the upper room—makes much more sense.

I have mentioned above (from Ephesians 5) three different types of songs. Historians tell us that *psalms* were devoted primarily to the praise of God, His name, His power, and all He has done for us. *Hymns* contained praise, thanksgiving, and petitions emphasizing our reliance on and need for God. The last group mentioned were *spiritual songs*, and these apparently were intended to arouse emotional responses as they sang about their devotion to God. All of these, especially the last of the three, were attempts to match the spirit of Man with the Spirit of God.

We also have singing again mentioned in Colossians 3:16. Just before this verse, Paul tells the church in Colossae to have good hearts (compassion, kindness, humility, gentleness, and patience), bearing with and forgiving one another. He tells them to put on love, which binds them together in special ways, and let the peace of Christ rule in their hearts. These things they can do in their daily lives—and should—but the times they come together as a group to formally worship God in their assemblies is when these attributes can be magnified. Paul is not finished, however; he then tells them to let the word of Christ dwell in them richly and with all wisdom. But he tells them *how* to do this in his next words: teaching and admonishing each other with psalms, hymns, and spiritual songs *singing* with thankfulness in their hearts to God.

Our conclusions are that we are to a) sing to *each other*, and this is achieved only when we are together (most likely in our worship assemblies); b) our songs should express thankfulness to God but also be of encouragement to each other (teaching and admonishing); c) these songs should reflect what is in Scripture (the word of Christ); and d) our hearts at the time are to be focused on the Lord. We do not have any of the songs they sang with us today; we do, however, have a treasure of all types of psalms, hymns, and spiritual songs created over the years that are both a) taken from Scripture or teach Scriptural concepts and b) allow us to teach and admonish each other as we sing. If a particular Scripture is not the foundation of a song, as long as its message does not contradict Scripture, that type of song would be acceptable also. Naturally, it should focus on God, Jesus Christ, The Word, converting others, or something similar.

One other point needs to be made, as long as we are focusing on the instructions and pattern we have provided for us. We are *commanded* to sing—*all of us*. It matters not the quality of voice, our ability to convey a story to others, or whatever the rationale might be. If we have a voice, we are to use it. If there is some medical restriction that does not allow us to use our voice, we can still *make melody in our hearts* (Ephesians 5:19). However, there are no authorizations for solos, duets, "special music," or any other additions to that which is authorized: all of us singing. We are only told to sing. Any additions to this—like musical instruments—would be an unauthorized enhancement where "necessary inference" would have to be invoked to justify. A cappella music is both natural and beautiful; most of our psalms, hymns, and spiritual songs are written in four-part harmony. A cappella music was the norm for centuries until, according to historians, the 10th or 12th Century with a few isolated references. It wasn't until the mid–19th Century that the practice of adding a piano or organ (and then other instruments) became popular among many denominations. Remember: God gives us patterns and He wants us to stick to them. The pattern mentioned in Scripture is singing and doing that with one another.

If what is being said here is something that doesn't comport with your current belief or practice, here is a challenge for you. Find the passage in the New Testament that commands the use of an instrument other than the human voice, an example that the early church employed musical instruments other than the human voice, or a truly *necessary* inference we should do so. An inference might be that we use hymnals of some sort, but a leap to a musical instrument inference is indeed not necessary. If it is not there, then we cannot do otherwise than acknowledge it is an addition by man ... and we have addressed how God views these.

The Lord's Supper

It is noted above that Jesus took the opportunity provided by the Passover feast observance to establish something that was to be initiated and carried out by the members of His church, Christians, whenever they met for formal worship. His only instructions concerned what the emblems stood for (bread—His body; wine—His blood) and that when partaking, they should be remembering Him and the sacrifice on the cross that He was, at the time, to shortly undergo. Some point to Acts 2:42 as the first mention of this ceremonial observance: "They were continually devoting themselves to the apostles' teaching and to fellowship, to the breaking of bread and to prayer." Teaching God's Word, fellowshipping, and prayer are things that would likely take place within a worship service, so the "breaking of bread" could mean the Lord's Supper if this is the context. On the other hand, Verse 46 suggests—using the same phrasing—sharing a common meal from house to house. Some believe Acts 2:42 is talking about the Lord's Supper and some don't. I am not attempting to settle that argument.

We do have two other passages we can examine to help us determine that the Lord's Supper was indeed a part of their worship service. The first is Acts 20:7, where we find Luke's words: "On the first day of the week, when we were gathered together to break bread, Paul began talking to them, intending to leave the next day, and he prolonged his message until midnight." The commentaries I consulted all suggested that this breaking of the bread was, indeed, observing the Lord's Supper. This is that approved, apostolic example that we seek as our pattern for what we do in our worship. Paul was present—obviously approving—especially since he apparently delayed his departure to worship with them. Otherwise, he was in a hurry to get to Jerusalem by Pentecost (v. 16).

Finally, we have in Paul's first letter to the church at Corinth a strong indictment of what they had let the Lord's Supper become. In 1 Corinthians 11:17, he says, "Now in giving this next instruction I do not praise you, because you come together not for the better, but for the worse." To summarize, there were divisions among them, something he had chastised them for in the early part of his letter. He tells them that when they came together, it was not to eat the Lord's Supper—*as it should have been*. So, this passage, like Acts 20:7, establishes that this was the primary purpose for assembling in the first place. Some came early and some came late; they were not "tarrying for one another" so they could participate in it together. On top of that, they had turned it into a common meal with some going without and some consuming too much. He reviews what this observance is and how it came about. He then tells them that by continuing to abuse this observance the way they have—in an "unworthy manner"—they would be "guilty of the body and the blood of the Lord." In other words, returning to an unsaved state; what they were doing was sin and, in no uncertain terms, Paul was setting them straight.

To conclude, we learn this from these passages: a) The New Testament church observed the Lord's Supper regularly when they came together; b) God had apparently transferred His emphasis from the Jewish Sabbath (seventh day of the week) to the Christian Sunday (the first day of the week) in commemoration of the resurrection of Jesus from the dead; c) There was a right way and a wrong way to do this, and we should do all we can to keep its observance a solemn feast focused on remembering Jesus; and d) it should contain the emblems Jesus used to institute it (unleavened bread and wine). Jesus also offered a prayer of blessing before passing each among His apostles, so that should be a part of our model as well. If we follow these components, we should be pretty close to the New Testament pattern.

These next two are less clear as being mandated *during* our worship assemblies. They are *giving* (or *making a financial offering* to support the work of the church) and *preaching*.

Giving

There are passages that tell us that we should contribute to the efforts undertaken by the local congregation. Acts 2 and 4 tell us that the church in Jerusalem did this so that no fellow Christian should suffer. Obviously, we have the "giving attitude" that Christians should have for the household of faith (Galatians 6:10). We have passages that talk about our attitude with which we carry this out (2 Corinthians 9:7) as well as our preparation for this (1 Corinthians 16:1–2), or so it would seem.

In 1 Corinthians 16, Paul appears to be making a shift from the latter verses of chapter 15. We do know that his letter to these Christians appears to be providing answers to questions they had sought from him. Here, he turns to the "collection for the saints" in areas of greatest need. He says,

> Now concerning the collection for the saints, as I directed the churches of Galatia, so you are to do as well. On the first day of every week, each of you is to put aside and save as he may prosper, so that no collections need to be made when I come.

He shortly says he and others they choose will take this "gift" to Jerusalem.

Some things to note here are the following. First, some say that this was a special need for those suffering elsewhere, and if that need hadn't existed, then would Paul have required the collection? That is a legitimate concern. He does the same, however, in 2 Corinthians 9:7 and talks about being a "cheerful giver." Paul spoke of others' generosity in giving to help spread the Word. Giving is what Christians do. They sacrifice self for others. If a special need is apparent, the Christian steps forward and the church does what it can for other Christians in need. This is an illustration of the attitude we should have concerning others in Phil 2:3–8.

However, above and beyond special situations, the local congregation must carry out the work that has been given them by the "apostles' doctrine." These would be evangelism, the edification of the members, and the benevolent activities for members and other Christians (the next chapter provides Scriptural references for these and other detail). We know they met on the first day of the week. Paul tells us to be willing, cheerful, and purposeful in our giving. Doing this on the first day of the week when we are already gathered makes sense. Is it mandatory? Is that the only time we can give? Those are questions left for a more detailed effort than we will undertake here. Let us agree that giving is part of the Christian obligation to support the work of the local church and that we are already gathered on Sunday; it makes sense to do it then.

Preaching

In the early verses of Acts, Luke shares with us a final meeting between Jesus and His apostles just prior to His ascension back to the Father. He tells them this: "You will be my witnesses both in Jerusalem, and in all Judea and Samaria, and even to the remotest part of the earth" (Acts 1:8). Mark's account tells us that "They went out and preached everywhere, while the Lord worked with them, and confirmed the word by the signs that followed" (Mark 16:20). Preaching the Gospel was what the apostles did. They were beaten and thrown in jail for it, and they all died for the message they delivered—according to secular history.

Paul, an apostle himself, preached to those in Troas before he left to meet with the elders from Ephesus, eventually ending up in Jerusalem. In Acts 20:7, we are told, "On the first day of the week, when we were gathered together to break bread, Paul began talking to them, intending to leave the next day, and he prolonged his message until midnight." Whether it was customary to have someone deliver a message during a worship service or not, we do not know. Paul did here, so it serves as a pattern that we should follow. As noted above, this is what the apostles and other inspired messengers of God did.

We also know that these men imparted gifts of the Holy Spirit to those who constituted the congregations they had established. These gifts included the word of wisdom, the word of knowledge, faith, healing, effecting miracles, prophecy, distinguishing spirits, tongues (languages), and interpretation of tongues (1 Cor. 12:8–11). It could be that in the absence of an inspired messenger of God (i.e., an apostle), these gifts were there for continued guidance and revelation. It is also likely that these gifts were demonstrated only during the worship service. Paul continues his message on these gifts a few chapters later in 1 Cor. 14:26 and writes, "When you assemble" before he lays out more instructions for the use of these gifts.

It is safe to conclude that at least *some message* was delivered during those early religious gatherings. Exactly what the content was is conjecture. We do know that earlier in Acts 2:42, we are told they were continually devoted to the apostles' doctrine. Written revelation of God's will for mankind continued through the end of the first century when the apostle John penned the book of Revelation. Whether it was carried out near a river, in a jail, within a house, in a synagogue, or even in a school (Acts 19:9), preaching was the vehicle by which the Gospel was spread. When people were gathered for worship, it makes sense that at least some message was shared.

Finally, Paul tells his young preaching companion this:

> I solemnly exhort you in the presence of God and of Christ Jesus, who is to judge the living and the dead, and by His appearing and His kingdom: preach the word; be ready in season and out of season; correct, rebuke, and exhort, with great patience and instruction (2 Timothy 4:1–2).

If this sounds urgent, it was; the next verses warn about a time coming soon when his listeners will not "tolerate sound doctrine," will want "to have their ears tickled," and will listen only to those who teach what they *want* to hear rather than "the truth." Finally, he tells Timothy to "Do the work of an evangelist, fulfill your ministry" (4:5). Preaching is what they did; Christians needed these inspired words as revelation at that time was incomplete. The first written works were recorded years later. Likewise, we need them today and preaching during the Lord's Day worship has precedent in Acts 20:7.

Chapter 11

Funding the Work of the Church

Appropriate questions might be the following: What exactly is the "work" of the local church? What is it to do and for whom? What is our authority for how these efforts are to be funded? Let's talk first about the purpose of the local congregation of Christ's people. (In the next chapter, I will discuss the differences between a church *local* and the church *universal*.)

In Ephesians 3, Paul is telling the church at Ephesus about his specific appointment by Jesus to testify of the things that had been revealed to him so that others could understand what he understands about salvation. Gentiles are now also legitimate candidates for God's blessings through the sacrifice of Jesus on the cross, just as the Jews had been under the Old Law. Not only could others understand and share in these blessings, it was apparently the obligation of the church to spread that good news to others, especially to rulers and authorities. In Ephesians 3:8–10, Paul says this (italics are mine):

> To me, the very least of all saints, this grace was given, to preach to the Gentiles the unfathomable riches of Christ, and to enlighten all people as to what the plan of the mystery is which for ages has been hidden in God, who created all things; so that the multifaceted wisdom of God might now be made known *through the church* to the rulers and the authorities in the heavenly places.

Paul says it is first his obligation to share what he has been given, through what he has written and that they can understand, so they, in turn, can transfer what they have learned to others. Evangelism of others is a fundamental responsibility of the church. Local groups should be all about sharing and discussing the gospel outside their own group to whatever extent they can.

In the next chapter (Ephesians 4), Paul talks about the first century church and how Christ "appointed" different individuals/groups to perform different tasks, so that the spreading of the gospel could take place, as well as another obligation. He says the following [my emphasis]:

> And He gave some as apostles, some as prophets, some as evangelists, some as pastors and teachers, for the *equipping of the saints for the work of ministry, for the building up of the body of Christ*; until we all attain to the unity of the faith, and of the knowledge of the Son of God, to a mature man, to the measure of the stature which belongs to the fullness of Christ.

The apostles were necessary to provide all of what had been revealed to them and was continuing to be revealed to them through the inspiration of the Holy Spirit. The "apostle's doctrine," mentioned back in Acts 2:42, was an ongoing and developing body of work. Prophets were those who were endowed with Holy Spirit inspiration who provided additional teaching for the early church (cf. 1 Corinthians 12, 14). Evangelists were those individuals who were most likely formally charged by the apostles and traveled with them (or alone) to spread the Gospel. Men like Timothy, Philip, Stephen, Luke, and others would certainly qualify. Today, evangelists (preachers, if you will) are not directly inspired by the Holy Spirit but certainly use the "tools" provided by the Holy Spirit in the Word of God to teach others through their preaching.

Pastors will be discussed in the next chapter in considerable detail, but it will suffice here to simply say that these individuals were the local church leaders who were responsible for the souls of that membership and for carrying out the work of the local church in a Scriptural manner. Today, the word "pastor" is commonly used in religious groups as the one person in charge of that congregation who preaches and tends to a host of other responsibilities. That is not how the Scriptures use the word, and this should not be our practice either. Lastly, teachers would be anyone "below" the level of assigned responsibility of the ones listed above who had been given the responsibility to share the gospel with others.

In the previous chapter, I examined one of the core features of what we do when we gather to worship God on the first day of the week: giving. The argument was made that 1 Corinthians 16:2 generally serves as our authorization for doing this. The instruction there was that each one of the members was told to put aside an amount of funds and reserve that for "the collection for the saints" Paul refers to in the first verse. Paul says he directed all the churches of Galatia to do the same. As I noted there, this could have been a special collection for the needy saints elsewhere, and that this is a special situation in the first century brought on by drought, persecution, or other oppressing circumstances. He does tell them, however, to do this when they were already coming together for the purpose of worship; this practice is set up for us in Acts 20:7 that tells us this is when they met to partake of the Lord's Supper. The context and logic tell us this was every first day of the week, just like the Sabbath was every Sabbath for the Jews in their religious observances.

Regardless of whether or not this was a "one time only" request by Paul for a special circumstance for the needy saints, local congregations had other financial needs that had to be met. A regular contribution would have been a logical way to address these needs and spread that responsibility across all members of that congregation. In the early chapters of Acts, for instance, we find that new converts likely still used the temple to meet (Acts 2:46), and in other places, we find groups of Christians meeting within houses (e.g., Romans 16:5; Colossians 4:15; Philemon 1:2). Obviously, thousands were converted on the Day of Pentecost (Acts 2:41, 47) when the church was established and thousands later were added as well (e.g., Acts 4:4; 5:14). At some point, growth necessitated larger and larger meeting places. This, however, is only one financial burden experienced by the local church that could be met with a regular contribution.

Treasury of the Local Church

The first examples we have of giving was shortly after the establishment of the church on that Day of Pentecost. Great things were occurring in the lives of the apostles (Acts 3 and 4), but the needs of the people, many of whom were still in Jerusalem to witness and participate in all that was happening there, were great. As a result, those who had possessions sold them to make sure that those who didn't have necessities were supplied with their needs (Acts 4:32–35). This sacrificing on the part of other Christians is a principle established at this point and reemphasized in the New Testament from time to time. It is an attitude that all Christians should have: the giving or sacrificing of self for others, with Christ as our example (Philippians 2:3–8).

In Acts 6, we have a situation where these needs had continued to the point where men had to be appointed to handle the distribution of food so that the apostles could devote themselves to "prayer and the ministry of the word" (Acts 6:1–6). Yet, the church and its work continued to increase, even to the point where many of the Jewish priests were even converted (Acts 6:7).

Large groups have needs and those needs are met by the generosity of those who can help with those necessities. Apparently, free–will giving on the part of righteous saints was the pattern for generating funds for these needs. Giving might not have been restricted to the first day of the week, but Paul noted that it was, at the very least, a convenient time to do so (1 Corinthians 16:1). We do have this example, so it can certainly serve as something we, too, can do when we come together for the needs of our congregations as they evangelize, edify the congregation, and take care of the benevolent opportunities that arise within the group. It should be noted that the only means mentioned of how to fund the work of the church is through these free–will offerings. If we are going to restrict ourselves to our established three means of how we derive authority for what we do religiously (command/direct statement; approved example; or necessary inference), then any other, more creative or adaptive means of raising these funds should fall under these guidelines for authority.

Benevolent Responsibilities of the Church

If you read closely in the paragraphs above, I mentioned that a congregation has the responsibility to address the needs of the saints *within that group*. First and foremost, the immediate context is their responsibility. Every example provided above deals with a local church addressing the needs of the local members of that group (or for needy Christians elsewhere). There is no suggestion that they were attempting to feed the rest of Jerusalem who might have been just as needy. Their responsibility was just to their own. In another section of this writing, we will find that the elders who were appointed to oversee local congregations were limited to the group over which they had been appointed, i.e., "the flock among you" (1 Peter 5:2).

It is not the local congregation's obligation to feed and provide for those outside that particular group. The community (world) outside is not their domain of responsibility. Their charge is to care for those within that body, and they are derelict in their obligations if they do not. The money collected from the sale of houses and properties in Acts 4 were distributed to fellow Christians within that group, not to the rest of Jerusalem or territories beyond. The church—that body of believers—was being built up by these efforts, not the world around them.

The only exception to this apparent pattern for doing things was what was highlighted in Paul's request in Acts 16:1–2. Congregations of God's people can use what they collect to help *other congregations* of God's people elsewhere. Where needs arise, we have the pattern, and thus the obligation if able, to help out in these circumstances. Some would say we should send these funds directly to the needy congregations; others say why not establish some "centralized distribution entity" to make sure that a) needs are known and b) needs can better be met. Those who say the funds should go straight to the churches in need suggest that by adding an *administrative layer* to the situation (whether there is a overhead cost or not), we add to or contradict the pattern we find. Paul was not a *collection agency*; he was a messenger or deliverer of the funds collected. Electronic bank transfers had not yet been developed. Someone had to get the funds from one place to the other; Paul traveled considerably and was a logical carrier of said funds to these other churches he would likely be visiting shortly.

In 2 Corinthians 8, Paul talks about this generosity found in particular congregations and in their willingness to go "above and beyond" what might be expected to help other congregations elsewhere. You cannot read 8:1–5 and not be impressed with the giving and sacrificing attitude of the churches located in Macedonia. Paul encourages the church at Corinth to exhibit similar efforts in 8:7–9, using Jesus as our perfect example of self-sacrifice on our behalf. He says he is not commanding them, but appealing to them (8:8); however, he ends this chapter with the following words: "Therefore, openly before the churches, show them the proof of your love and of our reason for boasting about you." This at least qualifies as a *challenge*.

Finally, he continues in chapter 9 with the same thoughts. He "presupposes" (9:2) that they will be generous to a fault and then notes in 9:7 the attitude with which this should be carried out: "not grudgingly" or as if "under compulsion." Given everything Paul says about our attitude and our actions on this particular subject, he is doing everything he can to stir up in them a generosity that will pay off for other faithful Christians. Paul is very persuasive noting that "God loves a cheerful giver" and then talks about the spiritual blessings they will receive having given of themselves first (8:5) and then of their funds.

I need to mention one point before moving to our responsibilities as individuals. As we work our way through these passages on giving and how we fund the work of the local church, it should strike us that the only way any money was ever generated within New Testament Scripture is through this means: *the free-will offering of generous Christians.* There is no mention of the local church—the only recognized structural entity within the Scriptures—employing *anything else* to generate funds. No bake sales, no car washes, no drives selling anything for profit … I am being facetious with these examples that certainly wouldn't apply to the early church had they had the opportunity. The point is just this: If we are going to stick to the Bible for our authority for how we raise money for the church, we need to stick to the pattern provided there.

Other needs likely existed within the local congregation other than just helping distant and more needy Christians. As congregations grew and larger groups were more tolerated, governments likely allowed buildings designed for worship to be built. In 1 Cor. 9:1–11, Paul makes the point that he has every right to be paid for preaching the gospel using Deut. 25:4 ("You shall not muzzle the ox while he is threshing") as evidence for this contention. So, paying a preacher—whether within your own midst or elsewhere (as Paul was)—is also a legitimate use of a church's treasury. He uses the same passage as authority to pay elders for the work they do in 1 Tim. 5:17–18. Edifying the congregation—building them up in the faith—through some means of teaching prompts the need for class materials (especially for children). The point here is that a local congregation has financial needs that use the weekly contribution to evangelize, edify, and provide benevolence for members in need. The only means of generating these funds in Scripture is the freewill offering of cheerful givers, Christians from that local body of believers.

Benevolent Responsibilities of Individual Christians

In Luke 10:25–37, Jesus encounters a lawyer who was likely a part of the group trying to trap Jesus into saying something contrary to the

Law so they could prosecute Him. He asks, "Teacher, what must I do to inherit eternal life?" Jesus asks him what the Law says; the lawyer replies with the passages Jesus points out in Matthew's account as "the greatest commandment" and the "second greatest commandment"—the latter being, "Love your neighbor as yourself." When the lawyer seeks clarification for who qualifies as "my neighbor," Jesus tells the parable of the Good Samaritan. Without going into that story's details, Jesus concludes by asking, "Which of these three do you think proved to be a neighbor to the man?" He answers, "The one who showed mercy toward him," to which Jesus responds, "Go and do the same."

Jesus invokes loving God and loving others as the two greatest commandments, and these are true under the Old Law as well as the New Law. In Galatians 6:10, Paul is addressing them as individuals from the first verses in the chapter: "Brothers and sisters . . ."; "Bear one another's burdens"; "the one who sows to the Spirit will reap eternal life"; "So then, while we have opportunity, let's do good to all people, and especially to those who are of the household of faith." Notice in that last one, he didn't restrict them to those in the household of faith, the church, but he said *for sure* to address their needs while looking to the needs of those outside the church. Notice also, he is speaking to them as individuals with individual responsibilities.

As Christians, we have not only the freedom but also the obligation to be "neighbors" to those around us. Like Paul and his "congregations argument" of not being under compulsion, we still are encouraged to do good to all men and will reap spiritual blessings if we do. Galatians 6:9 tells us to not lose heart in doing good to others. How do I generate the money I use to help others (and it does not always have to be through money)? Personally, unlike the church, I am not restricted in how I raise funds for doing good as long as the activity in itself is not sinful. Obviously, selling sexual favors, for example, would not be an acceptable source for generating income or for helping others. The point is that there is no approved pattern for generating and distributing funds to other individuals like there is for churches. *The treasury within a local congregation is restricted in how it is generated and in ways that it can be used; the individual Christian does not have these restrictions.*

As an individual Christian, I can give to religious institutions, though best to those that are teaching God's Word accurately. I can even give to nonreligious institutions. I can spend my money on anything I choose to spend it on unless that activity is a sin. I am a free, moral agent and have decision-making power over that which I earn or generate. Most would not dispute this assertion.

The difficulty comes when these *individual* freedoms encroach upon or are borrowed by the *local congregation*. Often, the justification is, "As long as it is doing good or teaching the Word, it should be OK." Nadab and Abihu (Leviticus 10) were still offering a sacrifice to God yet were consumed by the fire they were using because it was not authorized. Apparently, He wanted that done according to His instructions. Ananias and Sapphira (Acts 5) were stricken dead even though they were giving money—likely considerable amounts—to the apostles for the needy Christians. Getting only *close* to what God wants, but using our judgment to modify it, can have dire outcomes. "As long as it is doing good" may not be *close enough* to the pattern God has given us within Scripture. Local congregations are not free to use its treasury in any way they see fit; they are restricted by the pattern found for such usage in the Bible. Stepping beyond what is recorded there is dangerous.

Chapter 12

Leadership in the Church

Societies require laws and governance structures. God knew this from the beginning and has noted it in Scripture (Ecc. 8:1–8; Rom. 13:1–7; 1 Pet. 2:13). The Israelites needed Moses and others who followed him (Joshua, Judges, Kings, Prophets) to keep them in line and to make sure that things were conducted orderly and uniformly. Governments should provide for these conditions. As the passage in Romans above points out, someone or something has to keep those in check who would disrupt things. This is where government and formal laws come into play. God provided Israel with His laws and confirmed more than once that Moses was His selection for their leader. When others had a different idea (e.g., Numbers 12, 16), God was clear: He—not the people—would determine who would lead this nation. Even later, when He agreed to let them have a king, He still participated in the process through Samuel's anointings.

God Establishes His Authority

In Proverbs 14:12, we find this statement: "There is a way which seems right to a man, but its end is the way of death." In Isaiah 55:8–9, we have this: "'For My thoughts are not your thoughts, nor are your ways My ways,' declares the Lord. For as the heavens are higher than the earth, so are My ways higher than your ways and My thoughts than your thoughts." Over and over again in the Old Testament, God illustrates this to His people. Yet, somehow, man continues to think he has a *better way* than that which God has authorized, a common theme that keeps emerging here in this writing. When He had taken great pains to lay out His law for Israel, the two sons of Aaron (Nadab and Abihu) decided to alter a process that had been clearly established for an offering. God makes a dramatic statement on man's changing His rules and consumes the two with the strange fire they had offered, and the family was not even allowed to publicly mourn their deaths.

When the church was established in the first century, financial needs of the larger group were being met through the sacrifice and generosity of fellow Christians. People were selling possessions and donating those funds to the apostles to distribute so that no one suffered (Acts 4 and 5). Ananias and his wife Sapphira did the same—at least up to a point. While pretending to donate *all* they made on their sale—as others were indeed doing—they kept a portion back for themselves. They, like Nadab and Abihu earlier, experienced the wrath of God and were struck dead. Peter says, "You have not lied to men, but to God" and "You have agreed together to put the Spirit of the Lord to the test." It is interesting that at the initiation of both Laws—the Old and the New—He points out that corrupting these precepts will have ramifications. Man's ways are not God's ways; man needs to seek His pattern for doing things and follow that as closely as possible.

The "Business" of the Church

There are many things included in New Testament Scripture that provide guidance for how we as Christians are to carry out the work of the Lord. There are things we are told directly and should consider as commands (e.g., worship God in spirit and truth—John 4:24). There are examples of what the early church did that we should attempt to replicate (meet on the first day of the week for worship—Acts 20:7). Absent one of these, we are left to draw inferences in some cases and use our best judgment (Acts 8:35—Philip "preached Jesus" to the eunuch—next verse, the eunuch asks, "Look! Water! What prevents me from being baptized?"—we infer that "preaching Jesus" includes baptism). This pattern for establishing authority for what we do to become a Christian, to worship God acceptably, and to walk (i.e., live) in an acceptable manner is both common sense and how we communicate "instruction" to anyone at any time. You either tell them what to do, you show them what to do, or you imply something they understand as authoritative. We have introduced this concept in previous chapters.

Above, I introduced this chapter by talking about governance in society. The church is, by definition, a *society* (a collection or a community organized for a particular purpose). Like under the Old Law, God has provided instruction for how the New Law should be carried out. Governance is one of those things. Before I talk specifically about the local congregation, I need to discuss briefly about what has been called the "church universal."

When people render obedience to the Gospel and proceed through the steps of salvation noted in a Chapter 9, they are placed by God among the body of believers (See Acts 2:41, 47). They do not automatically "join" that particular group where they completed their conversion process; if they choose to remain and work with them, so be it. If they choose to move on and work with another congregation, that is their choice. Just realize that their initial "membership" is in the church *universal* and not a local congregation. This universal collective is the *group* that will be saved and has been predestined by God for that outcome (Ephesians 1:3–4, 11).

However, God realizes that a world–wide body of believers needs some structure and that in order to support each other in the Christian life, local congregations are needed to carry out His work. Paul and others established these as they traveled around preaching the Gospel; his letters to the churches he had established provide us with much of the New Testament as a whole and, more specifically, how these churches are to operate. The local congregation has the responsibility to spread God's Word (Ephesians 3:10), edify its members (Ephesians 4:11–12), and to make sure the needs of its members—and even other congregations, if necessary—can be met (1 Timothy 5:9–10, 16; Romans 15:25–26; 1 Corinthians 16:1; 2 Corinthians 9:13). The church, whether local or universal, has the additional (maybe related to spreading the Word) responsibility of glorifying God through our words and our actions—much like Jesus did while on earth—for all generations (Ephesians 3:21). Individual Christians are tasked with helping those outside the church (Matthew 25:40); the local congregation has responsibility for "saints"—i.e., other Christians.

Leadership in the Universal Church—*Jesus*

Now that we have a clear understanding of the difference between the *universal* church and the *local* church, let us examine God's pattern for how they are to be governed. Right up front, let us declare that there is no earthly organizational structure for the universal church of God. Jesus is the head of that body of believers (Ephesians 1:22; Colossians 1:18), and that body has been organized into smaller, local congregations for more effective work to be carried out. If there is a governance structure to be found in Scripture for the universal church, it needs to be exposed so we can see it and follow it. The fact that there is none provided in Scripture might be one of those things we, as Christians, are to infer: no instructions = no structure.

There is no situation where we find one local church overseeing or having authority over any other local church. There is no formal organization of groups of churches anywhere in the New Testament: no synod, no convention, no diocese, no conference, no *nothing*. The church at Philippi, Corinth, Thessalonica, and each of the churches in Galatia and Asia Minor—at least as far as we can determine from Scripture—all were independent, autonomous, and self-governing. No larger group existed, made decisions for them, or told them how to interpret the Truth as it had been delivered to them by Paul, one of the apostles, or another inspired preacher (e.g., Timothy). Obviously, some tried to come up with their own (Galatians 1:6–8), but Paul quickly corrected this situation in his rebuke to them. Yes, the apostles worked among different congregations and wielded power and influence in teaching them and instructing them. Paul even threatens a congregation if they do not take action against an erring member of their group (1 Cor. 4:21). However, that power died when the last apostle died and when the authority of God's Word took over.

The pattern we find in Scripture is for each congregation, each local church to be responsible for its own purity and adherence to the teaching provided to them at the time by inspired men of God. Any deviation from this pattern is a decision from man—not God—and the passages in Proverbs and Isaiah at the beginning of this section tell us that when these two conflict, we had better opt for God's will over man's will. Finally, if there is no authorized superstructure, then there is obviously no earthly figurehead at the top nor sub-figureheads leading up to that person.

In the absence of authority or policy, it is not up to man to devise it and declare it approved by God. Necessary inference cannot be invoked here as this superstructure is totally *unnecessary*. Independent congregations unified only in their adherence to the pattern established in the New Testament for becoming a Christian, living the Christian life, and worshiping God in spirit and in truth have existed for centuries.

Leadership in the Local Church—*Elders*

God has provided nothing for us concerning any sort of superstructure for the universal church, so our conclusion should naturally be, there is none. For the local congregation, however, we have solid information about God's plan for leading that entity. Paul, not long after being stoned (but not killed) by Jews from Antioch and Iconium, returned to the cities where he and Barnabas had established churches. They preached to them saying, "It is through many tribulations that we must enter the kingdom of God" (Acts 14:22). The very next verse says, "When they had appointed elders for them in every church, having prayed with fasting, they entrusted them to the Lord in whom they had believed."

When Paul wrote to Titus, his fellow-worker in the Lord, he opens the letter with a typical salutation and then said this: "I left you in Crete, that you would set in order what remains and appoint elders in every city as I directed you." (There is more in this quote that we will discuss shortly.) Apparently, what had been left undone—at least in part—was to appoint elders in those local congregations they had established through their preaching. To the church at Philippi, he addresses his letter to "all the saints in Christ Jesus who are in Philippi, including the overseers and deacons." More on deacons will be discussed later, but for now, notice the church there had all three: saints (or members), overseers (or elders), and deacons.

When Paul came to Miletus before traveling to Jerusalem for the last time, he called the elders from neighboring Ephesus to him for instruction and encouragement (Acts 20:17). He tells them a number of things is this passage, but in Verse 28, he says this: "Be on guard for yourselves and for all the flock, among which the Holy Spirit has made you overseers, to shepherd the church of God which He purchased with His own blood." He goes on to warn them of men *from among their own group* who would pervert the Gospel and lead others away. Their job is to watch for this and prevent it, if possible.

Peter, in his first epistle, ends Chapter 4 by warning them of the persecution they will undergo as a result of their faith in the Lord. He opens Chapter 5 this way:

> Therefore, I urge elders among you, as your fellow elder and a witness of the sufferings of Christ, and one who is also a fellow partaker of the glory that is to be revealed: shepherd the flock of God among you, exercising oversight, not under compulsion but voluntarily, according to the will of God; and not with greed but with eagerness; nor yet as domineering over those assigned to your care, but by proving to be examples to the flock.

Notice in this letter to churches in Asia Minor that he specifically speaks to the elders in those churches. What he tells them is to *shepherd the flock of God among them*—i.e., the local church—and do this by *exercising oversight ... according to the will of God*. He then addresses the younger men and tells them to be subject to their elders.

From these passages and others, it is safe to assume that a) elders were to be appointed in local churches; b) this was God's pattern (as communicated by inspired preachers) for overseeing the local congregations; and c) that the rest of us (obviously not only "younger men") are to submit ourselves to their leadership. This is the pattern we find in the New Testament, and it is the pattern we should be using in our local congregations. Any other form of church leadership or governance needs to be established through application of Scriptural teaching or else abandoned.

Elders—*The Greek*

The passage in 1 Peter 5 above reveals several things, but here, I want to focus on the various names, suggesting their roles, for elders. First, he calls them *elders*. The Greek word is *presbyterous* or *presbuteros*. At its core, it refers to one of age (also implying wisdom and maturity). Among the Jews (according to Thayer's Greek Lexicon), these men were members of the Sanhedrin and in the Gospels were often included within a phrase of those with authority: "chief priests and elders." Thayer also tells us that elders "presided over the assemblies or churches" and that other terms used were *bishops* and *overseers*.

Peter also tells these men to "shepherd the flock among you." The word *flock* suggests a pastoral role as well for these individuals. *Poimen* is our Greek word for *shepherd*, and its translation into Latin is *pastor*—someone who *cares* for the total well-being of God's "flock" (the people of the Lord) (Thayer).

These five words—*elder, bishop, overseer, shepherd,* and *pastor* (even *presbyter*)—all refer to the same group of individuals: those appointed to lead local congregations. They are not preachers (although a preacher could serve in a dual role as an elder—1 Timothy 5:17); they are not regional directors or coordinators for a group of churches; they are not anything other than local leaders in local congregations within God's universal body of believers. The passages and the Greek overlap of terms would be enough to assure us of the point being made here that this is God's plan for leadership within the body; it is *local* in scope, and it has its *designated responsibilities*. But there is even more.

Elders—Their Qualifications

Along with their roles of oversight and making sure that error does not enter the congregation through maintaining the sound doctrine provided them by their inspired teachers, we have even been provided the qualifications for those who would serve in these roles. The two passages providing us the most detailed information are 1 Timothy 3 and Titus 1. Here is a summary obtained by combining these two overlapping lists.

One who desires the office	Loves goodness and what is good
Blameless/above reproach	Has a good reputation outside the church
The husband of one wife	Just/fair/righteous
One who rules his own house well	Holy/devout/pious
Self–controlled/temperate/sober	Apt to teach
Sensible/sane/of sound mind	One who is faithful to the word and teaches it
Well behaved/orderly/decent	Not a drunkard/given to drink
Given to hospitality	Not greedy/covetous/a lover of money
Forbearing/considerate/moderate	Not a new convert/not a novice
Peaceable/not quick tempered/pugnacious/violent	Not arrogant/self-willed

I won't elaborate on these here. There is sufficient additional wording to help explain at least some of these within the passages themselves. Most are self-contained and self-explanatory. The list is weighty and demanding. God does not want individuals who cannot serve as good examples of what a Christian is and does serving in this role, nor does He want someone who does not have the capacity to carry out this extremely important role within the local body of believers. These are characteristics that all Christians should possess—at least most of them—but men appointed to these particular roles should be *role models* for the rest of the congregation where these are concerned. Do they have to have all of these? Probably. Do they have to be the perfect role model in all these areas? Probably not. Finding perfect elders is like finding perfect Christians; none of us measures up to that standard. However, these are the qualities and qualifications laid down by God for those who would serve in these roles. These individuals had better at least *minimally satisfy* them.

The points made above are clear. God wants His church on earth to be organized through local congregations of people coming together to do His will within a logistically convenient area. He wants them to preach the Word (evangelize), edify (build up) the members of that local body through teaching God's Word, and to care and provide for the needs of that group or other faithful congregations (benevolence).

God wants His church to worship Him in spirit and truth and according to the Gospel delivered to the apostles (and other inspired preachers and writers). Finally, He wants it organized and led by men who qualify for leadership roles—elders. Before leaving this topic of leadership within the local church, one other group needs our attention.

Deacons—*Role and Qualifications*

The role of the elder within the local congregation is both serious and potentially burdensome. Beyond the role of shepherding the flock and overseeing the souls of those within their charge, elders are responsible that all aspects of worship and work the church does is in accordance with the pattern placed before us in the New Testament. This would include making sure the facility used for gathering is at least minimally serviceable; monitoring the funds collected from the freewill offering of the members; and a host of other incidentals that would better qualify as managing *things* rather than leading *people*. At any rate, these details have to be addressed, as part of the charge for elders is running the house of God as well as they run their own houses and families (1 Tim. 3:5). Fortunately, the elders have help.

Some point to Acts 6:1–6 as the first instance of deacons being appointed. There was a need during the early church in Jerusalem, as noted above, to address the feeding of those who could not feed themselves. Hellenistic Jews—not native Judeans—were complaining that their widows were being overlooked in the daily distribution of meals. It is not necessary to address this in detail, but I use it here because it prompted the appointment of individuals to carry out this obligation. The apostles called the congregation together and stressed that their role of delivering the Gospel was their main responsibility, not the "serving of tables." They directed the people to select seven men "of good reputation, full of the Spirit and of wisdom" who could be appointed for the attention to details this feeding task required. Men were selected and duly appointed so the apostles could devote themselves "to prayer and the ministry of the word."

It could be that this selection was only an effort to solve an immediate problem. It is likely, however, that once this job was adequately addressed, these men continued in their support capacity for those in charge. If these were not the first deacons, then they at least served in that capacity without the title.

Paul addresses his letter to the church at Philippi specifically to three groups: the saints (or Christians); the elders; and the deacons. By this time, the role of the deacons had been established and warranted at least some attention by Paul. In his first letter to Timothy, he lays out not only the qualifications for elders but also those for deacons. These are found below.

Men of dignity	Hold to the mystery of the faith/clear conscience
Not double-tongued	Beyond reproach
Not addicted to much wine	Husband of one wife
Not fond of sordid gain	Good managers of children/households

The word *deacon* comes from the Greek work *diakonos* and suggests the notion of "service" or "servant." The root of the Greek means "to hasten after, pursue" (Vine's). There are other uses of words similar to this that speak of the servant in relation to his master, but *diakonos* speaks of the servant in relation to his work. Essentially, deacons within the local congregation serve the elders in whatever their needs might be, so that the elders—like the apostles in Acts 6—can attend to the more important role of shepherding the flock. These individuals are not specifically noted as having a leadership role within the congregation; they simply support—with an official role and title, however—the work the elders do.

It should be noted that some religious groups use the title of *deacon* to conduct the business of what the Scriptures point out as the role of *elders*. The qualifications laid out for elders are greater in number and more restrictive. The word itself suggests age, wisdom, and maturity so that these roles can be effectively carried out. Paul didn't call the Ephesian deacons to meet him at Miletus; he called the elders, the leaders. The Greek word for *deacon* suggests a role much different from that prescribed for elders. These two are clearly laid out for us in Scripture, and what is not clear is why some would place deacons over elders or simply use only deacons as their leaders.

[This concludes the second section on misunderstood or misapplied religious structures. The next chapters in this work will focus on general beliefs and their traditional interpretation compared to their more authentic application based on the features of context laid out in earlier chapters.]

Part 3

Misunderstood Religious Beliefs (General)

Chapter 13

Contradictions in the Bible

This chapter could easily or more accurately be entitled "The Accuracy of the Bible" or "The Reliability of the Bible," and indeed these issues will be covered. However, the most common complaint or attempt to discredit the Bible is the suggested "fact" that it contains "many, many contradictions and errors" and, as a result, "is unreliable" and "can't be trusted." If these claims are true, then I think all of us would have to agree: the Bible cannot be trusted as God's Word. Before we accept these claims as truth or reality, we need to be sure that they are accurate before we paint the Bible as unusable.

As noted elsewhere in this writing, the Bible is indeed ancient literature. The Old Testament was written over a period of about 1,000 years beginning about 3,400 years ago and "co–authored" by at least 40 individuals. The New Testament has that same characteristic of shared authorship, but it is considerably more recent. Its earliest books are traced to around AD 50, and its last one around AD 90. In both cases, however, they still fall into the category of "ancient writings," and they both have characteristics similar to other writings falling into this classification. Whether we are talking about religious or nonreligious writings, the process for studying them and validating them is exactly the same. Scholars of ancient writings are, if nothing else, *diligent* in applying their craft to the content they encounter. It is both an art and a science, and it is called *textual criticism*.

Textual Criticism

Anything written before the printing press was invented around 1500, was written by hand. Copies were sometimes made of those originals, and then copies of the copies were sometimes made. Be aware of this fact: no original versions (called "autographs") are available of any works that fall under the scrutiny of Bible textual critics. This includes those considered religious and those considered nonreligious. If originals are available, there is no need to certify the copies as accurate; the originals stand on their own. Also know that the word *criticism* does not imply a positive or negative predisposition toward any writing of any sort. It simply means to objectively evaluate all of the evidence that can be compiled on a particular writing *in an attempt to "recover" the original*. In other words, textual criticism is not an attempt to discredit the Bible any more than it is used to discredit any ancient work. It is simply the process used to make these assessments and its title involves a word commonly used in a more negative way; however, it simply means "an evaluation."

While the Bible is composed of both the Old and New Testaments, the discussion here will focus on the New Testament as that volume is the foundation of all I am discussing in this writing. As soon as a Gospel or other writing was penned in New Testament times, copies were made and circulated among the churches being established by the apostles and other evangelists throughout the region. As the number of copies grew, the likelihood that errors would be made grew as well, even though those doing the copying knew that they were handling the Word of God for future generations. Humans are indeed human, and errors will occur. The question is this: Are these errors significant, and do they damage the credibility of the document as a whole? I'll attend to these questions below.

In the first century, the language most commonly spoken across the Middle East was a form of Greek known as *Koine*, or "common" Greek. This was a holdover from the conquests and reforms put in place by

Alexander the Great who forced all people he conquered to learn the same language. Some point to this reality as part of God's plan to reveal His Son during this period of time in history so that everyone was using the same language and that the Gospel could more readily spread across the region. In Galatians 4:4, the phrase "in the fullness of time" is used for prompting these events, and these conditions likely contributed to God's choice. The *Koine* Greek is a very precise language with many variations or different forms for almost every noun and verb. This built–in *clarity* helps preserve the original language and intent behind the teachings found within the text. This is also why we in modern times frequently consult the Greek forms of words found in Scripture to more accurately discern appropriate definitions and subsequent understandings.

For a more detailed explanation of this information and other related content, I have recommended in a previous chapter a book by Neil Lightfoot ("How We Got the Bible") and do so here again. He does an outstanding job of covering numerous topics and issues related to the reliability of what we have in our hands today and why we can trust it as God's Word for mankind. After reading that work, one should come to where others who have studied God's Word in this fashion (textual criticism) have arrived. It is, by far, *the most reliable of any ancient work we have,* and we can have extreme confidence in the accounts and promises found there. In Chapter 6 ("The Canon and Non-Canonical Works") above, there is a chart evaluating the reliability of the Bible compared to other ancient works. This confidence is based on the overwhelming numbers of ancient *manuscripts* (copies of the originals) of the Bible compared to other ancient writings—as well as the proximity in time of those copies to the originals.

The "Conflicts"

Since none of the original autographs exist, the responsibility to pass down God's Word to future generations has fallen to individuals, many of whom devoted their adult lives to copying it in its truest form possible. A certain amount of respect should be granted to these individuals, though some have simply discredited their devotion to their task and labled variations in the texts as "human error." Their diligence should at least be mentioned.

Here is just one example from Lightfoot's book of how precise they were. For one particular group—the Massoretes—when a copying was completed, they would count the number of verses each contained to make sure it matched the original. However, they also counted the number of words and the number of letters of the text. Not only that, *they even counted the number of times each letter was used in each book*! If any discrepancies were found, they started back at the beginning; they did not have at their disposal a backspace, correct–o–tape, a bottle of white–out, or a delete key. This example is offered to illustrate how serious those who were charged with copying God's Word took their responsibility. This may be the extreme case, but it is at least an indication of how accurate copyists were attempting to be with the assignment they had been given.

Some other examples from history tell us how sacred this responsibility was. We are told that monks charged with copying the sacred books were exempted from working in the gardens of the monastery to preserve their hands and keep them from being damaged in any way. They sat at desks instead of on stools. They diligently prepared their materials for the task ahead and took both care and time to make sure they could do the job in the most professional manner. That understood, if they were occasionally guilty of an error, what types occurred and how important are they?

There were two types of errors contained in copied manuscripts: unintentional and intentional. Those of the unintentional type involve human frailties and the inability for everyone to hear and see the same thing and get everything down in script the same way. The difference between two words that sound very similar could be a problem. Distinct pronunciations at the end of words could make a difference. Many words in Greek differ by only one letter, so errors could have been made that way. Following along line by line in a text while copying it is difficult; sometimes skipping a line might occur unintentionally. Fortunately, some of the safeguards noted above would catch these. Also, when an error was found, as noted above, the page would be started over. This is another reason these copyists were diligent; no one wanted to make more work for himself by being sloppy or inaccurate in any way.

The second type of error would have been intentional, but not necessarily with a nefarious motive. In an attempt to help clarify a verse, a scribe might add something to help that effort. God guided the hands of the initial inspired writers, but there is little evidence (although some believe so) that He was working through the copyists as well. An example from Lightfoot tells us that the King James Version says in Acts 2:42, "the Lord added to the church." Earlier manuscripts (found after the KJV was created) use the word "number" rather than "church." These same people were called "the church" three chapters later, so while there is a difference, it has little significance in the reading. This is a pattern we find over and over where these *supposed* conflicts occur.

Daniel Wallace ("Revisiting the Corruption of the New Testament Text") offers these types of variances in manuscripts:

1. Spelling differences and nonsense errors (scribbles or "chicken scratches");
2. Minor differences that don't affect translations or those that involve synonyms;
3. Differences that affect meaning but are not viable (single manuscript or small group); and
4. Differences that both affect meaning and are viable (less than 1% of total text).

As one scholar noted (Greenlee: *Scribes, Scrolls, and Scripture*), these copyists were about copying, not about changing text or writing commentaries. They were not heretics attempting to influence doctrine.

As noted above, we have more evidence of authenticity for the Scriptures than we do of any other writing of that period or even anywhere close to that time period. Parts of over 5,300 manuscripts are available to us. Some claim that there are over 300,000 variations in those texts. Others, in answer, suggest that yes, anytime you have that many manuscripts, you will have errors—small and insignificant though they be—will be repeated. *Are they one error or one error repeated numerous times?* Also, the argument is effectively made that if there were only one manuscript, *there would be no errors.*

Estimates vary on exactly what percent of the Bible contains these "errors" or "contradictions" noted by those who want to discredit the work. Estimates from experts suggest a range from a low of .2% to a high of 1%. Those experts also suggest that none of these discrepancies affect the overall message, unity, or specifics of what is being taught within those pages. So really, is this conversation even worth the time or pages we have used on it? Well, yes. If deniers want to use these generalizations as scare tactics to drive others away from God's Word, we have to deal with it. Just know that much of what they say or evidence they provide can easily be answered with content like you have just read. While it is not the end of the issue or the complete story, there are numerous books and websites devoted to this topic. All objective treatments of the topic indicate that the suggestion the Bible contains so many errors or contradictions that it is unreliable in its claims ... is simply false.

Chapter 14

Universal Salvation, God Is All-Forgiving

The Christian Universalist Association has posted these statements on their website (https://christianuniversalist.org/beliefs/universal-salvation/):

- There is no such thing as eternal hell or annihilation because God has planned the universe to produce a positive outcome for all people of all times.
- The end of all things is a state of blessed reunion with God, the Creator — not eternal separation, misery, or destruction.
- (This is) based on a strong trust in God's omnipotence and benevolence.
- God is both powerful enough and loving enough to cause all souls to be rescued from a state of separation.
- Since no human being is totally bad, no human will perish eternally.
- God does not decide to condemn some people to hell because they sinned too much or they chose the wrong religious beliefs.
- Nor does God allow some people to remain in a hellish condition indefinitely because of making bad decisions of their own free will.
- Souls that leave this life on earth without experiencing salvation will have other opportunities for conversion, learning and growth after death.
- No one will ever run out of chances to return home to their Creator.

Where do I begin with this one? Since this organization speaks for "universalists" at large (my assumption), let me begin with some apparently contradicting passages for the assertions above; these are just a sample of what is available within Scripture.

Hell Is Real

Matthew 10:28—And do not be afraid of those who kill the body but are unable to kill the soul; but rather fear Him who is able to destroy both soul and body in hell.

Matthew 25:41—Then He will also say to those on His left, "Depart from Me, you accursed people, into the eternal fire which has been prepared for the devil and his angels."

Matthew 25:46—These will go away into eternal punishment, but the righteous into eternal life.

Mark 9:43—And if your hand causes you to sin, cut it off; it is better for you to enter life maimed, than, having your two hands, to go into hell, into the unquenchable fire.

2 Thessalonians 1:9—These people will pay the penalty of eternal destruction, away from the presence of the Lord and from the glory of His power.

Hebrews 2:2–3—For if the word spoken through angels proved unalterable, and every violation and act of disobedience received a just punishment, how will we escape if we neglect so great a salvation?

Jude 1:6–7—And angels who did not keep their own domain but abandoned their proper dwelling place, these He has kept in eternal restraints under darkness for the judgment of the great day, just as Sodom and Gomorrah and the cities around them, since they in the same way as these angels indulged in sexual perversion and went after strange flesh, are exhibited as an example in undergoing the punishment of eternal fire.

Revelation 21:8—But for the cowardly, and unbelieving, and abominable, and murderers, and sexually immoral persons, and sorcerers, and idolaters, and all liars, their part will be in the lake that burns with fire and brimstone, which is the second death.

God Cannot Lie

Hebrews 6:17–18—In the same way God, desiring even more to demonstrate to the heirs of the promise the fact that His purpose is unchangeable, confirmed it with an oath, so that by two unchangeable things in which it is impossible for God to lie, we who have taken refuge would have strong encouragement to hold firmly to the hope set before us.

Romans 3:4—God must prove to be true, though every person be found a liar.

1 John 1:10—If we say that we have not sinned, we make Him a liar and His word is not in us.

1 John 5:10—The one who believes in the Son of God has the testimony in himself; the one who does not believe God has made Him a liar, because he has not believed in the testimony that God has given concerning His Son.

Obedience Is Necessary

Matthew 7:21, 23—Not everyone who says to Me, "Lord, Lord," will enter the kingdom of heaven, but the one who does the will of My Father who is in heaven will enter … And then I will declare to them, "I never knew you; leave me, you who practice lawlessness."

Luke 11:28—Blessed are those who hear the word of God and observe it.

John 14:23–24—If anyone loves Me, he will follow My word; and My Father will love him, and We will come to him and make Our dwelling

with him. The one who does not love Me does not follow My words.
1 Timothy 6:14—Keep the commandment without fault or reproach until the appearing of our Lord Jesus Christ.

James 1:22—But prove yourselves doers of the word, and not just hearers who deceive themselves.

Finality of the Grave

Matthew 16:27—For the Son of Man is going to come in the glory of His Father with His angels, and will then repay every person according to his deeds.

Romans 2:15–16—In that they show the work of the Law written in their hearts, their conscience testifying and their thoughts alternately accusing or else defending them, on the day when, according to my gospel, God will judge the secrets of mankind through Christ Jesus.

Romans 14:10–12—For we will all appear before the judgment seat of God. For it is written: "As I live, says the Lord, to Me every knee will bow, and every tongue will give praise to God." So then each one of us will give an account of himself to God.

2 Corinthians 5:10–11—For we must all appear before the judgment seat of Christ, so that each one may receive compensation for his deeds done through the body, in accordance with what he has done, whether good or bad. Therefore, knowing the fear of the Lord, we persuade people.

Hebrews 9:27—Just as it is destined for people to die once, and after this comes judgment.

There are many who prefer to consider only one side of God. This is summed up in one of the tenets that universalists believe (and noted above): "God is both powerful enough and loving enough to cause all souls to be rescued from a state of separation." Well, of course He is powerful enough; the God of creation and the universe is powerful enough to do what He wills with His creation. But will He save us all because of His love and benevolence? There is a section below entitled "God Is All–Forgiving" that will go into more detail on this topic. For now, I'll just say that either God will condemn those to hell who are "not His," or He is a liar and has lied throughout the Scriptures. God is absolute justness, and this means that those who have rejected Him will "be recompensed for their deeds." Why say it so many times if it is not the truth?

The Old Testament is written for our learning, as a schoolmaster or tutor for us (Romans 15:4; 1 Corinthians 10:11; Galatians 3:24). If there is anything that we can learn from the Old Testament, it is that when God says something, He means it. When He says He will punish if His ways are not followed, He punishes. He demonstrates this over and over and over again with His chosen nation, Israel, when they—after repeated warnings and punishments—continue to leave His ways and pursue their own. The passage noted just above of 1 Corinthians 10:11 says this right after what we should learn from the Scriptures: "Therefore, let him who thinks he stands take heed lest he fall."

Elsewhere in this writing (Chapter 16) is the argument against the false notion of the impossibility of falling from grace. The Scriptures are very clear that just because you are at one point saved, this does not mean you cannot lose that state or condition. So, condemnation can be the result of never accepting God as well as accepting God and then leaving Him.

Free will is a principle established very early in Scripture. In the Garden of Eden, man was given one commandment: Do not eat of the tree of knowledge of good and evil. He disobeyed that commandment, and God punished him. Death would be the end of his existence on this earth, and he would have to work to produce things for himself. God reaffirmed His control over nature as well as His demand for allegiance to His commands in Genesis 6 when He destroys all of mankind except for eight righteous people. He reaffirms this throughout the time Moses (and then Joshua) was leading the Israelites: Follow Me and I will bless;

disobey Me and I will punish (Leviticus 26; Deut 28). Over 3,000 were slain following the Golden Calf situation (Exodus 32), and God sent a plague on them as well.

God has allowed mankind the choice to follow Him or not. Each individual must make up his or her mind; however, all must be willing to accept the outcome if they choose to deny Him as God. The Scriptures are entirely clear about this choice and about this outcome. I'll begin the closing this section with a passage, which, if nothing else, refutes the entire notion of universal salvation. If God can and will save everyone, then why even worry about a passage like this:

> For if we go on sinning willfully after receiving the knowledge of the truth, there no longer remains a sacrifice for sins, but a terrifying expectation of judgment and the fury of a fire which will consume the adversaries. Anyone who has ignored the Law of Moses is put to death without mercy on the testimony of two or three witnesses. How much more severe punishment do you think he will deserve who has trampled underfoot the Son of God, and has regarded as unclean the blood of the covenant by which he was sanctified, and has insulted the Spirit of grace? For we know Him who said, "Vengeance is mine, I will repay." And again, "The Lord will judge His people." It is a terrifying thing to fall into the hands of the living God (Hebrews 10:26–30).

There is no need to highlight, italicize, or underline any of it. All of it should be a sobering reminder that God is just, there will be a Judgment Day, and we will receive what is coming to us regarding how we treated Him, His Word, and His Son. Wanting to believe that the *mercy* of God will overrule the *justice* of God does not make it a reality. There are, indeed, two sides of our Creator that are illustrated over and over in both the Old Testament and the New Testament. One verse, however, speaks to both sides. In Romans 11:19–22, Paul is telling the Gentiles about how God will deal with His people, the Jews, and says that those "branches" will be broken off so that they (the Gentiles) can be grafted in. However, he also includes a warning:

You will say then, "Branches were broken off so that I might be grafted in." Quite right, they were broken off for their unbelief, but you stand by your faith. Do not be conceited, but fear; for if God did not spare the natural branches, He will not spare you, either. See then the *kindness* and *severity* of God: to those who fell, severity, but to you, God's kindness, if you continue in His kindness; for otherwise you too will be cut off.

If all will be saved, then there is no need to include "fear and trembling" as we work out our own salvation (Philippians 2:12), nor is there any reason to concern ourselves with the "severity of God" as the passage just above tells us to do. We could say the same for "It is a terrifying thing to fall into the hands of the living God" (Hebrews 10:31). These must be—according to universalists—just false bravado and bluster? I wouldn't stake my life on it, let alone my eternal life. A related feature of this universalist approach is the notion that God is so good that He just naturally forgives those who sin. The following section will address this notion.

God Is All-Forgiving

I had a friend in college who lived a life that was anything but "Christian." Mike swore like the proverbial sailor, using God's name in vain; he regularly was drunk to the point of not knowing where he was, he had a girlfriend but had sex with other girls; and he cheated in his classwork as well, assuming as little responsibility for himself as possible. None of us is perfect, and college is certainly a time to test one's faithfulness. Many of us hide the fact that we are Christians in those environments; I remember to this day as I walked across campus for my ride to worship services, I shamefully hid my Bible under my coat. I regret that; personally, I feel it is one of my greatest life sins (Mark 8:38; Romans 1:16). However, Mike—in spite of the life he led—proudly proclaimed that he was a Christian in good stead.

I asked him one day how he could claim such when so much of what he did and who he was ran counter to that assertion. He said, "God is all–

forgiving. I can do what I want, and He will forgive me." I think I said at the time something like, "Can you show me that passage in the Bible?" His response: "God is love."

I am afraid that Mike's understanding of God is more common than I would like to admit. The TULIP theory of John Calvin suggests that man is selected by God, not the other way around (Unconditional Election); it also teaches that once selected, we cannot reject the God's selection (Irresistible Grace); and finally, the fact that I cannot lose my "election" (Perseverance of the Saints) makes it pretty well impossible to fall from grace and lose my salvation. If you buy into any of this, then it makes sense to buy it all. The pieces build on one another and are logical, if you start down that road. If I cannot fall from grace and lose my salvation, then Mike was justified in living his life as he did. He might as well get as much pleasure out of life as possible.

The problem is that Mike's view, the TULIP theory, and anything else that supports that approach, is not found in the Bible. I will deal in more detail with falling from grace in a later chapter, so I'll hold comments on that for the argument presented there. However, I will at this point deal with what might be called the "dual nature" or the "two sides" of God.

The Love of God

The passage Mike was referring to in his response to my question is found in 1 John 4:7–8, 16 where the text says, "Beloved, let's love one another; for love is from God, and everyone who loves has been born of God and knows God. The one who does not love does not know God, because God is love" and "We have come to know and have believed the love which God has for us. God is love, and the one who remains in love remains in God, and God remains in him." Even without these verses, a strong theme in John's letters is *love*. After all, he referred to himself twice in his Gospel as "the disciple whom (Jesus) loved" and mentions *love* 45 times in his 5 chapters of 1 John.

If I listed all the evidence found in Scripture to support the assertion that God is the essence of love, this reading would go on much longer than interest would likely allow. However, I will mention a few, just to get a flavor of the all-consuming nature of His love for us,

- He created us in His own image, in His likeness. Although the comparison is weak, we "create" our children and love them at least partly because they are a part of us. We are God's offspring, and, as such, He loves us because we are His.
- He knows we will sin and separate ourselves from Him, yet He loves us and will always want us to return to Him. His will is that all will repent and be saved (2 Peter 3:9).
- He hates sin, yet He loves us despite our sins. His patience, longsuffering, and willingness to forgive is demonstrated over and over with Israel.
- He wants us to hate sin as much as He does, and He set up a system of sacrifices under the Old Law to remind Israel about how ugly sin should be to them.
- He sent His Son from heaven to this earth to undergo all that man undergoes (yet remain sinless) to be that perfect human sacrifice for all of mankind's sins.
- He allowed man to "see" Him—Jesus: "If you have seen me, you have seen the Father." We see the love of Jesus as He lived and died for mankind; this is the same love God has for us.
- He is not a mystery; He has given us His word that includes everything that pertains to "life and godliness" (2 Peter 1:3).
- God is faithful and will fulfill His promises (1 Corinthians 1:9; 1 Thessalonians 5:23–24).

The Justice of God

When John was a disciple, following Jesus, both he and his brother James were somewhat impulsive. Jesus even gave them the nickname "The Sons of Thunder" (Mark 3:17). One illustration of this was when they were traveling through Samaria and no one there would take them in and provide lodging for the night, which was much more of a social transgression than it would be today. These two said, "Lord, do You want us to command fire to come down from heaven and consume them?" Jesus rebuked (Luke 9:55) them just like He did when they asked to be seated on His right and left "when He comes in His kingdom" (Mark 10:37).

However, by the time John experiences what occurred on the Day of Pentecost, what he went through with Peter as they preached the Gospel in the early days of the church, and what he likely suffered at the hands of others as he led his life as an apostle, he is much more loving and caring than his earlier personality might have suggested. Indeed, John's letters are full of the love of God and the love of Jesus and the love that we should have for each other. It seems a major conversion has taken place.

On the other hand, love is not all John talked about in his letters. He is always stressing the importance of *truth*. Maybe a not-so-subtle message he is sending is that there are, indeed, two sides to God—*love* and *truth*—and both are extremely important. John stresses in these writings that if we claim to be "in fellowship with God and walk in darkness (sin), we lie and do not practice the truth" (1 John 1:6). The same is said for keeping His commandments (2:4); if we love only with our tongues (3:18); listening to the spirit of error instead of truth (4:6); walking in truth (2 John 1:4; 3 John 1:3–4). There are others, but these will do. So, why do we mention *truth* in the current context?

John was fully aware that there are two sides to Jesus (he personally experienced both) and two sides to God. He knew that just as much as God loved mankind, He also was a just God who could not lie. God had not only said He would reward those who obeyed Him and punish those who did not … He demonstrated that over and over again in the Old Testament as He dealt with a rebellious and stubborn people (Exodus 32:9; Deut 31:27). He wiped out thousands of them at the Golden Calf situation (Exodus 32–34) and during the Brazen Serpent purge (Numbers 21). He sent them into exile at the hands of pagan nations twice and wiped out an entire generation prior to entering the Land of

Canaan. God does what He says He will do; He has to. He cannot lie (Hebrews 6:17–18).

God demonstrated many times that He is an entirely just God. Those who do His will are rewarded; those who do not are punished, sometimes even destroyed. I have noted in sections above that God's people, the Children of Israel, were the first to receive the kindness of the Lord as He worked with them in the Old Testament. He also sent His Son to that group of people first when Jesus came to the house of Israel. As a nation, they rejected Him, and—as planned and prophesied—God offered salvation to the Gentiles as well (Romans 11:1–24).

Paul is saying, "Look, folks. God will do to you exactly as He has done to the Jews, those 'natural branches.' He will cut you off just like He did to them because of their unbelief." He is telling them that God is tremendously, overwhelmingly kind, but He is also a severe punisher of those who reject Him. Yes, He loves, and yes, He is just. That justness demands severity. Both are important; neither is more so than the other. The love should motivate us to love Him in return. The severity should motivate us to respect and revere the one who "can destroy both body and soul in hell" (Matthew 10:28).

As 1 John 1:9 tells us, God is indeed faithful to forgive us our sins. There is a stipulation to that in the opening phrase: "If we confess our sins." Paul, in Acts 26:20, testified to King Agrippa that he preached to the Gentiles and the Jews, "that they should repent and turn to God, performing deeds appropriate to repentance." The prophets preached repentance to Israel and Judah; John the Baptist preached repentance (Acts 13:24) to all those within his hearing during his ministry; and Jesus preached repentance as well (Matthew 4:17). Repentance is a "change of heart" and Paul tells us it is a commensurate change of action. My friend Mike's "blank check" approach to God's being "all-forgiving" is not without conditions.

God's covenant with man has always required obedience; blessings without compliance will not be forthcoming. "If we go on sinning willfully after receiving the knowledge of the truth, there no longer remains a sacrifice for sins" (Hebrews 10:26). Jesus's death on the cross was wasted, if we are not going to at least attempt to reform our lives and "be transformed by the renewing of our minds" (Romans 12:2). The parables of the marriage feast (Matthew 22:1–14: "Many are called, but few are chosen") and the 10 virgins (Matthew 25:1–13: "Lord, Lord, open up for us … Truly I say to you, I do not know you.") also illustrate that there will be some who will enter heaven and some who will not. Justice goes hand in hand with personal accountability; for God to be just, He must appropriately respond to those who have obeyed and those who have not.

Finally, at the end of what we have recorded of the Sermon on the Mount, Jesus talked about those who profess to be His but, in reality, are not because they don't do His will. These may even *acknowledge* Him as "Lord," but they are not His. They may even *claim* to do good works in His name, *but they are not His*. Hear His words in Matthew 7:21–23 and see if you can conclude that everyone is okay and that all will be saved:

> Not everyone who says to Me, "Lord, Lord," will enter the kingdom of heaven, but the one who does the will of My Father who is in heaven will enter. Many will say to Me on that day, "Lord, Lord, did we not prophesy in Your name, and in Your name cast out demons, and in Your name perform many miracles?" And then I will declare to them, "I never knew you; leave Me, you who practice lawlessness."

Chapter 15

Original Sin and Infant Baptism

Sin entered the world in Genesis 2 when Eve and then Adam broke God's only recorded law for them in Eden. This caused God to initiate the consequences He had established for them, should they break that law, and they were expelled from Eden (along with other consequences recounted in Genesis 3:16–19). Romans 5 and 1 Corinthians 15 lay out for us how, with Adam's action, sin was introduced to the world and later, with Christ's action of giving Himself for the sins of mankind, sin was "overcome." Man could, through obedience to Christ, remove his sins from his charge and experience the salvation that grace from God had afforded him. Sin places us in an unharmonious relationship with God (Isaiah 59:2); Jesus offered us the chance to be reconciled to God through His sacrifice on our behalf—both initially at our conversion and through our ongoing access to Him in prayer as we repent.

It is sin, then, that requires restorative action on our and God's part. Sin, in the Greek, literally means to "miss the mark" or to "go beyond" a target. Our target is perfect obedience to God's law, something that no one—except Jesus—has ever accomplished. In Romans 3, Paul discusses how we are all "under sin" (Verse 9) and that there is no distinction between Jew or Gentile, for "all have sinned and fall short of the glory of God, being justified as a gift by His grace through the redemption, which is in Christ Jesus, whom God displayed publicly as a propitiation in His blood through faith" (3:23–24). Even Paul speaks of the struggle he, as close as he was to God and Christ and as much as he was doing for the cause of Christ, experienced with his daily conflict between the spirit and the flesh (Romans 7:14–25). If Paul consciously struggled, then so *should* we, whether or not we actually do.

The doctrine of Original Sin tells us that we (all mankind) inherit the sin of Adam. Several passages are used to support this notion: Psalms 51:5; 5:12; 5:18; Ephesians 2:3; and 1 Corinthians 15:22. These passages admittedly establish that there is at least some *connection* of Adam's sin to our sins. That they suggest we are *born with his sin already on our account* is a different question altogether.

The Bible does not and cannot contradict itself. If it does, then it would be a safe assumption that it is not inspired of God and cannot be used for anything religious or spiritual. There are at least a couple of Old Testament passages that set the tone for this discussion.

In Jeremiah 31:30, the prophet says, "But everyone will die for his own wrongdoing." Each of us is accountable for our own behavior and actions committed in this life. The passage goes on with a real-life application of this principle and tells us only the man who eats sour grapes will have his teeth set on edge. Each of us is responsible for our sins; we do not inherit the sins of others.

Another passage that teaches this same enduring principle is found in Ezekiel 18 where the prophet refers to the passage in Jeremiah above and concludes in 18:4, "The soul who sins will die." In 18:17, after listing a number of sins the father committed—but not the son—the prophet says, "He will not die for his father's guilt, he will certainly live." In v. 20, he also repeats, "The person who sins will die," but then adds, "A son will not suffer the punishment for the father's guilt, nor will a father suffer the punishment for the son's guilt; the righteousness of the righteous will be upon himself, and the wickedness of the wicked will be upon himself."

The principle is clear. No matter how far back that lineage (i.e., fatherhood) goes (even all the way back to Adam), the son will be guilty of the sins *only he has committed*, not any that anyone before him has committed. Isaiah tells us in 59:2, "*Your* wrongdoings have caused a separation between *you* and *your* God, and your sins have hidden His face from you so that He does not hear." The emphasis is mine, but the message is clear. True, the prophet is speaking to Israel, a nation, but that group is composed of individuals who, by and large, were guilty of the sins that had separated them from God—as a nation and as individuals. Each of us separates ourself from God through *our* sins. We are not already separated at birth due to the sins of someone who came before us. This theme is repeated clearly throughout Scripture, and if God wanted us to know that we already had sin on our account even before we had a chance to sin, He would have made that clear. So, let's look at the passages that others say teach this notion of Original Sin. Since the Scriptures cannot contradict themselves, and I have attempted to established through Scriptures above that each of us is accountable for our own sins, let's see if there is another interpretation for what they assert is abundantly clear to them.

Psalm 51:5—*Behold, I was brought forth in guilt, and in sin my mother conceived me.*

Commentaries will differ on the meaning of this passage. Those who buy into the notion of Original Sin, assert that it is a proof text. Others, who do not, offer alternative interpretations. There is no indication that David's mother illegitimately conceived him, so it was not her sin that is under consideration. It is David's sin of which he is speaking here.

David was a great king and ancestor of Jesus. He is praised in 1 Kings 15:4–5 where it says, "But for David's sake the LORD his God gave him a lamp in Jerusalem, to raise up his son after him and to establish Jerusalem, because David did what was right in the sight of the LORD, and did not deviate from anything that He commanded him all the days of his life, except in the case of Uriah the Hittite." Scholars believe that Psalms 51 was written following the situation with Uriah, Bathsheba, and Nathan's indictment of David and his treachery. David's depth of regret and depression are discussed in the chapters following Nathan's revelation to David of how wretched his actions were. David responds by saying how vile he is and that to do something this horrid, his evil heart must go "way back"—even stretching it to the point he entered this world. His point is that for someone to do something this bad, he must have been practicing evil a long time. Albert Barnes in his commentary on this passage says,

> There is no statement that the sin of another was "imputed" to him; or that he was "responsible" for the sin of Adam; or that he was guilty "on account of" Adam's sin, for on these points the psalmist makes no assertion. It is worthy of remark, further, that the psalmist did not endeavor to "excuse" his guilt on the ground that he was "born" in iniquity; nor did he allude to that fact with any purpose of "exculpating" himself.

David is merely remarking at how utterly sinful he is to do what he has done. For a full week, until the child died (David's punishment for his sin), David lay on the ground, would not move, and would not eat. Contemplating what he had done and the ramifications of his sin was deep, and his guilt would not allow him to do anything else. It was in this state of mind (or shortly after) that David likely penned Psalms 51. As Barnes further notes, David was simply saying, "(1) that people are born with a propensity to sin; and (2) that this fact does not excuse us in sin, but rather tends to aggravate and deepen our guilt."

Romans 5:12, 18, 19—*Sin entered into the world, and death through sin, and so death spread to all mankind ... So then, as through one offense the result was condemnation to all mankind ... For as through the one man's disobedience the many were made sinners.*

Romans 5 is one of two passages that firmly illustrates the connection between Adam and Jesus; 1 Corinthians 15 is the other. In these somewhat extended comparisons, Paul affirms that what all lost on account of what Adam (and Eve) introduced into an otherwise sinless and perfect world, Jesus was the sole antidote for the consequences on their part. Taking these three verses as presented, it is understandable how one could conclude that Adam's sins are unavoidably connected to our sins. In reality, they indeed are, but not in the way others would want you to believe.

The warning to Adam (and shared with Eve) was that in the day they ate of the tree in the middle of the Garden, the tree of knowledge of good and evil, "you shall surely die" (Genesis 2:17). Eve repeats this to Satan when he tempts her to eat of it. In Genesis 3:19, part of God's curse to Adam (in reality, both of them) is that he will return to the ground (i.e., die). The knowledge of good and evil (or sin through violating God's commandments) cursed Adam to not only a spiritual death or separation from God, but it also meant that he would now at some point die and return to the dust from which he was created. This would not have been the outcome had he not sinned; he did, however, and it was indeed the consequence. In Romans 5, the full version of Verse 12 says this: "Therefore, just as through one man sin entered into the world, and death through sin, and so death spread to all mankind, because all sinned." Without that last phrase or explanation, we would think that yes, Adam sinned, and his sin passes to us. However, all Verse 12 is saying is that guilt is upon all men *because all men sin.*

In Romans 5:18–19, Paul is making the same point. Sin entered the world through one man and the consequences of this was that man now knew the difference between good and evil and would select evil from time to time. As a result, condemnation would be experienced by all mankind so that Christ could enter the picture—offering obedience and righteousness—and reverse—or at least mitigate—the things Adam had set in motion.

Prior to Chapter 5, Paul says in Romans 3:23, "All have sinned and fall short of the glory of God." Stark fact: all sin, and their guilt separates them from God and His glory. It is only through Jesus and the sacrifice of His blood on the cross that allows us to be justified in God's sight and be reconciled to Him.

Ephesians 2:1–3—*And you were dead in your offenses and sins, in which you previously walked according to the course of this world, according to the* *prince of the power of the air, of the spirit that is now working in the sons of disobedience. Among them we too all previously lived in the lusts of our flesh, indulging the desires of the flesh and of the mind, and were by nature children of wrath, just as the rest.*

Historically, Ephesus was a major stop on the trade routes crossing the Mediterranean from both directions. Its devotion to the Goddess Artemis (hunting, chastity, childbirth, wild animals, and the wilderness) were well known. A large temple and even three smaller ones were built to her hundreds of years before the first century. Paul points out that these Christians in Ephesus—just like the other pagans who turned to Christianity—had been dead in their sins due specifically to how they were walking "according to the course of this world." He says that we all were living "in the lusts of our flesh" as we were, by nature, sinful. His point is the same that we have been making. God, since the Garden of Eden, has allowed man to make choices in either serving Him or not serving Him.

If we choose the former, we are blessed and the blood of Christ saves us; if we choose the latter, then that "nature" which we all have within us overtakes us, and we bear the consequences, as a result. It is not that we were born with sin but that we were born with a nature that has to be subdued and put under subjection to a higher authority. Satisfying selfish desires is strong within man, but we must place God's will over our will in order to please Him and reap the rewards of those choices.

1 Corinthians 15:22—*For as in Adam all die, so also in Christ all will be made alive.*

As noted above, Romans 5 and 1 Corinthians 15 are similar if not parallel passages. Both talk about what was lost in Adam was found in Jesus and His sacrifice. Adam introduced sin into the world and all of us sin (Romans 3:23; 5:12); consequently, both Adam and all humans to ever live separated themselves from God through their sins. Jesus was necessary to rectify that "death" we had all incurred due to our sins. In the verse in 1 Corinthians 15 prior to the one provided above, Verse

21 tells us this: "For since by a man death came, by a man also came the resurrection of the dead." Adam introduced death into this world through his violation of God's command. Jesus was the antidote and the saving grace for what Adam introduced. Verse 22 is just a restatement of Verse 21. The Contemporary English Version presents it this way: "Adam brought death to all of us, and Christ will bring life to all of us."

This section will close by presenting, once again, Paul's explanation for how all of this fits together. Yes, Adam did introduce sin into the world (Romans 5 and 1 Corinthians 15); however, we do not assume his guilt when we are born any more than we assume the guilt of any of our other forefathers. Adam's sins were his and ours are no one's but ours. Paul says in Romans 5:12, "Just as through one man sin entered into the world, and death through sin, and so death spread to all mankind." If he had stopped there, we would still have all of what has been offered above refuting the notion of Original Sin. But he does not stop there. He says [my emphasis], "Death spread to all mankind, ***because all sinned***." That "because" is an awfully strong exception or qualifier to what precedes it. It also is a primary reason that infant baptism is not necessary. If babies are not born with the sin of Adam on their charge, then the question arises, "At what point do they sin?"

Accountability

There is no magical or scientific way to determine at what point in the cycle of maturity when children move from unaccountable to God for their sins to being accountable for them. It certainly has to do with their recognition of making decisions regarding right and wrong choices for some reason other than they will receive some temporal/earthly corrective measure for their poor choices. Once adolescents (the usual age demographic) become aware that they not only know the difference between right and wrong, but they also make choices that in some way negatively impact their conscience or self–concept ... they certainly have entered the ballpark of accountability. Even those raised in environments where standards of right and wrong are at best "loose,"

Scriptures tell us that even by nature, something inside of us functions as a guide for making right choices.

In Romans 2, Paul is addressing Jews and Gentiles and their treatment by God, depending on the laws by which they were governed. The first part of the chapter sets up the notion that we are *all* accountable to God and that "He will render to every man, according to his deeds" (2:6). Verse 9 stresses that both groups will be judged, and Verse 11 tells us that there is "no partiality with God." Verses 14–16 tell us that even those who were not beneficiaries of The Law (like the Jews) are still accountable:

> For when Gentiles who do not have the Law instinctively perform the requirements of the Law, these, though not having the Law, are a law to themselves, in that they show the work of the Law written in their hearts, their conscience testifying and their thoughts alternately accusing or else defending them, on the day when, according to my gospel, God will judge the secrets of mankind through Christ Jesus.

These verses tell us there is something either innate or developed and cultivated at some point in our lives that informs us concerning the difference between right and wrong. When we go against what we *instinctively* know we should do, that is a sin. (This principle is affirmed in James 4:17:) The argument is completed at the end of Romans 2 by telling the Jews that circumcision of the flesh will not save them, but circumcision of the heart (loving God and doing His will) is what is important. If the Gentile is more righteous than the Jew, then the Gentile's uncircumcision has become circumcision. Obedience is the qualifier, when the Jews were relying on fleshly ordinances and their heritage.

Interestingly, this issue was a point of argument of the serpent in his conversation with Eve in Genesis 3. When Eve says they can't eat of the tree in the middle of the garden—the tree of the knowledge of good and evil—because they would die, the serpent says this: "You surely shall not die! "For God knows that in the day you eat from it your eyes will be opened, and you will be like God, knowing good and evil" (3:4–5). A longer discussion on all of this needs our attention at some point, but for our purposes here, let's note the following: 1) Adam and Eve's eyes were opened and they indeed knew the difference between good and evil; 2) though their sin was not passed to us, apparently this feature of knowing the difference between good and evil was; and 3) this is an inherent trait in all mankind, according to Romans 2.

The point of the foregoing discussion is to illustrate that at some point in our lives, all of us become accountable to God, regardless of under what circumstances (or "law") we are raised. It is that point where decisions are made to follow or not follow what we know to be right. Infants, all would agree, are not accountable at birth. Likewise, they do not inherit the sins of their fathers, as this would throw them into the realm of accountability in dire need of forgiveness.

There are other reasons discussed in previous chapters concerning what it takes to have one's sins forgiven in the conversion process. The acceptable candidate for baptism, where sins are removed, has already demonstrated some cognitive processes that infants simply cannot demonstrate. The overwhelming evidence that *belief* is utterly foundational cannot be refuted. One has to acknowledge one's sins through repenting of them in order to be saved; *repentance* of sins is of utmost importance for one to be forgiven of them. *Confession* that Christ is the Son of God we are told is important for entry into heaven. Finally, *baptism* is available to those who have done these things. Babies and infants cannot do these things. Babies and infants are not born with anyone's sins on their account: "Everyone will die for *his own* wrongdoing" (Jeremiah 31:30).

Jesus said, "Leave the children alone, and do not forbid them to come to Me; for the kingdom of heaven belongs to such as these." He could say that because they had no sins on their account, and it wasn't because they had been baptized as infants (earliest historical references to such are around AD 220). He says this because those (adults) who come to

Him will be like these children: innocent and pure since their sins have been forgiven them.

Chapter 16

Falling from Grace

In Romans 2:17–24, Paul condemns the Jews because they think that, simply because they are Jews and are the children of Abraham, they are God's chosen and cannot lose what has been granted them. He tells them that their actions that are contrary to God's law make "the name of God blasphemed among the Gentiles" (2:24). In Chapter 11, he uses the pruning of branches and grafting in different ones to note that the "natural branches"—these would be the Jews—are not spared when the Gentiles are "grafted in." His warning is to the Gentiles, however, that if God spared not the *natural* branches, then He would not spare them (the new ones) either if they strayed from His Word (11:20–21). One more point: He is talking to the church at Rome, Christians who had obeyed the Gospel and were in Christ.

Although the Jews obviously felt they couldn't lose their salvation, this belief about not being able to lose one's salvation, once obtained, is the crowning assertion of John Calvin's TULIP theory. It is the "P" in the acronym and stands for "Perseverance of the Saints"; it has also been called "Impossibility of Apostasy." I'll not go into the other parts of the theory, although they are all flawed in one way or another, but I will focus here on the one that seems to have endured within groups that do not necessarily adhere to Calvin's other teachings.

One passage believers of this doctrine turn to is Romans 8:38–39. (It is interesting that they would use a passage from an inspired letter of Paul where I have already pointed out in two other places where this belief is condemned. Incidentally, this entire chapter in Romans will be examined for another point later in this writing.) This current examination, however, provides a conclusion to Paul's extended discussion of our being relieved from the bondage of the Old Law and being granted a victory over our sins in Jesus Christ. He says,

> For I am convinced that neither death, nor life, nor angels, nor principalities, nor things present, nor things to come, nor powers, nor height, nor depth, nor any other created thing will be able to separate us from the love of God that is in Christ Jesus our Lord.

Paul's point is focused on *external* threats; admittedly, nothing external to our relationship with God can cause Him to release His hold on us and our salvation. However, these other two points in Romans makes it clear that we can, indeed, lose our salvation if we, *ourselves*, cause the separation from God. The forces noted in the verse are outside the individual who, if strong enough, can resist them, even to the point of death in not denying Jesus. The Jews knew full well that the Israelites were sentenced to go back into the wilderness for 40 years until the unbelieving generation had died off. Surely, they didn't think they would be saved if they rejected the Son of God sent to them for their salvation. Besides these two references in Romans, the Scriptures are absolutely full of passages for our examination.

For instance, in Hebrews 3 and 4, the writer takes this exact situation with Israel, tells us that they lost what was within their grasp if only they had had faith, and then tells us that we, too, can fail to enter our "rest" just as they did. Part of the passage reads this way:

> Therefore, we must fear if, while a promise remains of entering His rest, any one of you may seem to have come short of it. For indeed we have had good news preached to us, just as they also did; but the word they heard did not benefit them, because they were not united with those who listened with faith (Hebrews 4:1–2).

In Verse 11, he says, "Therefore let's make every effort to enter that rest, so that no one will fall by following the same example of disobedience."

The writer is talking to Christians here, just like Paul was in Romans. They were saved, yet there was the possibility they could lose that salvation and not enter God's eternal rest—just like Israel failed to enter the rest of the Promised Land.

One more point on this passage and then I will move on to a few others. The Hebrew writer emphasizes the importance of following God's Word and describes it in extremely intense terms (Verse 12). He then ends in Verse 13 with what can only be viewed as a threat, should we think we will be able to discount the Son of God and get away with it: "There is no creature hidden from His sight, but all things are open and laid bare to the eyes of Him to whom we must answer." His justice is sure, and we will lose that on which our hold was—initially, at least—secure.

Peter talks about how extremely distasteful and repugnant it is and should be to us if we turn back again to the world after having received salvation and the forgiveness of sins. He says in 2 Peter 2:20,

> For if, after they have escaped the defilements of the world by the knowledge of the Lord and Savior Jesus Christ, they are again entangled in them and are overcome, the last state has become worse for them than the first.

He goes on in the next verse: "For it would be better for them not to have known the way of righteousness, than having known it, to turn away from the holy commandment delivered to them." He concludes with the repugnant comparison from Proverbs 26:11. "It has happened to them according to the true proverb, 'A dog returns to its own vomit,' and, 'A sow, after washing, returns to wallowing in the mire.'"

In another book I wrote (*Types in the Bible: Shadows of the True*), I compiled a list of passages that clearly teach, especially when taken as a group, that one who is a child of God, fully and completely in a saved condition, can lose that salvation through sin. This table is borrowed from that work. Read through these and see if you can come up with any other conclusion.

Conditions	
Matthew 10:22	1 John 2:15–16
John 3:16	1 John 3:9, 15
John 15:6	Longer Passages
Romans 11:22	Luke 8—Sower
1 Corinthians 6:9–11	Luke 9:62—Dedicated Discipleship
1 Corinthians 9:26–27	Acts 8—Simon
1 Corinthians 15:1–2	Acts 20—Elders
2 Corinthians 5:10	Galatians 2—Peter
Galatians 5:4	Galatians 6—Restoring the Lost
Galatians 6:8–9	1 Timothy 1—Shipwreck
Philippians 2:12	1 Timothy 4—Falling Away
2 Timothy 2:12	1 Timothy 6:10—Wandering away
Hebrews 4:2, 11	Hebrews 3:12—Falling away
Hebrews 4:6–7	Hebrews 10:38–39—Shrinking back
Hebrews 6:4–6	James 5:19–20—Straying from truth
Hebrews 10:26–27	1 Peter 5:8—Satan seeking victims
Hebrews 12:3	2 Peter 2:1—False prophets
Hebrews 12:12–13	2 John 8–11—Watching yourselves
2 Peter 2:20–21	Revelation 2/3—Churches in danger
1 John 1:6	

Calvinism says that if the Scriptures imply that one has lost his faith, he was never saved in the first place. That is the only conclusion—or excuse—that can be manufactured to explain that there are those who *appear* to be saved but now are not. Within the passages above, we have the case of Simon the Sorcerer in Acts 8. Philip was preaching and baptizing people in Samaria, including Simon. Peter and John were also sent to lay hands on others so that they could receive the gift of the Holy Spirit; most likely this included Simon as well. For whatever reason, Simon decides to offer the apostles money to have them give to him the same power they had to bestow gifts from the Holy Spirit. Peter pulls no punches, telling him that he can perish along with his silver, that he has no part in this matter, that his heart is not right before God, that he is in the "gall of bitterness and the bond of iniquity," and that he needs to immediately repent and pray that God will forgive him. From all appearances, Simon was a Christian even having received the gift of the Holy Spirit … and was in danger of losing it. We can lose our assurance as well. To say that Simon (or anyone) was "not saved in the first place" is allowing man to establish a judgment or a "truth" that apparently inspired men of God (God Himself) did not acknowledge.

In fact, the entire message of the Hebrew letter is framed as "Don't go back!" The author repeatedly warns them of losing the salvation they have in Christ if they go back into Judaism. Depending on how you count, he does this 13 or 14 times within the 13 chapters. If it was not a possibility to lose their salvation, why does he spend so much time telling them it is?

Two other passages from the chart above need examination particularly for their relevant wording. In Hebrews 6:4–6, the Hebrew writer stresses once again (after his Israel comparison in Chapters 3 and 4) the possibility of Christians losing their salvation. The words concerning those who have "once been enlightened and have tasted of the heavenly gift and have been made partakers of the Holy Spirit" sound convincingly that these folks were in a saved condition. He goes on, saying that they, "have tasted the good word of God and the powers of the age to come." But then he says, "And then have fallen away," they "again crucify to themselves the Son of God and put Him to open shame." Falling from a state of salvation *crucifies Christ all over again*, because you are rejecting the only means of salvation available to you. Notice the phrasing, they have "fallen away." You cannot fall *from* something you never had, were never on, or were never in.

Last, let's look at Galatians 5:4. In the first three verses of this chapter, Paul is telling these Christians to not go back into the "yoke of slavery" by going back to Judaism. If you do, he says this in Verse 4: "You have been severed from Christ, you who are seeking to be justified by the Law; you have fallen from grace." I do not know how you cannot equate "losing your salvation" with "falling from grace." How can you be severed from something of which you were never a part? Taking all of what I have said and offered on this point, how can anyone believe the opposite? Why would they? It is puzzling. You have to meet certain conditions to *get saved*; why wouldn't you have to meet certain conditions to *remain saved*?

Chapter 17

Preeminence of Peter

Many believe that Peter was something special among the apostles; some have even built their religious organizational superstructure on the assertion that Jesus pointed him out as being the "foundation" on which the early church was built. In this section, I will examine the source of this belief and practice to determine if that passage, indeed, teaches what some say it does about the "preeminence" of Peter.

Peter, the Leader

Before getting into any particular passage that may or may not point to Peter as any sort of foundation for the church, it must be acknowledged that he was, indeed, a leader—vocally if not even in other ways. There are several points to which I can allude to establish this.

First, John 1:40 tells us that Andrew (Peter's brother) is one of the two who first speak to Jesus after John the Baptist points Him out as "the Lamb of God." He and likely the gospel writer John, the "other disciple" of John the Baptist, follow Jesus, speak to Him, and go to where He is staying and talk with Him the rest of the day. Andrew brings his brother to Jesus, Simon Peter, after telling him, "We have found the Messiah." At that first encounter, Jesus tells Simon (his given name) that he will be called "Cephas." Luke (6:14) tells us "Peter." Both *Cephas* (Aramaic) and *Peter* (Greek) mean "rock"; throughout the gospels, Jesus refers to this individual by each of these two names, depending on the circumstance. *Simon* is used when Peter has done something that needs correcting or a rebuke; *Peter* is used when Jesus appears to be reminding him of what he ought to be: a rock. Jesus may have had "nicknames" for all of the apostles; we do not know. We do know the only other ones to receive something of this nature later were James and John who He called the "Sons of Thunder." (Well, we do have the various descriptions Jesus offers on Judas Iscariot, but the point is made; "Son of Perdition" is not really a friendly nickname.)

In Matthew's listing of the Twelve, he says, "Now the names of the 12 apostles are these: The first, Simon, who is called Peter." Interestingly, the Greek word used here for "first" is *protos*—and it does not refer to simply being first in the listing of the Twelve. Lexicons suggest "chief" or even "first in rank or influence." Indeed, in every listing (Matthew 10; Mark 3; Luke 6; and Acts 1) of the apostles, Peter's name comes first in the list. This is interesting as you might ask why—unless it is to point out that he, in some way, holds a position of importance among the group. It could be that he is the most outspoken and provides Jesus with so much "teaching material" that spawns from Peter's sometimes hasty responses to questions Jesus might ask. As a result, Peter, more than any other apostle, consumes text. We learn more about Peter than any other of the original 12 apostles. We have one-on-one conversations between Jesus and Peter. Other conversations, even though directed to an individual, appear to be in the presence of the group at large. Finally, there is the situation in the courtyard during the trial of Jesus where Peter denies the very Savior (he asserted earlier) he would defend to his death.

In addition to these bits of information, we also have Peter not only vocally leading the group following the ascension of Jesus, but he initiates the process for replacing Judas (Acts 1:15–26), speaking before a group of about 120 who had gathered in that upper room. He reviews the situation surrounding Judas and the qualification that his potential replacements must have been witnesses with them from the beginning until He departed. Matthias was selected. Another piece of support for Peter is that, although all of the apostles spoke in their variously assigned foreign languages preaching the same message as Peter was, it was Peter's sermon that is recorded on the Day of Pentecost (Acts 2). Just an observation. However, the next several chapters follow the activities of Peter and John who had apparently paired together for their early preaching efforts. There is a quote in Ch. 6 about appointing seven men to relieve the load of the apostles. It does not say that it is Peter, but it would not be a surprise to find out that it was. He, if any character, had received the most attention and appeared in more than one way to be the leader of the group and maybe even the effort to establish the church in Jerusalem.

With all of this said and recounted, we would have to acknowledge that Peter played a significant role in both the gospels and in the early chapters of the book of Acts. Some point to the unfounded contention that he was a bit older than the rest of the group. Regardless, he was a leader. Every group needs a leader for a variety of reasons, and Peter filled that role for the apostles and the early church. He apparently had the personality, the initiative, and the respect of the others to carry out this responsibility (self-assigned, likely) with all the skill of any natural leader. It does not mean, however, that Peter is any more important than any of the other apostles or that he holds any special or official (God-appointed) "status" in the first century church or any time thereafter.

The Rock: Peter or His Confession?

In Matthew 16, the Pharisees and Sadducees continued to push Jesus and test him; in this case they are asking for a sign of some sort that He is the Messiah. He has just completed a number of miracles (in the previous chapter) and He criticizes them for simply seeking a sign, saying, "An evil and adulterous generation wants a sign; and so a sign will not be given to it, except the sign of Jonah." This is an obvious reference to an earlier statement by Him in Matthew 12:40 where He compares the three days Jonah spent in the belly of the "sea monster" to His upcoming three days of being buried before His resurrection. Jesus tells His disciples (likely, the Twelve) to beware the "leaven of the Pharisees and Sadducees"; the text tells us they understand this as the influence of the *teaching* that comes from these groups.

Jesus later asks His disciples "Who do people say that the Son of Man is?" (Matthew 16:13). They offer that some say John the Baptist, others say Elijah, and still others Jeremiah or one of the prophets. He responds, "But who do you say that I am?" Peter, who seems to never be at a loss for words or for jumping in without thinking first, says this: "You are the Christ, the Son of the living God." In this particular case, Peter's gut-level response was, as they say, *spot on*. Whether absorbed from things Jesus had said about Himself or simply what he had come to conclude based on what he had observed—or both—Peter's response stirred Jesus to offer the following:

> Blessed are you, Simon Barjona, because flesh and blood did not reveal this to you, but My Father who is in heaven. And I also say to you that you are Peter, and upon this rock I will build My church; and the gates of Hades will not overpower it. I will give you the keys of the kingdom of heaven; and whatever you bind on earth shall have been bound in heaven, and whatever you loose on earth shall have been loosed in heaven (Matthew 16:17–19).

Let's unpack what Jesus has said here to His 12 apostles, as this passage appears to be where those who believe in the preeminence of Peter would turn for support.

The first part is, indeed, aimed directly at and addressed to Peter. Jesus says that he is blessed in this confession and the reason is that it has been revealed to him not by man but by God. Listening to man produces that "leaven of the Pharisees and Sadducees" noted above, and they certainly did not believe what Peter had asserted. Listening to God—opening one's heart to the Truth—produces statements such as this professing that Jesus is, for sure, the Son of God. Truth—with a capital "T"—about anything spiritual begins with an open mind that is receptive to the Word that can be planted there (Mark 4:1–20). So, our first point is that Jesus is targeting what Peter has said in his response to the question, rather than Peter himself. The *assertion* that Jesus is the Son of God is what is important.

Jesus then says something strange: "And I also say to you that you are Peter." He addresses him as Simon Barjona (son of Jonah, literally) first and yet says, "You are Peter." Was this a special christening of some sort lionizing the name Peter over how He had initially addressed him? Greek lexicons will tell you that the name *Peter* means "rock or stone"—even a *small rock or stone*—and others elaborate this way: *a piece of rock; a stone; a single stone; movable, insecure, shifting, or rolling.* Abraham means "father of nations"; Isaac means "laughter"; John means "Jehovah has shown favor." Names in Biblical times had meaning, and names assigned at birth usually had special meaning for the parents. Immanuel means "God with us." The name *Peter* in Greek means "a rock or a stone."

After saying "You are Peter," (more discussion below) Jesus then says, "and upon this rock I will build my church." The Greek word for "Peter" is *petros*, and the Greek word used for "rock" (used here by Jesus) is *petra*. Those same Greek lexicons tell us these are two different words, to begin with, but there is more. The Greek word for *rock* means "a rock; a cliff; a projecting rock; mother rock; huge mass; solid formation; fixed; immovable; enduring." I cannot find the original sources for these definitions, but any Greek dictionary or lexicon will tell you essentially the same. Also, in the Greek (and other languages), words have gender assigned to them. *Petros* is masculine; *petra* is feminine.

What appears to be happening here is that Jesus is making a play on words. (I can almost see the others smile or hear them chuckle as He makes this connection.) He is using the *meaning* of Peter's name and transferring that *meaning* to a similar word for something stronger and much more enduring than Peter himself. Jesus was not averse to using the language in this unique way to make a memorable point. In John 12:25, He says, "The one who loves his life loses it, and the one who hates his life in this world will keep it to eternal life." *Life* as two meanings here and Jesus plays on that to make the distinction between physical life and eternal life. Some point out the different words for *love* used by Jesus in John 21:15–17 when He is asking Peter if he loves Him as another instance where Jesus is pointing out something special about the words used. In our text, Jesus is obviously making a play on the fact that Peter "is a small rock" but the (big) *rock* on which His church is founded is something larger, more substantial, and more enduring.

If indeed Jesus wanted at this point to establish Peter as that rock on which the church would be built, He could have easily said something to the effect of, "and upon *you* I will build my church." He doesn't. Peter, neither before (Matthew 16:23; 26:58–76) nor after receiving the Holy Spirit (Galatians 2:11–13), displayed any special discernment or behavior that qualified him for such an honor. His abilities and responsibilities were identical to each of the other apostles, from everything we can derive from Scripture. Also, if Jesus were designating Peter as something special in these verses, there would have been no discussion about who would be the greatest in the kingdom that occurred more than once among them (Mark 9:33; 10:20–28, 41). They even do this in the presence of Jesus at the Last Supper just before they leave and go to the Garden where the events that led up to His crucifixion begin.

The true "rock" on which the church would be built was none other than Jesus Christ (1 Corinthians 3:11; 10:4; Ephesians 2:20; 1 Peter 2:6). The confession that Peter made—"You are the Christ, the Son of the living God"—was merely a statement that Jesus was that rock and that foundation, which Jesus points out. Yet, those who advocate that Peter was being anointed in some special way will also point out that Jesus told him that he would be given the "keys to the kingdom" (the church) and "whatever you bind on earth will be bound in heaven and whatever you loose will be loosed in heaven." In other words, whomever He was speaking to would have the same authority He had while on earth; they would be speaking for Him and for God who could assure these "bindings." Was He speaking only to Peter, or once He had used His play on words, was He now speaking to all the apostles? Were these words not true of all of them and not just Peter?

If what Jesus was saying would happen was indeed this authority they would eventually possess, once endowed with the Holy Spirit that He promises will come to them (John 16:13), that did occur on the Day of

Pentecost in Acts 2:1–13. Although Peter's sermon was recorded on that day for us, it is clear that the other eleven apostles were also teaching and preaching the same message (2:4, 6–8, 13). His instruction to the apostles at other times, as well, suggest that what they say through inspiration will be the same as if He Himself had said it. He is not speaking specifically to Peter in Matthew 18:18 when He says, "Truly I say to you, whatever you bind on earth shall have been bound in heaven; and whatever you loose on earth shall have been loosed in heaven." He also tells them after His resurrection that they will be able to forgive sins: "If you forgive the sins of any, their sins have been forgiven them; if you retain the sins of any, they have been retained."

These are the "keys to the kingdom" that *all* of the Twelve were prophesied by Jesus to receive. The power to work miracles, teach on His behalf, have the same authority He had … these were the weapons against which the "gates of Hades" could not even overcome. Peter, although likely the oldest of the apostles and, for sure, the most outspoken of the group, was indeed a leader among the Twelve. His and John's early work and adversity are presented following the establishment of the church. His name comes first when listing them possibly suggesting some sort of pecking order—or closeness to Jesus—among the group. Jesus singles him out just prior to His crucifixion—knowing that Peter would deny even knowing Him—to encourage Peter to return and be strong following that display of weakness (John 21:15–17).

Peter was indeed special, at least in some ways, among the apostles. However, there is no Scriptural support for the notion that he, in any way, was appointed "the first" anything as he and the other apostles established the kingdom on this earth and spread the Gospel for which the Son of God lived, died, and was risen to afford us forgiveness of our sins.

Chapter 18

Miracles and Spiritual Gifts

The first century was a very special period in the history of mankind. The Roman government and their various Caesars had ruled Europe and the middle east for at least a few centuries. There was relative peace, and when disturbances arose or rebellions occurred, Rome was quick to put them down. From a cultural standpoint, Greek was a commonly spoken language with Aramaic still spoken from time to time among the Jews. Greek was an extremely precise language that touches us still today as we attempt to understand God's Word in its proper context. In addition to the peace that Rome afforded, there were also improvements in transportation and communication during this time.

Paul, in Galatians 4:4–5, says,

> But when the fullness of the time came, God sent His Son, born of a woman, born under the Law, so that He might redeem those who were under the Law, that we might receive the adoption as sons and daughters.

This "fullness of time" notion suggests that it was the *perfect time* for God to fulfill the promises made to Satan (Genesis 3:15), to Abraham (Genesis 12:3), and through all those prophets who spoke of Messiah that was to appear one day in the future. That which was begun in the Garden of Eden, and corrupted through the sinful nature of man, would now have its rectification through the redemption of man and his reconciliation to God through His Son. God sent Jesus to be "the

Christ"—that Messiah promised—to save man from his sins and provide a hope of eternal salvation to him, if he would just obey.

However, even the Son of God would need something special if He were to get people to listen to Him. Just proclaiming He was the Son of God would do Him no good, and He readily admits this in John 5:31. "If I alone bear witness of Myself, My testimony is not true." Of course, it WAS true, but His point was that others would not believe it without supplemental confirmation (like at least a second witness—Matthew 18:16) to support who He was and that it was God who had sent Him. In that chapter, He mentions four things that "testify" of Him and that He is who He says He is. He mentions the preaching of John, the testimony of the Father, the testimony of the Scriptures (prophecies that He would completely fulfill), and He mentions His works. "But the testimony I have is greater than the testimony of John; for the works which the Father has given Me to accomplish—the very works that I do—testify about Me, that the Father has sent Me." These "works" are noted elsewhere in Scripture as "wonders" or as "miracles" or as "signs."

Miracles

The Latin word for *miracle* means "to wonder at." We wonder at miracles because they, by definition, are unnatural, supernatural, or beyond our range of experience and our ability to physically explain or bring into effect. Merriam/Webster dictionary says that a miracle is "an extraordinary event manifesting divine intervention in human affairs." When God set things into motion in Genesis 1 and pronounced it all "very good" (Genesis 1:31), that "natural order" continued until He or one of His agents interrupted that order for a specific purpose. Miracles were not indiscriminately thrown out; each was planned, was targeted, and had a message behind it. When what had become second nature to man (e.g., the sun rising and setting, the earth holding together, land and sea remaining separate entities, etc.) suddenly no longer existed, it got his attention and he knew, for a fact, that something unnatural or *super*natural was taking place.

In the Hebrew language, the word for *miracle* is *nes*, referring to "something raised up or elevated." That which is elevated above or outside normal circumstances is certainly supernatural and can only have divine origins. "The Miracle on Ice" is a description given to the match where the U.S. Hockey Team defeated the Russian Hockey Team in the 1980 Winter Olympics. Given the history of success (or lack of where the U.S. was concerned) for the two teams, betting against the Russians would have been foolish. Yet, the Americans won, and thus "The Miracle on Ice" is forever engraved in sports history. The point is that we sometimes toss around this word casually and use it in many ways in which it was never intended. On the other hand, there are some of us who use it in its correct sense—stating that God has intervened in the natural order. Unfortunately, we sometimes have erroneously attached special significance to a circumstance or situation that we cannot explain.

To put it bluntly, the time of miracles has passed. Miracles do not happen today. There was a time when they were needed and provided by God. That purpose has been fulfilled and completed. There is no further need for miracles. Before I look at passages that tell us this, let's look at the words and their meanings related to these supernatural events. This will help us understand why they no longer are needed nor exist. Vine's provides us the following from the original Greek. The Greek word for *miracle* is *dunamis*: "power, inherent ability, is used of works of a supernatural origin and character, such as could not be produced by natural agents and means." For *signs*, the Greek word is *semeion* and means "a sign, mark, indication, token of Divine authority and power." *Wonders* in Greek (*teras*) means "something strange, causing the beholder to marvel, is always used in the plural (wonders) and generally follows 'signs.'" So, a sign appeals to our understanding; a wonder appeals to our imagination; and a miracle indicates its source as supernatural.

The New Testament tells us that these individuals were able to work miracles: Jesus, the 72 disciples appointed by Jesus in Luke 10, the apostles (including Paul), and a few others (e.g., those casting out demons in Jesus's name—Mark 9:38; Stephen—Acts 6:8; possibly the companions of Paul in his preaching; etc.). However, these miracles were never intended to simply improve the lot of the one or ones on whom the miracles were performed. Yes, it did accomplish that, especially when the miracle was a healing of some sort or a raising from the dead. Yet, the healing—any miracle, in reality—was a way to get the audience's attention so that a *particular message* or an *overarching message* could be delivered.

The *message* was what was important. When Jesus commissions the 72 (Luke 10), He tells them to "Heal those who are sick" but adds also, "and tell them the kingdom of God has come near to you." Without the accompanying message, any of these gifted messengers would have been better described as *doctors with special healing powers* rather than special emissaries of God. Jesus tells us why miracles were incorporated within His ministry in John 5 (noted above), and that is re-emphasized in John 20:30–31 [my emphasis].

> So then, many other signs Jesus also performed in the presence of the disciples, which are not written in this book; but *these have been written so that you may believe* that Jesus is the Christ, the Son of God; and that by believing you may have life in His name.

It was this *overarching message* that Jesus was the Son of God that was important. The miracles were evidence of this truth, but they were incidental to the larger point being made. There are other passages, however, that tell us why miracles were used.

In Mark 16:15–18, Jesus commissions His apostles after He had risen from the dead and told them to "preach the gospel to all creation." He tells them that they will also have as evidence (that He has sent them out) the same types of miracles He performed in His ministry. Mark, in Verse 20 then says this: "And they went out and preached everywhere, while the Lord worked with them, and *confirmed the word* by the signs that followed." The emphasis is mine again but notice exactly what those signs (miracles and wonders) did for them. It told the *receivers* of the miracles that they were also the *hearers* of the words spoken, and it was the Gospel that was what was important for them. The power that granted them the ability to work miracles was the same power behind the message.

The establishment of the church started with a perfect example of all of this. In Acts 2, we find the apostles gathered together and the Holy Spirit descends upon them. A noise from heaven like a "violent, rushing wind" filled the house, tongues like fire rested on each of them, and they began speaking in other languages. This was the miracle that shortly gets the attention of all in attendance there in Jerusalem on Pentecost. The all-important message then followed: You have crucified the Son of God; repent and be baptized for the remission of your sins. This two-pronged approach—miracle and message—was initiated by Jesus and carried on by the apostles in carrying out their charge from Jesus. It was also effective; the church began with an overwhelming response and continued to grow accordingly.

Paul, in his first letter to the church at Thessalonica, said this in 1 Thessalonians 1:5: "Our gospel did not come to you in word only, but also in power and in the Holy Spirit and with full conviction; just as you know what kind of men we proved to be among you for your sakes." Paul essentially quotes Jesus in John 5 when he says that our words would likely not have been enough to convince you of our message. It took "power and the Holy Spirit"—i.e., miracles—to prove to you who we were, from Whom we came, and that our message was Truth.

Finally, on this point, we have the Hebrew writer offering the same rationale for this connection between the words spoken and the miracles performed in Hebrews 2:1-4 [the emphasis is mine]:

> For this reason we must pay much closer attention to what we have heard, so that we do not drift away from it. For if the word spoken through angels proved unalterable, and every violation and act of disobedience received a just punishment, how will

we escape if we neglect so great a salvation? After it was at first spoken through the Lord, it was *confirmed* to us by those who heard, God also testifying with them, both *by signs* and *wonders*, and by *various miracles* and by *gifts of the Holy Spirit* according to His own will.

He first stresses the importance of staying true to that which has been preached to them, saying that condemnation will result if they do not. He then mentions that this message was first spoken by Jesus and then *confirmed* and *testified* by God to them through signs, wonders, miracles, and gifts of the Holy Spirit. Again, the miracles were confirmation, proof, verification, authentication, etc. that they were indeed from God. Again, those wonders were not what was important; it was the *message* they brought affording them salvation that was critical.

This last quote emphasizes something that was noted above. The apostles not only could work miracles; they also had the power from the Holy Spirit to lay their hands on new Christians and allow them at least some measure of this power they possessed. Yes, the apostles are promised that the Holy Spirit (the Comforter—John 14:26; 15:13) will come to them and guide them into all truth—and this indeed happens in Acts 2—but they will also be able to impart "gifts of the Holy Spirit to others." What were these spiritual gifts; what was their purpose; how did they work; to whom were they given? Let's address these questions next.

Spiritual Gifts

Part of that which the Holy Spirit would provide to the apostles was the ability to impart "spiritual gifts" or "gifts of the Holy Spirit." The Holy Spirit inspired the apostles and the writers of the New Testament so that they could deliver God's word to mankind with the content and in the ways He desired. His Word will never pass away (Matthew 24:35), so He wanted it to be something that would be enduring and meaningful regardless of the time in the future when people would encounter it. The apostles were limited in number; there were only 12 of them with the specific commission to take the Gospel starting in "Jerusalem, and all Judea and Samaria, and even to the remotest pat of the earth" (Acts1:8). Sometimes they worked in pairs (e.g., Peter and John), but history and tradition tell us they fanned out to cover the area prescribed in their charge from Jesus. Paul, a thirteenth (actually "fourteenth" as Judas had been replaced by Matthias) appointment as an apostle, covered considerable territory establishing churches and appointing elders to lead them. He also had several companions (Aristarchus, Barnabas, Epaphras, Gaius, Jason, Sopater, John Mark, Luke, Onesimus, Silas, Timothy, and others) along the way to help him and often were left in places while he went on to another destination. Even with this help, Paul and his helpers could not be everywhere; something else was needed to sustain the new Christians in their absence. Apparently, these gifts of the Holy Spirit filled the void.

The best list of exactly what gifts were given is provided in 1 Corinthians 12:1–11. What won't be provided in this writing is a detailed explanation of each of these, their purposes, how they differed, and their relationships. That is for someone else at another time and place. My purpose here is to show the reader that these did, in fact, exist and were byproducts of being inspired of God for the purpose of revelation. The list in 1 Corinthians 12 includes variety but "all from the same Spirit" (12:4); some point to a couple of others in Verse 28 and some groups list as many as 25 spread out across other passages. Again, exposure to the concept and how it relates to this topic is my concern here. The list in 1 Corinthians 12 contains the following:

- The word of wisdom
- The word of knowledge
- Faith
- Healing
- Miracles
- Prophecy
- The distinguishing of spirits
- Various tongues (languages)
- The interpretation of tongues

We are first introduced to these gifts (in process and practice) in the early church in Acts 6 when the apostles laid their hands on the seven who had been identified as those who would serve the apostles in more mundane tasks so the apostles could attend to "prayer and the ministry of the word" (Acts 6:4). We are told in the previous verse that these men were to be "full of the Spirit and of wisdom." The next verses focus on Stephen—one of the seven—to say that he was "full of grace and power" and "was performing wonders and signs among the people" (Acts 6:8). He also demonstrated apparently miraculous wisdom and the ability to speak with the Spirit when confronted a few verses later (6:10).

We find the next mention of these gifts in Acts 8 where Philip had been preaching with considerable success in Samaria. Apparently, this Philip was one of those seven set aside to help the apostles back in Acts 6, but he was not an apostle himself. He was, however, able to perform miracles, as Acts 8:13 suggests. Word of Philip's success spread to the apostles in Jerusalem, and they sent Peter and John to Samaria so that these new Christians "could receive the Holy Spirit" (8:15). It is worthy of note that Verses 16 and 17 explicitly state, "For as yet He had fallen upon none of them. They had only been baptized in the name of the Lord Jesus. Then they laid hands on them, and they received the Holy Spirit." Philip, while he had been able to use miracles to confirm his words—just as the apostles were doing—could not lay hands on the new converts so that they could receive the Holy Spirit. Only true apostles could do this, and they did here.

It is also noteworthy, at this point, that Simon was so impressed with this power that he offered the apostles money so that he could have that same power they had to pass these powers on to others. That was a mistake. As they point out to him very pointedly, this is a spiritual matter, not a physical one, and that he, Simon, needs to repent and pray to God before he loses his soul. He apparently does so and asks them to do the same on his behalf. The larger point to take from this passage, however, is the sequencing of what occurred and what acts produced what outcomes. Receiving the Word and being baptized put them into Christ and saved their souls. However, to receive the gifts of the Holy

Spirit, an apostle of Jesus Christ had to lay hands on one who had otherwise already been obedient to the Gospel.

One other passage needs examination before continuing with this thought. In the latter part of Acts 18, we are introduced to Apollos, who was an impressive individual and was teaching all he knew about Jesus; his limitation was that he only knew the baptism of John. By this time, obviously, the church had been established and the "kingdom" that John proclaimed was "at hand" had indeed already come. Word traveled slowly in those days and Apollos apparently hadn't heard about the events on the Day of Pentecost. We are told that Priscilla and Aquila (acquaintances of Paul) heard Apollos and took him aside and taught him "the way of God more accurately" (Acts 18:26). We might assume that he also was re-baptized at this point when we consider what occurs in the next chapter.

At the beginning of Acts 19, Paul encounters a group who, like Apollos, had only heard of the baptism of John. He asks them if they had been able to experience what others elsewhere were in receiving "the Holy Spirit." Their response is that they hadn't even heard that the Holy Spirit even existed, let alone that it had done anything for them. Paul explained that John's baptism only addressed the coming of the Christ and His kingdom. It makes one wonder if they had even heard about Jesus and His completed mission. They were then baptized "in the name of Jesus." One would conclude from this that their initial baptism was deficient in some way as Paul apparently authorizes their second baptism. But notice what Paul does next: "And when Paul had laid hands upon them, the Holy Spirit came on them and they began speaking with tongues and prophesying" (Acts 19:6). Again, belief, then baptism. It was only after Paul laid his hands on them that they received the Holy Spirit and then began to speak in tongues and prophesy.

A Pattern for Us Today?

There are those who take Acts 2:38 and use it to teach that everyone who is baptized for the remission of sins will receive the "gift of the

Holy Spirit" mentioned there as being the same gifts mentioned in the two cases above. Either we have two different processes for receiving these "gifts" mentioned in Acts 8 and Acts 19, or we are looking at two different interpretations of the word "gift." Some view the gift in Acts 2:38 to be identical with those gifts detailed in 1 Corinthians 12. Others view it to be merely the salvation that comes when one renders obedience to those things required in Scripture to become a child of God. Yet others are somewhere between these two and hold that at our baptism, something special happens other than our sins being remitted. In some way, they say, the Holy Spirit enters us and works in tandem with our knowledge of God's Word to provide guidance and control in our lives of service to God.

I will not attempt to go any deeper on this topic than where I have gone at this point, other than to say that I am confident that it *does not mean* that upon our baptism we will receive the special and miraculous gifts of the Spirit noted elsewhere (Acts 6, Acts 8, 1 Corinthians 12). Aside from the two-step process early Christians went through when receiving these gifts (1—baptism and 2—laying on of apostle's hands), there are other reasons why I believe that Acts 2 does not teach that baptism produces special gifts of the Holy Spirit that extend to us today. Also, the next chapter in this reading delves into this particular aspect of the Holy Spirit in more detail.

The Word Is Confirmed

The revelation of the Gospel was occurring in real time in the first century. Once Jesus ascended back to His Father, the apostles were left to deliver the Gospel to those areas designated by Jesus in Acts 1:8. The Holy Spirit supplied them with the power to work miracles—just as the Father had supplied Jesus with the same—so that the message being delivered could demonstrate the same supernatural source, that being God in heaven. This continued until the Word of which they testified had been completely delivered. When that time had come, then the miracles—*that existed only to confirm the Word*—would cease, having performed the purpose for which they came into being in the first place. There are several places we can go to prove this.

In the first letter to the Corinthians, Paul spends a good deal of time on those spiritual gifts discussed above. Starting in 12:1, he appears to be answering another of the questions they had sought from him which had prompted the writing of this letter. He says, "Now concerning the spiritual gifts, brethren I do not want you to be unaware." He then goes on to list those gifts (also noted above). In the remainder of Chapter 12 and in 14, he addresses how these gifts should work together, and that no one should gloat due to their particular gift nor look down upon those who had a different gift. His point was the same that he made back at the beginning of this letter:

> So that there may be no division in the body, but that the parts may have the same care for one another. And if one part of the body suffers, all the parts suffer with it; if a part is honored, all the parts rejoice with it. Now you are Christ's body, and individually parts of it (1 Corinthians 12:25–27).

In Chapter 14, he talks about the differences among these gifts and even sets up conditions for how and when they can be used. He stresses that all of these are for *edification* (14:26) so that the church can be built up and concludes with, "But all things must be done properly and in an orderly way" (14:40).

Chapter 13 of 1 Corinthians is wedged between these two chapters that appear to be devoted to specifics concerning the endowment with, the differences between, and the orderly employment of these spiritual gifts by the early church. After his explanation in Chapter 12, as well as laying out various "appointments" in the church (12:28), he says this: "And yet, I am going to show you a far better way." He then begins Chapter 13.

Christians and scholars of the New Testament know this chapter as Paul's explanation on the preeminence of *love* and how it is more important than any spiritual gift, even more important than faith and hope. It is reminiscent of when Jesus cited the First and Second Commandments (those that supersede all others) when called to point out the most important commandment. It seems that within the context, Paul is chiding them for valuing one gift over another to the point where it was causing friction among them. Wedged in between these two "rulebooks" for spiritual gifts (Chapters 12 and 14), he pauses to emphasize how important love is and what part it plays in the process. He starts off by saying,

> If I speak with the tongues of men and of angels, but do not have love, I have become a noisy gong or a clanging cymbal. And if I have the gift of prophecy, and know all mysteries and all knowledge; and if I have all faith, so as to remove mountains, but do not have love, I am nothing. And if I give all my possessions to feed the poor, and if I deliver my body to be burned, but do not have love, it profits me nothing.

As impressive as these gifts were and in spite of all the good they did in revealing truth, they helped the ones possessing them *only if their use was framed by and encapsulated in love*. Again, he was discouraging division based on these differences and attempting to focus them on the real reason they were bestowed in the first place. Corinth apparently had a problem with allegiances to both people and spiritual things (1 Corinthians 1:10–13; 3:1–9). Paul was attempting to alter their inclinations and their focus. However, within his larger effort here, he reveals some things about inspiration in general and specifically about these spiritual gifts.

Starting in 1 Corinthians 13:8, he says, "Love never fails; but if there are gifts of prophecy, they will be done away with; if there are tongues, they will cease; if there is knowledge, it will be done away with." What are you saying, Paul? These gifts will not continue indefinitely? There is a *shelf life*, so to speak, on them? When will that happen, Paul, and why? He then says, "For we know in part and prophesy in part; but *when the perfect comes*, the partial will be done away with" (13:9). [My emphasis] We noted above that these gifts were to supplement the revelation being received from the apostles and other inspired individuals. What Paul is saying is that God's larger revelation of His *entire* Truth is *partial* in its delivery *at this time*; it is both progressive and incremental. The Old Testament was designed to be an introduction to His final plan, and as such, insufficient in and of itself; more was needed: His New Covenant. Similarly, this period of revelation taking place in the first century—complete with signs, miracles, and wonders as evidence—was also preliminary to a period where complete and final revelation would take place. We don't have just one letter or one book in the New Testament that contains the entire picture. He has chosen to reveal it in "pieces" and delivered by different inspired men who have those pieces that contribute to the whole. Paul comes right out and says that he and others with inspired teaching had *parts of the whole* and they presented what they had. However, when the "perfect"—that which would contain the whole, the completed, the total—Word of God was delivered, there would be no further need for partial revelations delivered through these pieces and portions. More importantly for our purposes here, there would also be no further need for confirming miracles of *the partial* they were delivering.

So, one might ask the following, "So how much of the larger picture did Paul or any inspired speaker on God's behalf possess?" I cannot answer that question. If they had the larger picture, they were only allowed to share what the Spirit moved them to at the time. He does say that he *knew in part and was prophesying in part.* He does mention in Ephesians 3 the *mystery* that was revealed to him that had been hidden until the current time that they could now possess as well. However, this could refer to the fact that God's favor is now extended to Jews and Gentiles alike (3:6). But let's not lose Paul's larger point in mentioning this partial revelation.

He points to something that is coming that will do away with not only the incomplete conditions under which they struggled, but that it would also do away with the need for this continued "partial revelation" that was in effect. The "dimness" or "darkness" he mentions will be done away. What could that be except *complete and perfect revelation* available for all mankind now and in the future? Read these passages and see if you don't come to the conclusions I provide next (1 Timothy 2:4; John 8:32; 2 Peter 1:3; 2 Timothy 3:16–17; Hebrews 13:21; James 1:21–25; and Jude 1:3).

1. The knowledge of the Truth can save us if we "receive" (accept and act on) it.
2. The Truth sets us free from our sins and can keep us from "eternal death."
3. The Truth was sent by God and delivered through Jesus and inspired men.
4. The Truth contains everything we need for both life and godliness.
5. The Truth (past/present/future) thoroughly prepares, equips, and completes us.
6. The Truth equips us with every good work to do His will.
7. The Truth is God's <u>perfect</u> law of liberty (Greek: *teleios*—finished, complete, perfect).
8. The Truth (also "the faith") *has been* delivered "once and for all."

In Hebrews 2:3–4 we find these words spoken of "the word" in Verse 2:

> After it was at first spoken through the Lord, it was confirmed to us by those who heard, God also testifying with them, both by signs and wonders, and by various miracles and by gifts of the Holy Spirit according to His own will.

If God's will is indeed complete and no further revelation is necessary, then there is no further need to confirm anyone's words with "miracles and by gifts of the Holy Spirit." Paul tells us that all of these things will cease when that "which is perfect is come." James tells us we have the "perfect law of liberty" by which we can shape our lives through hearing it *and through doing it.*

I'll mention one more point on this topic. Warnings are included within Scripture about "adding to or taking away" from that which has been delivered and what will befall those who present "any gospel other than that which has been delivered" (Galatians 1:6–9; Colossians 2:8; 1 Peter 4:11; Revelation 22:18–19). Any new revelation would have to be the same we already have and would be redundant (see Chapter 8 above). No more need for revelation? No more need for special works to confirm it. Miracles and spiritual gifts served their function at the time and when they were needed. They are no longer needed, and Paul tells us this very clearly.

"Evidences" of the Holy Spirit Today

If God is still using the Holy Spirit today to do the things the Holy Spirit did in the first century, then the passages above about His Word being "finished, complete, and perfect" are wrong. If further revelation is needed for us to know God's will for mankind, then He didn't provide us with "*everything* that pertains to life and godliness" (2 Peter 1:3). If there are those claiming to possess the Holy Spirit today in the same way that those in the early church did, then these points follow:

1. There are apostles still around laying hands on these folks so they can receive the Holy Spirit, because that is the only way Scripture tells us He, the Holy Spirit, was imparted.
2. If people are supernaturally healing individuals today (they aren't), then God has changed the purpose and function of that which was so specially and divinely used in the first century to prove Jesus was His Son. Also, He has not indicated anywhere that He was going to make this change in purpose or process in function.
3. The Holy Spirit was provided as a testimony of a miraculous presence, and that a message of Truth would be forthcoming. Remember Paul's restriction of "edification" on any gift of the Spirit (1 Corinthians 14:26–33). If some new revelation—not just the repeating of something already revealed—is not presented, there is no need for the expression of the gift. As noted elsewhere in this writing, if it is *new*, it is *another Gospel* (Galatians 2:8–9); if it is the *same*, it is *redundant and not needed*.
4. Those claiming to possess the Holy Spirit today—really anytime after the first century—fall under the same trilemma with which

we are faced concerning our conclusions about Jesus of Nazareth. Our options are that He was the biggest liar this world has ever known; or He was a lunatic so deranged that He was willing to die for His imagined deity He claimed; or He was what He claimed and demonstrated to be, the Son of God. Only one of these is possible, and we are faced with that choice.

5. For those who claim to be inspired of the Holy Spirit—similar to or like the apostles were and speaking on God's behalf—we are left with the same choices: a) they are deceiving others for whatever reason; b) they are so emotionally charged that they are deluded into thinking they are speaking for God; or c) all of us better start following them as they have "the Words of Life" that Jesus offered to those who followed Him. If these are indeed from God, then we are in a new era of revelation and all that has come before is out the window. Jesus and His miracles brought in a new era accompanied by the power of God. How might our current miracle workers be different?

Paul tells us clearly in 1 Corinthians 13 that these gifts were for revelation. He says that when the need for revelation was complete, the need for these gifts was over and in the past. If God's Word is not His complete revelation—as it professes to be—then He has some explaining to do. My points above are not to make fun of or denigrate those who claim to do special works in modern times and to be possessed of the Holy Spirit to accomplish them. There are some realities that accompany such claims, however. Short of their providing a Scriptural explanation that their experience either is or is not like that of the first century Christian, I am reluctant to provide them a forum for doing what they do, supposedly in the name of Jesus.

So what is the Holy Spirit? If He is not doing today what He did back earlier, then what is His role with us today? The next chapter will deal with these questions and others that arise when the Holy Spirit is under consideration for us in current times.

Chapter 19

The Indwelling of the Holy Spirit

The foregoing chapter introduced us to the Holy Spirit and the notion of "gifts of the Spirit" provided to Christians during the time when the church began and spread. I made an argument that "gifts of the Spirit" were similar to the miracles Jesus and His messengers worked to confirm their proclamations about God and the Gospel. There is no record of 24/7 news cycles, videotape of miraculous events, or even audio recordings of Jesus and the apostles. Every event was circumscribed by the people performing the miracle and people witnessing it. Of course, there was word of mouth; but as we know, its general reliability is questionable and "seeing is believing" (See Thomas's statements in John 20:24–29).

Wherever the apostles went, they converted people to Christianity, established churches, appointed elders, and laid their hands on people so that the gifts of the Holy Spirit could exist and thrive among this new local body of Christ. We are not privy to the content of what the Holy Spirit revealed to these people. We do know that Jesus did many other miracles that are not recorded for us in Scripture (John 20:30–31; 21:25), and I have attempted to show that the inspired words spoken were the reason for the existence of the miracle that supported them. This is likely true for the apostles as well. We simply do not have every piece of revelation made to mankind during this all–important period of revelation of God's Word, nor do we have all of the miracles that supported it. Finally, we are not aware of the types of things that emerged from sessions where the Holy Spirit was in evidence among early Christians.

We can be sure, however, that what we do have is all that we need; I'll not repeat what is laid out elsewhere here concerning the all-sufficiency of Scripture. What we can say, however, is that what occurred in the first century with the Holy Spirit is very different than what occurs today with the Holy Spirit. We can conclude from Scripture that He is still active in our lives—if we will let Him—but how He manifests on a day-to-day basis bears little resemblance to His manifestation in the early church. So, what is He and what does He do for us today?

The Holy Spirit Then

This may be an understatement, but it appears that the role of the Holy Spirit both in the past and today involves our guidance for following God's will and thus pleasing Him. As noted elsewhere, we are told that the Spirit sent Jesus into the wilderness following His baptism to be tempted of Satan (Matthew 4:1). We are also told that the Spirit exerted strong influences on Paul as to where he would and would not preach in his travels (Acts 16:6–8).

In Jesus's final words to the apostles before His arrest, He tells them that after He is gone, He will send them the "Helper"—the Holy Spirit—who will teach them all things and bring to their remembrance everything He has said to them (John 14:26). He repeats this promise in 15:26 and calls Him "the Spirit of truth" so that they can bear witness of Him because They both (He and the Holy Spirit) proceed from the Father. At least one more time in His final words to them, He says in 16:13–15 the Spirit will "guide them into all truth" and "disclose to them" what the Father has revealed to both of Them (Jesus and the Spirit).

Jesus has told them earlier (Luke 12:11–12) that when they speak on His behalf and are brought before "the synagogue, the rulers, and the authorities," they should not be concerned about how they will handle that situation or what they will say. The reason? "The Holy Spirit will teach you in that very hour what you ought to say."

These were fantastic assurances for the men who would carry on the work that Jesus had begun in introducing mankind to "the kingdom"; they would establish that kingdom on the Day of Pentecost and be the mouthpiece of God to deliver "the apostles' teaching"—that which they were receiving continually from the Holy Spirit and that which was promised to them and delivered to them initially in Acts 2:1–4. Without this persistent guidance and influence, the church as we know it today would not exist—or at least God would have had to use some other means of putting it into effect. Matthew 18:18–20 suggests that as long as they were attuned to God's will and sought His direction, He would provide it. That was then, however, when the church was in its infancy, when revelation was incomplete, and when it needed regular and persistent revelation from God through the Holy Spirit.

But what about today? Isn't the revelation of God's Word complete? Don't we have the "perfect law of liberty"? Haven't we been provided "everything that pertains to life and godliness"? Hasn't it once and for all "been delivered to the saints"? The answer to all of these questions is a resounding "Yes!" So, does that mean the Holy Spirit's work is complete? The answer to that question is a resounding "No!" Let me explain.

The Holy Spirit Now

Before delving into how the Holy Spirit carries out His work today, let me acknowledge up front that among believers in God's Word, there is a difference of opinion on this topic. The question is not *whether* the Spirit influences us as we attempt to do God's will—He does—but *how* the Spirit influences us. Let me provide some background.

In Acts 2:38, Peter tells the crowd, convinced they have crucified the Son of God and stand condemned, to "Repent and let each of you be baptized in the name of Jesus Christ for the forgiveness of your sins; and you shall receive the gift of the Holy Spirit." Those who repent of their sins and are baptized for the remission/forgiveness of their sins *will receive* the "gift of the Holy Spirit." Is this the same as "*gifts* of the

Holy Spirit" of which I spoke in the previous chapter? Is it something different? Is it the Holy Spirit Himself—like I might tell an organization who just hired me that I am 100% theirs; hiring me means getting all of me. In other words, I am giving myself to them. Those who claim to follow God's Word most likely align themselves across all three of these options. However, they are distinct and cannot all be true.

What Does the Holy Spirit Do?

An Internet search will yield websites claiming anywhere from 50 to 70 things the Holy Spirit did and/or does—passages are provided to supposedly support these claims. As noted above, there were roles the Holy Spirit performed in the first century that are no longer needed today, so the focus in this writing at this point will be on the passages that suggest an *ongoing* role for this part of deity. It should be noted that a good portion of the things these lists claim about the Holy Spirit are those relegated to the time when the church was being established and the Spirit was operating more actively and physically in the lives and teaching of the apostles. The overall outcomes have not changed; however, the roles have simply been reduced to those that are relevant post-first century. The first part below will focus on the roles, and the second part will focus on what is entailed as these roles are performed.

What follows is a list of the roles the Holy Spirit is still performing today and is the combination of several sources on the Internet as well as an examination of references that contain "Holy Spirit" or "Spirit" (when implying the Holy Spirit) in the New Testament. A quick search in a concordance will reveal that "Holy Spirit" or "Spirit" has 376 entries in the New Testament. The Word of God is both living and active (Hebrews 4:12) and is revealed by the Spirit, who obviously is both living and active as well. Consider the following, which is lengthy but may not be exhaustive. The roles are arranged sequentially (by first passage listed) according to how the New Testament is ordered.

1. Provides us a "new birth" (John 3:8; Titus 3:5)
2. Convicts the world of sin, righteousness, and judgment (John 16:8)
3. Provides guidance for truth (John 16:13)
4. Glorifies and reveals Jesus and God (John 16:14–15)
5. Pours God's love into our hearts (Romans 5:5)
6. His law frees us from the law of sin and death—the Law of Moses (Romans 8:2)
7. Provides a path where we can walk acceptably (Romans 8:5)
8. Dwells in us and gives us life (Romans 8:11; 1 Corinthians 3:16; 2 Timothy 1:14)
9. Helps us put to death the deeds of the flesh (Romans 8:13)
10. Leads us (Romans 8:14; Galatians 5:18)
11. Testifies that we are children of God (Romans 8:16)
12. Provides us with love to strive together (Romans 15:30)
13. Functions as the entity by which we are baptized into Christ (1 Corinthians 12:13)
14. Operates as a pledge of inheritance from God (2 Corinthians 1:22; 5:5; Ephesians 1:13–14)
15. Helps us wait for our hope (Galatians 5:5)
16. Produces fruit in us (Galatians 5:22–23)
17. Grants everlasting life (Galatians 6:8)
18. Brings unity to God through Jesus (Ephesians 2:18)
19. Operates as a vehicle for becoming a dwelling place in God (Ephesians 2:22)
20. Provides an inner strength (Ephesians 3:16)
21. Seals us for redemption in Christ (Ephesians 4:30)
22. Fills us (Ephesians 5:18)
23. Provides joy in tribulation (1 Thessalonians 1:6)
24. Sanctifies us (2 Thessalonians 2:13; 1 Peter 1:2)
25. Informs us that we abide in Jesus if we keep His commandments (1 John 3:24; 4:13)
26. Helps us test false prophets (1 John 4:1–2)

As you can see, the Holy Spirit plays a decisive and integral role in Christianity today. If you consider that a great number of roles carried out during the establishment of the church in the first century have been omitted for our purposes here, it is evident that this part of deity has played and continues to play an extremely important function for the cause of Jesus Christ. Since the age of miracles has passed (detailed in the previous chapter), we must conclude that the Holy Spirit's activity is not something supernatural or outside the bounds of what we have termed "the natural order." If this is true, then exactly how does the Spirit accomplish His work in our lives? He is responsible for much, so there must be an explanation. The answer is in one of the groups of passages above. The Holy Spirit "dwells" within us (Romans 8:11; 1 Corinthians 3:16; 2 Timothy 1:14), and much of what is accomplished occurs through the inner strength He provides from a spiritual aspect.

The "Gift of the Holy Spirit"

I have discussed that God endowed the apostles and early Christians with the Holy Spirit to both work miracles to confirm their teaching and to reveal truth to a needy and an essentially uninformed body of believers (both potential and real). Truth—all that was included not only in the Gospel but also that of the "apostles' doctrine" of Acts 2:42—was an evolving body of knowledge and was being delivered by a number of actors who were designated to carry out this revelation of God's plan for the church. In His omniscient wisdom, God provided the Holy Spirit to carry out not only the revelation of God's will during the infancy of the church but to make sure of the unity of the message and the teachings of those assigned to deliver it. The apostles were granted this gift on the Day of Pentecost (Acts 2:1–13), and they passed on at least a portion of that gift through the laying on of their hands (see Acts 8:9–24).

Yet, Acts 2:38 tells us the following: "Peter said to them, 'Repent, and each of you be baptized in the name of Jesus Christ for the forgiveness of your sins; and you will receive the gift of the Holy Spirit.'" What was this "gift of the Holy Spirit" and is it relevant today? Let's look at some possibilities.

1. A first view of the gift of the Holy Spirit is that it was a **literal indwelling of the Spirit in the saved believer**. This interpretation will be addressed in the next section below. The *literal* indwelling of the Holy Spirit is fraught with contradictions and inconsistencies. We are told that other things "dwell within us" and we do not use a literal interpretation for those. The terms "abide" and "dwell" in the Greek are used interchangeably. Jesus tells those in attendance in John 6:48–58 that they would abide in Him and He in them, if they ate His flesh and drank His blood. There is much figurative content included here but notice that He *would abide in them*. Was this literal or in a more representative way? Consider also the following passages that suggest other "abidings": John 8:31; 14:19–21; 15:4; Romans 8:9; Colossians 3:16; 1 John 4:15–16. None of these would be interpreted as literal, yet many will say that the Holy Spirit of Acts 2:38 is indeed literal.
2. A second view is that this gift of the Holy Spirit is **the *outcome* of our obedience and conversion**. Call it salvation, redemption, forgiveness, justification, reconciliation, sanctification, etc.—all point to the eternal consequences of our obedience as the gift the Holy Spirit confers on all who obey the Gospel according to the pattern found in Scripture. Salvation occurs at the point we are immersed and raised in baptism. It is at that point that we contact the blood of Christ (Romans 6:3; Revelation 1:5), our sins are forgiven (Acts 22:16), and we are raised to walk in the "newness of life" (Romans 6:4; Colossians 2:12). It is a gift *from* the Holy Spirit.
3. A third view is that it was **the same that the apostles and others received, but it was only for the first century and the period when revelation was in progress**. In other words, the Holy Spirit part of Acts 2:38 does not apply to us today. The argument is that the construction of the sentence does mean that one cannot enjoy the benefits of the first part without receiving the second part. That second part died with the death of the last apostle or last inspired person who revealed God's Truth in one form or another. Every time the terms "gift" and "Holy Spirit" are used together, the miraculous is under consideration (Acts 8:19–20; 10:45–46; 11:17; Ephesians

3:7; 4:8). It would be inconsistent to take Acts 2:38 out of this group to mean something else. Same verbiage; same interpretation: the miraculous. Finally, high priests and members of the Jewish council questioned the apostles why they continued to preach when they had been told not to. Peter and the others said this [my emphasis]:

The God of our fathers raised up Jesus, whom you had killed by hanging Him on a tree. God exalted Him to His right hand as Prince and Savior, in order to grant repentance and forgiveness of sins to Israel. *We are witnesses of these things, and so is the Holy Spirit, whom God has given to those who obey Him*" (Acts 5:30–32).

The apostles had witnessed the salvation experienced by those who responded, but they also were witness to the Holy Spirit when He was given to those on whom they laid their hands. They could only witness what they could see and that would be miraculous manifestations of the Holy Spirit.

More is needed for a more convincing argument on Acts 2:38, but the question of the "indwelling of the Holy Spirit" is a very real concept and the subject of this chapter. So, let's move to that aspect of the work of the Holy Spirit. Some of what is covered will support the contentions noted just above.

How the Holy Spirit Dwells within Us

As noted above, the Scriptures teach us that more than just the Holy Spirit dwells within us. We have God, Jesus, the Word of Christ, sin, nothing good, etc. Yet, none of these is ever interpreted as a physical, literal entity that somehow resides within our human and mortal bodies. To set up the points made below about the Holy Spirit, let's first look at Paul's statement in Galatians 2:19–20. In his ongoing efforts to demonstrate to the Jews that he had "died to the Law," he asserted that it no longer informed his behavior, guided him spiritually or physically in any way, or held him to any conformity that had held him in the past. In fact, he says that it was "through the Law" that he could now "live for God" under new circumstances. Paul was a legal Jewish scholar, and he was now telling Jews everywhere what it was that informed him, guided him, and conformed him—and that was Christ Himself. He puts it this way:

> For through the Law I died to the Law, so that I might live for God. I have been crucified with Christ; and it is no longer I who live, but Christ lives in me; and the life which I now live in the flesh I live by faith in the Son of God, who loved me and gave Himself up for me.

Did you catch that? Paul later says that he had lived his life as a good Jew with an "entirely good conscience before God" (Acts 23:1). In other places, he tells his readers that he was "a Hebrew of Hebrews; as to the Law, a Pharisee; as to zeal, a persecutor of the church; as to the righteousness which is in the Law, found blameless" (Philippians 3:5–6). Paul was as good a Jew as could be found; the Law was as much a part of him as anything. He would probably tell you that the Law "lived within him" as much as anything, and it drove his behavior in all that he did—even to the point of putting Christians to death for their faith.

However, he was shown the light (literally—on the road to Damascus—and figuratively), and that Light (John 1:4–9) is now driving all that he thinks and does in his current, converted life. Like the Law "lived within him" and influenced everything he did, he says that now he has "been crucified with Christ." Literally, no, but he might as well have been. He has said "goodbye" to all he ever knew and achieved in the Jewish world (Philippians 3:8) and counted those things as rubbish, dross, or even dung (depending on the translation). Living for Christ now drives him just as strongly as he was driven by the Law earlier. He then makes the confession under consideration here: "It is no longer I who live, but Christ lives in me."

Would that be physically? No, not any more than the Law "living in him" and controlling his every breath. True, Paul was an inspired apostle, so the Holy Spirit was providing him with inspired words. However, Paul was just like the rest of us and wrestled with fleshly desires just like we do (Romans 7:14–25). The Holy Spirit did not—nor Jesus dwelling in him—prevent these struggles from taking place. Christ "living in" Paul is the same as Christ living in us. Paul was human and had free will to make moral and spiritual choices. His allegiance and devotion to Christ helped him through those times of weakness. If we are truly His, and we come anywhere close to the faithfulness that Paul exhibited in his teaching and sacrifices, then we have Christ living in us as well. His Word dwells in us (Colossians 3:16) and it drives our behavior, our decisions, our thoughts in idle times, etc. to the point where we are no longer in control of our actions; his Word has taken over our volition and shapes every decision we make. We can still sin, of course, but if Christ and His Word are dwelling in us (even, "richly"), then certainly we can approach the condition of which Paul speaks where he is out of the picture; Christ is now living in us and influencing all we do. This is not a literal in-dwelling; it is a spiritual or *representative* in-dwelling.

The Holy Spirit's in-dwelling is similar, if not talking about the same type of direct, spiritual influence. The Scriptures tell us that God, Jesus, the Holy Spirit, and God's Word all "dwell within us." Can anyone point to distinct (or even casual) differences in how these entities affect us as they dwell within us? I can't. There are no Greek words to provide us with even nuanced differences. I might also assert that you cannot have one without the other three. They are a "package," so to speak. To be driven by God living in us and guiding our behavior is the same as any or all of the other three doing the same. It simply means that who they are, what they stand for, and the truth they teach … that is what is "in us" and is driving us to be and do what Paul tells the Romans:

> Therefore I urge you, brothers and sisters, by the mercies of God, to present your bodies as a living and holy sacrifice, acceptable to God, which is your spiritual service of worship. And do not be conformed to this world, but be transformed

by the renewing of your mind, so that you may prove what the will of God is, that which is good and acceptable and perfect (Romans 12:1–2).

Those last few phrases are Paul's exact point back in Galatians 2. Neither the world nor the Old Law controls us anymore. We are not conformed to that which is no longer relevant for us. God's will is relevant, *and all that is relevant*, as we let it transform us into servants in bondage (Romans 1:1) to Christ, doing everything we can to be acceptable, good, and perfect in His eyes. Our minds have been "renewed" to the reality that serving the Lord is our prime directive in this life. Armed with this knowledge and awareness, we now let Him and His Word (*provided to us by the inspiration and direction of the Holy Spirit*) work in us, just as if it is no longer us in control, but Christ in control. Literally? No, but in a representative manner? Absolutely!

The formula is pretty simple: W + OH → TH → C/C. The Word, operating on an Open Heart (the good soil of Luke 8:8), produces a Transformed Heart, that ultimately produces a Conformity to His Word that Controls our very being. The in-dwelling of the Holy Spirit cannot be explained—from a Scriptural standpoint—any differently than this. He is still "guiding us into all truth" kind of like He did for the apostles (John 16:13) in the initial revelation, but they have now transferred what they were given to us. Paul says more than once that he is simply delivering that which was delivered to him, so that "we can read and understand" the truth that was shared with him (2 Corinthians 1:13; Ephesians 3:4). Pretty simple, really.

One final request: Go back to the list of 26 things listed above that the New Testament says the Holy Spirit does. For each one of those ask the following questions:

1. Does He do this separate and apart from His influence on us through God's Word?
2. If He does, how would we establish that with a book, chapter, and verse?

3. If the Holy Spirit dwelling within us helps us in some supernatural way, has my volition or choice in doing right or wrong been influenced or compromised in some way?
4. Where does the supernatural help that I receive from the Holy Spirit start and my free will stop? Do they somehow merge to work together?

Personal and individual accountability on Judgment Day is a concept that is as clear as any single concept in Scripture (Matthew 12:36–37; Luke 12:47–48; Romans 2:12; Romans 12:1; Romans 14:10–12; 2 Corinthians 5:10; Galatians 6:1–5; Colossians 3:1–2; 1 Thessalonians 5:11; 1 Timothy 6:3–7; Hebrews 4:13; James 4:17; 1 Peter 4:4–5; 1 John 2:1–29; Revelation 20:12; etc.). God had plenty of opportunity to insert "except when the Holy Spirit is helping you" (or some similar stipulation) if that were indeed the case. Our God is a God of clarity and transparency. In a context where confusion was taking place (1 Corinthians 14:33), Paul said this: "God is not a God of confusion but of peace." To say the Holy Spirit influences us in any way, separate and apart from God's Word, introduces confusion concerning roles, free will, and even modern-day revelation.

Chapter 20

Providence

In sections above, it was illustrated that miracles were used by God and His agents for specific purposes: 1) to establish that the power observed was not of this earth (supernatural) and was indeed from God (John 3:2); 2) to focus the observer on the message being delivered as having the same power and authority as the miracle. The miracle was to get their attention; the message was what was important (convert/repent and save your souls). It was also shown that these supernatural events were to exist until the Word from God had been confirmed or established (1 Corinthians 13:9–10). At that point in the future, no more miracles were needed because revelation from God was complete (Jude 1:3).

Once we wrap our heads around this concept and firmly grasp it both physically and intellectually, then we are going to have to come up with something a little bit different if we say that God is still performing these kinds of events today where He interrupts the natural order. Not only do we have to develop a *different means* of accomplishing these events—as all of those who had that power have been dead for about 2000 years—we also have to develop a *different reason* for Him to continue to do this. Remember, the *reason* for the earlier miracles has passed on (i.e., died) just like the *individuals* who performed them. At the same time, we should be able to find somewhere in Scripture some mention of this shift and the motive behind it, just like Paul told us there would be a change in the use of miracles when revelation was complete. This would be another momentous modification, and a God of clarity would not leave it up to us to develop an explanation for either process or product.

Greek (and Roman) Mythology

Although other religious structures that man has labeled *mythology* have existed in history, our familiarity with those from the Greek and Roman cultures are the strongest. We study them in high schools and there are *Ancient Literature* courses offered to English majors in college as part of their curriculum. The gods of these two cultures were interwoven among the people's philosophies, their religion, and their lifestyles; their literature is full of references to these gods and their interpretations of respective influences over all aspects of their lives.

In the Scriptures, we find—after a point—essentially two groups: Jews and Gentiles (or nonJews). The Old Testament, for the most part, is about how God deals with His people (the patriarchs and then Israel) and His attempt to keep them from being influenced by the Gentile (pagan and idolatrous) nations around them. When finally allowed to enter Canaan, the Promised Land, He issued stern warnings through both Moses and Joshua against marrying those outside their group as well as entering into political alliances with them. He wanted those nations' influence completely obliterated before it had a chance to affect Israel's allegiance to Him.

Obviously, the entire system of polytheism was corrupt in concept and in practice. The core tenets, characters, and their activities and influences were concocted in the minds of storytellers dating as far back as 1000 BC. The stories of these gods had them display a number of "ungodly" characteristics that allowed for the celebration of their activities acted out by man in worship to them. Drunken orgies and temple prostitutes are only a couple of examples.

The point is this. The word *myth* itself refers to an idea that might have fairly broad support but is *false* and *untrue* at its core. Such is the case with the more formal system of *mythology* or *paganism*, practiced by the nations around Canaan, those nations God told Israel to utterly destroy as they entered the Promised Land (Deuteronomy 7:1–4). Another feature of most definitions of *mythology* is that these stories are attempts to explain some natural phenomenon or something that occurs within their society for which they have no other rational or logical explanation. "The gods must be angry" is a theme that spans much of Greek and Roman literature as the writers attempted to explain why events turned out as they did. This, in a way, allowed them the benefit of attributing outcomes to something other than their own actions or weaknesses. Deferring to "the unknown" allows for such. This examination of ancient mythology brings me to my point concerning the title of this chapter: Providence.

Definitions

From a non-Scriptural standpoint, we can examine what mankind has defined as *providence*. The word in Latin means "to see ahead" or "to have foresight and foreknowledge." Cicero, who lived 100 years before Jesus came along, coined the phrase *deorum providentia,* which meant "providence of the gods." *Providentia* was included in the list of personified virtues that contributed to the "Imperial cult of ancient Rome" and her face was even on the coins of the time. The Greek *pronoia* matches that which is offered by the Latin for Rome. Etymologies suggest its definition as "God as beneficent caretaker of His creatures."

The Cambridge Dictionary has this definition: "an influence that is not human in origin and is thought to control people's lives." Merriam/Webster's online dictionary provides this: "God conceived as the power sustaining and guiding human destiny." The word obviously is an extension of *provide* which simply means "to supply what is needed for sustenance or support." The Encyclopedia Britannica (which used to be our more scholarly source of information on things) offers these descriptions of *providence*:

- Benevolent intervention in the affairs of mankind and the world
- Religious answer for man's desire to feel significant in his world
- Divine beings responsible for the welfare of humans
- A Roman Stoic notion: God wills everything that happens to humans

- Dogmatic term rather than Biblical term: God created the world and cares for it
- Conflict between the free will of man and divine will

These entries are provided to illustrate that the concept is not new and that it has roots that stem from man's desire to feel that God cares for him and that he is important in the larger picture. These ideas are what man says about the notion of providence; let's see what the Scriptures say about it.

Providence in the Scriptures

Interestingly, though the concept and practice of employing providence in history and attributing divine connections to it, the Scriptures themselves only mention the word one time. In Acts 24:2, there is mention of Felix, a Roman governor, making provisions of reform for the people. He was "providing" for them. There is no other mention of the word *providence* in the Bible or God practicing it, separate and apart from his direct influence through miracles—about which the Scriptures contain much.

So, since man's use of *providence* is not mentioned in Scripture, let's propose several supposed explanations of how it supposedly works, at least as a belief in our world today:

1. If God has used miracles in the past, there is no reason to think He is not using them today.
2. God used miracles in the Old Testament to benefit His people directly, so why wouldn't He do that today?
3. Just because God's overt presence (i.e., miracles) is apparent in Old and New Testament miracles, it does not mean that He can't still be using them today, just not so obviously.
4. Yes, the purpose of miracles in Scripture was "to confirm the word," and that has been done; however, there is nothing in Scripture that says He won't do it for some other reason.

5. Today, God is working more behind the scenes rather than out in the open the way He did in the Bible; He is now just operating *through people* or by using *natural means.*
6. If God is not working miracles today, how do you account for the fact they still occur all around us every day? Doctors say, "Only a miracle saved this person from dying." Survivors of tragedies say, "I don't know why God spared me; everyone else died."
7. There is no other explanation for why things occur in this life other than the fact that God is still operating on our behalf—*it must be Providence.*

There is somewhat of a mantra that is used by those who believe in the inspiration and the authority found within the Scriptures: *Do Bible things in Bible ways; speak where the Bible speaks and keep silent where the Bible is silent; we need a book, chapter, and verse for authority for all we believe and do.* This attitude of sticking as closely to the Bible as possible as we seek to do God's will emanated from the Restoration Movement around the turn of the 20th Century with advocates like Alexander Campbell and Moses Lard. It had its roots, however, with Martin Luther and his 95 Theses he nailed on the door of the All–Saints' Church in Wittenberg, Germany (in AD 1517) in protest of perceived abuses by the Catholic Church.

Doing things the way God has set them in order for us is a fundamental concept if we want to please him. Jesus said, "If you love me, keep my commandments" (John 14:15) and "If anyone loves Me, he will keep My word ... He who does not love Me does not keep my word (John 14:23–24). *Keeping* God's Word implies a strict adherence to it both in word and deed; the closer we stay to God's way of doing things—found only in Scripture—is the only way to avoid introducing error, also known as "man's ways" in Isaiah 55:8. If *providence*, as presented in our list above is not found in Scripture, it is merely an accommodation developed in the mind of man for something he cannot—or chooses not to—explain. We will now look at the "support" (or standard examples for its rationale) for providence noted above.

The Standard Rationale

1. If God has used miracles in the past, there is no reason to think He is not using them today.

Am I suggesting by this that God has not dealt differently with His people in the past depending on the different dispensation or era of the time? If this is the case, then we can throw the books of Romans and Hebrews out the window as well as the rest of the New Testament. Just because God did something at one point in history is no foundation for carrying that practice automatically into a different point in history. The practice of animal sacrifices is just one example. His plan included a different way of dealing with our sins under the Law of Christ. God changed much from the Old Law to the New Law. Romans 10:4 tells us, "For Christ is the end of the Law for righteousness to everyone who believes," and Colossians 2:14 tells us that God has taken that law which "was hostile to us" out of the way and "nailed it to the cross." On the other hand, this supposed *law of consistency* is both contrived and artificial on its face; just because God has used miracles in the past, there is no reason to conclude that He is still using them today.

2. God used miracles in the Old Testament to benefit His people directly, so why wouldn't He do that today?

God used miracles in the Old Testament that indeed benefited His people (water in the wilderness, shoes that didn't wear out, etc.). However, the purpose of the miracles was always to demonstrate that they were dependent upon Him and that He would provide for them. It was their allegiance and hearts He really wanted, not their attachment merely for physical provisions. In the New Testament, this distinction is even more decisive. Sections within this writing lay out for us why miracles were used, and it was *always* to focus more on the message and messenger (Jesus, for example) rather than the fact that someone was incidentally benefiting from a miraculous event. The miracles were to get their attention so that the message could be more effectively heard and believed by those listening.

In John 6:26–40, Jesus in a way chastises the people for seeking Him for the wrong reason, that being physical benefit. He tells them,

> Truly, truly, I say to you, you seek Me, not because you saw signs, but because you ate some of the loaves and were filled. Do not work for the food that perishes, but for the food that lasts for eternal life, which the Son of Man will give you, for on Him the Father, God, has set His seal (6:26–27).

A few verses later, He tells them that the "bread" that Israel enjoyed in the wilderness was not from Moses, but from God who "gives you the true bread out of heaven." When they ask for this bread, He says,

> I am the bread of life; the one who comes to Me will not be hungry, and the one who believes in Me will never be thirsty. But I said to you that you have indeed seen Me, and yet you do not believe (6:35–36).

It is His message about Himself that should be important to them, not the physical benefits He might provide them because they simply follow Him around. Miracles in the New Testament were *illustrations* of something larger and more important, not simply *gifts* or *bounty* because you had an intimate interaction with Christ or one of His followers.

3. Just because God's overt presence is apparent in Old and New Testament miracles, it does not mean that He can't still be using them today, just not so obviously.

God never "hid" anything that He did; His purpose was to always let those in attendance fully and completely understand that He was at work in whatever was miraculously happening. Where His Word and His activity are concerned, He has always been extremely clear about things, never murky, clouded, or veiled in any way. When God acted, man knew that God had acted, whether directly or through an agent He had sent to them. God (or man through God) revealed that He had "raised up some ruler or king" in order to persecute His rebellious children, the Israelites. It may not have been known at the time, but God did reveal it. God never tells us that He is going to change the way He does miracles—that we will somehow have to *intuitively know* or *logically conclude* or *assign Him credit without evidence* that He is working them. In fact, He simply tells us a) why they were used in the first place in the New Testament (to *confirm* the words being spoken) and b) that they would cease when inspired revelation was complete. Revelation is complete; miracles have ceased; the reason for their necessity has disappeared. "Cease" and "done away with" are terms that are decisive and conclusive. Strong's Concordance offers, "Restrain, quit, desist, come to an end—cease, leave, refrain." Nowhere does any source, let alone God's Word, tells us that miracles *will be changed in both purpose and source transparency.*

4. Yes, the purpose of miracles in Scripture was "to confirm the word" and that has been done; however, there is nothing in Scripture that says He won't do it for some other reason.

Miracles play a major role in the Bible; to refute this assertion is to admit a significant misunderstanding of God's Word. Prophecies are made throughout the Scriptures on a number of topics and to demonstrate that God knows that things are going to happen and that, in many cases, God even *makes* things happen. Prophecies concerning the Messiah and that were fulfilled in Jesus to the precision we find are the perfect examples. Jesus made prophecies concerning the destruction of Jerusalem, the unification in Him of both Jew and Greek, His suffering and means of His death, as well as His resurrection and the establishment of the church—the kingdom of heaven on earth. If all of these could be accomplished with a simple notice that such would happen, surely the God of heaven should know that we would be needing some sort of heads–up that He was going to be making a major change in how miracles were going to occur and what their purposes were now going to be—at least at whatever point in the future this was going to happen.

He doesn't, and a change of this importance would be inconsistent without some notification. Any perceived change comes from our heads or from Scripture, and Scripture does not seem to be an option here. And as a final point where authority is concerned for what we believe and do, "It doesn't say we can't" has never been accepted among God's people for an excuse or reason for our beliefs and actions. The Bible's *silence* on a topic has never been accepted by God's people as authority for believing it or practicing it.

5. God is working more behind the scenes rather than out in the open the way He did in the Bible; He is just operating *through people* today or using *natural means*.

This one is easy. *Either He is doing it, or He is not.* God has always used natural means (i.e., something in our natural world) to show His power *over* nature—that is what a miracle is. You *interrupt* nature to show You have *power over* nature. You cannot develop an entire belief system of miracles today and justify it by saying He is operating through "natural means" or working them *through* humans. He has always used people to work His miracles, except for the ones He worked Himself in the Old Testament (e.g., the flood; miracles to convince Moses to lead His people out of Egypt). Again, either He is involved, or He is not. If He is involved, we are still experiencing miracles like in the Scriptures, just not so overtly. If He is not involved, then things that happen are *just things that happen*—whether we can explain them or not.

6. If God is not working miracles today, how do you account for the fact they still occur all around us every day? Doctors say, "Only a miracle saved this person from dying." Survivors of tragedies say, "I don't know why God spared me; everyone else died."

If you will, review the comments above on mythology that were used to set up this chapter. One of the justifications offered by historians for how this entire system came about in the first place was that man was unable to offer *reasons* why things happened to him. In his *desire to feel important in the larger picture* and that *something beyond himself cared about him*, he developed a system of gods and goddesses who not only oversaw what man did but also influenced activities and outcomes in which mankind participated. The explanation for "reality" was to create something outside of their control that they could wrap their heads around to *justify* why things happened as they did. When they lost a war, they didn't make the right sacrifices beforehand. When they won a war, the gods were looking favorably on them. *Everything happened for a reason, and that reason was largely outside of their control.* You can substitute man's use of *providence* for the Greek's use of gods and goddesses. "I don't understand it, so it must be other-worldly in origin and nature." Doctors are human beings: they are both limited in their knowledge (not omniscience) and they make mistakes. Just because a doctor calls upon deity as an explanation for why something happened, this does not make it so. And the indiscriminate nature of tornadoes is no reason to invoke God; science can explain why they generally move and "bounce" and are tremendously concentrated in wreaking their devastation. When I flush a toilet or pull the stopper in a sink of water, even that vortex moves around in the bowl; tornadoes do the same with considerably more force and resulting destruction.

7. There is no other explanation for why things occur in this life other than the fact that God is still operating on our behalf—*it must be Providence.*

Man is a finite creature; he does not know everything nor can he. We have our limitations. Understanding how our world around us works has been an ongoing challenge for mankind for thousands of years. Guess what? We still don't know everything about it. And here is an interesting conundrum: The more we learn, the more we find out how little we know—at least scientists have told us such. Just because we don't understand why something happened, we just don't throw up our hands and say, "Providence! That is the only answer." We set about studying what happened, applying all we know to a situation we cannot explain. In many cases, lo and behold, we do find out that there was a reason for why something resulted as it did—and it didn't require the action of any kind of deity. For others, it is just as easy to say, "Well, we just don't understand how that happened," as it is to say, "Providence! That is the only answer." What is offered above is an effort to show that man's view of God still acting and interfering in the natural order—but in a more "hidden way" than in Scripture—is a notion not found in Scripture and, as such, should be attributed to something other than God—who has been very clear about *when* He operates and *why*. It could be that *providence* is simply man's way of explaining what he does not know or cannot explain.

Chapter 21

Physical and Spiritual Blessings

It might be fruitful, as I begin this chapter, to go back and review the conditions for determining the *context* of a passage or a set of beliefs on a topic. The New Testament is filled with both conversations between individuals and between individuals and various groups. It also includes considerable narrative sections about people, places, sermons, etc. that don't properly fit the definition of a conversation. We still have to consider, in order to properly understand what is and is not being taught, the *who*, *to whom*, *why*, and the *how it would have been understood* features, whether it is a recorded conversation or a statement that someone had said.

A good example to illustrate this is Romans 8:28, a passage many use to tell us, "Everything works out for our good on this earth because God makes it so." More will be provided on this passage in a later chapter (Chapter 28), but suffice it to say here that the entire chapter of Romans 8 is concerned with *spiritual* blessings (most of those will come *after* this life), not *physical* blessings that will be granted in the here and now. For more information on that particular passage, refer to that chapter later in this writing. The point, however, is that if we do not consider context when Scriptures talk about "blessings" from God, then we might be guilty of setting up a false argument—at least as far as this and other passages are concerned.

Matthew 10—Sparrows

In Matthew 10, Jesus is sending out the Twelve on their first mission without Him present and as their leader. *They* will be doing the teaching, and *they* will be receiving the opposition with which He has been targeted up to this point. He tells them not to fear those who can kill the body, but fear the One who is able to destroy both body and soul: God the Father. He then offers them some comfort: "Are two sparrows not sold for an assarion? And yet not one of them will fall to the ground apart from your Father. But even the hairs of your head are all counted. So do not fear; you are more valuable than a great number of sparrows" (Matthew 10:29–31).

On the surface, this sounds like the reason that they don't need to fear persecution is because God will protect them. However, this is an assumption on the part of the reader. There is nothing here that says they will not face persecution, even to the point of death by those who can kill the body. He tells them one verse later, "Therefore, everyone who confesses Me before people, I will also confess him before My Father who is in heaven. But whoever denies Me before people, I will also deny him before My Father who is in heaven." That would include losing both body and soul. He is telling them to be bold exactly because there *are* those out there who are "wolves," and they as "sheep" will be in their midst (10:16). If that isn't danger, I don't know what is. He even tells them they will be charged in courts and be beaten in the synagogues (10:17). So, it is not protection from harm He is promising them. He then tells them, "You will be hated by all because of My name" but then He adds the important point: "But it is the one who has endured to the end who will be saved." He then offers this advice: "But whenever they persecute you in one city, flee to the next."

He is telling them about the cost of discipleship. The entire chapter is focused on the risks they will face but counters this aspect with the reward for those who are faithful.

> The one who does not take his cross and follow after Me is not worthy of Me. The one who has found his life will lose it, and the one who has lost his life on My account will find it" (Matthew 10:38–39).

This is not idle conversation; these are words they needed to hear from Him before they go out to face the persecution that is inevitable. So, what is that thing about the sparrows? Doesn't that say God will protect them? No, it simply says that He *is aware of* what they will go through on His behalf.

Consider some other translations of this phrase "apart from your Father": "outside your Father's care"; "without your Father knowing it"; "without your Father's will"; "without your Father's consent"; "your Father knows when any one of them falls to the ground"; etc. These suggest an *awareness, not a protection nor a prevention of the persecution they are about to face*. In fact, the rest of the chapter tells them exactly what they will face and why. The chapter is differentiating between the physical suffering they will undergo here but also on the spiritual blessings that will flow from their endurance in this life and finally awarded in the next life. The passage clearly does not teach that God will protect us from harm from religious persecution or any other hardship while here on this earth, but in fact, quite the opposite.

Matthew 7—Ask, Seek, and Knock

In Matthew 7:7–11, we are presented with the widely quoted passage summed up in its first verse: "Ask, and it will be given to you; seek, and you will find; knock, and it will be opened to you." Many believe that this passage tells us that we will be provided with everything we want or need; all we have to do is ask God for it. The next verse says, "For everyone who asks receives, and the one who seeks finds, and to the one who knocks it will be opened." Sounds pretty assured, right? All we have to do is ask, seek, or knock, and everything will work out for us. The question arises, however, "Is that how it happens?" Of course, on the surface and in the short term, this is not the case. I know a mother who prayed "unceasingly" for God to heal her daughter's cancer, yet He didn't; she would say, "He hasn't … yet." For that family and others, there is good news and then there is bad news … good news and then bad news. That is pretty much how cancer victims live their lives, of course, with some exceptions: some are cured and some die within a short time after diagnosis. That daughter died after suffering this cycle for 13 years.

The first question to be addressed is this: Is Jesus telling us 1) how to pray and 2) for what to pray? Most likely, He is. Prayer is my only avenue to talk to God in any way, so if He is instructing us to ask God for things, then yes, it must be through prayer. The second question requires a little more depth of discussion, however. Are these things sought *physical* in nature or *spiritual* in nature? Which of the two fits the *context* and which fits what we *know* we can count on and of which we can be *assured*?

This passage comes toward the end of Jesus's Sermon on the Mount where He addresses a great number of teachings. He is talking to the multitudes (Matthew 5:1), so His instruction here is not addressed to His apostles or those who will later be blessed with miraculous powers (Luke 10). On the other hand, Luke's version does include this information right after one of the disciples ask Jesus to teach them how to pray (Luke 11:1). At the end of that conversation, the same words from Matthew are used, but notice the last phrase: "So if you, despite being evil, know how to give good gifts to your children, how much more *will your heavenly Father give the Holy Spirit* to those who ask Him?" (11:13). We know that when He did send them out, He told them the Holy Spirit would provide them with miracles to support the words they would be given by that same Spirit. More than once in His final encouragement in the upper room before His arrest, Jesus tells the Twelve that anything they ask, He or the Father will provide it. Most who quote this verse leave out the Holy Spirit as the gift and generalize it to this: "If we know how to give good gifts (physical) to our children, then God surely knows how to bless us (physically) in the same way."

However, if we are indeed talking about miraculous provision for these men, then assuming those same support mechanisms are available for us would be an erroneous stretch. Arguments are made above in this writing discussing the notion that miracles were for a specific purpose (to confirm the Word) and were for a specific period of time (until that which is perfect—God's Word—was complete).

So, we are either talking about special provisions for emissaries of Christ, or we are talking about us as followers of Christ. The former does not apply to us as I note above, so let's deal with the latter option. We have decided that without miraculous intervention, we will not receive those things for which we ask, seek, and knock. Maybe, on the other hand, this passage only works if we are asking for or seeking the *right things*. Commentators will tell us this is indeed the case; the passage works when we focus on *spiritual* things instead of *physical* things.

Joseph Benson says,

> The spiritual blessings which you seek, in this way, you shall find; and the door of *mercy* and *salvation*, at which you knock, shall certainly be opened to you. For everyone that thus asketh, receiveth—Such is the goodness and faithfulness of God to his children.

Albert Barnes in his commentary says this:

> God is willing to provide for us, to *forgive* our sins, to *save* our souls, to *befriend us* in trial, to *comfort us* in death, to *extend the gospel* through the world. Man 'can' ask no higher things of God; and these he may ask, assured that he is willing to grant them.

Matthew Clarke offers this:

> Ask: turn, beggar at the door of mercy; thou art destitute of all spiritual good, and it is God alone who can give it to thee; and thou hast no claim but what his mercy has given thee on itself. Seek: Thou hast lost thy God, thy *paradise*, thy soul.—Look about thee—leave no stone unturned there is no peace, no final salvation for thee till thou get thy soul restored to the favor and image of God. Knock: Be in earnest—be importunate: *Eternity* is at hand!

These brief quotes support the interpretation Matthew 7:7 is speaking of asking, seeking, and knocking in pursuit of those things of which we can be certain that God can and will provide. He has never ignored or turned down the penitent believer who has responded as He has commanded, and His response deals with those things of *spiritual* and *eternal*—not *physical* and *time-bound*—importance.

Matthew 19:26, Mark 9:23, Philippians 4:3
All Things Are Possible

These three are dealt with together because they say essentially the same thing, and many use these to teach something not intended by the passages and their contexts. When considering something we might undertake in this life and in this world, many will say, "If we pray hard enough, God will hear our prayers and make it happen. 'With God all things are possible.'" Was Jesus talking about general efforts or undertakings in this life when He said this? Let's examine, once again, the context.

Jesus had just dealt with the "rich, young ruler" (Matthew 19:16) who had just asked Him what he had to do to inherit eternal life. After some preliminary questions, Jesus tells him to go and sell his possessions and give everything to the poor. The young man goes away "grieved" or "sorrowful"; the reason is offered: "He was one who owned much property." Jesus knew the man's heart and that he placed his possessions above his eternal life; this is why He presented *this* condition to *this* man. It is not intended as a condition for all of us; but it certainly is a consideration for those of us who value material possessions over spiritual blessings, especially our souls. Jesus tells His disciples how difficult it is for those who are rich to enter the kingdom of God. They respond, "Then who can be saved?"

His response points out how man needs to submit to God for salvation: "With men this is impossible, but with God all things are possible." Man cannot save himself—and he for sure cannot rely on his wealth and fame for entry into heaven. However, if one considers God as part of the equation, even the rich can be saved. Abraham in the Old Testament was extremely wealthy. In the New Testament, likely candidates include

Matthew himself, Nicodemus, Zacchaeus, and Joseph of Arimathea. The family of the apostles James and John were very influential and likely were well off. What they didn't do, apparently, was let their wealth interfere with spiritual priorities. They placed God *above* their riches, so with God involved in the picture, they were able to do that which many others in their position cannot do. This is the context that shapes our interpretation of the words from the mouth of Jesus. It has nothing to do with earthly, physical efforts; it has everything to do with priorities in this life so that we can obtain the reward promised us in the next life.

Physically in this life, yes, anything is possible with God—as long as He is willing to break with the commitment He has made to use miracles only as His inspired writers said He would: to confirm the words of the messenger using or performing the miracles. Either God is or He is not performing miracles—the interruption of the natural order in a supernatural way—today. When God performs a miracle today by supernaturally changing something that was going to happen or was not going to happen, then He has instituted a new *reason* for miracles beyond that which the New Testament teaches. This point is examined in greater detail in chapters above. He never told us or promised us He was going to do miracles in this new way, so claims of such should be suspect, especially if New Testament passages are used as evidence. *Spiritually*, in this life and the next, indeed God *can do* and *does* otherwise impossible things; saving our souls from eternal torment would be one simple yet obvious example.

Another example that requires an examination of context for similar wording is Mark 9:23. Jesus has just come down the mountain from the transfiguration (with Moses and Elijah) to hear some commotion in a crowd. A man's son has a demon; he has asked the other apostles (Peter, James, and John had been with Jesus on the mountain) to cast the demon out—something which they had been doing when Jesus earlier had sent them out without Him; they have been unable to accomplish this one, however. The man says to Jesus, "If You can do anything, take pity on us and help us!" With a note of unbelief, amazement, or even contempt (?), Jesus says, "If You can! All things are possible to him who believes." The man replies, "I do believe; help my unbelief." Jesus casts out the demon.

So, the context here is casting out demons, something that we don't have to deal with today. Casting out demons, like any other miraculous event, was a first century occurrence. Whether Jesus was speaking of the belief of the father or of the apostles who had been unsuccessful (probably both are applicable) is immaterial to our concern here. Miracles were for a specific purpose (noted repeatedly in this writing) and Jesus was commenting on conditions from a different day and time than ours today. To take this verse and apply it to anything and everything today is an injustice to the point Jesus was making and a misapplication of that situation to ours.

In Philippians 4:13, we have this rather impressive statement: "I can do all things through Him who strengthens me." Apparently, "all" doesn't mean "ALL." There are many things in this life that I will never be able to do and for a variety of reasons: physical limitations if for no other explanation. So, we must conclude that the interpretation is something other than what our first impression might be as well as for how many use this passage. Context, again, is our answer.

The verses leading up to Verse 13 say the following:

> Not that I speak from need, for I have learned to be content in whatever circumstances I am. I know how to get along with little, and I also know how live in prosperity; in any and every circumstance I have learned the secret of being filled and going hungry, both of having abundance and suffering need.

Paul had had his share of suffering for the cause of Christ. He is warned of this at his conversion (Acts 9:16), and two passages point out exactly what being a slave to the Gospel cost him: 2 Corinthians 4:7–11 and 11:23–28. You cannot read these two lists of trials he faced without wondering what kept him going and why he continued to believe in that which he was preaching.

The reason is that his sustenance was not drawn from *things*—he knew how to live with them and without them. His sustenance was drawn from the things he couldn't see that provided him the spiritual strength to endure whatever physically might come his way. His perspective was perfect. After one of the lists of "sufferings" he underwent on behalf of Jesus, he referred to them as "momentary, light afflictions" when compared to the glory awaiting him. Thus, he was able to confidently and with the voice of experience say, "I can do all things through Him who strengthens me." We could even insert the following to make it fit his overall point: "I can (*suffer*) all things (*physically*) through Him who strengthens me (*spiritually*)."

The points made by examining these three passages are not subtle. People claim daily that God has done something in their lives—either answered a prayer of some physical need or saved them from a terrible automobile accident. If this is true, and God continues to interrupt the natural order to physically bless His people, then the age of miracles is certainly not over. As stated elsewhere in this writing and just above, miracles were for a specific and limited purpose and for a specific and limited time period. Others will say that God has "changed" how He works now and that the New Testament pattern is no longer applicable. If this is the case, He never told us that He was going to do this, and He has always made it clear when He is involved in something and when He is not (in Scripture). In Biblical history, there was never a doubt. Today, there are likely "reasons why things happen" other than that God was directly operating on our behalf.

Finally, to those who make these claims, are His children the only ones that gain advantage from His beneficence? If He sheds blessings on only those who are His, then we ought to be able to see a decided difference in life outcomes for Christians compared to others. Seriously, do we see this or do both good things and bad things happen to the Christian and the atheist in fairly equal proportions?

We know, for a fact and from Scripture, that God continues to provide spiritual blessings for us. However, we need stronger evidence than these passages above, apparently taken out of context, to prove that God has continued His intervention in the natural order and in the lives of His people today like He did in Bible times.

Chapter 22

Stewardship

This will be a long chapter as it involves several pieces; I'll try to keep it reasonable in length. Regardless of whether or not your political views lined up with those of Rush Limbaugh, any objective observer would have to be in awe of his ability to draw millions to his daily radio program for somewhere around 33 years. One thing that many will remember about him was his unique signature phrase at some point in each program: "Talent on loan from God." Some say this is evidence of his over-the-top ego; others point to how the phrase displays the depths of his humility. He was a striking media figure in spite of what your views of him might have been. His point—if we take the *humility* approach—was that whatever he brought to the table had little to do with him and a lot to do with what he felt God had granted to him as a gift.

Maybe you have heard the following said either in a casual conversation, a Bible class, or even from the pulpit: "What you have is not yours; it is God's. We are just stewards of the gifts with which He has blessed us." The implications of these assertions involve a view of God and His direct interaction in our lives that has been mentioned in other chapters of this writing. These implications include the consideration of a trilemma that you may have heard posed before your encounter with this reading. Only one of these three can be true:

1. God is responsible for and controls *everything* physical in this life.
2. God is responsible for and controls *some things* physical in this life.
3. God is responsible for and controls *nothing* physical in this life.

Stewardship Defined

Bing.com defines "stewardship" as "the job of supervising or taking care of something, such as an organization or property." Merriam–Webster.com offers this: "the careful and responsible management of something entrusted to one's care." Dictionary.com provides the following: "the responsible overseeing and protection of something considered worth caring for and preserving." These definitions all imply three components: 1) a caretaker; 2) that entity which is cared for due to its perceived value; and 3) the act of diligent oversight.

If I am a steward, I have been placed in a position of supervision or oversight of something. My job is to care for it, preserve it, and likely eventually return it to the one who made me a steward in its original condition. The entity is not my own, yet I am to treat it as if it were. I provide and care for it until the time to return it to its owner arrives. There are many examples, but here are three:

1. A store owner and a manager (the steward) who runs the business.
2. An owner of a farm and the hired hand (steward) who works the land and/or cares for the animals.
3. A naval vessel operated by the admiral (steward) on behalf of the country's navy.

For a Biblical definition, we turn to our resident authority, Vine's. The word in Greek is *oikonomos* and "primarily denoted the manager of a household or estate"; stewards were "usually slaves or freedmen." Metaphorically, and "in a wider sense," a) "preachers of the Gospel and teachers of the Word of God," 1 Corinthians 4:1; b) "elders or bishops in churches," Titus 1:7; c) "of believers generally," 1 Peter 4:10.

Stewardship Passages

"Stewardship is a Biblical concept." Indeed, it is. I will refer to only two examples in the Old Testament to set up our thoughts in this section. The other four speak of a person who had the title of *steward* and served in the role of supporting a master. Of the two I will mention from the Old Testament, the first is the very first example of stewardship in Scripture, that being the appointment of Adam over various responsibilities in the Garden of Eden. In Genesis 2:15, we find that God placed man in the garden "to cultivate it and keep it."

God gives freely to Adam, but He does, however, also place one limitation to all that is in the garden. In the very next verses, God commands the following: "From any tree of the garden you may eat freely; but from the tree of the knowledge of good and evil you shall not eat, for in the day that you eat from it you shall surely die." This was a condition of Adam's stewardship. Essentially, God said, "You are in charge, but don't go beyond what I have allowed you to oversee." There is an addendum to what God allowed mankind to eat that comes later in Genesis.

Genesis 9:3

In the early chapters of Genesis, we have two accounts of the creation of man and then woman (Genesis 1:26–30; Genesis 2:7–25). In Genesis 1:29, God says to man, "Behold, I have given you every plant yielding seed that is on the surface of all the earth, and every tree which has fruit yielding seed; it shall be food for you." He later says in 2:16 the following: "From any tree of the garden you may eat freely." He says nothing about eating meat from animals until the time of Noah and the flood. In Genesis 9:3, God says to Noah following the flood, "Every moving thing that is alive shall be food for you; I give all to you, as I gave the green plant."

This is an obvious reference to the statement He made to Adam in the Garden of Eden. Man apparently was to eat only vegetation until God expanded his diet following the flood. When God says, "I give all to you," I think the rational interpretation would be that animals had been there the whole time—yes, created by God and given to man initially—but that now, He was allowing them to eat of those animals for the first time. I don't know if those who believe that God places our food before us use this passage to support that thought, but it really looks like He is just revising or expanding the menu already available to them. If it does mean that He was providing their daily food, then He certainly did that miraculously in the Old Testament on various occasions.

The following are the most relevant New Testament passages concerning this notion of stewardship for mankind, more specifically, God's people. Other passages not dealt with will be listed and summarized.

Luke 12:42–48

Jesus has just completed His warnings about being ready for the return of "the master." He iterates here what He later reiterates (Matthew 24:44), this being that "the Son of Man is coming at an hour that you do not expect." The example he provides is of a master who has gone to a wedding feast and left a slave in charge of his house. Peter (v. 41) asks Jesus if the parable is to them or to everyone. Jesus goes on to contrast the slave who is circumspect, diligent, and ready for his master's return with the one who lives cruelly and rebelliously. Jesus deals with the outcomes of these differing approaches to stewardship, and He closes with the passage "From everyone who has been given much shall much be required; and to whom they entrusted much, of him they will ask all the more" (Luke 12:48).

We will be held accountable for that with which we have been entrusted. This was a physical parable that had a spiritual meaning or application. All parables used by Jesus had these characteristics. What spiritual treasures have been committed to us?

1. God's grace
2. His forgiveness of our sins
3. His Son to die on the cross bearing those sins
4. The perfect and sinless example of His son
5. His Word, the Gospel, the power of salvation
6. His release from a law that could only produce sin, bondage, and death
7. Eternal life in heaven

The list could go on, but these are sufficient to illustrate the point being made. This parable was offered by Jesus to illustrate a spiritual warning: Be ready, always ready. You do not know when the Son of Man will return. You'd better have the *house* (i.e., our lives) in order.

1 Corinthians 4:1–2

Paul says in these two verses the following: "Let a man regard us in this manner, as servants of Christ, and stewards of the mysteries of God. In this case, moreover, it is required of stewards that one be found trustworthy." The "us" to whom Paul refers are he and his companions and, really, any person formally charged with sharing the Gospel with others. He specifically mentions himself and Apollos down in Verse 6. He goes on to stress the trustworthiness of these who have been entrusted with this extremely important responsibility. He talks about how unconcerned he is about being "examined" by those who might be criticizing him, even if in a human court. His allegiance is to the Lord and to God, and They are his judges.

His point is that, as a steward of the mysteries that have been revealed to him through inspiration, he understands his role, its privileges, its limits, and its consequences (4:6, 9–13) for them personally and physically. In other words, he takes his stewardship very seriously, as do all who suffer for their similar commitment. Stewardship of the Gospel for inspired men of God is the focus of this passage.

Ephesians 3:1–10

In this section of verses, Paul echoes what he told the church at Corinth in the passage we just considered above. He talks about being a "prisoner of Christ Jesus" for their sake; he says that God's grace given to him is part of his stewardship so that he could share that with them; he points out that it was the revelation given to him regarding the "mystery" that is now being revealed; he goes on to provide additional details on these points but ends up in Verse 10 saying that he is passing this obligation (and stewardship) on to the church so it can reveal "the manifold wisdom of God" to the world. Again, the emphasis on stewardship is that of the Gospel and Paul's responsibility to handle it according to what was given him to do, here specifically with the Gentiles, and for the Lords' church adopting that responsibility to take the Gospel to the world. He says this also in 1 Corinthians 9:12–18 and Colossians 1:25–26.

Titus 1:7

Here, Paul turns his thoughts on stewardship to the role of elders within the local body of believers. In this passage and a parallel version to Timothy (1 Timothy 3:1–7), he lays out the qualifications and characteristics of those who would serve in this extremely important position within congregations of God's people. This responsibility would obviously fit the *steward* role, as this person is entrusted with keeping the church in that locale pure and dedicated to God, as well as providing oversight of the souls of the individuals within that congregation. As "God's steward," the elder works in concert with others serving with him who make it their job to keep the congregation as spiritually focused as possible, so that Christ can include that group with the church as a whole when He presents it to Himself on the Day of Judgment (Ephesians 5:26–27).

1 Peter 4:7–10

Peter makes an interesting point at the beginning of this section: "The end of all things is at hand." Commentators differ on their interpretation of this assertion. Some feel it is their own deaths being imminent; some point to the destruction of Jerusalem and everything Jewish in the larger plan; others might point to the end of time, although "at hand" seems to cause this interpretation some problems. Regardless of the timing of this "end," Peter cautions them to maintain some things they have begun in their new relationship in Christ. Their love for one another is first and their hospitality and attitude toward that grace is next. He then mentions that each has received "a special gift" and encourages them to use it as a good steward should. We do know that it is at least related to a phrase we have heard in the passages discussed above: "the grace of God."

God's grace (unearned or unmerited favor) embodies many parts, some of which are listed under the discussion for the Luke 12 passage above. Part of God's grace that was given to the early church were gifts of the Holy Spirit, detailed for us in 1 Corinthians 12 and 14. Several of those gifts were employed in revealing enlightenment of the truth as it was being revealed in *real time* during that crucial first century following the establishment of the church on Pentecost (Acts 1 and 2).

Although Peter could have been referring to something else, it is interesting that he, in the very next verse, talks about speaking (before the group, we would guess) in harmony with "the utterances of God." He goes on to say those who serve should do so by the strength "which God supplies" for purpose (in both cases) so that God can be glorified through Jesus Christ. Vine's says this verse refers to the Greek word *charisma* or "His endowments upon believers by the operation of the Holy Spirit in the churches." Stewardship here refers to early Christians' appropriate use of miraculous spiritual gifts given only to those in the first century.

To this point, I have addressed the scriptures that specifically mention the words *steward* or *stewardship*. Note that all of them deal with that which was entrusted to apostles, inspired men of God, elders with oversight of a local congregation, or individual Christians who were given gifts of the Holy Spirit and encouraged to handle the word of God revealed to them very circumspectly. Yes, *stewardship* is a Biblical concept; however, we have not encountered anything yet that suggests God uses us as stewards for the physical blessings we receive from Him in this life. Let's look at some passages that might possibly suggest such and examine them in their context. Again, I will look at New Testament passages.

2 Corinthians 9:8

Starting at the beginning of Chapter 9, we find Paul praising the church at Corinth for their generosity of their "bountiful gift" in Verse 5. In fact, the entire chapter's context is their sacrifice for the physical benefit of others and that both groups benefit. The receivers, naturally, benefit through "the ministry of this service" that not only "supplies the needs of the saints" elsewhere but increases the thanksgivings to God for being the source of inspiration for this generosity.

In reality, this part of Paul's encouragement to them goes back to Chapter 8 (Verse 2), where he uses the churches in Macedonia to serve as an example of giving. Three things prompted their motives: their great ordeal of affliction, their abundance of joy, and their deep poverty. The first two are connected in Scripture elsewhere showing us that joy in the hereafter can motivate us to endure unbelievable affliction at the hand of others here in this life. The third one is explained in 8:5: "They first gave themselves to the Lord." Extreme sacrifice of self, when motivated by the love that God has shown first to us, comes more easily. He says in 8:8 that there is no command to give like these did, but he hopes they in Corinth will be motivated as well to do so. He then gives them the example of Jesus (8:9) who, though rich, for their sake "became poor" so that they "through His poverty" might become rich. Rich in eternal blessings is the obvious outcome spoken of here.

So, in 9:8, when Paul says, "And God is able to make all grace abound to you, that always having all sufficiency in everything, you may have an abundance for every good deed," what is he saying? "God grants you physical blessings so that having those blessings allows you to do good deeds for others?" Did those in Macedonia have "all sufficiency"? Doubtful, yet they still gave "out of their poverty." Does God's grace in Scripture ever refer to physical accommodations in this life? Jesus tells His followers that following Him ensures a life of discomfort as far as this world is concerned: "The foxes have holes, and the birds of the air have nests; but the Son of Man has nowhere to lay His head" (Matthew 8:20). "Sell all that you possess, and distribute it to the poor, and you shall have treasure in heaven; and come, follow Me" He says to a rich man in Luke 18:22.

The teachings of Christ are rich with denial of self in order that we might follow Him. For example, He says in Matthew 16:24, "If anyone wishes to come after Me, let him deny himself, and take up his cross, and follow Me." Jesus lived a life of self-denial, living in poverty, and existing off the generosity and provision from others. *Physical blessings in this life coming as a result of believing in Christ is a concept not found in the New Testament.* In fact, if anything, we might expect persecution, having our homes and possessions taken from us, and ending up in prison or even dead because of our belief in Him—at least in the first century.

The point made in the passage above (2 Corinthians 9:8), is that our liberality and generosity, as we give to the support of others, produces physical outcomes for them but spiritual outcomes for us. Reading past Verse 8, we find we will be able to do "good deeds," that the "harvest of our righteousness" will be increased, and the grace of God "in us" will be a cause for thanksgiving on the part of those that receive from us and that they "will yearn" for us due to our sacrifice for them. "Thanks be to God for His indescribable gift!" (2 Corinthians 9:15). That gift would be the sacrifice of His Son for us, who operates as the perfect model of self-denial and giving (2 Corinthians 8:9) so that we, too, can be motivated for "every good work" (9:8).

I have taken longer on this passage than the ones above. The reason why is that Verse 8 is often taken out of context to suggest that the "grace" that God abounds to us is *physical* capacity to help others. If that is the case, why are there even other Christians who need help? If He can provide physical abundance to us to help others, why wouldn't He just do the same for those who cannot help themselves? I am confident that grace, when used in Scripture, always means those spiritual blessings He does provide "in abundance" to all who would be obedient to Him. In context, these two chapters are about the spiritual influence of God on the heart of man to motivate him to be sacrificial and generous to others who have less than they do. It does not teach that everything physical we have on this earth and in this life comes directly from God, or else we would have nothing.

I must go on with one more point. God blesses His children in abundance and showers them with *spiritual* outcomes. There is what has been called the "Health and Wealth Gospel." This is the teaching that comes from those who make their living from the donations of others to their radio and TV programs. It works like this: You donate to them providing a "seed offering," (to their programs) and you will immediately find physical blessings or outcomes for yourself and your family. In fact, the more you sacrifice in this way, the more "blessings" you will receive. I would bet that a good research study or investigative reporting could find hundreds (maybe thousands) of people over the years who have given themselves right into poverty.

God and Jesus never in New Testament Scripture promise that you will be physically enhanced in any way for following them. As noted above, quite the opposite. Taking a passage about the spiritual blessings of giving to help others and transforming it into a passage about God's physically blessing you for your generosity comes awfully close to this Health and Wealth approach to Christianity, which most faithful Christians denounce. The abundant grace God grants to us in this life are His Son and the resulting *spiritual benefits* we enjoy as a consequence of that very precious gift. Is God the *author* or *ultimate source* of our sacrifice for others? Yes, but only through the demonstration of His love operating on tender hearts, so that we are able to willingly sacrifice for those less fortunate.

Matthew 7:11

"If you then, being evil, know how to give good gifts to your children, how much more shall your Father who is in heaven give what is good to those who ask Him!" The comparison is this: Humans know how to provide for the needs of their children in physical ways, and God knows how to provide for His children in spiritual ways. In fact, Luke's version of this passage (Luke 11:13) inserts "the Holy Spirit" for "good gifts" or "good things" (depending on the version used). Commentaries resoundingly indicate that these "gifts" are spiritual in nature.

Luke 12:22–34

I examined the latter part of Luke 12 above. Here, I look at what precedes Jesus's warnings to be diligent and always prepared for the return of the Master. Jesus has just been asked by someone in the crowd to "Tell my brother to divide the family inheritance with me." Jesus tells him that He is not a judge or an arbiter, but to "Beware and be on your guard against every form of greed; for not even when one has abundance does this life consist of his possessions." He then tells them a parable of a man who obviously had treasures in this life, not in heaven (Luke 12:16–21), and what would happen to him and to his earthly possessions.

The text then says, "And He said to His disciples. . . ." We might assume that Jesus simply continued to speak to the larger group, or that He began to speak to a smaller segment (true disciples of His) within the larger crowd. To be accurate, we could follow the next long speech (discussed earlier in this chapter above) and turn to where Peter just comes right out (as he often did) and says in 12:41, "Lord, are You addressing this parable to us, or to everyone else as well?"

Peter makes it clear for us that it is at least possible that Jesus's second group of comments were to the apostles and not to the group of His disciples or for sure, not to the larger crowd that was following Him. Indeed, Luke 12:54 later says, "And He was also saying to the multitudes."—suggesting, most likely, that his first thoughts were for the larger group (vv. 13–21), and then He speaks directly to the Twelve (vv. 22–53) before returning to the larger crowd once again. So, what does Jesus say that some would view as relevant to our topic at hand, that of God physically blessing those who follow Him?

The very first point of note from Jesus is that they are way too anxious about things of this life. If Jesus taught us anything, He taught us that our focus in this life should be on preparation for the next life to come, not this one. That fundamental principle is infused and dispersed throughout the Gospels as well as the rest of the New Testament. Verse 23 tells us that "Life is more the food, and the body than clothing." In Luke 12:25–26, He shows them how futile anxiety is and how little it can produce.

A *casual* reading of this part of Luke's Gospel might produce the following conclusions: Do not worry about food or clothing. Focus on God and seek His kingdom. Sell your possessions and give all to charity. He will provide your necessities.

Does this passage really teach that all we have to do is put all of our treasure (our hearts) in being "rich toward God" and "in heaven" (Luke 12:21, 33), and He will miraculously provide food and clothing for us? We don't have to worry about those things if we will just focus on heavenly things? Is this teaching consistent with other passages in the New Testament? Let's consider a few. And incidentally, I wonder why this approach hasn't been fully tested more often by those who believe this interpretation.

I just discussed above (2 Corinthians 9) how we should be sacrificial of the things we have for the benefit of others who are faithful and in need. Why are they in need if they are faithful? Why isn't God providing food and clothing for them? Why does Paul need to pause occasionally and work as a tentmaker (Acts 18:3) to provide for himself? Is he not focused enough on God and the kingdom? Why are we told to work, or we should not eat (2 Thessalonians 3:10)? Why is the man who doesn't provide for his family worse than an infidel (1 Timothy 5:8)? Why does Paul say that those who proclaim the Gospel have a right to be paid ("get their living") from that effort (1 Corinthians 9:14)? What do they need money for if God is going to (miraculously) provide for their physical needs? Other passages could be cited that apparently contradict a conclusion that all we have to do is be focused on heaven and our physical needs will be supplied miraculously by God.

Philippians 4:18–19

"I am amply supplied, having received from Epaphroditus what you have sent, a fragrant aroma, an acceptable sacrifice, well-pleasing to God. And my God shall supply all your needs according to His riches in glory in Christ Jesus." Paul is here thanking them for sending him support for the work he is doing. Like the argument presented above for 2 Corinthians 9:8, Paul is saying one of two things: 1) You give physically to the work of ministers and God will repay you *physically* for your every need, or 2) You sacrifice in this life for others and God will reward you with *spiritual* blessings.

I think if we can decipher what the "according to" means, this will aid greatly in our understanding of the passage. The Greek tells us that it is a preposition that is understood by what follows it. The word *kata* is translated in other passages with these renderings: as touching, concerning, by, by way of, etc. Whatever is selected, these *needs* are definitely "connected to" these *riches in glory in Christ Jesus*. Sounds spiritual, if you ask me.

While I don't generally like to rely on "living" or "contemporary" translations of Scripture, it is interesting that the only two from a list I have on Verse 19 say the following [my emphasis]:

1. New Living Translation: "And this same God who takes care of me will supply all your *needs from his glorious riches, which have been given to us in Christ Jesus.*"
2. Contemporary English Version: "I pray that God will take care of all your *needs with the wonderful blessings that come from Christ Jesus!*"

A *physical* sacrifice produces *spiritual* blessings interpretation makes sense here, and it keeps us from having to deal with explaining "The more physical you give, the more material you get," which has been addressed above. Many of the same arguments could be made for other passages (Matthew 6:31–32; Ephesians 2:8–10; James 4:1–2), which, on the surface, might seem to imply that all we have is simply "on loan from God" and that nothing we have done has caused things to come our way in this life.

What Reality Reveals

Many passages in the Bible talk of God rewarding His people. In the OT, He rewarded (blessed) them when they were faithful and punished them when they were not. Many times, He destroyed nations that were evil and that followed false gods. In fact, His explicit covenant with Israel was this: *Be faithful and follow me, and I will bless you; if you do not remain faithful, I will punish you.* In that era, blessings were predominantly physical in nature; miraculous provision of food; miraculously, shoes didn't wear out; against unbelievable odds, heathen nations were crushed. Christ had not come, sins had not been forgiven, and faithful children of God were still looking for a "city which has foundations, whose architect and builder is God" (Hebrews 11:10).

In the NT, however, it appears that the faithful are rewarded in spiritual ways and in the afterlife in eternity. Here are some passages that suggest such:

1. Whatever you do, do your work heartily, as for the Lord rather than for men, knowing that from the Lord you will receive the reward of

the inheritance (Colossians 3:23–24). Commentators suggest that "the inheritance" is eternal life.
2. And everyone who has left houses or brothers or sisters or father or mother or children or farms for My name's sake, shall receive many times as much, and shall inherit eternal life (Matthew 19:29). According to scholars (and logic) "manifold" or "hundredfold" or "many times as much" cannot be taken literally as some of these items cannot be stacked up that way. However, the spiritual blessings we enjoy in this life, as well as when we "inherit eternal life," are rewards indeed and are greater than any possessions or relationships in this life.
3. A few verses earlier (Matthew 19:21), Jesus tells someone the following: "If you wish to be complete, go and sell your possessions and give to the poor, and you will have treasure in heaven; and come, follow Me." This would have been a great time for Jesus to say this person would be taken care of physically by God. Our reward, however, is in heaven, not in the physical things of this material world. Additionally, if God is simply going to re-supply us with physical blessings because we just gave up some, then where is the sacrifice at all on our part, except maybe the brief interval while we await restoration?
4. The writer of Hebrews praises those who have "joyfully accepted the seizure of your property, knowing that you have for yourselves a better possession and a lasting one" (Hebrews 10:34).

There are others almost too numerous to provide here. The entire message of Jesus was that this world is not what matters; it is the next world and next life about which we should be concerned. While he did miraculously provide food for the 5,000 and the 4,000, those were unique situations, and, as always, He had a message for them about their responsibilities and why some might be following him. His more prominent message for them was that there was no promise of earthly benefits to following Him; in fact, they could expect that their lives would be *more* difficult *for* following him. He never says, "But don't worry, I will give you food and clothing and a house to live in." Nor should we expect that today.

Matthew 25:14–30

Last, we'll look at the Parable of the Talents (also found in Luke 19 where *minas* are used as the monetary unit under consideration). Many read this parable and conclude the following:

1. God provides us with our money/goods/etc. We are expected to use it correctly, or He will punish us. (If this story teaches us anything about the physical, we'd better be multiplying this world's goods in ways that many of us are not.)
2. Some mistakenly (at least stretch the meaning of "talent" here) include our abilities and personal "gifts" from God as application here.

As with all parables and noted above, Jesus uses a physical story to illustrate a spiritual teaching. Starting back in Matthew 24, Jesus begins some of His final instruction concerning the second coming and how important being ready for that event is and will be.

That chapter in Matthew lays out in relative detail how dire it will be for those who are not prepared and who are simply carrying out their day-to-day lives without a thought of being diligent and prepared for the Judgment. He concludes with Verses 42–51 about not knowing when the Master will return and offers a parable of the slave who is unprepared for the reality that will come his way (25:50–51). Chapter 25 begins with the parable of the 10 virgins to further illustrate the point that some will be prepared, and some will not, and Jesus then offers the parable under consideration in this section.

The points are these: a) Jesus is indeed a demanding Lord of our lives—He has promised that Judgment will take place and it will be sure (Matthew 25:31–46); b) our focus should always be on satisfying Him and personally (i.e., spiritually) being ready for His return; c) whether that occurs during our lifetime or sometime after, our chance to secure a place in heaven will be ended when our lives on this earth are over. The larger message is what is important; taking this parable in the context where it is found, we must draw the spiritual teaching of the reality of Judgment and the condition of our souls at that time. Parables teach spiritual lessons, not physical. The parable of the talents has spiritual implications, not physical implications about our earthly possessions and their source.

Chapter 23

God Has a Plan for Me

A friend recently told me that God talks to him—or at least provides direction for him in making life's decisions. Unfortunately, time did not allow for a follow-up discussion concerning this claim, but I am anxious to find out how this works for him. Several years ago, a fellow associate dean of the college in which we were employed told me that God was leading him to accept a position at another university in another state. We had talked about religion on occasions, so I felt comfortable saying, "How do you know that it isn't Satan instead of God?" He smiled and was gone at the end of the year. One year later, he was back in his original position, so I asked, "Was God just jerking your chain, or were you 'hearing' what you wanted to hear?" I cannot remember his response; maybe it was just another wry smile.

An earlier chapter in this writing deals with what is called "Latter Day Revelations." Points were made in that section that God's Word is complete, perfect, and fully sufficient to address our every need in this life as we prepare for the next life. Passages are referenced that contain dire warnings for those who would consider adding to or taking away from that which had been delivered us. God spoke directly to the patriarchs prior to the establishment of the Old Law, and He spoke directly to Moses and through Moses to the children of Israel. He communicated to the prophets who attempted to convince Israel to repent and return to God; the latter part of the Old Testament provides the history of good kings (relatively few) and bad kings (many) who were able to influence the people in one direction or the other.

In the first century, John the Baptist was moved by God to preach his message of repentance, followed by Jesus who spoke nothing that was not "from the Father" (John 5:19; 12:49–50). In Hebrews 1:1, we find the following statement:

> God, after He spoke long ago to the fathers in the prophets in many portions and in many ways, in these last days has spoken to us in His Son, whom He appointed heir of all things, through whom also He made the world.

God, likewise, spoke through the inspired writers after Jesus returned to heaven, and the words He wanted us to possess have been recorded in the New Testament. In 2 Peter 1:2–3, we find the following:

> Grace and peace be multiplied to you in the knowledge of God and of Jesus our Lord; seeing that His divine power has granted to us everything pertaining to life and godliness, through the true knowledge of Him who called us by His own glory and excellence.

We might expect that God, if He wants us to be faithful to Him (and He does), would provide us with His wishes and desires for us on how to follow Him and please Him in this life. Our sense of religion and how we carry out our worship for Him is thoroughly informed by what He has given us in His Word. How we get to heaven is also laid out in great detail there.

At the same time, however, Peter tells us that not only have we been given everything that pertains to godliness … we have also been provided "everything" that pertains to "life." In the teachings of Jesus, we have a handbook for social interactions with others; books like James provide a wealth of instruction on how to get along with others in this life. We don't need further revelation for us as a human race or for us as individual humans. At the same time there are other problems with God communicating with us today outside His Word and executing life plans for each of us. Many religious people contend that "God has a plan for my life; all we have to do is let it unfold for us."

Passages Used to Defend Against the Contention

If you conduct an Internet search on the first part of the quote just above, you will find passages that supposedly support this assertion. I will deal with them in groups, as they tend to cluster around three explanations: 1) God or His human mouthpiece was speaking to a larger group, not an individual; 2) The statement is obviously focusing on a larger, eternal outcome, not a day-by-day design; 3) God was indeed influencing the life of the individual involved, but that was during a period in Biblical history when He did such. As has been and will be throughout this writing, we will rely on context to determine the intent of the text under consideration.

Larger Group

In Jeremiah 29:10–11, God is speaking to His people through the prophet Jeremiah about how they will be restored to Israel following their bondage in Babylon. He says,

> When 70 years have been completed for Babylon, I will visit you and fulfill My good word to you, to bring you back to this place. For I know the plans that I have for you, plans for welfare and not for calamity to give you a future and a hope.

Those who advocate that God has individual life plans for us take this passage out of context; the point being made is that God sent them (as a group) into exile due to their disobedience, but when they have served their time, He will return them to Israel and to prominence. The *plans* God had for them were as a nation, not for each of them individually.

Ephesians 1:4–5, 9–10, and 2:10 are used to promote the belief that predestination is a Biblical concept. It is, I concede, but it is a truth for those who render obedience to God's will for man and that predestination is always focused on *any* who qualify through that faith and obedience, not to those arbitrarily selected by God. Individuals are indeed saved, but those individuals can be grouped into "the faithful"—regardless of epoch or era—who will be saved. In the verses noted above, we are told that we "are chosen from the foundation of the world" and that we "should be holy and blameless before (Christ)." We are "predestined … as sons through Jesus Christ," and that we are to "walk" in the "good works" that God has prepared beforehand. Clearly, the Bible teaches that those who are faithful and who are obedient to His law will be saved, regardless of the era in which they live. He does not select individuals; He selects those who are obedient. It is their *obedience* that qualifies them for their reward.

In the first chapter of Paul's letter to the church at Philippi, he says, "For I am confident of this very thing, that He who began a good work in you will perfect it until the day of Christ Jesus" (Philippians 1:6). He has not addressed this letter to any one individual; he has not singled out anyone in particular at this point in the text; but has only addressed this epistle to "all the saints in Christ Jesus who are in Philippi." The same could be said for 1 Thessalonians 4:3–4: "For this is the will of God, your sanctification; that is, that you abstain from sexual immorality; that each of you know how to possess his own vessel in sanctification and honor." The instruction is to the larger group as the very next verse contrasts their behavior (as a group) with that of the Gentiles. In neither passage is God pointing out individuals (by name or person) who will be saved, but those individuals who qualify to be included in a larger group that is obedient.

In Hebrews, we have two passages often used to contend that God selects us individually and has a personal plan for us that He completes in us. The first is found in Hebrews 10:36: "For you have need of endurance, so that when you have done the will of God, you may receive what was promised." The second is in Hebrews 13:20–21, and there it says,

> Now the God of peace, who brought up from the dead the great Shepherd of the sheep through the blood of the eternal

covenant, even Jesus our Lord, equip you in every good thing to do His will, working in us that which is pleasing in His sight, through Jesus Christ, to whom be the glory forever and ever. Amen.

In neither of these passages is there the indication the writer of Hebrews is writing to them as individuals or addressing these particular passages to individuals. Even Paul, in Galatians 2:20, suggests that it is his knowledge of Christ and what He had done for him that drives him to do what he does. We, like the Bereans, can search the Scriptures "daily" to find out what God expects of us and, as a result, has in store for us if we have been found faithful to Him. God's plan is not for individuals that only He selects, but for anyone and everyone who will follow His requirements for us: a) obtain salvation through obedience to the gospel and b) remain faithful until death. That is the plan; He does not deal with individual prescriptions for salvation; that grace is extended to all who will accept His Son as the Savior and obey His requirements for salvation. Those who contend otherwise need to provide scriptures that teach such, not just their feelings or impressions that this is the case.

Larger Outcome

First of all, I have an issue with using OT passages for NT concepts. The patriarchal era was unique in many ways as was the rest of the OT's account of Israel, Judah, and their prophets. However, let's look at a few OT passages that are commonly used to suggest the title of this chapter.

In Psalms 37:23, we have this statement: "The steps of a man are established by the LORD; and He delights in his way." God has always made clear to His creation His desires and how to make Him pleased or happy. What eternal God and Father would sanction a creation for not following rules that were left ambiguous and unclear? In fact, God has always made it clear how to please Him, regardless of the dispensation under which man found himself. How much more detailed could you get than the Law of Moses? The steps of man are indeed established by God—that is, how he *should step* rather than *will step*. From the beginning, God has made His laws, wishes, and desires very clear to man; from the beginning, it is man who breaks those laws with his behavior, his infidelities to his Creator, and his disregard for the law under which he finds himself. The *path* is established by God; the way man responds (i.e., *his steps through his free will*) is what either delights the Lord or condemns man.

Man has always had a choice: a) to do the will of God or b) to satisfy his own will and accomplish that instead. Both choices have consequences, but the latter one is a path toward destruction. If there is one enduring principle throughout the Bible, it is this: "Man must please God and satisfy His desires, or man will endure the consequences." Those consequences in the Old Testament were often short-termed and sometimes long-termed; under the law of Christ, most of those consequences are placed on hold until Judgment Day. In Proverbs 3:5–6, we have the following: "Trust in the LORD with all your heart, and do not lean on your own understanding. In all your ways acknowledge Him, and He will make your paths straight."

In the first century, humble, devout, committed converts to Christianity lost their homes/possessions, were abused, were tortured, and were put to death—all for their adherence to the law of Christ and the teachings that were coming from the apostles and other inspired individuals. The writer did not say that the path would be easy or that your journey would be free from troubles from nonbelievers. He said that they would be "straight." Greek authorities tell me that this means He will make them "smooth, straight, or right." Another interpretation of this term or phrase is that "he shall direct your paths." Jesus makes it clear in Mark 10:29–30:

> Truly I say to you, there is no one who has left house or brothers or sisters or mother or father or children or farms, for My sake and for the gospel's sake, who will not receive a hundred times as much now in the present age—houses and brothers and sisters and mothers and children and farms—along with persecutions; and in the age to come, eternal life.

Following Christ is not a bed of roses here on this earth. We are guaranteed that we will suffer on His behalf, or we ought to question whether we are actually one of His (2 Timothy 3:12).

In Romans 8:28, we have the following: "And we know that God causes all things to work together for good to those who love God, to those who are called according to His purpose." Some would say that all we have to do is love God (some would add "obey Him"), and everything in this life just works out positively for us. We just mentioned in the paragraph above how this was not the case in the first century, so why would we think this in the 21st century? Romans 8—the context for v. 28—is *entirely spiritual*. The spiritual blessings are those under consideration, and to thrust a physical interpretation to this one verse in the middle of the chapter is an attempt to make a point without Scriptural backing. Ultimate good? Of course. His promises are sure, but never does Jesus nor any of the divinely-inspired men who wrote in the New Testament promise a proverbial "bed of roses" here on this earth. If anything, the persecution mentioned in 2 Timothy 3:12, as well as those losses mentioned in Mark 10 just above, are what we should expect. *This* life is not what Christianity is all about; it is the *next* life.

In 1 Corinthians 2:9, we have a quote from Isaiah 64:4: "Things which eye has not seen and ear has not heard, and which have not entered the heart of man, all that God has prepared for those who love him." Yes, God has prepared heaven and all of its glories for man. Eternal life and eternal rest is in store for those who love Him and keep His commandments. If we truly love Him, we will keep His commandments, for they are not difficult (1 John 3:5). The plan that He has for me is the same one He has for any who are obedient to the law under which we find ourselves.

Micah 6:8 reminds his readers of what God has already told them: "He has told you, O man, what is good; and what does the Lord require of you but to do justice, to love kindness, and to walk humbly with your God?" This is pretty straightforward information. In 1 John 5:14–15, we also have this statement:

> And this is the confidence which we have before Him, that, if we ask anything according to His will, He hears us. And if we know that He hears us in whatever we ask, we know that we have the requests which we have asked from Him.

Does this mean we will get everything we seek in this life, and all we have to do is ask for it? Well, if this is the interpretation of these verses, then we certainly do not see it born out in this life, do we? The first century Christians didn't either. Putting these two passages together, we see that we have an obligation to live according to the "path" that God has laid out for us. Follow His commandments and in this life follow the perfect example left for us by Christ, the epitome of justice, loving kindness, and humility before God and man. There is also a key phrase in the passage from 1 John—"if we ask anything according to His will." If you overlook that phrase, you can take from this passage that God will provide everything for us in this life; all we have to do is just ask. It does not say we will get "an answer"; it says we "have the requests we have asked." The condition for these blessings is that phrase "if we ask according to His will." I tend to think of these blessings as spiritual; I am guaranteed of those. If we go to the physical, then we have difficulty explaining mixed outcomes. You cannot use the excuse, "He answered; He just said 'No.'" The passage says, "we know we have" them.

Special Cases

Last, there are a few cases where God *did* directly influence outcomes for individuals, but these individuals played a role in the larger outcomes God had designed from the beginning. The question is this: Is His plan for situations and revelation complete; or is He still manipulating outcomes on this earth and in our lives? Have we truly *been given* "everything that pertains to life and godliness" or have we not (2 Peter 1:3)?

In Psalms 139:16, we have the following: "Thine eyes have seen my unformed substance; and in Thy book they were all written, the days that were ordained for me, when as yet there was not one of them." This psalm is attributed to David, King of Israel. God selected David as Israel's second king after the first one failed to follow Him. David, we find in Acts 13:22, was a "man after God's own heart." God worked with and through David to lead Israel to heights formerly unachieved. The nation of Israel was indeed established as God's people under the leadership of David. David was a special person and a special case for God working through an individual for the success of His chosen people.

God used numerous individuals throughout the Old and New Testaments to effect His will for mankind. This is accomplished through battles won, strong empires overthrown, miracles performed to preserve the lives of both individuals and groups, and a host of other evidences that, in times past, God has interrupted the natural order of things to accomplish His larger purposes for the crown of His creation: man. The question is this: Is God still interrupting and interfering in the lives of men with signs, miracles, and wonders (Acts 2:22; 2 Corinthians 12:12), or has the time for these demonstrations of power through God a thing of the past? Scripture teaches us that these were for a specific period of time and for a specific purpose: to confirm the words of those who were speaking them. They needed miracles to get the attention of the audience (wonder), to demonstrate a power uncommon to man (the miracle itself), and finally, its source (sign from a power beyond that of man). [See Chapter 18 for more detail.]

God's plan for me (title of this chapter) is the same as that for every person today. It is found in many verses, but one that sums it up well is 1 Timothy 2:4, where Paul says, "This is good and acceptable in the sight of God our Savior, who desires all men to be saved and to come to the knowledge of the truth." God has not individualized all of our lives on the earth now any more than He has done so since the complete revelation of His will during the first century. God's plan for each of us is simply to learn what we have to do to be saved ("come to a knowledge of the truth") and simply render obedience to that edict for salvation. The blood of Jesus Christ covers all who have been faithful, regardless under which dispensation they lived and died (Hebrews 9:15).

Chapter 24

Discipline of the Lord

There are those who believe that God actively sends tests/trials/tribulations to His people as a means of *proving* their faith. After all, did He not test Abraham by telling him to offer Isaac—the son of his old age and the "son of promise"—as he would a dumb animal? Didn't God say that He now knew that Abraham would hold nothing back from Him as he served his God? The logic is that if He would do that to Abraham, why wouldn't He do that to us today?

Likewise, wasn't Jesus led (*driven* or *impelled* in Mark 1) by the Holy Spirit into the wilderness to first, be weakened by His fasting, and second, to be tempted by Satan? God wants us to be strong, and one way to facilitate that is to send us problems and issues that, once we overcome them, make us stronger in His service. Right? Before getting fully into this assertion and all it implies, let us look at the definition of *discipline* to make sure we understand it fully. The word itself is used in the most important passage cited when this contention arises.

Discipline

Vine's provides this: Discipline—primarily, "an admonishing or calling to soundness of mind, or to self-control." Strong's *Analytical Concordance* offers the following: "the rearing of a child, training, discipline" and also "instruction that trains someone to reach full development (maturity)." Thayer's *Greek Lexicon* says, "tutorage, i.e., education or training; by implication disciplinary correction." Finally, etymologyonline.com provides suggestions of teaching, suffering, instruction given, learning, knowledge, and the order that is necessary for instruction.

There are two sides to the word *discipline*. There is the notion that it is a corrective activity exercised on one to make that person conform to whatever is desired by the one administering it. Words like *chastisement, punishment,* and *admonishment* emerge when this part of the definition is used. Granted, God did discipline (i.e., punish) Israel over and over again for their idolatry and transgression of His covenant with them. You should be reminded in earlier chapters of this writing about how and when God intervened in the Old Testament, how He did so in the New Testament, and how He has provided for our correction post-first century. In 2 Timothy 3:16–17, Paul tells us that Scripture is our guide, our tutor, our "disciplinarian" so that we can be fully equipped to do God's will: "All Scripture is inspired by God and beneficial for teaching, for rebuke, for correction, for training in righteousness; so that the man or woman of God may be fully capable, equipped for every good work."

However, the other part of the definition, where words or phrases like *soundness of mind, training, reaching full development,* and *instruction* are used, is where I will be spending my time. This is because of the context of Hebrews 12 and the verses found there that are probably the longest passage on topic of "the discipline of the Lord."

Context for Hebrews 12

The book of Hebrews is impressive for a number of reasons but mainly because of the contrast provided there concerning everything that has come before compared to everything found in the Son of God. Passage after passage declares and illustrates the superiority of Christ and all He is and did over anything else under the patriarchal age or God's dealings with the nation of Israel. In Chapter 11, the writer seems to shift gears a bit but still drives home the preeminence of Jesus in the faith illustrated by those mentioned there. He starts with a definition of *faith* (v. 1): "the assurance of things hoped for, the conviction of things not seen." He provides a few examples of those who demonstrated great faith, and then he says (v. 6), "Without faith it is impossible to please Him." He provides some more examples and says this in v. 10 (speaking of Abraham): "For he was looking for the city which has foundations, whose architect and builder is God."

Verses 13, 16 offer the following: "All these died in faith, without receiving the promises, but having seen them and having welcomed them from a distance, and having confessed that they were strangers and exiles on the earth" and "But as it is, they desire a better country, that is a heavenly one. Therefore, God is not ashamed to be called their God; for He has prepared a city for them." Finally, after listing a host of other heroes and heroines from the Old Testament who exhibited great faith, the writer says this: "And all these, having gained approval through their faith, did not receive what was promised, because God had provided something better for us, so that apart from us they should not be made perfect" (vv. 39–40).

As faithful as they were; as convicted in their minds that something better was coming; and even though it was not going to happen within their lives … their efforts to please God were bolstered by a promise of a day in the future that would affect their salvation. Christ came during the first century, and all that had been planned from the beginning began to take shape in the incarnation of the Son of God.

So, what do all of these things have to do with the "discipline of the Lord"? After laying out all of these Old Testament figures who were revered by the Jews in the first century, the writer revisits a theme he has mentioned numerous times within the letter already. In a nutshell, he has told these Christians who came out of Judaism, regardless of whatever persecution or temptation was befalling them, to hold fast, be strong, and resist the pull to go back to that which has nothing to offer, especially compared to what they have realized in Christ. A later chapter in this book will go into much greater detail concerning the warnings the Hebrew writer includes, but let it be said that he does not treat the subject lightly. Multiple times and in multiple ways he attempts to keep these Jewish converts to Christianity within the fold despite what they might be suffering.

Content of Hebrews 12

The twelfth chapter of Hebrews begins with a challenge. The writer tells them they have just been reminded of a great "cloud of witnesses" who overcame unbelievable odds and situations through their faith in that which they could not visibly see—that city whose "architect and builder is God." He refers to the "encumbrances and sin" that influence his readers but also instructs them to "run the race with endurance." He then presents Jesus as the perfect example of enduring all He did and ultimately received the reward of returning to heaven and rejoining the Father at His right hand. He then says, "For consider Him who has endured such hostility by sinners against Himself, so that you may not grow weary and lose heart." These words are used to introduce to them, once again here toward the end of the letter, that they, too, are going to undergo suffering because of their faith. He now turns to their situation.

His first words (12:4) are essentially, "Yes, you have suffered, but not to the point of death." Of course, the "shedding of blood" could just be physical torture, but the phrase more commonly means *dying*. When we say that there was "so much bloodshed," we are talking about a body count. He also uses the same verbiage that he did in the previous verse concerning Jesus "enduring the hostility of sinners" when he refers to their "striving against sin." If he simply meant sins in general, why bring up the blood issue? "Sinner" of v. 3 has become "sin" in v. 4 and represents those who would be tempting them to deny Christ and return to Judaism. He then quotes a principle (found in Job 5:17 and Prov. 3:11) about the "discipline of the Lord." He says this is addressed to them and they have forgotten it: "My son, do not regard lightly the discipline of the Lord, nor faint when you are reproved by Him; for those whom the Lord loves he disciplines, and He scourges every son whom He receives."

Remember the context and the example the writer has just provided in Jesus who endured even though that persecution did result in His death. He now appears to refer to the oppression they were experiencing as "the discipline of the Lord." He asks the rhetorical question, "What father doesn't discipline his son?" He tells them that if they are not receiving this "discipline," then they are not sons at all. In 2 Timothy 3:12, we find the statement that all "who desire to live godly in Christ Jesus will suffer." The context there is the persecutions Paul had undergone at Antioch, Iconium, and Lystra. The context of Hebrews 12 is suffering for the cause of Christ and the writer calls this "the discipline of the Lord." He says (v. 10) that we experience this discipline because He does it "for our good, that we may share His holiness."

The Hebrew writer then makes the point that discipline, from our earthly fathers or our Heavenly Father, is never pleasant. Suffering is never "joyful, but sorrowful." However, it is the outcome on which we should focus during these times of persecution; we "share His holiness" and experience the "peaceful fruit of righteousness." How can suffering produce these results? Listen to the writer in v. 11—he says discipline "trains us." Part of our definition of *discipline* above was the notion that it includes *training* and *instruction* that leads to a *soundness of mind* and allows us to *reach full development*.

The point is this. When we suffer for the cause of Christ—and endure it by overcoming temptations to sin by giving in—it has an effect on us that those who persecute us do not anticipate. In their efforts to weaken us, they in reality make us stronger. Consider the following passages that proclaim such. In James 1:2–4, we have "Consider it all joy, my brethren, when you encounter various trials, knowing that the testing of your faith produces endurance. And let endurance have its perfect result, that you may be perfect and complete, lacking in nothing."

In Romans 5:3–5, we find,

> And not only this, but we also exult in our tribulations, knowing that tribulation brings about perseverance; and perseverance, proven character; and proven character, hope; and hope does not disappoint, because the love of God has been poured out within our hearts through the Holy Spirit who was given to us.

In 1 Peter 4:15–16, 19, we are told,

> By no means let any of you suffer as a murderer, or thief, or evildoer, or a troublesome meddler; but if anyone suffers as a Christian, let him not feel ashamed, but in that name let him glorify God. … Therefore, let those also who suffer according to the will of God entrust their souls to a faithful Creator in doing what is right.

These passages entirely support the point being made by the Hebrew writer in the twelfth chapter. Following his statements and advocacy of the benefits of this type of discipline we received "from God"—because we are children of His—he then returns to a point he made back in Hebrews 10:22–25. In these times of trials and tribulations at the hands of others, it is extremely important to stay together, to support one another, to overcome these difficult times through their common goal of the final reward guaranteed them if they will only endure and not "go back" into that condition which has absolutely no hope of anything beyond this life. He drives this point home instructing them (12:12–15) to do the following:

> Therefore, strengthen the hands that are weak and the knees that are feeble, and make straight paths for your feet, so that the limb which is lame may not be put out of joint, but rather be healed. Pursue peace with all men, and the sanctification without which no one will see the Lord. See to it that no (*anyone of the group?*) one comes short of the grace of God; that no root of bitterness springing up causes trouble, and by it many be defiled.

Admonishments prior to this point have been directed to the individual concerning his or her efforts to resist pressures to fall back. Here, the writer focuses on their responsibility as a collective to each individual in the group in providing whatever support is needed to help others [my emphasis above] overcome and be as successful as they are. *Strengthen* that person; if spiritually weak, *heal* that person; make sure *no one comes short of the grace of God* (that salvation afforded us by the sacrifice of His Son on the cross).

Let me include two final points before closing this chapter. First, some might say that it is splitting hairs as to whether the discipline we receive is from the Lord or simply because we are His followers. Either way, the Lord is involved. However, and second, we should consider the implications and potential outcomes. Let's say that deity does indeed *send* individual trials to individual people on a regular basis. I assume these would be external to the natural order if they are directly from Them. Our context says that we also will have trials through those who persecute us for being faithful. Does God use others to persecute us? I discussed elsewhere how this gets awfully close to notions found in mythology literature and likewise impacts their free will. Our response should be the same, regardless of which, but how will we know the source? However, the larger question is this: Why would God send us opportunities to sin? Doesn't scripture tell us that He tempts no man (James 1:13)? If you buy the notion that the discipline of the Lord mentioned in Hebrews 12 is a potential stumbling block placed before us by the Lord, how is this not antithetical to His stated desire to save mankind and not condemn it?

In talking with educators over the years, I would ask them the following question: "What is the ultimate goal of discipline?" Naturally, the context was in their roles as educators within educational environments, but they could have taken it back to the parent who is, as they say, a child's "first teacher." Answers revolved around maintaining order and proper focus so that learning could take place, or something similar. I would stress *ultimately* and not for the others but for *that individual*. Eventually, we would all agree that discipline's essential function was to help the individual, over time, become *self-disciplined*. When discipline is administered, whether in the form of correction or punishment or simply as instruction, there is an external force employed to help shape the child, the student, or (if you will) "the disciple." At some point, those external influences (parents, teachers, trainers, etc.) will disappear, and the one who has been disciplined will now be responsible for his or her behavior without that external help.

If the discipline has been appropriately administered and has had its desired effect, the individual should be able to make this transition. Naturally, each of us is different, and some adapt more quickly and/or better than others. However, numerous passages in Scripture address the reality that each of us will face on the Day of Judgment when our individual accountability is under consideration. No one is responsible for my salvation but me; others can help and provide support, but when it comes down to it, it is *my* responsibility and *mine* alone. If we have learned the lessons that our earthly and spiritual discipline efforts are designed to teach us, God will be faithful to reward us according to the promises He has made in His Word.

Chapter 25

Praying to Jesus

Prayer is an important feature in the Bible. Of the 66 books found there, 61 of them mention it or include a prayer, and there are over 1,000 times prayers are or praying is noted. The New Testament mentions the activity 132 times. Jesus often separated Himself from the others to pray, and He offers an extended prayer on their behalf just prior to His arrest and crucifixion (John 17). We are commanded to pray (e.g., Colossians 4:2; 1 Thessalonians 5:17) and told how to and how not to pray (e.g., Matthew 6:6; James 4:2–3). It is not an overstatement to say that prayer is a thread or theme that runs throughout the Gospels and the New Testament church as it began and grew.

The apostles said to Jesus, "Teach us to pray, Lord," and His response is recorded in both Matthew 6 and Luke 11. His content, if outlined, would include the following:

- Acknowledging God's greatness/power/etc.
- Alignment between God's will (heaven) and man's will (earth)
- Provision
- Pardon
- Protection

We should be mindful of the fact that Jesus was praying to the Father, but He was responding to the question about how they should pray.

We often hear people saying, "Thank you, Jesus," whether they really are giving Him credit for making something happen or just remarking they are happy about some outcome. It could even be within the context of a more formal prayer to Him. The question, however, is this: To whom do we Scripturally pray? Is it God; is it Jesus; is it either; is it both? What about the Holy Spirit, we don't want to ignore that part of the Godhead. What about angels, or Mary, or "canonized saints"? Is there a limit to whom we can pray? Can we turn to Scripture to determine who it is that warrants our prayers and if there are other roles for those who are not the direct target? If God wants us to pray (He does), then surely, He wouldn't leave us out in the cold on how to go about this important part of being a child of His. Let's look at Scripture and see what we can find.

Praying to Jesus

Some might point to statements from Jesus to establish that we can pray to Him. For example, in John 14:13–14, He says, "If you ask Me anything in My name, I will do it." If we take this as instruction to all of us, then we have taken the statement out of context. The speaker is Jesus, obviously, but the hearers of the words are only His apostles. At this point in the narrative, they are in the upper room where He washes their feet, shares the Passover with them, institutes the Lord's Supper as the new "remembrance feast," provides instruction for them as they will shortly undertake the responsibility of continuing His ministry, promises them the help of the Comforter (the Holy Spirit), and prays to God on their behalf.

The immediate context is miracles. He has just said in the previous verse that His works are sufficient for belief in Him but that those who believe (those to whom He is speaking) will work even greater works, "because I go to the Father." He then tells them, in practically the same breath, to ask whatever they want or need from Him (to do these works), and it will be granted to them. If speaking directly to Jesus was something they could do in their ministry, that privilege should not automatically be extended to all Christians. Miracles were the topic under consideration and were the domain of those who were specifically appointed by Jesus to perform them.

Likewise, in John 15:16, He uses similar but different phrasing saying, "Whatever you ask of the Father in My name, He may give it to you." In John 16:23, we also have these words from Jesus [my emphasis]: "In that day you will ask Me no question. Truly, truly, I say to you, if you shall *ask the Father* for anything, He will give it to you *in My name*." So, even in the case of the apostles themselves, their plea for aid in their ministry is to the Father, but *in the name (or authority) of Jesus*. If it was to Jesus directly, then that was a special situation for them and the works they would do on His behalf.

Some would say that Paul "prayed" to Jesus in 2 Corinthians 12:8 concerning the thorn in his flesh that he wanted removed. We do not know what that thorn was, and it is not important for us to consider at this point. Did Paul pray to Jesus or not, and if he did, why can't I? Other versions say "entreated," which means *pleaded, begged, besought,* or *implored*. Right away, we can acknowledge that Paul had a unique relationship with Jesus. Verses 1–6 in this passage talks about a man taken up to the third heaven to hear inexpressible words. This was a vision he had about someone else; it was something he heard from someone else; or this was Paul putting it in third person about himself. Most commentaries would opt for the third choice, and Verse 8 suggests he was talking about himself. Certainly, in a situation where you were speaking one-on-one with the Lord, you could address him personally. Whether or not this is even a prayer is doubtful. Paul speaks of "preparation" he had for his ministry in Galatians 1:11–12, and Jesus says to Ananias when He sends him to Saul of Tarsus (Paul's earlier name), "I will show him how much he must suffer for My name's sake." We are likely talking about the same situation with Paul being with Jesus in that third heaven.

Stephen, after reviewing how the people of God came to that point in history, roundly condemns the Council of Jewish leaders for murdering the Son of God. He gazes intently into heaven and sees "the glory of God, and Jesus standing at the right hand of God" (Acts 7:55). He tells them this and they immediately take him outside the city and stone him. Just before he dies, he says, "Lord Jesus, receive my spirit" as well as "Lord, do not hold this sin against them." The questions are these: a) Were these prayers and b) If they were, was this a special case? I think we would agree that this was indeed a special case. Stephen was "full of the Holy Spirit" when he uttered the first one. Seeing into heaven is not a common human experience even at the point of death—at least of which I am aware. These are apparently requests spoken to deity in a special situation and involving a special agent of God. Extending this privilege to us would, again, be another stretch.

Jesus—Our Access to God

In John 14:6, Jesus says, "I am the way, and the truth, and the life; no one comes to the Father but through Me." The only way we can access the Father is *through* Jesus. Does this exclusively mean prayer? No, being a child of God comes through the sacrifice of Jesus, so this likely does not mean prayer, at least exclusively. However, in Ephesians 2:18, Paul tells us, "For through Him (Jesus) we have our access in one Spirit to the Father." In Ephesians 3:11–12, he says, "Christ Jesus our Lord in whom we have boldness and confident access through faith in Him" and in the next verse, he says, "For this reason, I bow my knees before the Father"—which obviously is prayer.

In Matthew 27:51, when Jesus yields His spirit to God in death, the veil of the temple was torn in two from top to bottom. This event was both literal and symbolic. The veil was that entity which separated man from God; only the high priest, and only once per year, was he able to enter this "Holy of Holies" to appear in the presence of God for man and to make an offering for his sins. This veil separated man from God; Jesus tore it in two, allowing us access to God through His sacrifice. In Hebrews 10:10–12, we are told He removed the function of the high priest to offer sacrifices for our sins, and in vv. 19–22, we are told we can now draw near to God because Jesus has abolished that which separated us. Back in Hebrews 7, we are told that Jesus lives forever, has established a permanent priesthood, and lives to intercede for us.

Praying to God

When asked to show His apostles how to pray, Jesus starts with "Father." He commonly prayed to His Father, so this is likely how He commonly addressed Him in those prayers as well. In Matthew 6:6–8, He tells the crowd to "Pray to your Father" and "Your Father knows what you need before you ask." He never tells us to pray to Him while on earth, and He never tells us to pray to Him when He returns to heaven. In Acts 4:24–30, the early church was persecuted and prayed to God mentioning the works done in the name of Jesus.

Paul says in Colossians 1:3, "We always thank God, the Father of our Lord Jesus Christ, when we pray for you." In Philippians 4:6, he says, "Be anxious for nothing, but in everything by prayer and supplication with thanksgiving let your requests be made known to God." In Ephesians 5:20, he tells them the following: "Giving thanks always and for everything *to God* the Father *in the name of our Lord Jesus Christ*." The emphasis is mine, but this verse sets up the rest of the argument presented here. Jesus provided the access to God with His sacrifice and obtain that access through our prayers. It is *through* Him and by His authority that we can even hope to come into the presence of the God of Creation. Look at the following list of verses for the consistency presented on this topic:

- Romans 1:8—"I thank my God through Jesus Christ for you all."
- Romans 7:25—"Thanks be to God through Jesus Christ our Lord."
- Romans 16:27—"To the only wise God, through Jesus Christ, be the glory forever. Amen."
- Colossians 3:17—"Whatever you do in word or deed, do all in the name of the Lord Jesus, giving thanks through Him to God the Father."
- 1 Peter 2:5—"You also, as living stones, are being built up as a spiritual house for a holy priesthood, to offer up spiritual sacrifices (*prayers?*) acceptable to God through Jesus Christ."

- Jude 25—"To the only God our Savior, through Jesus Christ our Lord, be glory, majesty, dominion and authority, before all time and now and forever. Amen."

I have likely said (at least implied), "I sure do thank the apostles for having the courage to do what they did in the early church." I have also said, "I thank whoever invented the microwave." Paul says in 1 Timothy 1:12, "I thank Christ Jesus our Lord, who has strengthened me, because He considered me faithful, putting me into service, even though I was previously a blasphemer and a persecutor and a violent aggressor." Paul could simply have been saying to Timothy that we all owe an extreme debt of gratitude to Jesus for what He did, but that in Paul's case, he was particularly grateful for the special dispensation granted to him, considering what he was doing and where he was headed in his life. He does not say, "Thank you, Lord Jesus, for saving me." If he did, then that would have indeed been a prayer, even though, as we know, apostles had special access to powers that we do not have through Jesus or the Holy Spirit. However, it would have come closer to a prayer. But he does not address Jesus as we address God directly in our prayers, so I doubt we can use this as an example of praying to Jesus. Even if he did, Paul had a direct encounter with Jesus from heaven on the road to Damascus and also in that "third heaven" (also "Paradise"), if Paul is speaking of himself in 2 Corinthians 12.

Conclusions

We are never told to pray to Jesus; any examples I might point to appear to be more in the vein of conversations rather than formal prayers to Him and from individuals in circumstances that do not apply to us today (i.e., endowed with the Holy Spirit; able to appeal for help in performing miracles). While Jesus is certainly worthy of praise, we can do that through prayer to God. We are told to pray to God by both Jesus and inspired writers. His sacrifice clearly allows us access to God; see also Hebrews 10:19–22 for confirmation of this access and the attitude with which we can approach God.

One might ask the following: "Is it wrong to pray to Jesus; is it a sin?" Also, "After all He's done for us, I can't thank Him for it directly?" The point here is that it is just not according to the pattern we find or in the instructions from Jesus Himself or the inspired writers. Also, just because it doesn't make sense to us should not be the issue. If this is indeed how God wants it, then that alone should be the criterion we use to carry out this important blessing we are afforded.

Finally, here is a list of passages to check for yourself to see that praying to God was the norm in the instructions from Jesus and in the early church as well as to help us conclude that we should do the same: Matthew 6:6; Matthew 6:9; Matthew 9:37–39; Matthew 18:19; Luke 18:11; John 15:16; John 16:23; Acts 1:24; 4:23; 10:2; 12:5; 14:26; 16:25; 27:35; 28:15; Romans 1:9–10; 8:15; 10:1; 15:30; 2 Corinthians 1:3–4; Ephesians 1:15; 2:18; 3:14; 5:20; Philippians 1:3–4; 4:6; 4:19; Colossians 1:3; 1:9–10; 4:3; 1 Thessalonians 1:2; 3:9; 2 Thessalonians 1:3; 1:11; 2:13; James 1:5; 5:18.

Chapter 26

The Unforgivable Sin

One might say, "I thought all sins are forgivable. You mean there is one that is not? Tell me so that I don't commit it." Yes, God can forgive any sin, but it is not as simple as naming this "one sin." I will look at some points for foundation before I get to the passages that talk about "the unforgivable sin," "the unpardonable sin," "the sin that leads to death," or "blasphemy of the Holy Spirit," all of which are likely talking about the same issue.

Proverbs 6:16–19 lists seven sins that God hates: haughty eyes, a lying tongue, hands that shed innocent blood, a heart that devises wicked plans, feet that run rapidly to evil, a false witness who utters lies, and one who spreads strife among brothers. This is an Old Testament verse, but I am confident that these, in one form or another, are repeated in the New Testament. The list is not, however, all inclusive of every sin that God hates or finds an abomination. That list would include every sin known to man and some that probably aren't. Isaiah 59:2 tells us Israel's sins had separated them from God, so it is safe to say that ours do the same. At the very least, unforgiven sins put us "at odds" with God. Something is amiss and needs to be corrected.

Sin, simply put, is breaking God's law. God could not hold man to a standard, i.e., His law, and then allow him to break it without consequences (Matthew 16:27; Galatians 2:6). If nothing else (of course He is much more), God is just. A God who created man with a free will to follow His commandments or not follow them must render to mankind his due in this regard. God has set things up this way, and it is up to man to make the right choices for the desired outcome. God and sin are incompatible.

Many like to think that God will ultimately save everyone and that He is too good to let anyone suffer just because they made some bad choices. This approach, called *Universal Salvation* (dealt with in Chapter 14) ignores much of what Scriptures tell us directly and of how He regularly demonstrated His consistency in punishing those who sinned and rewarding those who were faithful. We learn from these situations to help us conform ourselves to His Word. Romans 11:22 is clear on this point: "See then the kindness and severity of God: to those who fell, severity, but to you, God's kindness, if you continue in His kindness; for otherwise you too will be cut off." God's favor is indeed conditional, as this passage (and many others) demonstrates.

God, most assuredly, hates sin; He has proven this over and over again for us in the Old Testament and in the New Testament as well. He doesn't want anyone to bear the consequences of their sins (2 Peter 3:9) and only asks they repent of them and comply with His plan for forgiveness. He hates sin so much that He developed a plan for us to escape our sins—at least their consequences. He willingly offered His Son to come to this earth, live a sinless life, and be put to death by the very people who give expression to this notion of a sin that is "unforgivable." So, if God is willing to forgive men if they repent of their sins, then why is there a sin that falls outside this formula? How can a sin be *unforgivable*?

The Unforgivable Sin

There are essentially two passages that use this particular wording, and they are parallel passages in the Gospels of Matthew (12:30–32) and Mark (3:28–29). Jesus has been casting out demons (among other miracles), and the scribes and Pharisees accuse Him of having this power through "Beelzebul, the ruler of the demons" and even declared that Jesus Himself was possessed by Beelzebul (a god of the Philistines and known as "the prince of the devils"). Jesus first points out a flaw in their logic: a kingdom divided against itself cannot stand. He broadens their thoughts to Satan himself, likely the point they were making anyway:

"And if Satan is casting out Satan, he has become divided against himself; how then will his kingdom stand?" He then provides them the logical alternative (that which He has been teaching) that His power is from elsewhere: "But if I cast out the demons by the Spirit of God, then the kingdom of God has come upon you."

It is at this point that Jesus points out the condition of their hearts that places them into a situation that has dire consequences. In Matthew 12:30–32, He says,

> The one who is not with Me is against Me; and the one who does not gather with Me scatters. Therefore, I say to you, every sin and blasphemy shall be forgiven people, but blasphemy against the Spirit shall not be forgiven. And whoever speaks a word against the Son of Man, it shall be forgiven him; but whoever speaks against the Holy Spirit, it shall not be forgiven him, either in this age or in the age to come.

Here we have from the mouth of the Son of God the declaration that a) there is a sin (a condition) that will not be forgiven, and b) they who deny the Spirit of God as the source of His miracles have committed it. Notice, they can speak against the Son of Man and be forgiven, but "blasphemy against the Holy Spirit" places one into an entirely different category. So, why is this the case? Why does God place a greater outcome on this sin "over others"?

Sin, Repentance, and Forgiveness

Paul makes it clear to those in Athens that things have changed. With the giving of His Son and the offering of salvation to all mankind through that sacrifice, He is now requiring everyone everywhere to repent (Acts 17:30). Peter's version of the sermon to all those gathered on the Day of Pentecost is recorded (Acts 2:27–38), and he says they are guilty of killing the Son of God on the cross. They desperately ask,

"What shall we do?" The first word out of Peter's mouth is "repent." Both John the Baptist and Jesus preached repentance, with Jesus making the undeniable link between repentance and our salvation: "Unless you repent, you will all likewise perish" (Luke 13:3, 5). On the cross, Jesus forgives the thief who speaks of his sins and confesses Jesus, but there is no record that He forgives the other one who does not repent (Luke 23:43).

We know that we all sin; that is a given (Romans 3:23). Man is self-willed and will violate the will of God—some more often than others and—at least in man's eyes, some more seriously than others. Sin is sin and God hates all sin; it is our attitude toward our sins that is important. James 2 (Verses 1–10) tells us that, if we treat even one aspect of God's law lightly or with contempt, we are guilty of all of it. If we sin without the slightest regard for how it affects us or our relationship with God, then repentance will not be forthcoming … and God will not forgive us. If, on the other hand, we acknowledge that our sins damage our relationship with God, this is the beginning to making that relationship whole again. Our sorrow (or grief) concerning how we have treated God in these cases lead us to repent. If we repent, God is faithful to forgive us (1 John 1:9).

Jesus on the cross did ask God to forgive those who were crucifying Him, "for they do not know what they are doing." Was He going against what has been noted above—that repentance is necessary for forgiveness of sins—or was He asking that forgiveness be granted *when they do repent* of their sins? In order to avoid a contradiction, I will select the latter. Jesus knew that at some point, many of these would realize their error and do what was necessary to correct it. It was these—on the Day of Pentecost and afterward—about whom He spoke. They repented and did what was required of them that day to obtain that which was promised as a result: forgiveness of this sin and all those before (Acts 2:38, 41, 47). As long as man is willing to repent, God is willing and eager to forgive him of those sins. So, why is there mention of a sin that is "unforgivable"? Isn't that a contradiction?

The Unforgivable Sin Is Not an Single Sin

First, it should be noted that the unforgivable sin is not a single thought or a single action, the way all other sins are. I can commit covetousness with a single state of mind and in an instant. For whatever reason, I might slander someone and damage their reputation, when I otherwise have no ill will toward them. Human impulse is difficult to control (see James 3 for thoughts on the tongue and its dangers). Sins like these are committed in an instant; however, even if I plan over the course of time to commit some sin, this sense of spontaneity evaporates, but I can still obtain forgiveness. Man makes a distinction between *premeditated murder* and other levels of murder; this is not so with God. He will judge those who willfully sin planning on the fact that God will forgive them. Seems a bit presumptuous, but I am glad that this is His domain.

In Genesis 4:7, God told Cain to be careful because "sin is crouching at the door." Most likely, He knew what Cain was thinking and getting ready to do. The very fact that he might have been plotting his brother's death at that point shows that he had already sinned in his heart but that it was going to expand to an action even worse. Sin was already at his door, and he was about to embrace it. What Jesus was talking about to these individuals in Matthew 12 and Mark 3 was a *condition of the heart* more serious than a heart that was planning to kill another human.

The Holy Spirit is that part of the Godhead whose role, at least in part, is to provide information to man about how to please God by following His instruction. Jesus was led by the Holy Spirit into the wilderness following His baptism to be tempted of the devil (Matthew 4:1). Jesus notes that He casts out demons not by the power of Satan but by the Spirit of God (Matthew 12:28). It would be that Holy Spirit that would function as a Comforter to the apostles as they take up the ministry begun by Jesus and establish His church on this earth (John 14:26). We are told that the Holy Spirit "dwells within us" (1 Corinthians 3:16; 6:19) and helps us produce the Spirit's fruit (Galatians 5:22–23). We are told to let the word of Christ "dwell within us" as well (Colossians 3:16), and since the Holy Spirit is at least responsible for guiding the apostles into "all truth" (John 15:26; 16:13), it is that truth they would share that would convert the world.

The role of the Holy Spirit, at a minimum, included providing God's Word to mankind. It is that content we "consume," and it becomes that which influences us as we become the temple of God. Jesus said we could speak against Him and receive forgiveness (Matthew 12:32), but if we speak against (blaspheme) the Holy Spirit, then we shall not be forgiven "either in this age or the age to come." So, why is that? Again, why the difference?

The Role of the Holy Spirit

From things noted above, it is safe to say that the role—at least the primary role—of the Holy Spirit is to operate on the hearts of mankind (our spiritual minds) to provoke us to follow God's Word. Just how much else the Holy Spirit does is up for discussion, and this writing has an earlier chapter on this discussion (Chapter 19). For the current chapter, I will simply acknowledge that the Spirit's influence operates on us to do God's will. This gives rise to the following question: What had the Pharisees of Matthew 12 done that placed their souls in jeopardy and of which they could not be forgiven?

Jesus indicated that there were things that functioned as testimonials or witnesses that He was who He said He was. In John 5:31, He makes the statement that if He alone testifies of Himself, then His "testimony is not true"—or, it has no backing for convincing others. As support, He first offers John the Baptist (vv. 33–35), then His works (v. 36), the Father (vv. 37–38), and finally, the Scriptures (vv. 39, 47–47). He implies with this much "testimony" of Him, why would they not believe? Yet, the majority of the world has failed to accept Him as the Son of God, who He proclaimed (and demonstrated) He was. Any of those who have rejected Him could have at any time, before they passed from this earth, changed their minds and accepted Him. However, the Pharisees fell into a different category.

Not only did they not accept Jesus as the Son of God (for which they were condemned, and their souls were in peril), they had gone beyond just mere rejection of the evidence offered by Jesus in John 5. They had gone beyond not only rejecting Him as the Son of God, but they would also in time falsely charge Him, hire false witnesses, select a known criminal to be released instead of Him, have Him beaten severely, and ultimately hung on the cross to die among the company of common criminals. Yet not even all of this was what placed them into the category of "unforgivable." Consider the following sequence laid out above:

Holy Spirit → Word of God/Truth → Convicted Heart → Grief/Godly Sorrow → Repentance/ Obedience → Forgiveness of Sins → Salvation

The Holy Spirit, as the source of Truth (i.e., the Gospel that is "the power of God for salvation"—Romans 1:16), is that entity which motivates man to let the Word of God operate on him. It is the Spirit's influence on the heart of man through his encounter with Truth that prompts man to respond to what he hears or encounters regarding the Word of God. If the heart of an individual is *so cold, so unmovable, so obstinate,* and *so steeped* in rejection of *anything* that Truth might offer, then none of the rest of the steps noted above even have a chance of taking place. When one rejects the very notion that this Truth even exists, then he becomes one who has eyes that do not see, ears that do not hear, and, as a result, will not understand (Matthew 13:14–15).

In Matthew 13, Jesus shares the Parable of the Sower (or the Soils). If the Pharisees even qualify for one of the types of soil Jesus mentions, it would be the first one—the seed lands and does not even have a chance to take root before Satan infiltrates their hearts in rejection. Right after Jesus mentions blasphemy of the Holy Spirit in Matthew 12, He uses the very next statements to continue His line of condemnation for the Pharisees. They accuse Him of being in league with Satan (12:24); He exposes their flawed logic and attitudes (vv. 25–29); charges them with the unforgivable sin (vv. 30–32); and then tells them how rotten to their core they are (vv. 33–34).

> The tree is known by its fruit. You brood of vipers, how can you, being evil, speak what is good? From the mouth speaks out of that which fills the heart. ... For by your words you shall be justified and by your words you shall be condemned (Matthew 12:33–34, 37).

As Jesus so accurately points out, the Pharisees—along with the other ruling groups of the Jews—had entered their encounters with Him with hearts that simply *could not* accept Him for what He obviously was. Their hearts were in such a condition that it would not have made *any difference* whatever Jesus might have done to convince them. They simply were not going to let His teachings, His personal actions, His words directly to them, His repudiations of their thoughts and actions, or His indictments of them before the multitudes have any sort of positive impact on them at all. What impact Jesus did have on them was to drive them to putting Him out of their misery by humiliating Him through the lowest form of death the Romans had conceived, that of death on the cross.

Two verses in John (11:48 and 12:19) tell us all we need to know about these enemies of God. They are apparently motivated by jealousy and pride where Jesus is concerned, and later, we are told directly that jealousy was at work when they punished the apostles for preaching the Gospel (Acts 5:17). Not only did Jesus expose their hypocrisy from His earliest teachings (Matthew 5:20), He Himself was everything that they were not where a religious leader is concerned. You cannot read Matthew 23:2–36 and come away without a very clear picture of the hearts of these Jewish leaders and where they stood, condemned by Jesus from top to bottom, inside and out. It was to these individuals He was speaking in Matthew 12 (and Mark 3).

Their souls were so corroded that nothing Jesus said or did was going to change them. It was not *any single sin* that they had committed; *it was who they were* from the inside out. If your character is of such a nature that absolutely nothing would sway you to change your heart, then you have denied (blasphemed) the Holy Spirit and have reached a point where you are unredeemable—or your sin is unforgivable. It is similar to receiving a diagnosis of a serious disease; it could be *curable* or it could be *terminal*. All other sins are *curable*; blasphemy of the Holy Spirit is *terminal*.

Whose Call?

No matter how fair-minded, objective, or spiritually informed I am, there is no way in this world that I am qualified to make a judgment on the eternal destiny of someone's soul. That domain is entirely in the hands of deity—so far above my "pay grade" it is hardly worth mentioning. As Jesus said, "The tree is known by its fruit" (Matthew 7:16). Yes, we can see the actions of others and make observations—even judgments—about some things. However, we absolutely cannot see their hearts (that spiritual portion of their intellect) and make judgments about them, their motivations, or the outcome of their souls. That is entirely in the hands of Those who will participate on the Day of Judgment—and that does not include mankind, at least on the judging side of the table.

God knows the hearts of men (Jeremiah 20:12; Luke 16:15). Jesus knows the hearts of men (Matthew 9:4; Luke 5:22). The Holy Spirit is intimately aware of who we are (Romans 8:26–27). Blasphemy of the Holy Spirit—that sin which God has deemed as unforgivable and "leads to death"—is a state of the heart that is irretrievable. No matter what might occur, that person is a lost cause where salvation is concerned. We cannot make that determination; but those who are responsible for the creation of this world and judging it in the final day, certainly can … and have already done so. It is a terrible state to be found in this condition, and "It is a terrifying thing to fall into the hands of the living God" (Hebrews 10:31). Our sins separate us from God until we repent; the *unforgivable sin* separates us from God for eternity.

Part 4

Misunderstood Religious Beliefs (Specific)

Chapter 27

Pray, Believe, Receive
Mark 11:24

We often hear about the "power of prayer," the importance of having a "prayer life," and the encouragement to be a "prayer warrior." Prayer was an important part of the life of Jesus, as well as the apostles and the New Testament writers. It is mentioned often and is deemed an important part of exercising that right and that access to God afforded us by the sacrifice Jesus made on the cross. Most likely, how intimate our relationship is with God is initiated, maintained, and intensified through our communication with Him in prayer. Our regular study of His Word contributes to this intimacy as well.

Chapters above have already dealt with the targets and some types of content of our prayers, but in this section, I want to deal with a scripture that is often taken out of context and applied to all circumstances. In Mark 11, Jesus has come into the city of Jerusalem supported and cheered by the crowds of people. In Mark 11:11, we are told that following this, he departs for Bethany with the 12 apostles as it was late. Bethany was about a mile and a half from Jerusalem, and this short journey occurred more than once.

The next day as they departed Bethany, Jesus was hungry, approached a fig tree, and finding no figs, said, "May no one ever eat fruit from you again." The text notes that the apostles were listening. That evening, they again left the city and returned the next day. As they passed the fig tree, Peter noted its withered condition and said, "Rabbi, behold the fig tree which You cursed has withered." Jesus responds with the following in 11:22–23:

> Have faith in God. Truly I say to you, whoever says to this mountain, 'Be taken up and thrown into the sea,' and does not doubt in his heart, but believes that what he says is going to happen, it will be granted to him.

Jesus follows this amazing statement with another: "Therefore, I say to you, all things for which you pray and ask, believe that you have received them, and they will be granted to you." Let it be noted that Jesus was speaking apparently and directly to His 12 apostles. We are not told that anyone else had joined them in these trips to Jerusalem and return to Bethany each day. As we know, these men were specifically selected by Jesus to walk with Him daily, hear His teachings, watch His miracles, and even experience the ability to perform these types of miracles themselves on occasion (Matthew 10:5–15).

As noted elsewhere in this writing, He also gave them the same authority He had to speak on behalf of His Father (through the inspiration they received) and that He would give to them "the keys of the kingdom of heaven, and whatever (they) bind on earth will be bound in heaven, and whatever (they) loose on earth will be loosed in heaven" (Matthew 16:19; 18:18). They were to be God's mouthpiece; inspiration of the Holy Spirit would provide them with everything they needed. They still would need considerable faith, not only to endure what they would at the hands of the Jews and the Romans, but also to apparently work the miracles He said would follow them to confirm the words they were speaking concerning the Gospel.

It is with this understanding that Jesus spoke the words in Mark 11 to them. Peter (and likely the others) was astonished at how quickly the fig tree had withered—not just the leaves, but "from the roots up" (11:20). Most commentators refer to this action by Jesus as a sign of what would take place shortly when the Jews rejected Jesus as Messiah and then later, when Rome finally destroyed Jerusalem and everything Jewish in AD 70. Right after He cursed the fig tree, they enter Jerusalem, and Jesus has to cleanse the temple a second time due to the corruption in and around "His Father's house." It was immediately after this action that the chief priests and the scribes began "seeking how to destroy Him; for they were afraid of Him, for all the multitude was astonished at His teaching" (Mark 11:18). They had talked about it before, but now they knew they had to do something … and soon. A few days later, they arrest Him, have Him beaten, and then turn Him over to the Romans for scourging and have Him nailed to a cross to die.

The reason this passage is offered in this section is that many will talk about the power of prayer and quote these verses (Mark 11:22-24) as proof that anything we ask for, God will make it happen. First, this is not true on face value. If it were, many people who suffer would not be suffering. Second, many people would be asking for and getting things that God obviously does not have in mind for our best interest. Third, Jesus was speaking directly to His 12 apostles who (with the exception of Judas) would be actually doing some of the things He is talking about in these verses. We do not have any accounts that mountains were thrown into a sea somewhere, but Jesus was merely stressing the *absolute power* of what they were to have within their hands, if only their faith in God were strong enough. These were words to them—not us.

In Matthew 10, after He officially appoints them as apostles, He says they will "Heal the sick, raise the dead, cleanse the lepers, (and) cast out demons" (Matthew 10:8). Words to them—not us. In Mark 16:17-18, we have,

> In My name they will cast out demons, they will speak with new tongues; they will pick up serpents, and if they drink any deadly poison, it will not harm them; they will lay hands on the sick, and they will recover.

And "They went out and preached everywhere, while the Lord worked with them, and confirmed the word by the signs that followed" (Mark 16:20). Words about them—not us.

The final point of this, once again, is to be cautious about taking instruction, prophecy, promises, etc. out of context—especially when it was intended for a New Testament audience and in a New Testament situation—in an attempt to apply it to us today. Prayer is important, but we need to be careful—and Scriptural—concerning the things we seek from God through this avenue of speaking directly to Him through His Son, Jesus Christ.

Chapter 28

The Prayer of a Righteous Man
James 5:16

Theme and Content

The Book of James in the New Testament is an interesting diversion from many of the other letters of Paul and Peter, let alone Acts and the Gospels. James is a handbook for practical living in an age of trials and temptations, and I have even seen it called the "bossiest" book in the New Testament. Some of these instructions early on are the following:

1. Purpose and outcome of testing our faith
2. Sin's origins and progression
3. Listening and speaking
4. Both hearing *and* doing the Word
5. Dangers of showing partiality
6. Relationship between faith and works
7. Dangers of the tongue

The first one above sets the tone and much of the content for the entire work. In James 1:2–4, he writes, "Consider it all joy, my brethren, when you encounter various trials, knowing that the testing of your faith produces endurance. And let endurance have its perfect result, that you may be perfect and complete, lacking in nothing." His encouragement to those who were undergoing persecution and would undergo more, most likely, was to adopt an attitude that would benefit them rather than one that might lead to doubts and giving in to these trials. He tells them to look to these *opportunities* with "joy" by understanding they had a purpose: testing or sharpening their faith that would produce greater endurance—and ultimate payoff in their salvation. This resulting endurance would provide them the strength to resist giving in to those who would want them to renounce their faith and return to Judaism.

James then returns a few verses later (12–15) to point out from where our weaknesses emanate when we are tempted: our own lusts. There are other allusions for how to "keep oneself unspotted from the world" in the letter, but the last chapter hits this theme decisively with several related points. In James 4:3–7, he offers a scathing indictment of those who would attempt to be both friend to the world and servant to God. This pride they were exhibiting was not only unseemly, it was condemnable, and he refers to them as "adulteresses," "enemies of God," and "sinners." He says their focus is on their "pleasures" (v. 3), and their motives are corrupt.

In James 5, the author begins with a scathing indictment of the rich and lays out what their riches have done to them. Remember to whom he has addressed this letter: "To the twelve tribes who are dispersed abroad" (1:1). These are Jewish Christians who, due to the persecution of the church, have spread out across the region. They have, however, continued to live lavish and prosperous lives, a possible indication that their faithfulness to Christ is not producing the persecution in their new homes that it is among others elsewhere. It could be that they are able to straddle the fence enough to continue their lifestyle (*pleasures*, noted above) and avoid the more stringent trials and temptations faced by those who are more committed.

The author continues in this last chapter with more indictments and encouragements. In v. 5, he refers to dangers of giving into the pleasures and riches of this life instead of resisting these to avoid sin. Paul tells Timothy (2 Timothy 2:12) that those in that day and time who desired to live godly would indeed suffer persecution. If these were Christians to whom James was speaking in chapter 5, then they had found a way to avoid the persecution the rest of the Christian world was experiencing. They were able to maintain their rich and lavish lifestyle, which strongly suggests that their faith was not being tested due to their adherence to God and His will for them.

James goes on by stressing that they be patient and persistent in their waiting for the Lord (7–8); that they should not grumble and complain at those who supposedly were persecuting them (9); that they use the prophets and Job as role models for suffering (10–11); and, finally, that they must be firm in their convictions and never waiver or equivocate in their declarations and vows (12). We then come to the verses focusing on what happens when one at least comes close to capitulating his faith, if not going totally over the edge, falling into sin. These verses (13–20) have caused confusion for many, and at least part of the confusion is not understanding the terms used by James and to what particular circumstance he is referring.

Physical or Spiritual Circumstance?

Here is the text for James 5:13–16:

> Is anyone among you suffering? Let him pray. Is anyone cheerful? Let him sing praises. Is anyone among you sick? Let him call for the elders of the church, and let them pray over him, anointing him with oil in the name of the Lord; and the prayer offered in faith will restore the one who is sick, and the Lord will raise him up, and if he has committed sins, they will be forgiven him. Therefore, confess your sins to one another, and pray for one another, so that you may be healed. The effective prayer of a righteous man can accomplish much.

The first term we must deal with is *suffering*. There are two kinds of suffering in Scripture: 1) physical or mental misery resulting from simply being a human; 2) being persecuted for the cause of Christ. All of us, at one time or another, will suffer physically; as humans we encounter accidents and diseases or our bodies simply wear out as we age. These physical issues can cause us mental anguish as well. Depression, anxiety, and anger are all potential outcomes of the physical suffering our bodies are undergoing. Pain and misery are part of inhabiting this earthly tabernacle of flesh, and some of us experience more than others, unfortunately. Much of what we experience in this regard is not caused by any particular lifestyle or decisions we have made; life and its frailties just happen. We have no wall of protection around us, and, indeed, all of us experience both the ills and joys that come with being human.

On the other hand, there is something we consciously decide to do that can, indeed, cause us to suffer. Jesus talks about the cost of following Him (Luke 9:23–27; 14:26–33); noted above, Paul tells Timothy that if you are godly, you are going to be persecuted. Those words carried considerably more weight in the first century than they do today; persecution was part and parcel of the Christian's lot in life. Numerous examples from both Scripture and history could be cited here, but at this point, I'll just acknowledge that reality. Suffering for the cause of Christ is self–inflicted from the choice we made and is just a part of being one of His.

So, which of these two types of suffering is James 5:13 addressing? The "answer" for this suffering is "Let him pray." If this is simple human suffering (not as a Christian), then for what might one pray? Possibilities might be for relief, the strength to endure, that those treating your malady will be successful. This does assume that one has consulted a doctor or at least one who has more medical knowledge than does the one who is ailing. Paul suggests to Timothy a "home remedy" for his stomach that was obviously causing him a problem (1 Timothy 5:23).

On the other hand, if the suffering was for the cause of Christ, then prayer would indeed be a source of strength for such; however, there are other remedies that are available that James mentions back at the beginning of his letter. Change your attitude toward your suffering from possibly one of depression or self-pity into one of a more positive orientation. Peter writes to his readers (1 Peter 3:14) to count their suffering for Christ as a "blessing." The apostles rejoiced for the opportunity to be counted worthy to suffer shame on His behalf (Acts 5:41). Historians record how early Christians actually smiled in the face of imminent death as a result of their belief. Attitude is important and one of the means they employed (and we can, too) for enduring under the worst physical, human outcomes possible: torture and death. The "joy" they were experiencing was the assurance that their faithfulness was producing a home in heaven for them.

It is interesting that the next contrasting question and answer are these: "Is anyone cheerful? Let him sing praises." I'll just suggest that it sounds like he is saying, "Things not going well? Pray. Things going well? Sing praises." Human suffering can be either physical or mental or both at the same time and interacting. At this point, however, I don't know we can say which type of suffering is under consideration in this verse. Let's see if further examination helps.

In v. 14, James seems to shift to another point, seemingly related, but offers a different response: "Is anyone among you sick? Let him call for the elders of the church, and let them pray over him, anointing him with oil in the name of the Lord." So, I just said that one of the types of suffering in v. 13 could be some sort of physical or mental malady. Is James just adding to that point with another option, or is he moving to another kind of suffering here? If the same issue, he is just including an additional step for the person to take with the elders. It does seem odd to stick in the "cheerful" piece, and it does seem odd to use a different word (*suffering* and *sick*).

On the other hand, he could have changed the subject a bit here as he introduces a different remedy and the decisiveness of the outcome. First, for the two words under consideration, let's look at the Greek. For *suffering*, we have *kakopatheia*, which is rendered "experiencing evil, trouble, distress, affliction." Certainly, this could be a physical illness. For *sick*, the Greek word is *asthenes*, defined as "without strength, weak; not strong, weak physically or morally, infirm. Nothing here about being ill, unless you lock on to *infirm*. However, a dictionary definition of *infirm* offers this: "not physically or mentally strong, especially through age or illness." It could be age or illness causing one to be physically or mentally weak, but it doesn't have to be the cause or reason.

Paul refers to the brother who is influenced to violate his conscience by Paul's exercising his personal liberty (1 Corinthians 8:9)—in this case, to eat meat offered to idols—as "weak." The word is not used in the parallel passages on this topic (Romans 14 and 1 Corinthians 10), but it could be. The same Greek word is used as in James 5 to describe the person under consideration: *asthenes*, or a form of it. The point here is that in 1 Corinthians, Paul is addressing one who is not as informed on an issue as he (Paul) is. As a result, that person's conscience is violated (and he commits sin) when, in reality, it shouldn't be; it is just a deficit in knowing more fully the truth on the issue.

In James, it appears that the person under consideration has a different kind of deficit, but at least part of the impact is the same: the person's spiritual condition is in jeopardy. If indeed James is talking about one who is spiritually weak and not physically ill, then much of the rest of this passage—as well as the chapter as a whole—makes more sense. Let's consider a few things to see if this is the case.

The remedy for this one who is "sick" is to "call for the elders, and let them pray over him, anointing him with oil in the name of the Lord." If the sickness here is a physical malady of some sort, then a physician would be possibly more appropriate—even those whose understanding of how the body works and of diseases and injuries was limited to first century information and training. Paul, referring to Timothy's "frequent ailments," suggests a bit of apparent medical advice advising him to leave off water and consume a "little wine" for the sake of his stomach. If the one under consideration here in James 5 was physically ailing, then something medicinal might have been in order. However, James recommends calling the elders, having them pray over him, and having them anoint him. On the surface, this seems an extreme measure, especially if something short of this hadn't been already attempted. Granted, it could have been, and we just are not informed of that.

Elders in the early church most likely had the power to perform miracles. The listing of spiritual gifts granted to Christians and listed for us in 1 Corinthians 12:8–10 include the following: wisdom, knowledge, faith, healing, miracles, prophecy, distinguishing of spirits, tongues, and the interpretation of tongues. Notice that "healing" and "miracles" are in the middle of that listing, and if the *elders* of a congregation didn't qualify for receiving such, then I don't know who would. So, yes, elders most likely had the power to perform miracles. The question is this: Is James talking about physical healing (involving a miracle from God) or about a spiritual weakness in one who is restored?

Jesus sometimes prayed before He healed or raised someone from the dead. This appears to be more for the benefit of those in attendance (e.g., John 11:41–42) rather than a prayer for any special power to work the miracle. Jesus does say that, at least in some cases, prayer is necessary (Mark 9:29), but it appears that this would be an acknowledgment that the power was from God and not from their own efforts.

James instructs the elders to pray and anoint the individual "in the name of the Lord." It could be that the same instruction is under consideration here as in Mark (6:13). If indeed this individual is physically ill—and at this point we are making it a consideration—then having spiritually-endowed elders intervene, pray over him, and anoint him while publicly acknowledging all was being done with the authority (or in the name) of the Lord would make sense. Using oil to anoint someone had a few different purposes:

1. A mark of respect a host would pay to guests (Luke 7:46)
2. A formal act during an inauguration to an office (e.g., prophets, priests, kings)
3. A ritualistic or ceremonial pronouncement following a healing (Mark 6:13)
4. A physical, defensive benefit in preparation for war (Isaiah 21:5)
5. A physical benefit to help heal someone (oils, medicines, fragrances from plant extracts possessed calming and therapeutic properties)

If indeed this was a physical illness in James 5, then we are likely looking at #3 above like the instructions for those who went out healing in Mark 6.

The foregoing points are offered in support of the one under consideration in James 5:13–18 being physically ill and that the elders are called in to perform a miracle in order to save him. On the other hand, however, let us now consider that this situation is *not* a physical situation at all, but one where the person is simply *spiritually* "sick" or "weak"—as I pointed out above the term is more accurately rendered. What are the ramifications of this approach to the passage? Do we lose anything or gain anything from this perspective?

The Argument for a Spiritual Context

Let's once again look at the passage:

> Is anyone among you sick? Let him call for the elders of the church, and let them pray over him, anointing him with oil in the name of the Lord; and the prayer offered in faith will restore the one who is sick, and the Lord will raise him up, and if he has committed sins, they will be forgiven him. Therefore, confess your sins to one another, and pray for one another, so that you may be healed. The effective prayer of a righteous man can accomplish much.

First, let's look at logic and custom. The Scriptures are replete with those who are spiritually weak turning to God in prayer seeking strength, wisdom, perseverance, and other physical benefits from that exercise. The Psalms are full of examples. Paul regularly mentions this *strategy* for dealing with all he went through on behalf of Christ (Romans 8:26; 2 Cor 12:9–10; Ephesians 6:18; Philippians 4:12–13). So, an individual praying for strength is entirely Scriptural and, as such, fully authorized. In James 5, we have the individual being instructed to take an additional step in helping secure additional strength to overcome whatever is facing him. He is told to call in the elders to pray for him as well. I have posed some questions above about determining the context in James 5 as a physical illness. If we use *spiritual weakness* instead, the argument only gets stronger as we continue. Notice the outcome.

"The prayer offered in faith will restore the one who is sick." Notice the absoluteness of the result: "<u>will restore</u> the one who is sick." First, if this is a physical illness, we are left to conclude that James 5 is strictly a first century situation and not applicable for circumstances where that list of spiritual gifts including "healing" and "miracles"no longer exist. Elsewhere in this writing, the argument is made that miracles had three predetermined purposes: 1) to grab the attention of those present ("wonder"); 2) to perform a feat that required supernatural intervention ("miracle"); and 3) to confirm the words ("sign") that always preceded or immediately followed the miracle (Mark 16:20; 1 Thessalonians 1:5; Hebrews 2:2–4). When the Word was completed and confirmed, there was no longer any need for miracles to confirm it (1 Corinthians 13:8–10; James 1:25). If James 5 is speaking of a physical illness that the elders today can cure by prayer and anointing, then miracles still occur, and these men are endowed with spiritual power beyond the norm. As well, these prayers *will produce a massive, positive outcome*. Physical restoration will occur, absolutely. Also, this example might be the only one in the New Testament where the miracle was performed solely for the benefit of the one healed and not secondary to a message of some sort; such is not the case elsewhere, and we have noted Scriptural reasoning for the ability to perform miracles (confirm the Word). Hospitals, otherwise, would be empty.

Unfortunately, our experiences today tell us this is not the case. Prayer does not always heal the person under consideration, regardless of who is offering the prayer or how many of us are praying. James 5 says the outcome is *guaranteed*. So, maybe we are talking about something other than a physical illness. The text says that the one will be both "restored" by the prayer and "raised up" by the Lord. Does a spiritual context work here? Entirely. First, let's look at the two words found in this section of the passage.

The Greek word for "restore" (*sosei*) means "save, material or temporal deliverance from danger or suffering." For "raise up" (*egerei*), we have "to waken, to arouse from sleep, cause to rise." Does this sound like a physical situation or does a spiritual situation make more sense? If I find myself in doubt, being tempted, unable to deflect persecution, etc., then a) praying for strength makes sense, b) asking for additional prayers from those who are possibly more spiritual than I (at least currently) makes sense, and c) receiving absolute relief from my situation makes sense. Additionally, James throws in another piece of support for a spiritual weakness at this point: "and if he has committed sins, they will be forgiven him." The question is this: Is this an additional benefit from confessing your spiritual weakness to others and being restored as a result? Or is it more incidental to a *physical* interpretation of the passage? *Spiritual* makes entirely more sense and even better completes the thought James has started.

Remember, first century Christians were regularly abused in public and in private. Their homes and their lands were confiscated; their livelihoods were abolished; they were rejected by former religious leaders and even by members of their families. They were, in many cases, social and professional outcasts. On top of these types of persecution, you had those who operated like Saul of Tarsus before his conversion whose job it was to seek out participants of "The Way" and bring them to justice in Jerusalem that often included imprisonment, torture, and even death. Being *weak* in the face of such persecution was not uncommon. The book of Hebrews was written specifically to those who were encountering such pressures and strongly encouraged them to persevere and endure these earthly trials for the heavenly and eternal payoff after this life. James even alludes to this in his first chapter within the first few verses.

Moments of weakness would have been expected. Strength drawn from the support and prayers of others, I am sure, were regularly needed. The writer of Hebrews tells his readers, "Let us hold fast the confession of our hope without wavering, for He who promised is faithful; and let us consider how to stimulate one another to love and good deeds"

(Hebrews 10:23–24). There must have been a reason for this warning and encouragement, as well as other admonishments in Hebrews to remain faithful. Remember also Peter's reference to the dog and its vomit and sow and its mud. Weakness is one thing; carrying that weakness to the point of sin is another. I can be weak, and I can pray; I can even call on others to pray with and for me; I might even have crossed the line in my weakness and sinned. If this is the case, I am told in James 5 that all is not lost. If I share my weakness and confess those sins to God and others, I can *know* that I will be forgiven, restored, and raised up (see also 1 John 1:9).

If that were not enough, James gives us more reason to interpret this passage and context as a spiritual and not a physical situation: "Therefore, confess your sins to one another, and pray for one another, so that you may be healed" (James 5:16). Why all of this talk about sins if this is a physical illness the elders are called in to remedy? Also, notice that really important word "Therefore." In conclusion, in summary, the point of all written above ... is what James is telling us with that word. The point of all of this?

1. Spiritual weakness is not a death sentence; in fact, in the current situation, it is expected.
2. In addition to your prayers, you have the benefit of faithful *others* who can offer additional support and prayers on your behalf.
3. You can be guaranteed that the prayers (yours and others') offered in faith *will have the desired outcome*; you will be restored (lifted out of danger) and raised up (awakened from your slumber).
4. Additionally, if there are sins involved, your confession of those to God and to others will absolutely produce forgiveness and you will be "healed" (made whole) from your "sickness" (weakness).
5. The reason? Prayers of sincere, committed individuals produce results. Righteous people praying with and for sincerely repentant individuals accomplishes much.

Notice James 5:19–20: "My brethren, if any among you strays from the truth, and one turns him back, let him know that he who turns a sinner from the error of his way will save his soul from death and will cover a multitude of sins."

Finally, James concludes his points from the text above. The context is clearly spiritual weakness in the one under consideration and has indeed "strayed from the truth." The ones called in to help him get "turned back" and on course will have participated in saving that erring child of God from his untenable position of having his soul in danger of death (eternal). This reversal, of course, has caused the one here to repent and confess his sins to cover past (recent?) sins and potentially those that might have occurred in the future, had not this intervention taken place. "Multitude" of sins might even be an understatement.

Additional Support for a Spiritual Context

The Greek word for "sick" is rendered "weak" in 12 of the 15 times it is used in the New Testament. I am not pulling this definition into use here; it is established elsewhere as legitimate. Paul tells us to "receive the one who is weak in faith" in Romans 14:1. In Hebrews 12:12–15, the writer is talking about suffering for the cause of Christ and acknowledges that there are those who might not be as strong as others in this regard. He tells them, "Strengthen the hands that are weak and the knees that are feeble." He follows this up with "Make straight paths for your feet, so that the limb which is lame may not be put out of joint but rather be healed." This really sounds like the writer is using physical insufficiencies (weak hands, feeble knees, lameness, having bones out of joint) as a metaphor for spiritual "weakness" that can be "healed."

Earlier in James 5, he refers to the dangers of giving into pleasures and the riches of this life, instead of resisting these sins. If individuals were holding on to their possessions instead of having them taken from them, it could be that they were compromising their faith in order to make this happen. He mentions that they should be patient (and faithful) in waiting for the return of the Lord (5:7–8) and that any grumbling should be directed at those who persecute them (5:9).

He then uses both the prophets and Job as examples of suffering persecution related to one's faith (5:10–11) and instructs them to be consistent in their faith and their conversation (5:12). He next lays out his argument for what to do when they find themselves compromised in one way or another regarding their faith (5:13–16; 19–20). The context forces us to look at these latter verses as one who has found himself weakened, doubting, and even possibly sinning as a result. When we allow others to share in our weakness and confess our sins, then we can truly know that prayer has the power to save a soul from death. Righteous people, united in faith and effort, can accomplish much (James 5:16).

We see just how effective our efforts to help others who are struggling spiritually can accomplish with James 5:19–20:

> My brethren, if any among you strays from the truth, and one turns him back, let him know that he who turns a sinner from the error of his way will save his soul from death, and will cover a multitude of sins.

These are the last verses in the entire epistle and come at the conclusion of a passage that strongly suggests a spiritual weakness context. Participating in "saving a soul from death" is just as important of leading someone to Christ in the first place. You are saving souls, and there is no higher calling than that.

The Insertion of Elijah

The naysayer of the argument for a spiritual context for James 5 would say, "Well, what about Elijah here? Doesn't this example of a *righteous man availing much* count for anything? Physical miracle for Elijah; same for the one mentioned here." Elijah prays for a drought, which occurs with the aid of a supernatural God. He then prays for rain to end the drought, which occurs with the aid of a supernatural God. Yes, this is a physical example of a physical miracle. In reality, this *pro*-physical argument could indeed be the case; however, we are then thrown back into some of the issues that particular type of context and interpretation causes for us with the passage as a whole

I might suggest that the use of Elijah here is a physical example to illustrate how faithful men praying in *any situation* can accomplish much. God intervened regularly in physical and supernatural ways in the Old Testament—at least through a good portion of it. He also provided for miracles in the New Testament as well, and I have pointed out the reasons for that above. God accomplishes much through miracles in a physical way, and He accomplishes much through the prayers of devout, repentant people in spiritual ways. In doing so, He covers a multitude of sins (James 5:19–20; 1 Peter 4:8): physical actions (sins) with spiritual ramifications (condemnation), if not resolved.

Finally, James begins his letter focusing on persecution and its benefits for those who persevere. He says, "Consider it all joy, my brethren, when you encounter various trials, knowing that the testing of your faith produces endurance. And let endurance have its perfect result, that you may be perfect and complete, lacking in nothing" (James 1:2–4). He ends his letter focusing on what we are to do *when we do not persevere.* When weak, call on the support mechanism God has provided us in those around us who are faithful, who can identify with our weaknesses, who can support us, and who can pray with us to receive forgiveness and reignite the passions necessary to live faithfully, even though the world around us mitigates against such. It is important that we acknowledge we are weak and that we need the help of fellow Christians and God to make it through. Paul confesses the following in illustration of this point:

> And He has said to me, "My grace is sufficient for you, for power is perfected in weakness." Most gladly, therefore, I will rather boast about my weaknesses, that the power of Christ may dwell in me. Therefore, I am well content with weaknesses,

with insults, with distresses, with persecutions, with difficulties, for Christ's sake; for when I am weak, then I am strong (2 Corinthians 12:9–10).

Chapter 29

Judging Others
Matthew 7:1

You have often heard it said, "Who are you to judge me? Your own Bible tells you not to judge others." This passage is likely one of the few, if not the only passage, that nonbelievers have memorized. These assertions are offered, obviously, when it is pointed out that what someone is doing is in conflict with Scripture, has consequences, and should be stopped. "When they make a law preventing me, then I'll stop" is another response commonly offered. Often the behavior under consideration is deemed a moral or ethical issue, and these are considered "mushy" depending on who is making the judgment. The truth is that there are a number of controversial *moral* issues for which there are no civil *laws* forbidding them. A quick example would be hating someone. No law against it, although current "hate speech" restrictions are becoming popular on college campuses and in the public square. Regardless, hate itself is not a crime. But, back on topic, let's talk about "judging others."

The longest sermon presented by Jesus that we have recorded is His "Sermon on the Mount" provided in the most detail in Matthew 5–7. Jesus covers a number of subjects, but in Chapter 7, He turns his attention to the topic of judging. In Matthew 7:1, He says, "Judge not, that ye be not judged." Many interpret this to mean, "Don't judge others and they (or even He) won't judge you." This tacit agreement to essentially scratch each other's back where our behaviors are concerned is a *quid pro quo*. You leave me alone, and I'll leave you alone. Many stop with just the first two words: "Judge not." You can't judge me; Jesus forbids it. Well, does He?

In the very next verse, He provides an elaboration on what He means. In Matthew 7:2, he says the following [my emphasis]: "For in *the way* you judge, you will be judged; and by your *standard of measure*, it will be measured to you." Jesus is trying to get us to examine ourselves before we point out the shortcomings of others. The more modern version of this would be "People in glass houses shouldn't throw stones" or "Clean up your own back yard before complaining about others." He warns that using a standard—whether it be God's Word (likely here) or some other measure—opens one up to being measured by that same standard. He goes on in the next verses with even greater clarity. In Matthew 7:3–5, Jesus continues,

> Why do you look at the speck that is in your brother's eye, but do not notice the log that is in your own eye? Or how can you say to your brother, 'Let me take the speck out of your eye,' and look, the log is in your own eye? You hypocrite, first take the log out of your own eye, and then you will see clearly to take the speck out of your brother's eye!

What? You mean we *can* address our brother's shortcomings; all we have to do is make sure that we are circumspect in our lives or, more particularly, in that regard? Yes, He is saying that, or He wouldn't use the word *hypocrite*. Same issue, but we are just as guilty (even more so?) and complaining about others? That is indeed hypocrisy. So, Jesus is saying just be careful; if you are going to find fault with another—or make judgments about or judge that person—make sure you are not guilty of the same thing or something similar. However, there are other reasons that God's Word tells not only that we *can judge others* but that we *must judge others*.

Just a few verses later, He talks about the general ratio between those who will be saved and those who will face eternal destruction. While no real numbers are cited, He says,

> Enter through the narrow gate; for the gate is wide and the way is broad that leads to destruction, and there are many who enter

through it. For the gate is narrow and the way is constricted (*or narrow*) that leads to life, and there are few who find it (Matt. 7:13–14).

Many will be led to destruction and only a *few* (by comparison) will follow the way that leads to life. His next words actually point out *our responsibility to judge others* and the obvious reason is to help us determine who to and who not to follow that leads to these disparate outcomes.

He tells us to beware of false prophets, those who look acceptable but have anything but honest and noble deeds as their intent. He then says, "You will know them by their fruits" and provides us with examples: thorn bushes don't produce grapes; thistles don't produce figs; good trees bear good fruit; bad trees bear bad fruit. He says, "Every tree that does not bear good fruit is cut down and thrown into the fire." In other words, these are the false prophets and wolves in sheep's clothing we are to avoid. He again says, "So then, you will know them by their fruits." The obvious question is this: How can we identify them without at least *examining* their "fruit"? We have to view their work, *make a judgment,* and then avoid them.

Jesus does not contradict Himself here in Chapter 7 of Matthew. He is not telling us *not* to judge others. He is telling us a) to be careful in doing so as we ourselves will be judged similarly and b) to use that same measure to judge others who would lead us on a path to destruction ... and avoid them. These thoughts are echoed in Romans 14:10–13. However, there are other passages in the larger context of the Scriptures that confirm the notion that we not only *can* judge others but that we *must* judge them.

The purity of the local church is of paramount importance. God wants His people to be examples of the teachings they are supposedly supporting and preaching. Paul, in his first letter to the church at Corinth, tells them that they are in trouble. The situation is introduced in the latter verses of Chapter 4—at least Paul's attitude toward it—and is laid out in detail in Chapter 5. Without going into detail about the particulars, the situation was one of immorality within that group that Paul says, "does not even exist among the (heathen) Gentiles" (1 Corinthians 5:1). Paul says that he has already judged this person (v. 3) and that their obligation to do so is long overdue. In vv. 9–10, he says we have to associate with immoral people *in the world*, but *not within the body of Christ*. He tells them, in no uncertain terms, to remove that person from among their group. In other words, notify him and punish him. How can we do this if we are not to judge others?

The apostle John writes to his "children"—or those who he likely converted and still felt an obligation to lead or at least to offer inspired instruction. In 1 John 4:1–6, he makes a distinction between those who are from God and those who are not and the criterion they should use to determine such: those who confess that Jesus Christ has come in the flesh versus those who do not confess such. He says, "We are from God. The one who knows God listens to us; the one who is not from God does not listen to us. By this we know the spirit of truth and the spirit of error" (4:6). These are his concluding thoughts on the issue after he boldly tells them up front to "not believe every spirit, but test the spirits to see whether they are from God, because many false prophets have gone out into the world" (4:1). *Testing* the spirits would be exactly the same as *judging* them. We have to judge others, especially if they are presenting something as God's Word that is clearly not such.

There are other passages that tell us outright or suggest that judging is part of what we are to do as children of God (e.g., Matthew 18:15–17; Luke 17:3; Romans 16:17; 1 Timothy 5:20). The New Testament is God's Word, and it is our standard of measurement to use against other standards offered by the world. When these two are in conflict, we are to use the intelligence granted to us to determine if practices encouraged by the world should be called out or not. We obviously have the responsibility to make that distinction and make application in our lives. God has given us the *ability* to make judgments and also the *authority* to make the same, using His Word as the standard. We are not judging the souls of others; we are simply examining their words and actions and comparing them to God's standard.

Chapter 30

The Rising Sun and Falling Rain
Matthew 5:45

After His temptation in the wilderness by Satan and the arrest of John the Baptist, Jesus begins His earthly ministry in Matthew 4:12–17. He gathers a considerable multitude from across the region including Jerusalem, Galilee, Syria, Decapolis, Judea, and beyond the Jordan (Matthew 4:23–25). It was to this group of followers that He delivers what has come to be known as "The Sermon on the Mount." Jesus taught from other hillsides and mountains, but this sermon—the first extended one we have on record—stands out among others. After beginning with what is commonly called "The Beatitudes," he stresses His mission's relationship with the Law and the Prophets—not abolishing them but *fulfilling them*. He then focuses the majority of the rest of His sermon on the Jewish leaders of the day and how they had corrupted the law (5:19–20) with His "You have heard … but I say …" series of contrasts to illustrate the false "righteousness" of these scribes and Pharisees.

Toward the end of chapter 5 (in vv. 38–42), Jesus turns to our relationships with others. He contrasts what the Jewish leaders have pulled from the Old Law with what our attitudes and behaviors towards others should really be. If one strikes you on the cheek, turn the other. If one wants to sue you and take your shirt, give him your cloak also. Those who force us to "go one mile, go two." Do not turn away those who need goods we can supply. Apparently, the scribes and Pharisees told the people to hate their enemies, but Jesus told them "Love your enemies and pray for those who persecute you in order that you may be sons of your Father." He already told them to rejoice under persecution (5:11–12) as these He is indicting persecuted the prophets before them.

A "son" in this regard is not a blood relative, but one who follows the example set by the father (or Father, in this case). Jesus is making the point that God does not hate His enemies but loves them and forgives them. If we want to be like Him (i.e., sons), then we will do the same. Two verses later, Jesus points out that we are no better than the tax–gatherers or the Gentiles who love only those who love them. Our job is to be more like our heavenly Father: "You are to be perfect, as your heavenly Father is perfect." Obviously, this cannot mean sinless perfection, but is more focused on a more mature and forgiving attitude than those mentioned as negative examples we are to shun.

The Sun and the Rain

A verse was omitted in the discussion above and is right in the middle of these admonishments to treat everyone with the same generous, smiling, and go–the–extra–mile attitude, exemplified by our Father in heaven. Here is what it says (5:44–45):

> But I say to you, love your enemies and pray for those who persecute you, so that you may prove yourselves to be sons of your Father who is in heaven; for He causes His sun to rise on the evil and the good, and sends rain on the righteous and the unrighteous.

Obviously, Jesus is telling His listeners that all of God's creation, especially all of mankind, has worth. One's soul is not deemed less valuable simply because he or she is unresponsive to God's invitation to believe in Him. All creatures have worth. As a result, the other part of creation dealing with the "natural order," He has ordained and set forth in Genesis 1, and that continues undeterred and indiscriminately across both the evil and the good, the righteous and the unrighteous. That which was pronounced as "Good" by the Creator was being approved by Him for conditions until the end of time (of course, except during times when He sovereignly interrupted that order to perform miracles as a reminder of His absolute power over all).

God wants all of humanity to respond to the mercy and grace He has extended to them through the giving of His Son: "The Lord is not slow about His promise, as some count slowness, but is patient toward you, not willing for any to perish, but for all to come to repentance" (2 Peter 3:9).

However, this verse in Matthew 5 is sandwiched between two passages; one talks about the "day of judgment" and "destruction of ungodly people" and the other "the day of the Lord" and "the heavens will pass away with a roar and the elements will be destroyed with intense heat." Verse 11 asks, "Since all these things are to be destroyed in this way, what sort of people ought you to be in holy conduct and godliness," and v. 14 tells us to "be diligent to be found spotless and blameless by Him." Obviously, there will be ungodly people who will face eternal judgment unprepared to meet their Maker. So, why is Matthew 5:45 misunderstood and how is it taken out of context?

In a previous section of this writing (Chapter 14), I dealt with a notion called *universal salvation*. At the beginning of that chapter, there are several bullets advocating the belief that our Creator is "both powerful enough and loving enough" to rescue all souls from any sort of eternal separation from Him. They declare that there is "no such thing as eternal hell or annihilation" because God intended the universe "to produce a positive outcome for all people of all times." That chapter deals with this larger issue in detail, so I won't repeat that here.

The passage in Matthew 5:38–48 is primarily aimed at our attitudes towards our enemies and those who mistreat us or need what we can offer them. It is a change from the attitude promoted by the scribes and Pharisees, and that is the only point Jesus was making here. It is an attitude that He possesses and that God possesses. All humans have worth; particularly, their souls have value, and we need to set proper examples before unbelievers. There is benefit to this sort of response; 1 Peter 3:16–17 says,

> Keep a good conscience so that in the thing in which you are slandered, those who disparage your good behavior in Christ will be put to shame. For it is better, if God should will it so, that you suffer for doing what is right rather than for doing what is wrong.

Peter also provides this as an outcome: "Keep your behavior excellent among the Gentiles, so that in the thing in which they slander you as evildoers, they may because of your good deeds, as they observe them, glorify God on the day of visitation" (1 Peter 2:12).

Many take our passage under consideration out of context to show that both the evil people and the good people will have their share of misfortune—interpreting the "rain" in the passage to be the bad side of life. Rain, for the most part in Scripture, is viewed as an extremely positive event and its absence is even viewed as punishment in some cases (e.g., Leviticus 26:4; 1 Kings 8:35; Job 5:10; Prov 16:15; Jeremiah 5:24).

Do bad things happen to good people as well as bad people? Of course, and I would estimate in relatively equal portions over the course of history—that is, unless the bad people experience bad outcomes as a direct result of their wickedness. This could tip the scales in their direction, if this is the case. However, the point made here and by this entire writing is that we cannot take passages out of context and without being guilty of misusing or corrupting them. Is this notion—that everyone suffers—viable and supported by God's Word? You cannot look at the lives of individuals presented to us in the Bible as a whole and not recognize that being a child of God is no special shelter or prevention against the evils and disappointments in this life. Heaven will be a place where these earthly experiences will disappear (Revelation 21:4). Our job as children of His is to do His will while we are here and not suffer due to our disobeying it (1 Peter 4:15). On the contrary, let your suffering here be due to your unrelenting faith in God and His promises. Handle the disappointments in this life with grace, endure persecution due to our convictions from others willing and joyfully, and do both by placing more emphasis in the life hereafter than in the one we are currently living (e.g., Romans 5:3–5; 2 Corinthians 4:17–18; Hebrews 10:32–34; James 1:2–4; 1 Peter 4:16–19).

Yes, this passage does call into play a physical reality: both rain and sun are experienced by both good people and bad people in equal amounts. However, the context is that we, as imitators of God and Christ, should treat those who are righteous and those who are unrighteous just as equally as the sun and rain do. Do not favor only the righteous; every soul has worth, and we should treat those "who despitefully use us" the same as Christ does. Pray for them and do what you can to facilitate their conversion to the other side of the situation.

It would indeed be a stretch—more like an injustice or even slander—to lift this passage (Matthew 5:45) out of its immediate context and apply it to a position that is roundly disputed in the larger context of the New Testament (that of *universal salvation*). God's Word is clear: all will come before Him and be judged according to our words and our deeds in this life; those who are found faithful will be rewarded, and those who are not will be punished. The support for this conclusion is overwhelming in the New Testament. Jesus, Himself, in the very sermon under consideration, tells His listeners the following:

> Enter through the narrow gate; for the gate is wide and the way is broad that leads to destruction, and there are many who enter through it. For the gate is narrow and the way is constricted that leads to life, and there are few who find it.

He also says a few verses later,

> Not everyone who says to Me, 'Lord, Lord,' will enter the kingdom of heaven, but the one who does the will of My

Father who is in heaven will enter. Many will say to Me on that day, 'Lord, Lord, did we not prophesy in Your name, and in Your name cast out demons, and in Your name perform many miracles?' And then I will declare to them, 'I never knew you; leave Me, you who practice lawlessness" (Matthew 7:13–14).

God's Word is clear. There will be a Day of Judgment where all of mankind will be judged. The outcome is binary: reward or punishment. No in between, no crossing over, no second chances.

And just as it is destined for people to die once, and after this comes judgment,
so Christ also, having been offered once to bear the sins of many,
will appear a second time for salvation without reference to sin,
to those who eagerly await Him (Hebrews 9:27–28).

Chapter 31

God Is in Control
Romans 8:28

In sections above, I discussed the fact that the age of miracles came to an end with the death of John, the last apostle. As noted there, miracles throughout both the Old Testament and New Testament were for demonstrating the power of God or the power of the one operating on behalf of God, but this demonstration also carried a not-so-subtle point that the person was also *speaking* on behalf of God. The *message* was what was important, not that the person could work a miracle—a *supernatural* interruption in the *natural* order. This was even more apparent in the New Testament where God had restricted Himself to operating through others (inspiring John the Baptist, the miracles of Jesus and His disciples, the miracles that accompanied those who preached the Word in the early church, and the gifts of the Holy Spirit realized through the laying on of hands of the apostles).

To review, wonders, miracles, and signs were used to a) get their attention with something very much out of the ordinary (wonder); b) work the supernatural with the help of the power of God (miracle); and c) use this resulting attention to teach the Truth from God to those who needed it (sign). The power and authority to work the miracle had the same source of the power and authority in that which was taught: God. If the miracles were worth watching, then the prior, concurrent, or subsequent teaching was worth hearing and obeying.

However, once this new Word being delivered at that time was over and the revelations taking place were complete, there was no longer any need for miracles. The all-sufficiency of the Word, "once for all delivered to the saints" (Jude 1:3), was all that was needed. From there, faith was the primary operator on the hearts of people as they heard the Gospel in a second-hand format. As Jesus said to Thomas, "Because you have seen me, have you believed? Blessed are they who did not see, and yet believed." I think Jesus was saying that it takes *greater faith* for those of us who were not there to see the risen Christ, not there to witness the mighty works and hear the first-hand testimony of the apostles, and not there to witness the Holy Spirit operating in those early worship services with wisdom, knowledge, prophecies, tongues, etc. We no longer have those; what we do have, however, is what they did not have: God's perfect Word that provides "everything that pertains to life and godliness" (2 Pet1:3).

If this argument is adopted and fully believed, then why do many today still believe that God is working miracles on their behalf and for their benefit today? *Did God (or His agents) ever work a miracle solely for the purpose of benefiting the one on whom the miracle was focused*? One of the reasons for this belief is a misunderstanding of Romans 8:28. I noted early on in this writing that context is extremely important when attempting to understand a passage of Scripture; this is one of those cases. Hear what the passage says, how it is usually interpreted, and what the context tells us instead: "God causes all things to work together for good to those who love God, to those called according to His purpose."

Taken out of context and on face value, one would have to agree that for those who are His, those who love Him, and those who are abiding in His Word ... He is actively and physically making things in this life and this world work for their benefit. I just dealt with this issue at the end of an earlier chapter, but let's look further. First, let's look at the rest of the chapter to see what is really meant by Paul. Romans 8 is all about *spiritual* (not physical) blessings. There are two ways in which God has shown favor to man: physically and spiritually. He made Abraham a very wealthy man as he sojourned through Canaan and Egypt (physical). He likewise took care of the Israelites as they wandered in the wilderness before entering Canaan, their Promised Land (physical provision).

There are, however, more important blessings God affords those who are His. These blessings are found in Christ and, for the most part but not entirely, will be realized when this life is over. These are *spiritual* blessings that are the ultimate "payoff" for a life devoted to God. These were not possible or fully realized prior to the sacrifice of Jesus on the cross and His resurrection, but now they have been granted to all who have been faithful to God, regardless in which dispensation they lived or what covenant they obeyed (Hebrews 9:15; 11:39–40).

Let's look specifically at the context of Romans 8 for a proper understanding of what it is telling us. In v. 1, Paul tells us there is "no condemnation for those in Christ"; this is a spiritual blessing as our reward will come after this life is over (spiritual). Verse 2 tells us that we are no longer in bondage to sin anymore through Jesus; our sins have been forgiven (spiritual). Verses 4–11 play out for us how the flesh and the spirit are at odds within ourselves and how each appeals to us. If Christ is in us, sin is dead to us, and the spirit is alive due to righteousness. Verse 14 tells them that if you are led by the Spirit of God, you are sons of God (spiritual). Verse 17 says that if we are children of God, then we are heirs with Christ and glorified with Him (spiritual). Verse 18 reminds us that whatever current sufferings we are undergoing, they are nothing compared to glory to be revealed in us at His coming (spiritual). We might note that these were *the faithful*, but things were not "working together for good" (depending on the interpretation of "good") for them at the moment.

In vv. 20–25, we are told that in this life, we groan (discomfort) and hope for redemption (spiritual). Verses 26–27 point out that the Spirit provides hope for us and intercedes for us in our prayers (spiritual). Verses 29–30 note that He predestined us to be like His Son: called, justified, and glorified (spiritual). In vv. 31–34 we find the following: "If God be for us, who can be against us?" He delivered up His son for us (our souls), so "How will He not also with Him freely give us *all things*?" Can this be anything but spiritual, given what we have just read? Finally, in vv. 35–39, "Nothing can separate us from the love of God in Christ Jesus" (spiritual).

Nothing in the entire chapter speaks of physical blessings or rewards or favors of any kind from God while on this earth. The focus is entirely on the spiritual blessings that we have in Christ and with which God has blessed and will richly bless us. To take v. 28 in the midst of this context and force its interpretation for a physical outcome is putting the proverbial square peg in a round hole; it just does not fit. "And we know that God causes all things to work together for good to those who love God, to those who are called according to his purpose." Of course, He does ... *ultimately* and when Jesus comes again. God absolutely does not "cause all things to work together" for our good in this life. Not how I count "good" anyway, and my trials and tribulations in this life can only be interpreted as "good" when their result is realized in glory. Also, what we suffer today cannot hold a candle to that which was suffered by those for the cause of Christ in the first century. Either "good" means something else or I don't understand its meaning.

Or maybe I do and just understand it to mean "ultimate good." Our salvation, that for which we labor earnestly here on this earth, is our spiritual reward. And while I cannot describe for you what heaven will be other than that which we have been provided within Scripture, I know for a fact, it will indeed be "good." Romans 8, and especially v. 28, is talking about heaven and the spiritual rewards we will experience there for having been faithful here. To interpret it otherwise is abusing both the verse and the chapter.

Chapter 32

Forsaking the Assembly
Hebrews 10:25

The letter (epistle) to the Hebrews contains a treasure of valuable information for Christians. It was written to Jews who had converted to Christianity, but who, for various reasons, needed reassurance a) that their faith was not in vain; b) that they had truly obtained salvation through their obedience; c) that Judaism, regardless of how dear it was to them in the past, was gone; and d) that Jesus and everything He offered was indeed far superior to everything offered under the Old Law. The writer acknowledges the current pressures under which they find themselves to return to Judaism, but he also stresses what a colossal mistake that would be. The danger of losing the salvation once achieved was real, and they should consider the consequences of such an outcome. Likewise, we non-Jewish converts can learn from this that turning our backs on the only sacrifice that will ever reconcile us to God would indeed have serious and eternal consequences.

There are several passages in the book that contain warnings or allusions to warnings. The first mention is Hebrews 2:1–3:

> For this reason we must pay much closer attention to what we have heard, lest we drift away from it. For if the word spoken through angels proved unalterable, and every transgression and disobedience received a just recompense, how shall we escape if we neglect so great a salvation?

What they "have heard" is the Gospel and what they won't escape is eternal damnation. The question is rhetorical; God is sure in His promises to both reward and punish.

Hebrews 3 has several passages that are relevant here. First, Hebrews 3:6 tells us "Christ was faithful as a Son over His house whose house we are, if we hold fast our confidence and the boast of our hope firm until the end." Notice the condition in the last phrase: "if" predicates the rest. If you don't hold fast *to the end*, the other will not follow or be true. A few verses later, another warning is given:

> Take care, brethren, lest there should be in any one of you an evil, unbelieving heart, in falling away from the living God. But encourage one another day after day, as long as it is still called "Today," lest any one of you be hardened by the deceitfulness of sin. For we have become partakers of Christ, if we hold fast the beginning of our assurance firm until the end (3:12–14).

Remember the point in the middle about encouraging one another; that activity will come up again. However, the initial point is that they not only *can* fall away from God … they *are falling away* if they go back into Judaism! Also, you have that conditional "if" offered again at the end. Verse 19 tells us that, like Israel, we too can be denied entry into eternal rest.

In the very next verses (Hebrews 4:1–2), the thought is continued:

> Therefore, let us fear lest, while a promise remains of entering His rest, any one of you should seem to have come short of it. For indeed we have had good news preached to us, just as they also; but the word they heard did not profit them, because it was not united by faith in those who heard.

Verse 11, again stresses their situation's likeness to that of Israel, saying, "Let us therefore be diligent to enter that rest, lest anyone fall through following the same example of disobedience." I think it is apparent a theme is developing here.

In Hebrews 6:4–8, we have probably the most severe and graphic warning of where these Jews were headed on their current path:

> For in the case of those who have once been enlightened and have tasted of the heavenly gift and have been made partakers of the Holy Spirit, and have tasted the good word of God and the powers of the age to come, and then have fallen away, it is impossible to renew them again to repentance, since they again crucify to themselves the Son of God, and put Him to open shame. For ground that drinks the rain which often falls upon it and brings forth vegetation useful to those for whose sake it is also tilled, receives a blessing from God; but if it yields thorns and thistles, it is worthless and close to being cursed, and it ends up being burned.

They are reminded of all the blessings found in Christ and then told if they reject that, there is no further sacrifice made on their behalf. They have rejected the only one offered. Essentially, they are crucifying Him all over again with their actions. The latter part offers a threat concerning their outcome if they continue. Remember the Parable of the Sower/Soils (Matthew 13; Luke 8) that had a very similar message.

Finally, Chapter 9 lays out in considerable detail exactly why returning to Judaism would be so fatal and tragic. Everything under the Old Law is laid side by side with that which Jesus offers, and in all cases, there is no comparison. Christ is superior to the Old Law. It was designed to be replaced and Christ is that replacement. The latter verses refer to "death" and then the "judgment." As we come to Chapter 10, the writer continues with why Christ's sacrifice was the perfect sacrifice and that He needed to do it only once "for all" (10:10). This section ends in Verse 18, saying, "Now where there is forgiveness of these things, there is no longer any offering for sin." It is at this point, the writer seems to shift gears and provide some conclusions to the points he has been making. Before examining that portion of the passage, let's make a comparison to another passage with similar concomitant circumstances.

Parallel Conditions of 1 Corinthians 7

Persecution of early Christians is well-documented in both religious and secular writings, and I have referred to it in this writing several times. The Bible refers to it numerous times; the apostles experienced it firsthand; and Paul certainly did so himself. He and others often offer encouragement to endure with patience, count it all joy, etc. under the pressures from both the Jews and the Romans. One of those situations where Paul is teaching about something else is framed under these conditions. In 1 Corinthians 7, Paul is apparently responding to another question on which this congregation has sought an answer (i.e., his "Now concerning" introduction which he uses several times in this letter). The topic appears to be marriage and relationships; these are some of the instructions he offers:

1— "It is good for a man not to touch a woman";
7—"I wish that all men were even as I am" (single);
8—"To the unmarried and the widows, it is good for them to remain even as I";
20, 24—"Let each man remain in that condition in which he was called";
29—"Those who have wives should be as though they have none";
33—"The one who is married is concerned about the things of the world"; and
39—"If her husband is dead, she is free to marry … but in my opinion she is happier if she remains as she is" (single).

These are strange instructions, especially in light of what else is found in Scripture that would appear to contradict these. In fact, many assert that Paul was *anti-marriage*. Marriage as an institution is established early in Scripture (Gen. 2:24) and touted throughout the New Testament as a model for the relationship between Christ (bridegroom) and the church (the bride) in Matt. 9:15; John 3:29; 2 Cor. 11:2; Eph. 5:22–28; and Rev. 19:7. There must be a reason for this, and indeed there is. Paul's "conditions" under which he offers these are also included in 1 Cor. 7:

26—"This is good in view of the present distress";
28—"Such will have trouble in this life, and I am trying to spare you";
29—"The time has been shortened"; and
31—"The form of this world is passing away."

It is apparent that these people were under severe oppression, and Paul is trying to keep them focused on "undistracted devotion to the Lord" (v. 35). So, why do I mention this situation in 1 Corinthians to compare it to the letter to the Hebrews? The comparison should be obvious; both situations involve persecution and its impact on present conditions. Paul would never have offered these thoughts on marriage had they not been in their "present distress" as these contradict so many other New Testament passages that both sanction and praise the institution of marriage. Likewise, in Hebrews, he is using their current situation to prescribe other, possibly unconventional behavior in an attempt to endure the conditions under which they find themselves. Here is what he says to them in Hebrews 10:32–36:

> But remember the former days, when, after being enlightened, *you endured a great conflict of sufferings, partly by being made a public spectacle through insults and distress, and partly by becoming companions with those who were so treated.* For you showed sympathy to the prisoners and *accepted joyfully the seizure of your property*, knowing that you have for yourselves a better and lasting possession. Therefore, do not throw away your confidence, which has a great reward. For you have need of endurance, so that when you have done the will of God, you may receive what was promised.

Notice the italicized phrases indicating conditions similar to what the church at Corinth was experiencing. He warns them not to throw away this "confidence (of a) great reward" by giving in to these pressures. Not only this, but he also says just above these verses the following:

> For if we go on sinning willfully after receiving the knowledge of the truth, there no longer remains a sacrifice for sins, but a

terrifying expectation of judgment and the fury of a fire which will consume the adversaries. Anyone who has ignored the Law of Moses is put to death without mercy on the testimony of two or three witnesses. How much more severe punishment do you think he will deserve who has trampled underfoot the Son of God, and has regarded as unclean the blood of the covenant by which he was sanctified, and has insulted the Spirit of grace? For we know Him who said, "Vengeance is mine, I will repay." And again, "The lord will judge his people." It is a terrifying thing to fall into the hands of the living God (Hebrews 10:26–31).

The verbiage the writer uses here is the same as in all the other passages in Hebrews warning them not to go back into Judaism, not to turn their back on the only hope they have, not to give up what is already within their grasp—that being salvation. He ramps up his threats here to show them the extremely dire situation in which they will find themselves if they do give in and return to their previous belief system (Judaism) and condition (unsaved).

"Forsaking the Assembly"— Hebrews 10:25

With all the Hebrew writer has offered up to this point (review is unnecessary), he now begins in Hebrews 10:19 with another statement of encouragement to a) resist the temptation to revert to Judaism but b) use our association with each other as fellow–believers and fellow–Christians as a source of strength. Isolating oneself from others of like faith will only weaken you, making it easier to totally withdraw and fall away—the danger of which he has warned them repeatedly in this letter, both before and after this key verse. "We have confidence to enter the holy place by the blood of Jesus"; "Let us draw near with a sincere heart in full assurance of faith"; "Let us hold fast the confession of our hope without wavering"; and "Let us consider how to stimulate one another to love and good deeds." These are all things we do *together*; notice the employment of the plural pronouns of "we" and "us."

(Remember an earlier comment about Hebrews 3:13. Here is what the text says about turning back and a possible preventive measure [emphasis is mine]: "But *encourage one another day after day*, as long as it is still called "Today," lest any one of you be hardened by the deceitfulness of sin." The writer sets up points he makes in Chapter 10 about the strength drawn from others of like faith, especially in those trying and stressful times of persecution. Notice also that this was to be a *daily activity*.)

The next phrase, however, is the one that brings us to the point of our discussion here and reads as follows: "not forsaking our own assembling together, as is the habit of some, but encouraging one another; and all the more, as you see the day drawing near" (NASB). Let's begin with the last phrase here as we attempt to understand the true meaning of this verse *in context*. Remember, the writer is stressing the superiority of Jesus to *everything* the Old Law has to offer; he is telling them to do everything they can to resist the temptation to be pulled away from Christ and back into Judaism; and he is setting up Chapter 11 (which we have not mentioned yet) to show them how Hebrew *icons* of the past made sure their entry into the Promised Land (i.e., both Canaan and heaven) through their persistence and endurance, energized by their faith.

All the More As You See the Day Drawing Near

This phrase is an add-on to what has just been said, sort of as a multiplier or "stressor" because of an additional condition. I'll come back to that condition in a moment, but for now, let's consider the meaning of "the day" mentioned toward the end of the sentence. There are at least three possible interpretations of this "day" that is under consideration here.

The first interpretation is that it is the Lord's Day or The First Day of the Week that, elsewhere, I have mentioned as the New Testament's establishing this day—as opposed to the Sabbath Day of the Jews—for special attention to and worship of God. It is not that the other days are not important for acknowledging God; it is just that the New Testament appears to establish the first day of the week, Sunday, for being set aside to formally come together to worship Him. Not coincidentally, this is the day of the week that Jesus rose from the dead, and from a logical standpoint, this one would be special if we were going to set one aside.

The second option for "day" might possibly be Judgment Day or the End of Time. This day is forecast numerous times and even some detail is provided in New Testament passages (Matt. 10:15; 12:36; John 12:48; Acts 17:31; Rom. 2:16; 1 Cor. 3:13; 4:5; 2 Cor. 5:10; 2 Thess. 4:13–18; Heb. 9:27; James 5:5; 2 Pet. 2:4–9; 3:7; 1 John 4:17). There are others, but these will do to establish that there will be a day of reckoning and that each of us who has ever lived on this earth will account for the deeds committed in our life here (Rom. 14:12).

The third possibility for "day" could possibly be referring to the Destruction of Jerusalem that occurred in AD 70. The Roman army comes at that time to put down the insurrections that have been occurring, and this, too, was forecast in Scripture (Matt. 24:1–28; Luke 19:41–44; 21:20–24). This was not the first time Jerusalem had been destroyed, but it was the last time—at least as far as New Testament history is concerned. Along with the destruction of Jerusalem and the Temple, the Jewish economy and nation as a viable entity were destroyed as well. Israel would never again become what it had been, and this is the judgment that was placed upon the Jews following their national rejection of Jesus as Messiah. Jesus wept over Jerusalem just before He enters it for the last time and alludes to its future demise (Luke 19:41–44). So, let's examine each of these three days to see which fits best in this context in Hebrews 10.

The Lord's Day

Many read this passage without really looking at what it is saying. They read it to say, "Don't forsake the Lord's Day assembly as you see the Lord's Day drawing near." That is not what it says, and that would not make sense. I guess you could say, "Remember that the Lord's Day is approaching, so be sure you observe it." Even that twists the apparent intention of the passage. Does it mean we are to be more righteous on Friday than we were on Monday, the closer it gets to Sunday? Of course not. Paul would not put a stipulation of heeding the fact that Sunday is approaching just to get them to not forsake assembling together on that day. If that is what he meant, there are other, clearer ways to deliver that message.

The only way this choice of "days" would make sense would be if he was saying to them, "Stay close together during the week so that on Sunday you will still be together for worship." This interpretation seems really forced and unlikely.

Judgment Day

If they can "see the day approaching," then it is something visual and contextual that they will indeed be able to take in and process intellectually. Paul was speaking of an event to be seen by the Hebrew Christians in the first century. Judgment Day has not yet occurred, so how could an event happening some 2,000 years (and counting) after all those in Jerusalem died, be a warning for them? It couldn't.

Some try to answer this objection by saying that Christians have always viewed the Lord's return as possibly happening at any moment, so we should always anticipate that it is near. While that is true, there is that little word "see" in Heb. 10:25. Also, Jesus said there would be no signs of His Second Coming since He will come as a "thief" in the night (Matt. 24:41–44). No "seeing it ahead of time" in that phrasing. This warning to the Christians in Jerusalem is for them to be prepared for a very significant event to take place in their lifetime and that they will be able to see it coming.

The Destruction of Jerusalem in A.D. 70

In Matthew 24, Luke 19, and Luke 21, Jesus predicts and talks about the destruction of Jerusalem. He weeps over it as He enters it for the last time and says,

> Jerusalem, Jerusalem, who kills the prophets and stones those who have been sent to her! How often I wanted to gather your children together, the way a hen gathers her chicks under her wings, and you were unwilling. Behold, your house is being left to you desolate (Matt. 23:37–38).

Estimates are that Matthew's Gospel was written one to two years prior to AD 70, when Jerusalem fell to the Roman army and these prophecies by Jesus came true. Jesus even tells them in Matthew 24:15–25 to heed the warnings they will be able to "see" (v. 15). Like Matthew, Bible scholars date the book of Hebrews between AD 68 and AD 70, just prior to Jerusalem's destruction.

Remember, the Jewish Christians who read the Hebrew letter were being persecuted not only by Rome to denounce their Christianity, but they were also being persecuted by Judaizing teachers who were pulling them back into Judaism. Numerous times and in various ways, the Hebrew writer warns them of this destructive folly. If they indeed fell back, the warnings in successive verses spell out their destiny, especially where God is concerned (Heb. 10:26–31). They needed to be especially diligent in their faithfulness and prevent this drastic outcome from renouncing their faith in Christ and losing their salvation.

We can only stimulate one another to love and good deeds (10:24) through our mutual association and interpersonal personal contact. If there is danger of falling away due to persecution (there was: 10:32–36), then these people needed to stick together and draw strength from each other's faith. The writer was telling them to "stay tight"; keep your associations; don't neglect getting together for this mutual support network you have going. And here is the "kicker": You haven't seen anything yet—the destruction of everything you know is about to happen. Stay faithful; don't turn back; stay together in the Lord. Remember also, that Hebrews 3:13 tells them to do this *day by day*, not just when they came together for worship assembly. The early church did so, and it unified them (Acts 2:43–47).

Analysis of Hebrews 10:25

My conclusion, from the options presented above, is that "day" spoken of in Hebrews 10:25 is the destruction of Jerusalem in AD 70. The "current distress" invoked by Paul in 1 Corinthians 7, as he made some otherwise odd recommendations, is the same "current distress" these folks are facing in Hebrews 10. Normally, these instructions would not be made or at least have to be offered as intensely. However, under the existing persecutions, both Paul and the Hebrew writer lay out some strategies that will help them cope with these extremely trying circumstances. I have noted where the writer of Hebrews has warned them about falling away, and now, we have a really focused and drastic picture painted for them if they do (10:26–31).

Forsake

Vine's tells us this about the word "forsake" for our consideration here:

> "Forsake"—*enkataleipo*—denotes (a) "to leave behind, among, leave surviving," Romans 9:29; (b) "to forsake, abandon, leave in straits, or helpless," said by, or of, Christ, Matt. 27:46; Mark 15:34; Acts 2:27, 31; of men, 2 Cor. 4:9; 2 Tim. 4:10, 16; by God, Heb. 13:5; of things, by Christians (negatively), Heb. 10:25. See LEAVE.

In each of the passages noted here, there is a strong implication—if not outright declaration—that we are talking *total* desertion, *total* abandonment, *total* leaving behind when this word is used. This definition fits this passage but only if you adopt the context as meaning, "Do not go back into that which you left." Again, the retribution that will follow those who do in vv. 26–31 fits this approach to "forsake."

Assembling Together

Let's look at the next phrase in the passage. The combined words "assembling together" is from one Greek word—*episunagōgē*. This word is a noun, and it is found in only one other place:

> Now we beseech you, brethren, by the coming of our Lord Jesus Christ, and by our *gathering together* unto him, that ye be not soon shaken in mind, or be troubled, neither by spirit, nor by word, nor by letter as from us, as that the day of Christ is at hand (2 Thess. 2:1–2).

"Gathering together" is translated from *episunagōgē*. It is obvious in this passage that *episunagōgē* refers to our being gathered to Christ at His coming where we will meet Him in the air (1 Thessalonians 4:17), not our gathering on a regular basis for worship.

There is a verb form of this word. It is *episunagō*. It is found in several verses. Let's look at them.

- Matthew 23:37. Jerusalem, Jerusalem, who kills the prophets and stones those who have been sent to her! How often I wanted to *gather your children together*, the way a hen gathers her chicks under her wings, and you were unwilling (parallel verse in Luke 13:34).
- Matthew 24:30–31. And then the sign of the Son of Man will appear in the sky, and then all the tribes of the earth will mourn, and they will see the son of man coming on the clouds of the sky with power and great glory. And He will send forth His angels with a great trumpet blast, and *they will gather together* His elect from the four winds, from one end of the sky to the other (the parallel verse is in Mark 13:26–27).
- Mark 1:33. And the *whole city had gathered* at the door.
- Luke 12:1. Under these circumstances, after so many *thousands of people had gathered together* that they were stepping on one another, He began saying to His disciples first of all, "Beware of the leaven of the Pharisees, which is hypocrisy."

In every place where we find the verb *episunagō*, it is used to refer to a gathering of some sort to Christ. And in the only other place where the noun form *episunagōgē* is used, it is used for that great gathering to

Christ on the day of His return and our resurrection. Thus, when we see *episunagōgē* used in Hebrews 10:25, we must begin to suspect that perhaps it does not automatically refer to going to worship on Sunday (or any other day of the week) but to something greater (like staying faithful and unified in faith).

Even in Acts 20:7, where we can be certain that Luke was talking about the Lord's Day, the Greek word *synēgmenōn* is used. The definition offered by Strong and others is very similar to that for *episunagō*: simply to "gather together, draw together, bring together, join together." There is nothing special about "the assembly"—at least from an original Greek perspective—in Hebrews 10:25. In fact, with the limited knowledge I have of Greek, I have been unable to track down within the New Testament a Greek word officially designating what Christians did on the first day of the week. What we do on that day to formally honor, praise, and worship God, sing songs of praise and devotion, and observe the Lord's Supper *ought to have* a Greek word of some sort, but it does not appear to be so. Vine's says this in his notes under the entry for *worship*: "The worship of God is nowhere defined in Scripture."

Traditional Argument

All of us have heard from the pulpit that attending worship services—even gatherings for Bible Study—are important. Some will even go so far as to say that missing *any* of these opportunities is a violation of the command found in Hebrews 10:25 to "forsake not the assembly." At the very minimum, this passage is used as some sort of proof text for the importance of not missing that particular gathering, "unless Providentially hindered" (see earlier thoughts on the word *providence*). On the contrary, it simply does not say that. It does not say, "Do not miss worship services."

The argument presented above leads us to these more accurate conclusions about the meaning of this verse in its context:

- "The day" we are talking about is the destruction of Jerusalem in AD 70 and not Sunday, the Lord's Day, when we come to worship.
- *Forsake* means "totally abandoning" rather than "occasionally missing" and fits the context here for what these Jewish Christians were being threatened with in successive verses if they "totally abandoned" Jesus for Judaism. Most verses elsewhere for the Greek word used here refer to "don't abandon" or "totally leave" something.
- *Assembling together*—according to how the Greek word is used elsewhere in the New Testament—means our ultimate coming together to be with Jesus or simply "a gathering" of some sort.

The point is this: does the context support using this passage as a *proof text* for not missing worship services? No, it does not. Look at the context.

- The *larger* context is Christ's superiority to everything Jewish or under the Old Law
- The larger context is that going back to Judaism kicks in an entire world of ramifications these Jews do not want to face.
- The larger context is that they will lose their salvation after having gained it.
- The *immediate* context is that they have just been shown Christ's superiority and 10:18 says, "Where there is forgiveness (only in Christ) of these things, there is no longer any offering for sin." Not the regular and repeated ones under the Law nor a second offering—like that of Jesus's—will be forthcoming.
- The immediate context tells them to "have confidence" (v. 19); "draw near" (v. 22); "hold fast without wavering" (v. 23); and "stimulate one another" (v. 24).
- All of those verses lead us to "don't forsake"—abandon, desert, leave off from, etc.—your associating together, your coming together, your relationships that strengthen you … or you will fall away.
- The immediate context then tells them what will happen if they do go back to Judaism:
  - This is sinning after having received forgiveness.
  - They are turning their back on the sacrifice Jesus made.

- They can expect a terrifying judgment.
- They have trampled underfoot the Son of God.
- They have regarded His blood unclean.
- They have insulted the Spirit of grace.
- They have invited God's vengeance .
- They have thrown away their reward.
- They have "shrunk back to destruction."

These are the things that will occur when you *truly forsake* (totally abandon) Jesus Christ for anything else as a substitute. Missing a worship service is not the issue here.

Final Points

To artificially thrust "missing worship services" into this context for one verse, in a way, insults the larger point being made. He is talking about drawing strength from one another and what we as a collective can do to prevent the sad affair when one falls away. In this context, the *falling away* was going back into Judaism. In ours, it could be a number of things we "go back into," but any reason is insufficient and incurs a rejection of the salvation that they (and we) had within their hands. Peter tells his readers this in his second letter: "For it would be better for them not to have known the way of righteousness, than having known it, to turn away from the holy commandment handed on to them" (2 Pet. 2:21). Why is that? Because they *had it* and *lost it*. It is sad when people never come to a knowledge of the truth and render obedience to the Gospel. However, it is much sadder when they do have it and then turn from it to lose that salvation which was once theirs.

With all of this said, these questions are legitimate: 1) Is worshiping regularly with fellow Christians important and something we should habitually do? 2) Isn't worshiping regularly with fellow Christians one of the ways that we can "assemble," "have confidence," "draw near," "hold fast," and "stimulate each other to love and good deeds"? Both questions can be answered with, "Of course."

For these questions, let me offer these points.

- Christ came to this earth to die for and establish His kingdom, the church. He accomplished that, and the body of believers the world over constitutes that church.
- The apostles were selected and *ordained* to carry out the spreading of the Gospel. Although Jesus never said anywhere, "Establish local congregations to do this," the apostles apparently understood this through inspiration of the Holy Spirit or something Jesus might have said that was not recorded. Maybe it was a logical deduction on their part that we take as an approved apostolic example we should follow.
- The bulk of the apostles' doctrine (Acts 2:42) is found in Luke's history of their Acts and the letters that inspired men wrote to both individuals and churches. Without these instructions to these two entities, we would know little about what churches, or local congregations, are to do.
- We conclude from Scripture that local congregations came together on the first day of the week to observe the Lord's supper; teach and admonish each other by singing psalms, hymns, and spiritual songs; more than likely study God's revelation (His Word) to mankind; and very likely donate a portion of their earnings so that this group could continue to evangelize others, edify the group, and provide for the needs of other Christians.
- I would contend that Christ died both for the church *universal*, and He died for the church *local*—that entity designated to carry out His Word on a day-to-day basis. If this is the pattern we are to follow to carry out His work on this earth, then why would the local church not be a part of the picture when considering why Jesus died and rose?
- Our passage under consideration (Hebrews 10:25) tells us the kinds of benefits these types of gatherings for worship *can* indeed supply, but it is likely talking about the larger relationships drawn even outside these times we come together for worship. So yes, assembling ourselves together for worship is *one way* that we can do all those things we as a group should do for each other.

Finally, Paul's commitment to the church at large was manifest in his efforts to establish churches at the local level. He knew this was God's plan for spreading the Gospel to the world. His teachings and admonishments to these groups was an attempt to hold them together, especially during times of temptations and persecutions. I will close this section with a couple of quotes, one from Ephesians 3:8–12 that talks about our obligations as local congregations and the implication that we as individuals should be contributing members of these efforts.

> To me, who am less than the least of all the saints, this grace was given, that I should preach among the Gentiles the unsearchable riches of Christ, and to make all see what is the fellowship of the mystery, which from the beginning of the ages has been hidden in God who created all things through Jesus Christ; to the intent that now *the manifold wisdom of God might be made known by the church* to the principalities and powers in the heavenly places, according to the eternal purpose which He accomplished in Christ Jesus our Lord, in whom we have boldness and access with confidence through faith in Him.

The second quote is from Paul's first letter to the young evangelist, Timothy. In the third chapter of that letter, Paul lays out the qualifications for both elders—those who have the charge leading local congregations—and deacons—those who have the charge to help the elders do their job of leading and caring for the souls of the congregation's membership. The mere fact that leadership is clearly defined for local congregations speaks strongly for the importance of these groups' existence and function. In fact, part of that function is included in our last quote. Upon conclusion of Paul's list of qualifications and characteristics of elders and deacons, he says this:

> I am writing these things to you, hoping to come to you before long; but in case I am delayed, I write so that you may know how one ought to conduct himself in *the household of God, which is the church of the living God, the pillar and support of the truth.*

Yes, the church as a larger body (universal) certainly has the responsibility to preach the gospel—each of us individually—but that is most effectively carried out by God's implementation of the *local congregation concept,* initiated by the apostles in the first century. Both the church local and the church universal are the "pillar and support of the truth" (i.e., the Gospel of the "church of the living God").

Chapter 33

The Presence of the Lord
Matthew 18:20

You just read an extended chapter on "the assembling of yourselves together" noting that the passage *might possibly be* referring to when we meet to worship. However, I noted it also is more likely *anytime* those Christians—in that time of persecution and temptation to return to Judaism—met together to "stimulate one another to love and good deeds," wherever that might take place. From what we can conclude, the early church met every Lord's Day, the first day of the week, to worship and to do the things that churches did in that day.

From apostolic examples, we know they observed the Lord's Supper—apparently the primary reason they came together as suggested by the wording in Acts 20:7. More than likely, someone delivered some sort of message, or inspired writings were read (Paul preached in Acts 20). I am also assuming that, at least during these first century sessions, spiritual gifts were on display by various members of the group and some revelation took place through these. (I have discussed elsewhere how these gifts are no longer needed nor are there any apostles around to "gift" others with these powers.) We are told to sing to one another, and this can only be done when we are together. Prayer would be another logical activity and Scripture could be found for such. Finally, Paul tells the church at Corinth (1 Cor. 16:1–2)—as well as the churches of Galatia—to give of their means through a free-will offering, commonly known as a *collection*, for the support of the work of spreading the Gospel, or helping other needy Christians. This was apparently also done on the first day of the week, at least in that example, but was likely a common or regular time to take care of this obligation.

Where Two or Three Are Gathered

The passage under consideration for this chapter is Matthew 18:20, which says the following: "For where two or three have gathered together in My name, I am there in their midst." The most common employment of this passage is to teach that when we assemble in corporate worship—as noted above—Jesus in there in our midst, certainly in a spiritual sense rather than physical. This could conceivably extend to anytime that Christians are gathered to focus on deity regardless of how formal or inclusive. For example, a small group that gathers to offer prayers for something specific (or general) could work; a home Bible study might also work.

The point being made is that Jesus (and obviously, God) approves His people gathering in His name—or by His authority, and He signals this by stating that His spirit is present. Anytime people are turning their attention to God's Word or doing things that Scriptures tell us to do, that activity is approved of by the Father and the Son. He even mentions eating of the Lord's Supper with them "in the kingdom" (i.e., the church), indicating He is spiritually present when we observe this memorial feast. Let's be clear, however, that if the results of that gathering should conclude in doctrinal error in some way, the *outcomes* are not approved. How and when Jesus would leave the group is undecipherable; He is not going to spiritually sanction something with His *presence* that obviously was misguided or contained error.

That the Father and the Son can be and are spiritually "in our midst" when we gather to Scripturally worship is not really debatable. We'll look at some passages suggesting such below. However, the question is this: Does Matthew 18:20 teach this or is it taken out of context (its real purpose) to promote a concept that is supported elsewhere?

Context for Matthew 18:20

At the beginning of Matthew 18, the *disciples* (commentaries, due to the larger context, tell us these were the 12 apostles) come to Jesus asking a question that is recorded in other Gospels and arises even again later during that final Passover meal when Jesus institutes the Lord's Supper. For one reason or another, there appears to be some sort of power struggle among the apostles, and they sought a statement from Jesus about which of them would be the greatest in His kingdom. True, this could be some good-natured ribbing among the guys, but Jesus treats it as a serious topic, regardless. This also, of course, suggests a continuation of their misconception about that kingdom (the church) and that it was not going to be a physical returning of Jews to world dominance with Him reigning on David's throne. No matter how many times He told them differently and that He would be dying soon, their indoctrination in this Jewish belief was too strong to overcome. Only His death, burial, and resurrection—along with the empowerment of the Holy Spirit on Pentecost—could overcome these deep-seated tendencies.

That they would be petty enough to argue over who among them was the greatest suggests a level of egotism that Jesus more than once had spoken against. Nevertheless, they persisted, and Matthew 18 is one of those times. He proceeds to talk to them about humility by using a child as an example (18:2–6) saying that one cannot enter the kingdom unless he or she is humble like this child. He then says that whoever causes "stumbling blocks" for these (including the current group's lack of humility, most likely), that action would keep that person from salvation. The well-known examples of the hand and eye that might cause one to burn in hell are provided; better to eliminate one of these than suffer eternal torment with two. "For the Son of Man has come to save that which was lost" (18:11).

Continuing this thought, He goes on to discuss how valuable each soul is to the Father and how one lost soul that was saved causes greater joy than 99 that were already saved. God wants no one to perish, an assertion that we find elsewhere in Scripture (John 5:34; 1 Timothy 2:4; 2 Timothy 2:25–26). Jesus then begins the context for the statement of our focus here.

He inserts a few thoughts about how a group can exert pressure on an individual who is guilty of sin. He says that there is a "formula" for the process that is a principle found in the Old Law: "By the mouth of two or three witnesses every fact may be confirmed." First, He says, go to the brother in private, one on one, and reprove (correct) him. If that works, you have won him back. If he doesn't respond, take one or two more with you (the principle noted above). If that does not work, He tells them to tell it to the church, and if that doesn't work, then the brother is to be treated as a Gentile or tax-gatherer (heathen or publican). In that day, one could not go much lower in the eyes of Jews. Remember, it appears the immediate context is that Jesus is speaking to the 12 apostles.

He then says to them something that He has said to them relatively recently. Although some think that Jesus is speaking only to Peter in Matthew 16:19, He is apparently speaking to all of them, as He speaks the same words to them here in Matthew 18:18: "Truly I say to you, whatever you bind on earth shall have been bound in heaven; and whatever you loose on earth shall have been loosed in heaven." Personally, I believe the case is made elsewhere in this writing (Chapter 17 on the "Preeminence of Peter") that Jesus was speaking to all of them in Matthew 16:19, but even if He was only speaking to Peter at that point (because Peter was the one who responded to the question), He has now certainly expanded that promise to all of His apostles in Matthew 18:18.

Now, what does "the church" have to do with this (v. 17)? The church at this point does not exist, as I have noted that it came into existence on the Day of Pentecost, 50 days after Passover, that time when Jesus made His sacrifice on the cross and rose from the dead. Some say that He was speaking to Jews to take these issues to the leaders in the local synagogue. Some say He was speaking at the point when the church *would be* in existence and they, the Twelve, would play not only the chief role in establishing that church, but they would also be the initiators of doctrine and *enforcers* of those who fall out of line with their teaching. We have examples of this.

In the church at Corinth, there were several issues going on that Paul attempted to correct in his letters to them. For one in particular, he threatens to come and take care of the issue personally if they do not. You can read the details in 1 Corinthians 5:1–13, but the instructions are essentially the same as what we find in Matthew 18: the person straightens up or that person is to be disciplined by the group. They are to withdraw themselves from him until he realizes his error and repents. However, notice what Paul says to make sure that they understand 1) how serious this issue is and 2) his level of authority (1 Cor. 4:18–21):

> Now some have become arrogant, as though I were not coming to you. But I will come to you soon, if the Lord wills, and I shall find out, not the words of those who are arrogant, but their power. For the kingdom of God is not in words, but in power. What do you desire? That I come to you with a rod, or with love and a spirit of gentleness?

Paul meant business and spoke with the authority that all the apostles had from Jesus. This power to determine policy and doctrine moving forward from the establishment of the church was wielded in other cases as well.

Most are familiar with the situation with Ananias and his wife, Sapphira. Both were struck dead for lying to the apostles, to the Holy Spirit, and to God. Peter pronounces the judgment on these two in Acts 5:4, 9; notice the response of those who saw or heard about this situation:

> And great fear came over the whole church, and over all who heard about these things. At the hands of the apostles many signs and wonders were taking place among the people; and they were all together in Solomon's portico. But none of the rest dared to associate with them; however, the people held them in high esteem.

The people recognized the power these 12 men had been given and responded accordingly. Peter and John condemn the thoughts and actions of Simon the Sorcerer in Acts 8:20–22 and essentially tell him he has lost his salvation. Paul strikes Elymas, the magician, blind for opposing them in Acts 13:8–12. There were likely other demonstrations of both the power and authority these men had been given by Jesus, and through the Holy Spirit, to carry out the important work they had undertaken.

The Passage Under Consideration

As Jesus continues His thought after reiterating His assertions concerning the apostles' authority and power, He repeats something in v. 19 He has said elsewhere. In His final meeting with His apostles, He demonstrates the kind of humility He wants them to have in serving others by washing their feet; He institutes the Lord's Supper; He talks with them about unity and other topics; and then He offers a prayer to His Father on their behalf. In this extended account of His last meeting with them, John (chs. 13–17) offers us three times when Jesus assures them that they will have the support of the Father and the Holy Spirit in their charge following His departure.

In John 14:13–14, He says, "And whatever you ask in My name, this I will do, so that the Father may be glorified in the Son. If you ask Me anything in My name, I will do it." In John 15:7, He again says, "If you remain in Me, and My words remain in you, ask whatever you wish, and it will be done for you." Finally, He tells them in John 17:23–24, "Truly, truly I say to you, if you ask the Father for anything in My name, He will give it to you. Until now you have asked for nothing in My name; ask and you will receive, so that your joy may be made full." He is assuring them that this power they will be granted will produce just as much power as He demonstrated in His miracles and His words.

I am not sure, however, why He inserted the piece about two or more of them agreeing on things that would be sought. This stipulation—if indeed that is what it is—is not offered in the passages in John noted above where the same promise is made. We do know that when Jesus sent out the 72 back in Luke 10, He sent them out in pairs. Likewise, we see both Peter and John apparently pairing up in the early chapters of Acts. So, it could be that this was part of His instruction to them before He ascended back to the Father: start out in pairs, at least at the beginning. We do know that Paul was seldom alone in his travels and teaching and was accompanied by a variety of individuals.

One thing Jesus did require of His apostles, and prayed for in the Upper Room, was unity. It was their love for one another that would provide the evidence for others that they were from Him (John 13:35). It could be that Jesus is simply reminding them of this fact and that their unity is of paramount importance. Not only their unity when they make determinations like the one under consideration in this passage (discipline of an erring brother), but also submission to and unity with the Spirit that would be guiding them.

Now, let's look at the particular verse under consideration, Matthew 18:20. Matthew ends and sums up this discussion with these words of Jesus: "For where two or three have gathered together in My name, I am there in their midst." The passage, as noted above, is often used to simply assure worshipers that Jesus is in their presence when they worship him; whether or not this declaration is true will be addressed below. The immediate concern is this: *Is this what the passage in context is truly teaching?* The answer, after analyzing the context as we just concluded, would have to be in the negative.

Jesus is continuing His line of thought here in v. 20; we even have the word "for" that begins this concluding thought recorded by Matthew. You could insert "And therefore" and not change the meaning. Jesus is simply putting a conceptual "exclamation point" on the fact that, not only do they have the authority to speak for Him and the Father on all issues, but that He indeed is in their midst as they do. Physically, no, but it would be the same as if He were. He is simply transferring His power to them, and this is what the entire passage is teaching and nothing else.

Is Deity in Our Midst in Worship?

In John 4, Jesus encounters the Samaritan woman at the well. Jesus demonstrates knowledge about her that prompts her to say, "Sir, I perceive that You are a prophet. Our fathers worshiped on this mountain, and yet you Jews say that in Jerusalem is the place where one must worship" (4:19–20). Jesus responds this way:

> Believe Me, woman, that a time is coming when you will worship the Father neither on this mountain nor in Jerusalem. You Samaritans worship what you do not know; we worship what we do know, because salvation is from the Jews. But a time is coming, and even now has arrived, when the true worshipers will worship the Father in spirit and truth; for such people the Father seeks to be His worshipers. God is spirit, and those who worship Him must worship in spirit and truth.

Jesus was proclaiming to her that the *place* for worshiping God—regardless of how misplaced (for the Samaritans) it might be—was coming to an end. These "true worshipers"—those soon to be in the new kingdom, the church—would worship God in spirit and truth, for "God is a spirit." Jesus is proclaiming to all the world—Jewish, Samaritan, and Gentile—that a major change is about to take place. He forecasts elsewhere that Jerusalem will no longer hold any special place in God's heart as the Jews had left Him long ago and that He had withdrawn His presence from them in that place (1 Chronicles 7:19–21; Ezekiel 10:18–19). He also noted that Jerusalem would be destroyed and all that represented physical Judaism would be destroyed with it (Matthew 24; Mark 13; Luke 21). It is something He had alluded to concerning the spiritual nature of His kingdom that would be established, but few if any comprehended it, not even the apostles until after His resurrection, particularly on the Day of Pentecost.

In the OT, God's presence was represented by the pillars of cloud and fire that guided the Israelites in their journeys in the wilderness. It sat over the tabernacle that was moved from place to place as they traveled.

It was a constant reminder that God was with them, protecting them, and providing for them. When the temple was finally completed, God again demonstrated His presence this way: "And it happened that when the priests came from the holy place, the cloud filled the house of the Lord, so that the priests could not stand to minister because of the cloud, for the glory of the Lord filled the house of the Lord" (1 Kings 8:11). During this time and in generations before, the Ark of the Covenant was the physical representation of God's presence with Israel.

However, things are different in the kingdom of God now. Peter, in his first letter to a group of Christians across a considerable geographic area (1:1), tells them this: "And coming to Him as to a living stone which has been rejected by people, but is choice and precious in the sight of God, you also, as living stones, are being built up as a spiritual house for a holy priesthood, to offer spiritual sacrifices that are acceptable to God through Jesus Christ" (2:4–5). He states this again in 1 Peter 2:9–10. Christians are God's chosen people now, not the Jews, and he calls them "a royal priesthood, a holy nation, a people for God's own possession." We are that "spiritual house"—like the temple under the Old Law— where God resides. Paul calls the church "the Israel of God" (Galatians 6:16). We, the church, are now where God resides.

Paul also tells us in 1 Corinthians 3:16–17 that the Spirit of God dwells within us individually and that we are a temple of God; the temple of God is holy "and that is what you are." In that same letter, he tells us that our bodies are temples "of the Holy Spirit" within us (6:19), and in 2 Corinthians 6:16, he says, "We are the temple of the living God." There are other passages to consider in this regard (Ephesians 2:21–22; 1 Timothy 3:15; Hebrews 3:6; 1 John 4:13), but whether we are talking about Christians as individuals or Christians as a corporate group (universal or local), *we are the temple of God*. The only way we can approach His throne of grace (Hebrews 4:16; 7:19) is by being a member of His church, that body of believers who have availed themselves of the sacrifice of Jesus on the cross. It is this group that He will deliver to the Father on Judgment Day (1 Corinthians 15:24) to reign with Him in glory.

Finally, if Christ lives within us individually (passages above as well as Galatians 2:20), then He certainly is present with us when we meet together in His name. If God's presence over and in the tabernacle and temple were assured for Israel when they were faithful, then there is no reason to think that He would not provide the same (or similar) *presence* for us when we meet in His name and do so according to His Word. If this is our group worship sessions, then yes, He is there. If we are in a Bible study group, attempting to learn more about Him and God's Word, then He is there in our midst. The Holy Spirit guides us into all truth—not like the apostles who directly were inspired—when we read God's Word and let it work through us to shape us and conform us to His will for us.

If what we have said above is true, Matthew 18:20 is not our proof text for establishing that Jesus is in our midst when we worship, like many assert. However, other passages convincingly support this notion. The point here is not to say He doesn't; it is just to point out that we need to make sure we are using the right Scriptures for the right conclusions.

Chapter 34

Whatever Is Not of Faith
Romans 10:17 / 14:23

"If it is not in the Bible, it is sin!" If you have been attending relatively conservative worship services or Bible classes, you have likely heard this one. The argument seems logical, and there may even be elements of truth to it. However, the passages used to support the argument—at least one of them—is taken out of context to make the argument. Let's examine the two passages in context to see where the error occurs.

Romans 10:17

In an earlier section, I discussed the steps necessary for one to become a child of God. Before that can even have a chance as an outcome, the very first step is to have some sort of encounter with the Gospel. The *Gospel*, loosely interpreted, means "the good news" and refers to the life of Jesus Christ and all that relates to Him and His importance to our salvation. It contains information found in the four Gospels (Matthew, Mark, Luke, and John) as well as the supporting information found in the rest of the New Testament concerning the establishment and growth of the church, what it takes to become a Christian, the structure and function of local congregations, living the Christian life, and a host of other related pieces of information.

Today, we can encounter this information in a number of ways (reading, radio, TV, social media, street corners, etc.). In the first century, however, contact was primarily through hearing it from the mouth of a witness to those events, a second-hand verbal account, or even a written letter from an inspired writer. I suppose other personal letters would have contained this important information as well. "Hearing"—in other words—can mean more than the vocal/aural interaction.

In the 10th chapter of Romans, Paul is stressing to the church in Rome that *faith in Jesus* is the basis on which salvation is realized. He speaks of the confession that God raised Jesus from the dead as the foundation of our faith and that we must be willing to confess our belief in that truth if salvation is even a possibility for us. Part of his effort in this letter is to convince them that there is no Jew and Greek distinction; he has spent the better part of the previous chapter talking about this. In Romans 10:13, Paul quotes Joel 2:32 but applies it to the Jew/Gentile merging in the mind of God into one body when Joel says [my emphasis], "*Whoever* will call upon the name of the Lord will be saved."

Paul then asks a series of rather rhetorical questions:

> How then shall they call upon Him in whom they have not believed? And how shall they believe in Him whom they have not heard? And how shall they hear without a preacher? And how shall they preach unless they are sent?

His point is rather obvious, but it is found in one of our key verses under consideration in this section. He says, "So faith comes from hearing and hearing by the word of Christ" (Romans 10:17). For me, this wording is a little strange. The New International Version, I believe, makes it clearer and reads more smoothly: "Consequently, faith comes from hearing the message, and the message is heard through the word about Christ." In other words, *faith comes by hearing the message about Christ*. We have to encounter it at some point and by some means if it is to even enter our consciousness; at that point, it is up to us as to how we receive it and respond to it.

Romans 14:23
(1 Corinthians 8 and 10)

Most students of the Bible would link Romans 14 to the two passages in 1 Corinthians 8 (1–13) and 1 Corinthians 10 (23–33). The subject in all three passages (Romans 14:1–23) is the Christian's influence on a weaker brother. The *weakness* has to do with the brother's uninformed or misinformed understanding of eating meat offered to idols. Having either come from an idolatrous background or a background that might be inordinately offended by the concept, this individual is a *total abstinence* advocate who still believes there is something forbidden about the meat itself. Paul teaches us here that, since there is no such thing as an idol (false gods are just that: false), then any meat offered to them does not become tainted in any way and thus, unfit for consumption. In 1 Corinthians 8:4–6, we have Paul telling the church at Corinth the following:

> Therefore, concerning the eating of food sacrificed to idols, we know that an idol is nothing at all in the world, and that there is no God but one. For even if there are so-called gods whether in heaven or on earth, as indeed there are many gods and many lords, yet for us there is only one God, the Father, from whom are all things, and we exist for Him; and one Lord, Jesus Christ, by whom are all things, and we exist through Him.

For Paul, the inspired writer, the argument of whether to eat meat offered to idols is framed by the reality that there is no such thing as a false god or an idol representing it. They just don't exist. There is only "one God"—as he says—and any attempt to create other "so-called gods" are simply in people's minds. Elijah had a contest with the prophets of Baal in 1 Kings 18 to demonstrate to Israel how utterly foolish a belief in these other gods was.

Paul, however, is acutely aware that there are those who come from one of the two backgrounds noted above who still have some leftover sensibilities concerning these idols and the meat that came from the sacrifices that were offered to them. In 1 Corinthians 10:25, he says, "Eat anything that is sold in the meat market without asking questions, for the sake of conscience." Apparently, the meat from these pagan sacrifices was taken to the market and sold as common food as a profit to someone. Since there is no such thing as an idol, a sacrifice to an idol, sanctified (or contaminated, depending on your view) meat, etc., Paul says that it should not violate the conscience of a Christian to eat this meat. It is just meat, and God has sanctioned the eating of meat. So, Paul is confident that he has the right or liberty to eat such meat.

On the other hand, he also knows about the weaker brother who still feels even a bit reluctant to eat, is possibly emboldened by Paul in his status as an apostle who does so, and then this one violates his conscience and partakes of food that, at least to some degree, is *forbidden* to him. Paul sums up the reality of this situation in Romans 14:22–23:

> The faith which you have, have as your own conviction before God. Happy is the one who does not condemn himself in what he approves. But the one who doubts is condemned if he eats, because his eating is not from faith; and *whatever is not from faith is sin.*

I have italicized that last phrase as it is key to our overall argument on these passages. I'll come back to this point shortly.

Paul concludes not only has the person above violated his conscience and sinned, but Paul also now has a part in this transgression. Even though Paul has the conscience-free liberty to eat the meat, he says he will forego it on behalf of the one who might be influenced to sin—as that person does not have the same "conscience" that he does. In the verses just above in Romans 14:16–21, he explains:

> Therefore, do not let what is for you a good thing be spoken of as evil; for the kingdom of God is not eating and drinking, but righteousness and peace and joy in the Holy Spirit. For the one

who serves Christ in this way is acceptable to God and approved by other people. So then we pursue the things which make for peace and the building up of one another. Do not tear down the work of God for the sake of food. All things indeed are clean, but they are evil for the person who eats and causes offense. It is good not to eat meat or to drink wine, or to do anything by which your brother or sister stumbles.

Notice Paul's context here is meat offered to idols, a common problem in his day due to the number of people coming out of paganism into Christianity. However, he makes it clear that a *principle* is being established here and not just a circumstance. He includes the drinking of wine as another possibility and then says, "*anything* by which your brother or sister stumbles." In reality, we can have the absolute right, or liberty, to do a number of things. However, if doing them influences an uninformed brother or sister to do so and violates his or her conscience, then we have caused that person to sin and, as a result, we have as well. Paul says, if this is the case, he would go so far as to give up meat, at least in that situation (I am assuming). In 1 Corinthians 10:27–33, he mentions such a situation: a) you are invited to an unbeliever's house and b) eat whatever you want. However, if one says something about the meat being offered as a sacrifice, then do not eat it. It is not your conscience under concern but the one who made note of the meat's origin. He concludes in v. 33 that our goal is the saving of others' souls.

The Misuse

While Romans 10:17 is a very important passage, especially when considering the spread of the Gospel and its sharing among those unfamiliar with it, using it in juxtaposition with the passage at the end of our Romans 14 topic in v. 23 simply cannot be legitimately accomplished. Now that we have visited both passages (as well as the two related ones in 1 Corinthians), here is the argument as it is commonly presented in terms of a well-known mathematical (used in logic) theorem.

> If "a" (the word of God) = "b" (faith), and if "not a" (not in the word of God) = "not b" (not faith), then "not b" (not of faith) = "c" (sin).

If that is more confusing than helpful, then ignore it; here is what is important. While both of these passages have their context and proper application, you cannot take the conclusion in Romans 14 and force it into an unscriptural *marriage* with Romans 10. Romans 14 is wholly dedicated to violating one's conscience—i.e., that which is not of faith (or conviction of the heart on something)—and Romans 10 is talking about spreading the Gospel. This is important: *Regardless of how true the overall statement might be, it is a violation of Scripture to put these two together to attempt to make a strong or stronger point.*

Generally speaking, the Bible is our guide for all things pertaining to life and godliness (2 Pet. 1:3). It provides us all we need; it is thorough, complete, and "perfect" (James 1:25). We have talked in earlier sections about "going beyond" what is found there or "deleting" something established as ordained of God. We have mentioned that the Scriptures are readable and understandable (2 Cor. 1:13), so there should be little "wiggle room" for what is indeed "adding to" or "taking away." There are plenty of Scriptural ways to make that point that God's Word is all-sufficient, sanctified, and self-contained without distorting these two passages because they *sound alike* and *make your point*.

Finally, if you abuse the context of Romans 14 and take "of faith" to mean simply "found in the Bible," you open yourself to all sorts of oh-yeah-well-what-about questions. If we can do absolutely nothing in our worship, for example, other than what we find in Scripture, then we do away with anything we like to call *an expediency*. As noted in another section, we derive our authority for how we worship (among other things) from three sources: direct statements or commands; approved apostolic examples; or necessary inferences or conclusions based on the context. This last group, *necessary inferences*, allows us to use the context to make assumptions about things that likely occurred but are not specifically spelled out. If you use Romans 14:23 to say, "If you can't find it in the Bible, then you cannot do it," this would call into question things that we take for granted, like a) a church building; b) air conditioning in that building; c) padded pews; d) hymnals; e) an electronic system for projecting sounds or PowerPoint slides to a screen; f) individual classrooms for children … and on and on.

The passage does not say this, so to put it with another passage to make it *sound like* it does commits two errors, not just one. You have misinterpreted the passage's point *and* you have incorrectly coupled it with another passage and essentially corrupted *both* in doing so. No matter how noble our intentions are, we should not and cannot allow fellow–Christians to misuse Scripture. Our silence is tacit agreement, and that is sin (Romans 1:32; Ephesians 5:11; James 4:17).

Chapter 35

Bearing Fruit
John 15:1–11

In John 13–17, Jesus is addressing some things with His apostles just before He is taken from them to undergo His arrest, trial, beating, and crucifixion. Once that happens—and after He appears to large numbers following His resurrection—He commissions them to continue His work for which they have been prepared and in which they will be aided by the Holy Spirit. During these final hours with these chosen individuals, He attempts to prepare them for the task ahead, fully acknowledging they do not completely comprehend what is ahead of them and knowing full well that they will not be "perfect" as He was in His ministry. When the mother of James and John comes to Jesus to request special places for them in the kingdom, He says this to them: "You do not know what you are asking."

He later washes their feet to illustrate the serving attitude they need to adopt. He tells them that others will know they are His if they have love for one another. He predicts Peter's denial. He chastises them for wanting to see the Father when they have seen Him—and that He and the Father are one. He tells them that if they love Him, they will keep his commandments and then later, His word. He commands them to love one another. He warns them that the world will hate them for His sake.

In the midst of all of these warnings and encouragements, Jesus makes the following statements in John 15:1–11.

- I am the true vine, and My Father is the vinedresser. Every branch in Me that does not bear fruit, He takes away; and every branch that bears fruit, He prunes it so that it may bear more fruit.

- I am the vine, you are the branches; the one who remains in Me, and I in him bears much fruit, for apart from Me you can do nothing.
- My Father is glorified by this, that you bear much fruit, and so prove to be My disciples.

Some have taken this passage and employed it in the effort to convince us that it teaches we have the responsibility to convert others to the cause of Christ. While this may not be a widely practiced use of this passage—I haven't heard it in many years—it is an erroneous use of the passage. Just as Hebrews 10:25 (discussed above) is often misused to "threaten" those who miss worship services, this passage is used to tell us that if we are not producing other Christians, we are subject to some of the outcomes Jesus mentions here that certainly approach condemnation. While attending worship services is indeed important, we should not misuse scripture to teach it. Likewise, while sharing the Gospel with others in an attempt to convert them is also important, we should not misuse passages to convince us to do so. Let's look at what Jesus was really saying here.

Again, context is important. As I have noted above, this is during that final session Jesus has with His apostles who will—without Him physically present—establish the church, spread the Gospel, be persecuted for His name's sake, and ultimately die (tradition tells us) for their efforts. He uses an agrarian example, something which all of them would understand, to illustrate who they are and what they will be. He sets up a series of relationships: God is the vinedresser, the one who plants and oversees; Jesus is the vine, that source from which produce flows; and they are the branches, those entities from which the fruit will emerge. They are being charged with establishing a movement that is dependent on its growth in spirit and in number. Surely, converting others is what Jesus is talking about here. But is He?

Bearing Fruit

First of all, if the analogy is going to hold up under scrutiny, the apostles, followers of Christ, would have to bear other followers of Christ, i.e., other *branches*, and not *fruit*. Jesus could have easily said, "I am the vine and you are the branches; produce other branches." He didn't; He said to produce *fruit*. Some might say that we would be over–analyzing if we suggest such, but let's look further at what "producing fruit" means within Scripture elsewhere.

We could first look at Romans 11:17–24 where Paul is laying out for the Gentiles how they were *branches* that were "grafted in" when the Jewish *branches* were "cut off." The "natural branches" (Jews) were not spared and neither would He spare the "grafted in branches" (Gentiles) if they fall away. Branches for branches are discussed here; but there are better arguments in this discussion about branches and fruit.

Much has been said in Scripture about "bearing fruit" or "producing fruit." It should be noted that in all of the following places where this terminology is used, it does *not* mean to convert others to Christianity. Is that one way that we can bear fruit? Of course, but notice what these passages say about the more immediate application of this agrarian analogy. Vine's tells us that the symbolic *fruit* under discussion here is "the visible expression of power working inwardly and invisibly, the character of the 'fruit' being evidence of the character of the power producing it." Vine's points to Philippians 1:11 for Paul's "fruit of righteousness" as well as Hebrews 12:11 that says this righteousness produces "peaceable fruit."

Earlier, we can look at what John the Baptist said about bearing fruit. In Matthew 3:8–10, John warns the Pharisees and Sadducees in the crowd (after calling them "vipers"), "Therefore produce fruit consistent with repentance," and "The axe is already laid at the root of the trees; therefore, every tree that does not bear good fruit is being cut down and thrown into the fire." Fruit obviously means actions that are godly rather than ungodly, like those of the Jewish leadership had been.

Next, we can turn to Galatians 5:19–23 where Paul lays out for us the differences between the "works (or deeds) of the flesh" and the "fruit of the Spirit." His deeds of the flesh are listed in vv. 19–20 and cover a wide variety of sins of those who "will not inherit the kingdom of God." He then contrasts these with the "fruit of the Spirit"—love, joy, peace, patience, kindness, goodness, faithfulness, gentleness, and self-control—and suggests that we belong to Christ if we practice these. In Ephesians 5:5–10, Paul tells us, first, that "No immoral person or covetous man, who is an idolater, has an inheritance in the kingdom of Christ and God." He tells them that they were formerly in darkness, but they are not currently and now walk as "children of light." He then says that "the fruit of the light consists in all goodness, righteousness, and truth" and doing what is pleasing to the Lord.

So, we can conclude from these verses and other passages that talk about this analogy of "bearing fruit" that they are focusing on living our lives according to those things produced by the Spirit of God (i.e., love, goodness, kindness, etc.) rather than on the self-satisfying works of the flesh that lead to our destruction. These attitudes and actions on our part should be visible to others around us and should indicate that we are, indeed, led by the Spirit instead of our own selfish desires. Jesus tells us in Matthew 7:15–20 that we can spot false prophets "by their fruits." He tells them that "good trees bear good fruit" and "the bad tree bears bad fruit." Finally, He says that trees (people) who do not produce good fruit will be "cut down and thrown into the fire," a statement noted by John the Baptist and reiterated by Jesus in our home text for this section.

Jesus is not talking about converting others to Christianity in John 15:1–11; He is talking ultimately about *being a Christian* and living a life that would exemplify such. Do we have the responsibility, however, to share the Gospel with others in hopes that they too will see the light and render obedience to what the Gospel teaches about becoming a child of God? Of course, we do. While we don't have that more "global command" the apostles received from Jesus, we do have a responsibility to explain to others why we have this hope of an eternal existence in heaven after this life is over (1 Peter 3:15). More is offered on this topic a couple of chapters below in this writing.

Chapter 36

Wall of Separation
Ephesians 2:14–16

The Scriptures provide us with a very stark and pointed argument concerning what the death of Jesus (and the subsequent burial and resurrection) provides for us. That act and those events prevent us from being eternally damned as a result of our sins that separate us from God. So much could be written at this point to prove this assertion, but I think that most believers would grant that contention without going into detail in this section, especially since this section is making a different point altogether. A little background is necessary to set up the argument made here.

The Torn Veil

Scripture tells us that at the moment Jesus died on the cross, several things happened. Even though it was noon, darkness covered the land. Three hours later, at the point when He commits His spirit into God's hands, there is an earthquake and rocks were split. Tombs were opened and the bodies of dead holy people were raised to life. Also, the veil between the Holy Place and the Most Holy Place was torn into two pieces from top to bottom. These are all mentioned in Matthew 27, but are confirmed, at least in part, in both Mark and Luke.

While the veil being torn in two is significant—a miracle that otherwise would not have occurred—its overarching implication is that Jesus has provided us the access to God through His death that was previously experienced only by the high priest of the Jews. This access was granted only one time each year to offer sacrifices for himself and for the sins of the people. This was part of the Old Law and had been practiced for centuries. Jesus, however, made that practice, along with the Old Law, obsolete by "nailing it to the cross" (Colossians 2:13–14).

The tearing of the veil was indeed a symbolic event representing our new-found access to God through Jesus's blood, but it was also a very real fact—not merely symbolic. Other passages found below tell us this more directly or strongly.

We could, for example, turn to 2 Corinthians 5:17–19. This is one of several passages explaining not only that we are separated from God through our sins but that we must be reconciled to Him. This can only be accomplished through the blood of His Son that was shed on the cross. This is only available to us if we are "in Christ," and that comes through complete obedience to the examples and commands we find in the New Testament: hear, believe He is the Son of God, make that confession, repent, and be baptized for the remission of our sins. We could also use Colossians 1:19–23, which makes the same point about this reconciliation provided through the blood of Jesus and its necessity for our salvation.

For a more explicit reference, we can also use Hebrews 6:19–20 which says Christ "entered the veil" as a forerunner for us, He had access to God, and we now have it because He provides it to us. We essentially go "through the veil" when we access God in prayer. The high priest offered sacrifices for his sins and the people's sins. Jesus is our perfect substitution for this shedding of blood required for forgiveness (Heb. 9:22), and our bodies are a living sacrifice to God (Rom. 12:1). Prayer is now how we come face to face with our sins, and this is the medium through which we obtain forgiveness from God (1 John 1:9). We also have another passage in Hebrews that speaks to this same issue and privilege. In the first part of Hebrews 10, the chapter is talking about the contrast between the high priest of the Jews and that of our high priest, Jesus. This culminates in vv. 19–22 when it tells us that we "have confidence to enter the holy place" and go "through the veil" because the blood of Jesus allows such.

There are other passages we could go to for establishing that Jesus's death is what now allows us the access to God as did the high priest under the Old Law, but in ways far superior and more significant than that under that Law. However, the point of this section is to address the misuse of another passage that some will call on to prove the point made above.

The Wall of Separation

I have heard it mentioned many times in my life of the "wall of separation" that separates man from God and how Jesus broke down that wall in His death. While this is indeed true, for which we make argument above, it is my contention that we are mixing up two metaphors here, especially when we go to Ephesians 2 for evidence. Again, I am not refuting the point being made here; our sins have indeed separated us from God and for which we are in dire need of reconciliation through Jesus's sacrifice. My point below will show why other passages are better suited for proving this than Ephesians 2 that talks about an entirely different separation.

The way I read that chapter in Paul's letter is that he is explaining to these Gentiles how they were "once this" and are now "not this." If you read down through the first 13 verses, it is easy to see that he is telling them that they "had no hope" as sinful Gentiles, but now, as Christians, they most assuredly do. He makes much of the contrast of their old lives in vv. 1–3 with the benefits they now have been afforded through the grace offered by God through Jesus (vv. 4–10). In v. 13, he tells them that they were "far away from God" but now are "brought near" by the blood of Christ. Indeed, Paul sets up the latter part of his point by noting the reconciliation to God they experienced in going from *lost* to *saved*. This, however, is not the only "division" Paul addresses. Most of the rest of the chapter is devoted to a discussion about the consequences of the blood of Christ from another perspective.

Paul turns to an obvious reality of the "enmity" that has existed for generations between these Gentiles and their counterparts, the Jews. He notes that the Jews ("the circumcision") referred to the Gentiles as "the uncircumcision" and placed them on the same level of contempt as they had for the Samaritans and the traitorous tax-collectors. Jesus, somewhat mockingly, points out this disdain the Jews had for Gentiles in Matthew 15:21–28 when a Canaanite woman implored Him to save her demon-possessed daughter. Jesus engages her and explains, in so many words, that His offering is to the Jews and not to "dogs." Personally, I am confident He was referring to the Jews' *perception* of those who were not Jews and not His personal perception.

Paul continues this thought with vv. 14–16. First, "Christ is our peace." Peace between what and what? Obviously, the Jews and the Gentile was what he was just discussing. He also made "the two one and has torn down the dividing wall of hostility." The two: Jews and Gentiles. The wall of hostility: that of the disdain of the one (Jews) for the other (Gentiles), and likely vice versa—although that is not highlighted in Scripture, but it surely had to exist. Jesus did this "by abolishing in His flesh the law of the commandments and decrees" —and nailing the Old Law to the cross (Colossians 2:14). Nothing so far about the division between man and God or the veil and the high priest.

Next, Paul notes, "He did this to create in Himself one new man out of the two, making peace" between them. No longer Jews/Gentiles; just one, and both now one in Him (see also Galatians 3:28). In doing so, "He reconciled both of them to God in one body through the Cross." This is where you might bring in the torn veil as an event that signified and supported what Paul says at this juncture; however, that is not Paul's point. He finishes with "the cross, by which He (Jesus) extinguished their (Jews/Gentiles) hostility." The final two verses reiterate what he has just said.

So, while we can agree that there was a wall of separation between God and man, and also agree that the tearing of the veil in the temple at the death of Jesus symbolized the destruction of that wall … I think the point being made here that using passages other than those from Ephesians 2 makes considerably more sense to support this enduring truth. Yes, God broke down a barrier in the death of Jesus that indeed separated Him from us. However, the wall addressed in Ephesians 2 is specifically the *enmity* that had traditionally existed between the Jews and Gentiles, but now the blood of Jesus had removed that wall and made them "one" (i.e., both saved) in Him.

Chapter 37

The "Great Commission"
Matthew 28:19 and Mark 16:15

This one is another one that has some truth behind it, but advocates use it outside of its context. Obviously, these two passages are orders from Jesus to His eleven apostles (at this point) to continue His teachings and to establish His kingdom on earth, the church. Shortly after speaking these words to them, He is "received up into heaven" to sit at the right hand of God (Mark 16:19). His time on earth was over; His ministry was completed, and their ministry was just beginning. He had arisen from the dead and was seen by hundreds (1 Corinthians 15:5–8) who functioned as witnesses. Many of these died confessing they had witnessed the risen Christ, so their conviction on that event was firm. Let's look at these two passages, and then I'll talk about their use.

> But the eleven disciples proceeded to Galilee, to the mountain which Jesus had designated to them. And when they saw Him, they worshiped Him; but some were doubtful. And Jesus came up and spoke to them, saying, "All authority in heaven and on earth has been given to Me. Go, therefore, and make disciples of all the nations, baptizing them in the name of the Father and the Son and the Holy Spirit, teaching them to follow all that I commanded you; and behold, I am with you always, to the end of the age" (Matthew 28:16–20).

Later, He appeared to the eleven disciples themselves as they were reclining at the table; and He reprimanded them for their unbelief and hardness of heart, because they had not believed those who had seen Him after He had risen from the dead.

> And He said to them, "Go into all the world and preach the gospel to all creation. The one who has believed and has been baptized will be saved; but the one who has not believed will be condemned. These signs will accompany those who have believed: in My name they will cast out demons, they will speak with new tongues; they will pick up serpents, and if they drink any deadly poison, it will not harm them; they will lay hands on the sick, and they will recover" (Mark 16:14–18).

Remember, at least some of these men had been followers of John the Baptist whose reputation was known far and wide. Also, Jesus had led these men almost daily for approximately three years. He had taught publicly when they were in attendance. He also had private conversations with them on numerous occasions concerning what He had said publicly or on some other issue that either He or they brought up. They had seen him publicly indict the Jewish leaders for their hypocrisy and corruption of the Law, and they had seen how these leaders had tried to take Him forcefully and put Him to death—at first, unsuccessfully and then later accomplishing the task. They had seen Him work all kinds of miracles demonstrating His power over nature with the authority granted to Him by His Father. They, themselves, had experienced this power on occasion as well. However, their rabbi, their master, their teacher, and their leader is now leaving them and giving them the responsibility to finish the work He began. It is my assumption that anxieties were high in the group; they needed some assurance, once again, that they were up to the task.

He had already told them prior to His death that they would have The Helper, the Comforter, the Holy Spirit, to guide them into all truth (John 16:13). They really wouldn't even have to worry about what they would say, as this Comforter would provide them with appropriate utterings to be shared with even those in high places (Matthew 10:19–20). They apparently had already experienced this in His first commission after they were officially designated as apostles (Matthew 10), or else He was preparing them for this later, even greater challenge after He is gone. Likely, it is both. In these two passages under consideration and quoted just above, here are His points:

1. My Father has granted to Me all authority; I am commissioning you to do the following.
2. Go into all the world and teach all nations (all creation/every creature) the Gospel.
3. Make disciples of them by baptizing those who believe in the name of the Father, the Son, and the Holy Spirit.
4. Teach them to follow the things I have taught you.
5. I am with you always in this charge; you will have special powers to support and confirm the words you will speak to them.

The Issue

If you have spent any time in worship services over the years, most likely you have heard these words read to you as personal instructions, just like the apostles received them. On the surface, there are some things that definitely do not apply to us today or even in the past after the first century. Once again, we have lifted something out of context and applied it in a much broader sense where it simply does not fit. Either it is direct instruction for us, or it is not for us but limited to those to whom it was spoken at the time. What *does not apply* to us should be obvious:

- We are not officially "commissioned" to *go into all the world* to teach; those who suggest that this applies to us had better sign up for frequent flyer programs and get on it. We say this, but we apparently do not, in reality, believe it. "All the world" is *all the world*. Jesus told them to spread out from Jerusalem, to Judea and Samaria, and to the *remotest parts of the earth* (Acts 1:8)—and history tells us the apostles did. That was their charge, not ours.
- Even if we did go into all the world, the signs that followed them (Mark 16:20) would not be there for us. As discussed in previous sections of what you are reading, the purpose of these miracles was to confirm the words that Jesus spoke and the words His apostles spoke on His behalf. Words are just words without some signal that an authority higher than the one speaking those words is behind

them (John 5:31–32). The Word *has been* confirmed; it is complete and perfect; all partial revelation is brought together and made known in God's totally revealed Word.

So, at least part of the Great Commission does not apply to us. Does that mean that none of it does, and that we have no responsibility to spread God's Word to anyone anywhere? Absolutely not, and that is not what I am saying. The point noted above is simply to be careful of lifting a passage to say that it applies to us without considering the rest of the passage that does not. Our responsibility to teach others is documented in Scripture without misusing Matthew 28 and Mark 16 in support of such.

Another Offering

Just recently, I was in a Bible class and heard another one that I need to include here in this discussion. Again, the point being made was that we as Christians have the obligation to share with others the Gospel. With this assertion, I have no quarrel, as I have contended and will contend below. However, I do value context—as has been noted within this writing—and I do sincerely believe we should not take passages out of their context to a) prove something new and different or b) artificially strengthen something that is already taken for granted as a truth. The passage under consideration at this point is Matthew 9:35–38.

Jesus has concluded His "Sermon on the Mount" and is now going about healing all sorts of diseases, casting out demons, and performing a host of other miracles. Toward the end of Matthew 9, He looks upon the multitude following Him perceives they were "distressed and downcast like a sheep without a shepherd." Jesus then says to His disciples the following: "The harvest is plentiful, but the workers are few. Therefore, plead with the Lord of the harvest to send out workers into His harvest."

The very next verse begins Chapter 10, but it is obvious that no break in the action occurs from one chapter to the next. The text says, "And having summoned His twelve disciples (*apparently those same disciples he spoke to in the previous verse*), He gave them authority over unclean spirits, to cast them out, and to heal every kind of disease and every kind of sickness." Matthew then verbally "anoints" these 12 "disciples" and calls them "apostles." He then returns to the action, saying "These twelve Jesus sent out after instructing them … ." Matthew then records a long narrative of instructions Jesus had for these men who would be responsible—it would appear—for fulfilling the request Jesus makes just above concerning the need for workers and that the harvest is ready.

One point should be restated here concerning what these men would be taking with them for their effort. It is the same package noted above when we discussed Mark 16:20. He tells them to first, go only to Israel, not to the Samaritans and Gentiles; next, He tells them to preach that the kingdom of heaven is at hand—what both He and John the Baptist had been preaching. Next, He tells them what they will have at their disposal to convince their hearers that they had been sent out by One with authority:

> Heal the sick, raise the dead, cleanse the lepers, cast out demons; freely you received, freely give. Do not acquire gold, or silver, or copper for your money belts, or a bag for your journey, or even two tunics, or sandals, or a staff; for the worker is worthy of his support. And into whatever city or village you enter, inquire who is worthy in it; and abide there until you go away. And as you enter the house, give it your greeting. And if the house is worthy, let your greeting of peace come upon it; but if it is not worthy, let your greeting of peace return to you. And whoever does not receive you, nor heed your words, as you go out of that house or that city, shake off the dust of your feet. Truly I say to you, it will be more tolerable for the land of Sodom and Gomorrah in the day of judgment, than for that city. Behold, I send you out as sheep in the midst of wolves; therefore be shrewd as serpents, and innocent as doves. But beware of men; for they will deliver you up to the courts, and scourge you in their synagogues; and

you shall even be brought before governors and kings for My sake, as a testimony to them and to the Gentiles. But when they deliver you up, do not become anxious about how or what you will speak; for it shall be given you in that hour what you are to speak. For it is not you who speak, but it is the Spirit of your Father who speaks in you (Matthew 10:5–20).

It was not necessary to include that entire passage, but I wanted to offer the entire content and feel for what Jesus was telling they would experience and how they should handle it. My point here is in the beginning and end of what Jesus says.

He first tells them to share the Gospel concerning the kingdom of heaven that will be arriving soon. He then tells them to do what they have seen Him doing: "Heal the sick; raise the dead, cleanse the lepers, cast out demons." In other words, they will have exactly what He has had to convince others of His authority, not only to do these works, but, more importantly, to preach the all–important words of the Gospel. The words are what are important; the miracles are simply testimony of the Source of both.

However, He also tells them that—concerning those words they will be speaking—they should not worry about their message. Yes, they will suffer for what they will be speaking, but regardless of the situation or to whom they might be called before, they should not worry: "Do not become anxious about how or what you will speak; for it shall be given you in that hour what you are to speak. For it is not you who speak, but it is the Spirit of your Father who speaks in you." They are armed with miracles of all sorts *and the very words they will speak*. These are comforting thoughts considering the persecution that is also included in Jesus's warnings.

So, like the "Great Commission" (for all nations) noted above in Matthew 28 and Mark 16, this "Limited Commission" (to only the Jews) is spoken directly to those within the immediate hearing of Jesus. He is with only them when He makes these statements, and, more importantly, He promises them comforts and assurances not offered nor guaranteed to those outside this immediate group. To take this passage and/or the others noted above and say they are spoken either directly or *indirectly* to all Christians (then or now) and bind these words to this larger group is, most assuredly, taking them out of context, ignoring very relevant "accommodations" of the real receivers of these instructions, and binding them on us where we cannot be bound. God does not give us miracles as confirmation of our words, nor does He give us—by direct inspiration of the Spirit—whatever words we speak. And, He certainly hasn't either restricted our preaching to just the Jews nor expanded it to the entire world.

With this said, as Christians we do have the responsibility to teach others. The next section will address more accurately where we can find this obligation.

Our Responsibility to Teach

Becoming a child of God is the most important accomplishment that anyone anywhere in this life will ever achieve. Everything else pales in comparison to this responsibility: being a success; making money and giving it all to the poor; raising a godly family; influencing others for good; even saving others' souls. Paul speaks to this in 1 Corinthians 9:27 where he notes that while he might preach—even successfully—to others, he still could lose his soul in the process. Jesus tells us the 2nd Greatest Commandment is to "Love others as you love yourself." If you love others, you will share the Gospel with them. However, the precondition to this is loving yourself and caring for your own soul. Take care of No. 1 and then do what you can for others. The advice in the airplane is to "Place the mask on your own face before attempting to help others." The point is this: becoming a child of God through obedience to His Word is the only thing that matters in this world. Jesus says,

> If anyone wants to come after Me, he must deny himself, take up his cross, and follow Me. For whoever wants to save his life will lose it, but whoever loses his life for My sake and the gospel's will save it. For what does it benefit a person to gain the whole world, and forfeit his soul? For what could a person give in exchange for his soul? For whoever is ashamed of Me and My words in this adulterous and sinful generation, the Son of Man will also be ashamed of him when He comes in the glory of His Father with the holy angels (Mark 8:34–38).

So, our first responsibility is to save ourselves; we are directly told to do so in Philippians 2:12. Peter tells them on the Day of Pentecost, "Save yourselves from this corrupt generation" (Acts 2:40). But what about our responsibility to teach others? Jesus's words in the quote just above suggest our attitude toward Him and how that attitude might affect our willingness to share "Him" with others.

In Romans 10:10, we find that confession is truly "good for the soul." The previous verse explains the content of this confession: Jesus is Lord and God raised Him from the dead. This confession is part of what potential Christians assert just prior to their baptism that place them into Christ (Acts 8:37; Galatians 3:27). However, this confessional "event" is only the beginning of a *lifetime of confessing Him* to and before others. Jesus, in the midst of a passage detailing how belief in Him would do anything but provide for peace, said the following in Matthew 10:32–33: "Everyone who confesses Me before people, I will also confess him before My Father who is in heaven. But whoever denies Me before people, I will also deny him before My Father who is in heaven." This sounds like more than a one-time event.

At the end of a long warning against being swayed to return to Judaism, the Hebrew writer warns against "shrinking back" and the fact that God will have nothing to do with those who do:

> But my righteous one will live by faith; and if he shrinks back, my soul has no pleasure in him. But we are not among those who

shrink back to destruction, but of those who have faith for the safekeeping of the soul (Hebrews 10:38–39).

A lifetime of defending the faith is what the early Christians were charged with, and what they had to endure in the way of persecution far exceeds anything we are likely to face in our lives. That charge is the same for us. "Be faithful unto death and you will receive a crown of life." These words were spoken to individuals within some of the churches of Asia in Revelation 2 and 3.

In 1 Peter 3:14–17, the author says the following:

> But even if you should suffer for the sake of righteousness, you are blessed. And do not fear their intimidation, and do not be in dread, but sanctify Christ as Lord in your hearts, always being ready to make a defense to everyone who asks you to give an account for the hope that is in you, but with gentleness and respect; and keep a good conscience so that in the thing in which you are slandered, those who disparage your good behavior in Christ will be put to shame. For it is better, if God should will it so, that you suffer for doing what is right rather than for doing what is wrong.

The passage stresses the endurance we must possess to bear up under those who would persecute us in various ways. If we have to suffer for doing right, then so be it; better that than to suffer for doing wrong. But notice what Peter says in 3:15 in particular: "Sanctify Christ as Lord in your hearts, always being ready to make a defense to everyone who asks you to give an account for the hope that is in you, but with gentleness and respect." We are *charged* with the responsibility to defend our faith and the hope we have in Christ. Two other points are included here, however: 1) do it with gentleness and respect and 2) in doing so, we sanctify Christ as Lord in our hearts. I would say this goes both before and after our testimony concerning our hope. The fact that we sanctify Him in our hearts provides us the boldness to declare our convictions, yet, once we do so, we are strengthened by the fact that we were able to confess our faith before others. We find that in James 1:2–4, these experiences *build* our faith rather than weaken it. This, of course, presumes that we know why we believe what we believe and are able to share that convincingly with others.

In Heb. 5:12 and 1 Cor. 3:1–2, we find the writers admonishing the people for not having grown in their maturity in the Gospel and that the Hebrew writer was at least concerned, if not dismayed, by the fact that his readers *should have been* **teachers** by now but were in need of being taught themselves on the very basic and fundamental issues of faith. Growth in the Word of God is a persistent theme/commandment in the New Testament, and it is only our confidence in our knowledge of that Word that will give us the conviction to share that belief before others (1 Cor. 1:5; Eph. 1:17; 4:13–15; Phil. 1:9; Col. 1:9; 2 Tim. 2:15; 2 Pet. 1:2–3; 3:18). Remember, if we don't confess that belief before others, Jesus will not confess us before our Father in heaven. That suggests dire outcomes for any who fail in this regard. Do not shrink back. Know the Scriptures; speak with boldness and conviction; your salvation could depend on it.

So, the point of this discussion is not to assert that we don't have the responsibility to teach others concerning the good news found in the life, death, and resurrection of Jesus Christ. Of course, we do. Chapter 35 discusses how important bearing fruit is, and this is certainly one way we can do it. The problem pointed out in this discussion is using the passages found in Matthew (28:19) and Mark (16:15) to establish that responsibility. These two passages—when accurately considered within their contexts—were for the ears of those present and who would, indeed, be charged with changing the world through their teaching and demonstration of the power of the Holy Spirit despite the opposition they would face.

Chapter 38

Jesus: Advocate or Judge?
1 John 2:1 and Acts 10:42

Many religious people take comfort in the notion that on Judgment Day, Jesus will be pleading our case before God and "advocating" on our behalf to help us enter heaven. As odd as this seems—God the Father seeking to condemn while God the Son advocating against it—it is apparent that many have taken passages out of context, or they have at least misunderstood this "role" and its timing. On the other hand, there are numerous passages that suggest or outright state that Jesus will indeed have an active role on that day, not as an advocate pleading our cases to God, but participating in the judging itself taking place at that monumental event.

The picture I get with this view is almost as if Jesus will be moving back and forth from His position at the right hand of God as He judges, and then He jumps up from that position to stand beside each of us as we come before the throne of judgment. It is like He has a judging hat that he removes to replace it with His advocacy or lawyer hat. Rather silly, but such is the case when we don't examine closely what these terms mean and when each took place or will take place. First, let's look at the definition and common role of advocates or mediators.

The Advocate and Mediator

In 1 John 2:1, we have the following statement: "My little children, I am writing these things to you that you may not sin. And if anyone sins, we have an Advocate with the Father, Jesus Christ the righteous." This certainly sounds like He will be operating on our behalf in our lives and even before God in judgment. However, the very next verse tells us how He accomplished that "advocate" role: "And He Himself is the propitiation for our sins; and not for ours only, but also for those of the whole world." Several passages below will explain how this works and that Jesus will be operating as Judge in that day, not as a lawyer on our behalf.

The Greek word rendered *advocate* in 1 John 2:1 is *parakletos* (one called alongside to help) and is used in other passages to describe the Holy Spirit, most notably in Jesus's final words to His apostles in the upper room. There, it is most often translated as *comforter* instead of *advocate*. The notion there is more of a *helper* or an *aide*. When Greek writers used the term *advocate*, however, they usually were referring to one who stands beside us to defend us, like in a courtroom. Albert Barnes in his commentary lays out the responsibility of a courtroom advocate:

1. First, he demonstrates his client is not guilty of whatever charge is made against him. There are a number of ways this can be done; however, the advocate never admits to his client's guilt.
2. Second, if his client is indeed convicted of the crime, then the advocate's responsibility is to mitigate impact on his client by appealing to all the law allows in way of explanation.

Though the object of the action may be essentially the same—that of seeking good on our behalf—the advocacy of Jesus is very different. Here is how Barnes presents this part of the comparison:

1. Jesus admits to our guilt whether direct violation of the law or by our own conscience condemning us. He does not apologize, nor does He attempt to conceal any facts in the case.
2. He argues that justice will be sure and absolute; we will receive what we deserve. The "mitigating factor" He presents, however, is that there has been a substitute provided for us so that we do not have to undergo the deserved punishment for our crimes (our sins). That substitute is Jesus Himself and is fully recognized (even planned) by God as such.
3. The only determination, then, is whether or not we have availed ourselves of that substitution through obedience to the Gospel and

continued application of His blood by living lives of conformity to His will or what He has laid out for us to do to be one of His.

Below are a few passages that are referenced when people want to say the Scriptures justify that Jesus will advocate as a lawyer would on Judgment Day. Let's look at a few.

Luke 23:34

As Jesus hung on the cross bearing the sins for all mankind, His thoughts were not on himself but on those who were crucifying Him. His thoughts were not of condemnation or revenge; they spoke to the depth of His character and commitment to His teaching recorded in Matthew 5:44: "Love your enemies and pray for those who persecute you." After Jesus is lifted up with the two criminals, the very first thing He says is, "Father, forgive them; for they do not know what they are doing."
As the Son of God here on this earth, Jesus was very clear about the choices we make and how they affect our eternal destiny. "If you love me, keep my commandments." We are told to confess Him before men, but "Whoever shall deny Me before men, I will also deny him before My Father who is in heaven." Elsewhere in this writing, the steps for obtaining forgiveness of our sins are detailed and supported from Scripture. Even under the Old Law, repentance and obedience was necessary to receive any recognition from God concerning their sins (Psalms 51:17; 1 Samuel 15:22; Joel 2:13).

Even in His physical torture of crucifixion and His spiritual distress of bearing the sins of all mankind, He was acutely aware of God's unwillingness to forgive those who do not repent. The importance of repentance was the essence of both His and John the Baptist's initial message (Matthew 3:2; 4:17). To say that Jesus was directly asking God—without their repentance—to forgive those who crucified Him would have contradicted so much of what He taught while here on this earth. In 2 Peter 3:9, we are told that God wants all to "come to repentance." The very next verse talks about the "Day of the Lord" and how destruction of everything is sure.

The Jews most likely knew what they were doing, at least the Jewish leaders. They had been on the receiving end of scathing indictments from Jesus (Matthew 23), and they feared they would lose their position and their power if He were to succeed (John 11:48; 12:19). The Roman soldiers were simply carrying out the commands of their superiors. The mob who yelled, "Crucify Him, crucify Him!" would also be included in this group. It is not clear to which group Jesus is referring, but possibly all three. However, their coming to a knowledge of the sin they were committing, repenting of it, and confessing Him as Lord is obviously implied or taken for granted. Also in this writing, the importance of baptism and its connection to the forgiveness of sins has been stressed. Jesus is obviously implying that these conditions would naturally be a part of God's forgiveness for what they were doing to Him.

Romans 5:9–10

"Since we have now been justified by his blood, how much more shall we be saved from God's wrath through him!" In an earlier chapter, the notion of *universal salvation* was discussed and demonstrated to be a false doctrine. Our salvation has always been conditional on our acceptance and completion of the requirements God has placed on us that can be found in His Word. Yes, without Jesus coming to this earth and dying for our sins, we could not be justified. Even under the Old Law, faithful followers of God could only show their penitence through their sacrifices, but those efforts could not remove or forgive their sins (Hebrews 10:3–4). It took Jesus to allow us to be justified before God, having had our sins removed through obedience.

All the verses under consideration here are saying is that without Jesus and His sacrifice, we could never be justified. He has allowed us to escape the wrath of God that we all deserve due to our sins. Through obedience to the Gospel, we can not only have our sins removed, but we can stand justified before God and experience eternal salvation.

Romans 8:34

In Mark 16:19, we are told that when Jesus had said His final words to the apostles, He was "received up into heaven, and sat down at the right hand of God." Stephen testifies of this fact as well in Acts 7:55–56. The passage under consideration here says, "Christ Jesus is He who died, yes, rather who was raised, who is at the right hand of God, who also intercedes for us." In Hebrews 7:25, we have a similar assertion. The question is, "How does He do this?" Will it be on the Day of Judgment as suggested above or is it due to something He has already done?

Our sins are forgiven when we believe, repent, confess, and are baptized. The sacrifice of the Son of God who left heaven to come to earth to save us from our sins is that *interceding event*. Without His sacrifice and His subsequent resurrection, we would have no hope and still be dead in our sins (1 Corinthians 15:17). However, no one remains sinless following that forgiveness; we all sin, but we are also told that His sacrifice covers us even after that initial cleansing of our souls (1 John 1:7), if we are faithful and "walk in the light." His initial sacrifice and our initial obedience allows us to be cleansed, but His sacrifice didn't stop there. If we remain "in Him," that blood continues to cleanse us if we are repentant and seek forgiveness from God. In Revelation 2:10 we are told that if we are faithful until we die, we will receive that crown of eternal life.

1 Timothy 2:5

"There is only one God and one Mediator who can reconcile God and humanity… Christ Jesus." This is true. As noted above, without His atoning blood, we could never stand justified before God nor even have access to God through prayer for the forgiveness of our sins. It took His willingness to leave heaven and do what He did for us to even have a chance at salvation. This was the plan from the beginning (1 Peter 1:20). He did this once—not regularly as the priests under the Old Law had to—and it was for all mankind (Hebrews 9:28; 1 Peter 3:18).

Hebrews 9:24

"For Christ did not enter a holy place made with hands, a mere copy of the true one, but into heaven itself, now to appear in the presence of God for us." Yes, when Jesus said on the cross, "It is finished," at least part of what He might have meant was that His mission was complete. He had left heaven, lived a sinless life before men, and was crucified bearing the sins of mankind so that we all could be reconciled to God (2 Cor. 5:18–19).

Be returning to heaven and being seated at the right hand of God, He has indeed "appeared before God" and on our behalf, having completed His mission on earth. 9:28 talks about when we will be judged and says the following: "So Christ also, having been offered once to bear the sins of many, shall appear a second time for salvation without reference to sin, to those who eagerly await Him." His appearance this time will not be to save us from our sins; it will be to judge us (Acts 10:42). If we are faithful, we can eagerly await His appearing. If we are not, His second appearance will be anything but eagerly anticipated.

Chapter 39

Summary and Conclusions

So, that is what this writing has to offer. Is there more? Very likely, there is enough religious error, misguided understanding, and erroneous application of Scripture to fill volumes. In John 21:25, we find these words that John offers concerning the recording of the actions and teachings of Jesus while on the earth: "And there are also many other things which Jesus did, which if they were written in detail, I suppose that even the world itself would not contain the books which were written." Man's mistreatment of God's Word is similar.

Mankind has had somewhere around 2,000 years to deal with the NT and apply its teaching for what they do religiously and how they live their lives. Some changes made by man have been a deliberate corruption of those teachings and for ignoble motives (Titus 1:11). Some have been the result of many who simply took the words written there as *advice* rather than *prescription for absolute and unalterable Truth*. Others were just careless with the instruction found in Scripture and let personal preferences or simple inattention slip in and be later adopted as Truth, much the way the Pharisees and scribes had added their traditions to the Old Law (Mark 7:6–9).

Regardless of how error entered the picture, it is still error. This writing has been an attempt to highlight and discuss at least some of those beliefs and practices carried out by well-meaning individuals in their respect for and worship of God. In that attempt, there has been a concerted effort to accomplish the following: 1) use the Bible to let it speak to us about what we believe and what we do in life and in religion; 2) take a book/chapter/verse approach to suggesting needed corrections; 3) use all the tools (i.e., the original Greek; knowledgeable authorities; recorded history; etc.) available to us to decipher the *true* meaning of passages that might otherwise have multiple interpretations; and finally, 4) employ both the immediate and broader context of a passage to ensure its interpretation matches and comports with its surroundings in Scripture.

Intended outcomes from this writing are these:

1. We will accept the Word of God as both authoritative (directly from God Himself) and that which contains absolute Truth.
2. We will treat God's Word with the honor and respect it deserves as we attempt to mold all that we do in accordance with what we find there.
3. We will study what has been included here to make sure that it does not contain errors.
4. We will reexamine our thoughts on these and possibly other religious beliefs and practices to make sure they are *sound* handlings of God's Word and based on the context surrounding targeted scriptures.
5. We will use this writing as a springboard to inspire us to more deeply research and consider Scripture as we improve our knowledge of this all-important text.
6. We will do everything we can to make sure that what we believe and what we practice in our service to God is guided by an *accurate* understanding of His will for us found only in the Bible.
7. We will, as a result, be able to hear on the Day of Judgment these words: "Well done, good and faithful servant; enter into the joy of your master" or something similar.

www.ingramcontent.com/pod-product-compliance
Lightning Source LLC
Chambersburg PA
CBHW040302170426
43194CB00021B/2860